ORACLE®   *Oracle Press*™

Oracle8*i* for Linux
Starter Kit

D1405344

ORACLE® *Oracle Press*™

Oracle8*i* for Linux Starter Kit

Steve Bobrowski

Osborne/**McGraw-Hill**

Berkeley New York St. Louis San Francisco
Auckland Bogotá Hamburg London Madrid
Mexico City Milan Montreal New Delhi Panama City
Paris São Paulo Singapore Sydney Tokyo Toronto

Osborne/**McGraw-Hill**
2600 Tenth Street
Berkeley, California 94710
U.S.A.

For information on translations or book distributors outside the U.S.A., or to arrange
bulk purchase discounts for sales promotions, premiums, or fund-raisers, please
contact Osborne/**McGraw-Hill** at the above address.

Oracle8*i* for Linux Starter Kit

1234567890 DOC DOC 019876543210

Book p/n 0-07-212440-7   and   CD p/n 0-07-212441-5
parts of
ISBN 0-07-212442-3

Publisher	**Copy Editor**
Brandon A. Nordin	Andy Carroll
Vice President & Associate Publisher	**Proofreader**
Scott Rogers	Mike McGee
Acquisitions Editor	**Indexer**
Jeremy Judson	David Heiret
Project Editor	**Computer Designer**
Janet Walden	Lucie Ericksen
Acquisitions Coordinator	**Illustrator**
Monika Faltiss	Michael Mueller
Technical Editor	**Series Design**
Ravi Animi	Jani Beckwith

This book was composed with Corel VENTURA ™ Publisher.

To Lou and Lorraine,

the best parents that anyone
could ever wish for.

About the Author

Steve Bobrowski is CEO of Animated Learning, Inc., which manages the widely popular web service The Database Domain (www.dbdomain.com), an information hub dedicated to teaching database administrators and application developers the challenging concepts of high-end database management systems, such as Oracle. In addition to writing for several major industry publications, such as *Oracle Magazine*, Steve is also the author of the award-winning book, *Mastering Oracle7 & Client/Server Computing* (Sybex; 1994, 1996) and of Oracle Press's (Osborne/McGraw-Hill) *Oracle8 Architecture* (1997) and *Oracle8i for Windows NT Starter Kit* (2000). Previously, Steve worked for Oracle Corporation, where he assisted in the development of Oracle Server and Oracle's own documentation on Oracle7 and Oracle8.

Contents at a Glance

vii

PART III
Basic Database Administration

Contents

PART II
Fundamentals of Application Development

PART III
Basic Database Administration

Acknowledgments

Typically, the author of a book gets all or most of the credit for writing the masterpiece itself—think about it, how many of you can name Stephen King's editor? However, what most people do not understand is that producing a book is the collective effort of several people working toward a common goal. The words that follow are an attempt to thank formally the many people who have helped me write, edit, and print this, my fourth commercial book. Hopefully, our work has produced a publication that helps you accomplish your own personal goals in working with Oracle8i.

First of all, I'd like to thank my partner Kathleen O'Connor. Without Kathleen to help me, I'm afraid that my writing and organization of thoughts would not be nearly as clean as they exist on the pages of this book. There were many long days and late nights necessary to produce this book, and Kathleen challenged me to be the best that I could be in putting my words together so that everyone who reads this book has a clear understanding of Oracle8i and its concepts. I owe her an immeasurable debt of gratitude.

Next, I'd like to thank my many colleagues at Oracle whom I am happy to also call my friends. The technical expertise and reviews of Mike Hartstein and Filiz Dogan were instrumental in making this book a comprehensive and accurate guide on Oracle8i. Numerous others at Oracle, knowingly or not, also made significant contributions to this book, including Marsha Bazley, Tom Bishop, Kevin Canady,

Sandy Dreskin, Julie Gibbs, Ed Miner, Tom Portfolio, Gordon Smith, Leslie Steere, Milton Wan, and Wynne White.

The folks at Osborne/McGraw-Hill also deserve many thanks for publishing this book. I'd like to thank Scott Rogers and Jeremy Judson, who demonstrated enormous patience as the pages of this book trickled in. Monika Faltiss was instrumental in getting all of the book material to the correct place at the right time. Andy Carroll and Janet Walden were a pleasure to work with in editing the prose in this book.

Introduction

This book is a concise, intermediate-level presentation of the terminology and concepts related to Oracle8i. This book also includes a trial version of Oracle8i Enterprise Edition for Linux. Once you install Oracle8i on your Linux computer, you can follow the practice exercises in each chapter to quickly learn, with a hands-on approach, the most typically used features of Oracle8i Enterprise Edition on Linux. The following sections explain important additional information that you should understand before beginning to read the body of this book.

What This Book Covers

Oracle8i Starter Kit for Linux teaches you the concepts of Oracle8i and then provides you with hands-on exercises so that you can quickly learn the skills necessary to work with Oracle8i. Whether you are a database administrator, application developer, or an application user who simply wants to understand more about how Oracle8i functions, this book is for you. Oracle8i is a sophisticated database management product that is challenging to master, no matter what background you have with computers, software, or information management technology. After reading this book, you will have a tremendous perspective of everything Oracle8i, including the structure of Oracle8i databases, how Oracle8i's software architecture manages access to shared databases, and other concepts about Oracle8i.

What This Book Assumes

Oracle8i Starter Kit for Linux assumes that you are new to Oracle8i and want to learn all about its features and functionality in some depth. However, given the intended scope of this book, it also assumes that you have a general knowledge of database systems, especially relational database systems. Because Oracle8i is a relational database management system, some general experience with relational database systems will most certainly make this book easier to read. For example, if you already understand some of the basic concepts of a relational database system such as tables and views, you will simply have to focus on how Oracle8i implements the relational database model. If you have no background with database systems, I suggest you read the recently updated classic work, *An Introduction to Database Systems* (Addison Wesley, 1999), written by one of the founders of the relational database model, C.J. Date.

Conventions Used Throughout This Book

Throughout this book's hands-on exercises, you'll be interacting with Oracle8i using SQL commands—for introductory information about SQL, see Chapters 1 and 4. This section explains the conventions that this book uses while presenting SQL command syntax listings and examples.

Except in clauses that contain case-sensitive conditional tests, Oracle8i ignores the case of letters throughout SQL commands. However, as you read this book you'll notice that SQL command examples include a mix of uppercase and lowercase keywords and variables. For clarity, all SQL keywords are listed in uppercase letters, and all command variables (command components not actually part of the SQL language) are listed in lowercase letters. For example, consider the following example of the SQL command CREATE TABLE.

```
CREATE TABLE salesreps (
  id   INTEGER,
  lastname   VARCHAR2(100),
  firstname   VARCHAR2(50),
  commission   NUMBER(38)
);
```

In the preceding example, the keywords such as CREATE TABLE and datatype names (INTEGER, VARCHAR2, and NUMBER) are all in uppercase letters. Alternatively, all command variables such as the name of the table (salesreps) and the names of the table's columns (id, lastname, firstname, and commission) are all in lowercase letters.

This book also includes syntax listings for many SQL commands so that you know how to structure corresponding SQL statements. For example, the following is an abbreviated syntax listing for the SQL command ALTER TABLE.

```
ALTER TABLE [schema.]table
  ADD [CONSTRAINT constraint]
   { {UNIQUE|PRIMARY KEY} (column [, column] ... )
   | FOREIGN KEY (column [, column] ... )
      REFERENCES [schema.]table [(column [, column] ... )]
      [ON DELETE {CASCADE|SET NULL}]
   | CHECK (condition)   }
```

The conventions used for the syntax listings in this book are consistent with those that you will find in many language reference books. If you are not familiar with reading these types of syntax listings, here is a brief guide to the conventions used in the syntax listings that this book presents:

- All SQL keywords appear in uppercase letters (for example, ALTER TABLE, ADD).

- All command variables appear in lowercase italic letters (for example, *schema*, *table*, *constraint*).

- All optional command components appear between brackets [ ]. Do not enter brackets when building a command.

- All required command components appear between { }. Do not enter braces when building a command.

- A vertical bar | indicates an option in a list of an optional or required command component. Do not enter | when building a command.

- Unless otherwise stated, all parentheses, commas, operators (for example, =, :=), and other symbols are part of the command itself and must be entered when building a command.

- Ellipses (...) indicate that the preceding command component can be repeated. Do not enter ellipses when building a command.

Onward...

Now that you know where this book will take you and how it will present information, let's begin learning all about Oracle8i and how you can use it to manage information.

PART

I

Getting Started

CHAPTER
1

Introducing Oracle8*i*

ost everyone has heard the cliché, "information is power." And is this ever true. When you think about it, one of the most important assets of any institution is its information. For example, a typical business must keep track of its customers, orders, product inventory, and employee information for obvious reasons. Additionally, the analysis of pertinent business information can help make a company more competitive. For example, a sales analyst can use current sales data to forecast future sales and identify trends that might help to improve overall business profitability.

Information Management

In today's world of high technology, computers manage most information because they make it easy to organize, store, and protect valuable data. The proliferation of powerful personal computers and networks has made it possible for all businesses, large and small alike, to quickly and safely make information readily available to people that require access to it.

Databases

Computers typically store and organize large amounts of information within a database. A *database*, whether or not a computer manages it, is nothing more than an orderly collection of related information. A database safely stores information and organizes it for fast retrieval. For example, a business can use a database to store tables of customer records, corresponding sales orders, product parts, and employee lists. Various workers can then use the database to efficiently perform their jobs. For example, salespeople can quickly enter or look up sales orders, advertising executives can study and forecast product sales, and warehouse personnel can efficiently manage product inventories.

Types of Databases

Databases come in many varieties. *Inverted list*, *hierarchic*, and *network* database models are older types of database systems that, in general, are inflexible and difficult to work with. These types of database systems were originally designed primarily for prescribed transactions that input data rather than dynamic environments where data analysis is critical.

The very weaknesses of these earlier systems are exactly why *relational* database systems now dominate newer information management systems. Relational databases are easy to understand, design, and build. Relational databases store and present all information in tables, an easily understood concept. Furthermore, relational databases hide the complexities of data access from the user, making application development relatively simple when compared to other types of database systems.

Object-oriented databases are a relatively new type of system that supports the object-oriented development paradigm. The primary goal of object-oriented thinking is to raise the level of abstraction so that it is more natural to design and build an information management system. For example, in an object-oriented database, complex data structures called *objects* closely model the entities in a business system, while *methods* match the business operations that act upon the objects in the system. So, rather than store tables of, say, customers, orders, and order line items, a database stores instances of customers and sales order objects. Associated methods stored in the database describe how to add, change, and delete customer and sales order objects.

Database Management Systems

A *database management system (DBMS)* is computer software that manages access to databases. A typical multiuser DBMS performs the following tasks, and more:

- A DBMS safely manages shared access to a single database among multiple concurrent users. For example, a DBMS locks data as users add and update information, so that users do not destructively interfere with one another's work.

- A DBMS uses computer resources wisely so that a large number of application users can perform work with fast response times for maximum productivity.

- A DBMS protects database information in such a way that it can reconstruct work lost due to anything from a simple power outage to catastrophic site disasters.

You can purchase any one of several commercially available DBMSs to build and manage databases. The market-leading DBMS in use today is Oracle Corporation's Oracle Data Server, also known simply as *Oracle*. The latest version of Oracle is Oracle8i, and it is an *object-relational database management system (ORDBMS)*. That is, Oracle8i is a database server that offers the capabilities of both relational and object-oriented database systems. The goal of this book is to teach you how Oracle8i works and how to get started using the software's most typically used features.

Oracle8i, Building on Oracle7 and Oracle8

Oracle8i builds on the strengths of its predecessors, Oracle7 and Oracle8.0. Oracle7, originally released in early 1993, set a lofty standard for high-end relational database management systems. Oracle7's many features made it a potent database server for all types of common business applications, including:

- **Online transaction processing (OLTP)**   Applications that process many small update transactions, such as banking, reservation, and order-entry systems

- **Decision support systems (DSS)** Applications that query targeted information from a database for the purposes of data analysis

- **Data warehousing** Applications that access large, read-only databases that are specifically optimized for fast access to even the most esoteric bits of information

Oracle8.0, released in the summer of 1997, added many new features to extend the power of Oracle7 and make Oracle suitable for even the most demanding and complex application environments. New Oracle8.0 features included data partitioning, object types and methods, large object (LOB) datatypes, password management, the Recovery Manager utility, and more.

Oracle8*i*, released in the spring of 1999, is the most recent release of Oracle. Oracle8*i* enhances the original release of Oracle8 in two primary areas: data warehousing and Web-based application development. For data warehousing, Oracle8*i* includes many new features specifically designed to increase the performance of complex query processing, such as materialized views, automatic query rewrite, and function-based indexes. For Web-based application development, Oracle8*i* ships with a Java VM (virtual machine) so that developers can build all application components using Java (including Java-based stored procedures, functions, and packages), or access existing database information using Java applications. A future release of Oracle8*i* will also include Oracle's Internet File System (IFS), which is essentially a drag-and-drop interface for manipulating database information. Subsequent chapters in this book will teach you how to use several of Oracle8*i*'s new features.

Oracle8*i* License Options
Oracle8*i* is available in several different license formats:

- **Oracle8*i*** The basic version of Oracle8*i* that includes the most commonly used options and features available with Oracle8*i*.

- **Oracle8*i* Enterprise Edition** The complete version of Oracle8*i* that provides multiuser access to all features, including features for high-end database processing, Web-based database access, and data warehousing.

- **Oracle8*i* Personal Edition** A single-user development database license that provides access to most of the Oracle8*i* Enterprise Edition features.

- **Oracle8*i* Lite** An Oracle8*i*-compatible database designed for use in mobile computing environments. Oracle8*i* Lite is not discussed in this book.

Oracle8*i* Enterprise Edition for Linux
Oracle8*i* is available on most popular operating systems. The goal of this book is to teach you how to get started using Oracle8*i* Enterprise Edition operating on top of

one of the most popular server operating systems in use today, Linux. This book teaches you about the operating system–independent features of Oracle8i, as well as several Oracle8i features available only with Linux.

NOTE
For the most part, Oracle operates the same way, no matter what operating system you choose. Therefore, the large majority of this book will be useful even if you are using Oracle8i on a different operating system.

Oracle Fundamentals

Before proceeding to the next chapter to install Oracle8i Enterprise Edition for Linux on your computer, you should understand some of the basic terms related to Oracle and relational database systems. If you already have experience working with Oracle, the following sections contain information that you might already know.

Databases and Instances

An *Oracle database* is a collection of related operating system files that Oracle8i uses to store and manage a set of related information. Structurally, an Oracle database has three primary types of files: data files, log files, and control files. Subsequent chapters of this book will explain more about the purpose and management of each type of database file.

A *database instance* is the set of operating system processes and memory areas that Oracle8i uses to manage database access. You cannot access an Oracle database until after you "start up" an instance that associates itself with the physical database files.

NOTE
Sometimes, people use the terms "database service" or "server" as synonyms for a database instance.

For now, this is all that you need to understand about Oracle databases and instances. You'll learn more about databases and instances in Chapter 3.

Tables

Tables are the basic data structure in any relational database. A *table* is nothing more than an organized collection of *records*, or *rows*, that all have the same *attributes*, or *columns*. Figure 1-1 illustrates a typical CUSTOMERS table in a

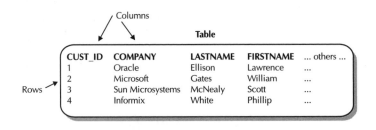

FIGURE 1-1. *A table is a set of records with the same attributes*

relational database. Notice that each customer record in the example CUSTOMERS table has the same attributes, including an ID, a company name, a last name, a first name, and so on.

For now, this is all that you need to understand about tables. You'll learn more about building and using tables in an Oracle database in Chapters 4 through 8.

SQL and Data Access

To work with a commercial relational database system, such as Oracle, applications must use *Structured Query Language* (*SQL*) commands. SQL (pronounced both "sequel" and "ess-que-ell") is a simple command language that allows database administrators, developers, and application users to:

- Retrieve, enter, update, and delete database data
- Create, alter, and drop database objects, such as tables

In fact, the only way that an application can interact with an Oracle database is to issue a SQL command. Sophisticated graphical user interfaces might hide the complexities of SQL commands from users, but under the covers, an application always communicates with Oracle using SQL.

If you currently do not have any experience with SQL, don't panic. SQL is a relatively simple language to learn because you build SQL commands by combining intuitive keywords and clauses that ask Oracle to perform specific tasks. For example, the following SQL statement is a simple query that retrieves specific columns of all rows in the PARTS table.

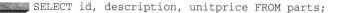`SELECT id, description, unitprice FROM parts;`

```
    ID DESCRIPTION           UNITPRICE
--------- -------------------- ---------
     1 Fax Machine                 299
     2 Copy Machine               4895
     3 Laptop PC                  2100
     4 Desktop PC                 1200
     5 Scanner                      99
```

At this point, you don't need to know much more about SQL. In almost every other chapter of this book, you will use SQL statements to access Oracle and perform tasks. Chapter 4, itself, provides you with a complete introduction to the basics of the most commonly used SQL commands.

Database Users and Sessions

Oracle is a DBMS that manages shared access to a database among one or more users. To provide database access to someone, you or an administrator must create a *database user account* for the person. To perform work with Oracle, you must start an application and establish a connection to Oracle using your account's username and password. A *database session* starts when you establish a connection to an Oracle database, and ends when you disconnect.

You will learn more about database users and database security in Chapter 9.

SQL*Plus

One type of application that you can use to enter SQL commands and interact with an Oracle database system is an ad hoc query tool, such as Oracle's SQL*Plus. SQL*Plus provides you with a very simple command-line interface that you can use to enter SQL statements and then view the results of each statement's execution. In effect, SQL*Plus lets you talk with an Oracle database server so that you can either query the database for information, or input, update, or delete data in the database. For example, the following commands demonstrate a simple SQL*Plus session that connects to an Oracle database, retrieves some data from the CUSTOMERS table, and then terminates the session by disconnecting from the database.

```
SQL> CONNECT scott/tiger;
Connected.
SQL> SELECT empno, ename
  2    FROM emp
  3    WHERE deptno = 10;

     EMPNO ENAME
--------- ----------
      7782 CLARK
      7839 KING
      7934 MILLER

SQL> DISCONNECT;
Disconnected from Oracle8i Enterprise Edition
```

The examples and practice exercises throughout the chapters in this book use SQL*Plus to communicate with Oracle. Chapters 3 and 4 begin teaching you how to get started with SQL*Plus.

Onward...

Oracle8i is a powerful product that you will use to manage information. Now that you have a general idea of what Oracle8i is all about, the remaining chapters in this book are a tutorial that present essential Oracle concepts and corresponding practice exercises so that you can quickly become proficient using Oracle8i for information management.

CHAPTER
2

Installing Oracle8i Enterprise Edition for Linux

efore you can start using this book to learn how to use the Oracle8i database management system, you must install the software on a computer that uses Linux. This chapter teaches you how to install the version of Oracle8i Enterprise Edition for Linux (8.1.6) that comes with this book. This chapter also explains the steps necessary for preparing to use the practice exercises in this courseware.

Overview and Planning for Oracle8i Installation

To successfully install Oracle8i Enterprise Edition for Linux, you need to take the time to understand and plan for the installation process. You should have a good understanding of the products, product options, and installation options that will be available to you during an installation session. Once you decide exactly what you are going to install, make sure that your system meets the necessary requirements to complete the installation and that you have all the information you will need as you proceed through the installation. The next several sections provide you with an overview of what you should understand and the information that you should have available before actually installing Oracle8i Enterprise Edition for Linux.

The Focus of This Chapter

When you install Oracle8i Enterprise Edition on Linux, you can perform a Typical, Minimal, or Custom installation. This chapter teaches you how to accomplish a Typical installation of Oracle8i Enterprise Edition on Linux. Furthermore, the subsequent sections in this chapter implicitly focus on performing a Typical installation. Should you need help with other types of installation options, please read the Oracle8i Installation Guide on your CD-ROM.

NOTE

To access the Oracle documentation on the CD-ROM that comes with this book, mount the CD-ROM and then access the file /mnt/cdrom/doc/ unixdoc/index.htm, assuming that /mnt/cdrom is the mount point for your CD-ROM.

The Oracle Universal Installer

To install Oracle8i on your computer, you will use the *Oracle Universal Installer* (henceforth referred to in this book as "the installer"). The installer is a Java-based program that looks and operates the same, no matter what operating system you happen to be using. The installer is the tool that you use to install various Oracle products onto your computer, and subsequently to remove them, if necessary.

Available Products and Options

Oracle8i Enterprise Edition for Linux is not just one product. Rather, it is a set of interrelated products that all work together to provide you with a powerful database management system. A Typical installation of Oracle8i Enterprise Edition for Linux will install the products and product options shown in Table 2-1.

NOTE
This book teaches you how to use the products that appear in italics.

Primary Product	Related Products and Product Options
Oracle8i Server *(Oracle 8.1.6)*	*Oracle Partitioning* Oracle interMedia Oracle Time Series Oracle Spatial Oracle Advanced Security
Net8	*Net8 Server* *Net8 Client* *Net8 Assistant*
Oracle Utilities	*SQL*Plus* SQL*Loader Export/Import Oracle Recovery Manager [†]
Oracle Configuration Assistants	Oracle Database Configuration Assistant [†] Oracle Data Migration Assistant
Development Tools	Oracle Call Interface (OCI) Object Type Translator

[†] Not fully functional in this release.

TABLE 2-1.   *Products and Product Options Installed with a Typical Oracle8i Enterprise Edition Installation*

Primary Product	Related Products and Product Options
Oracle Java Products	*Oracle JDBC Drivers* *Oracle SQLJ* Oracle Enterprise Java Beans and CORBA Tools *Java Runtime Environment (JRE)*
Oracle Enterprise Manager Products [††]	Oracle Intelligent Agent
Oracle Installation Products	*Oracle Universal Installer*
Product Documentation	Oracle8i for Linux Documentation

[††] A complete version of Oracle Enterprise Manager (OEM) is not included on the CD-ROM that accompanies this book.

TABLE 2-1. *Products and Product Options Installed with a Typical Oracle8i Enterprise Edition Installation* (continued)

Installation Options to Consider

When you install Oracle8i Enterprise Edition on Linux, there are several options to consider. The following sections explain some simple choices that you must make before actually starting an installation.

Oracle's Home Location

One of the first things to decide before you install Oracle8i is where you want the software and related files to reside on your computer. In general, you can pick any partition on a hard disk of your computer that has at least 750MB of available disk space. The root directory where you install Oracle8i is referred to in both the Oracle documentation and this book as the *Oracle home location* and is pointed to by the Linux environment variable *$ORACLE_HOME*. This book will use the /usr/oracle directory as the Oracle home location—if you choose a different $ORACLE_HOME, you'll need to make adjustments to many of the file specifications in subsequent exercises of this book.

Oracle's Base Location

When you install one or more Oracle products in a computer, the installer creates an inventory of products that have been installed. The root location where the inventory is kept is known as the Oracle base location and is pointed to by the Linux environment variable *$ORACLE_BASE*. This book will use the /usr/oraInventory directory as the Oracle base location.

The Starter Database

During a Typical installation, the installer will build a starter database on your computer after all of the software has been installed. The practice exercises in this chapter assume the presence of the starter database and use it extensively to help you quickly learn the fundamentals of working with Oracle8i.

NOTE
If you choose a Minimal or Custom install, a starter database might not be installed on your system. See your Oracle documentation for more information.

Before you start an installation, you should pick a name that you will use for the starter database. If you want your database name to match the results shown in many of this book's hands-on exercises, you should choose to name the starter database *oralin* (short for Oracle on Linux).

Additionally, the installer will prompt you to enter the network location of your computer so that it can configure several network-related settings, including the starter database's name in the network. In TCP/IP networks, Linux systems use standard dot notation to indicate the network node and the domains that encompass the node for your computer, such as mydb.mycompany.com. For example, the test Linux starter database that I used to write this book is named oralin.animatedlearning.com—the database name is oralin, and my company's domain name is animatedlearning.com. If you are not familiar with network naming schemes and the network name of your computer, take some time to read your Linux and network system documentation regarding this topic.

Documentation

Unfortunately, the version of Oracle8i Enterprise Edition for Linux that ships with this book (8.1.6.1.0) does not include a complete documentation library—only an installation guide and release notes are available on the CD-ROM. To access the complete Oracle8i generic documentation set, you'll have to surf Oracle's Technology Network Web site. After loading the home page at http://technet.oracle.com, click on Documentation, and then work your way to the generic Oracle8i documentation set.

NOTE
You'll need to sign up for a free membership to Technet to access the documentation area of the Web site. See the license agreement in the back of this book for more information about a Technet membership.

System Requirements

The following table briefly explains the system requirements necessary to perform a Typical installation of the copy of Oracle8i Enterprise Edition for Linux that comes with this book. Ensure that your system can meet these requirements before proceeding with the installation steps outlined later in this chapter—if you fail to meet these requirements, do not be upset if your installation fails!

System Component	Requirements
Operating system	Linux kernel 2.2 or greater, GLIBC package 2.1, Window manager that supports Motif 1.2
Web browser	Support for Java and frames (for documentation)
Physical and virtual memory	128MB RAM minimum; 256MB swap space minimum
Disk storage	A disk partition 750MB or more for Typical installation, including the starter database (recommended)
CD-ROM drive	A CD-ROM mount point for the Oracle8i Enterprise Edition for Linux CD-ROM shipped with this book

A Note About Your Linux Kernel

Many distributions of the Linux kernel are available—some free, some not so free. In any case, your computer must be using a Linux kernel version 2.2 or greater with GLIBC packages version 2.1. In writing this edition of the book, I chose to use Red Hat Linux 6.1, which meets all operating system requirements for the version of Oracle8i distributed with this book (8.1.6).

The root Account

During the installation for Oracle8i, you will need to perform several operations using the root account. This book assumes that you have complete access and control of your Linux computer, including the capability to use the root account.

Additional System Requirements to Consider

In addition to the requirements already mentioned, the Oracle8i Installation Guide for Linux also discusses several Linux kernel parameter settings to consider, such as the shared memory kernel parameters SHMMAX, SHMMIN, SHMMNI, and SHMSEG. If you are using Red Hat Linux 6.1 and do not plan to use the database that you install with this book for anything but learning how to use Oracle8i, you do not need to concern yourself with these kernel parameters. However, before you use Oracle8i Enterprise Edition on Linux to support a production database environment, you should take the time to meet the requirements that the Oracle documentation suggests.

And finally, the Oracle documentation also discusses special requirements for installing an Oracle Flexible Architecture (OFA)-compliant starter database such that the database's data files are distributed among at least four different mount points on your computer. This book assumes that you are installing Oracle8i for educational purposes only, and for simplicity, teaches you how to install all of the starter database's files on a single partition (mount point).

Preparing to Install Oracle8i

Before actually installing Oracle8i Enterprise Edition on your Linux computer, you need to complete several preparatory steps to ensure a smooth installation:

- Create the sysdba, sysoper, and oinstall groups.

- Create the oracle user.

- Create the directory for the Oracle inventory.

- Set the environment for the oracle user account.

Creating Operating System Groups

The first preparatory step to complete is to create several operating system groups necessary to support Oracle8i:

- Create the sysdba operating system group to support the Oracle sysdba database role.

- Create the sysoper operating system group to support the Oracle sysoper database role.

- Create the oinstall group to support the ownership of all Oracle homes and the Oracle base location. You must install all Oracle products, including Oracle8i, with oinstall set as the current group.

To complete the previous steps, *establish a session as the root user,* and then enter the following commands from your shell prompt in a terminal window:

```
groupadd sysdba
groupadd sysoper
groupadd oinstall
```

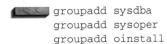

NOTE
If you are not familiar with the groupadd command, see your Linux documentation or man page.

Creating the oracle User

The next step is to create a Linux account that will own the installation of Oracle8i Enterprise Edition. To follow along with the installation described in subsequent exercises in this book, *establish a session as the root user,* and then create the Linux user account oracle using the following command:

```
useradd oracle -d /usr/oracle -g oinstall -G sysdba,sysoper
```

Note that the preceding command creates the oracle user account with the home directory set as /usr/oracle, the default group set as oinstall, and assigns the account the supplementary groups sysdba and sysoper. Don't forget to use the passwd command to set the initial password for the new oracle account:

```
passwd oracle
```

NOTE
If you are not familiar with the useradd command, see your Linux documentation or man page.

Finally, use the chmod command to set the correct permissions for oracle account's home directory, which will also serve as the Oracle home directory.

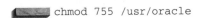
```
chmod 755 /usr/oracle
```

NOTE
The Oracle8i Installation Guide for Linux does not document what permissions are correct for the Oracle home directory. The permissions indicated above should be correct.

Creating the Oracle Base Location

Although it is not mentioned in the Oracle documentation, I found it necessary to create the directory that you plan to use for the Oracle inventory before installation. *Establish a session as the root user*, and then enter the following commands from your shell prompt in a terminal window:

```
cd /usr
mkdir oraInventory
chown oracle.oinstall oraInventory
```

Notice that after creating the /usr/oraInventory directory, you must use the chown command to assign the directory's ownership to the user oracle and the group oinstall.

Setting the Environment for the oracle User

The final preparatory step to complete before commencing installation is to set the proper environment for the oracle user account. *After establishing a session as the oracle user*, the first step is to check the setting for umask so that the files created by the installer have the proper permissions. From a shell prompt, enter the umask command:

```
umask
```

The umask command should return 022—if it does not, you will need to set it properly when you add several environment variable settings to the oracle account's login file.

Next, use a text editor such as vi to edit the account's login file. For example, if you are using the /bin/bash shell, open the $HOME/.bash_profile file in an editor such as vi—if you are using a different shell, edit the appropriate file.

Once you open the oracle account's login file for editing, you need to set several environment variables as follows:

```
DISPLAY=localhost:0.0; export DISPLAY
ORACLE_BASE=/usr/oraInventory; export ORACLE_BASE
ORACLE_HOME=/usr/oracle; export ORACLE_HOME
ORACLE_SID=oralin; export ORACLE_SID
PATH=$PATH:$ORACLE_HOME/bin; export PATH
```

Please note the following about the preceding example:

■ If you are using a different shell than /bin/bash, use the appropriate syntax for setting environment variables.

- If you choose a different directory for your Oracle inventory, set the $ORACLE_BASE environment variable properly.

- If you choose a different directory for your Oracle home location, set the $ORACLE_HOME environment variable properly.

- If you choose a different database name for your database, set the $ORACLE_SID environment variable properly.

- If you plan to store data in your Oracle8i database with a character set of anything other than the default US7ASCII character set, you should also set the $NLS_LANG and $ORA_NLS33 environment variables—see your Oracle documentation for more information about database character sets. The examples in this book assume that you use the default US7ASCII character set.

NOTE

If you plan to try the examples in Chapter 6 of this book that teach you how to use Java with Oracle8i, you can save yourself some time later by also setting the $CLASSPATH and $LD_LIBRARY_PATH environment variables now, as described in Exercises 6.1 and 6.4.

Once you edit the oracle account's login file, save the edited file and then logout and login again as oracle to establish a session with the proper environment.

Installing Oracle8i

At this point, you are ready to begin installing Oracle8i Enterprise Edition on your Linux computer. The following sequence of exercises takes you step by step through the installation process.

EXERCISE 2.1: Mounting the CD-ROM

Insert the Oracle8i for Linux CD-ROM (which comes with this book) into your computer's CD-ROM drive. If necessary, mount the CD-ROM *as the root user* using the following commands:

```
su root
mount -t iso9660 /dev/cdrom /mnt/cdrom
exit
```

NOTE
If Linux is configured to automatically mount your CD drive when you insert a CD-ROM, you can skip this exercise.

EXERCISE 2.2: Starting the Oracle Universal Installer

To start the installer, *start an X-Windows session as the oracle user.* From a terminal window, start the installer using the following commands:

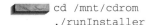
```
cd /mnt/cdrom
./runInstaller
```

Once the installer starts, it presents the Welcome page, as shown in Figure 2-1.

NOTE
When you execute the runInstaller script from your terminal window, ignore the warnings—they are normal.

FIGURE 2-1. *The Welcome page of the Oracle Universal Installer*

EXERCISE 2.3: Installing Oracle8i—Step by Step

Once you have the installer up and running, you can proceed with the installation of Oracle8i Enterprise Edition. The installer is essentially a wizard that presents a number of pages to you to complete the installation of Oracle8i. This exercise explains each of the pages that you should see as you install Oracle8i.

The first page that the installer presents is the Welcome page (see Figure 2-1). To continue with the installation, click Next to display the File Locations page, shown in Figure 2-2.

The Source section of the File Locations page lets you specify the source location that the installer will use to install Oracle8i. You should not have to edit the file specification in the Path field—the default setting for this field points to the installer file on your Oracle8i for Linux CD-ROM.

The Path field in the Destination section of the File Locations page lets you specify the destination for your installation. Carefully choose the setting for the Path field—the location that you choose is where the installer will install the Oracle8i Enterprise Edition software, as well as the default starter database for your installation. Set the Path field to the same directory that you specified for the $ORACLE_HOME environment variable earlier in this chapter when you configured the environment for the oracle user.

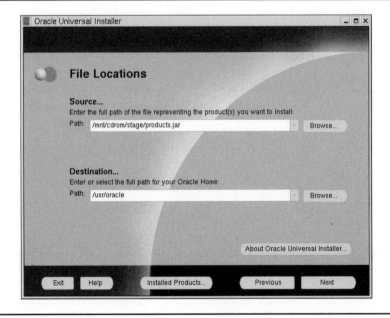

FIGURE 2-2. *The File Locations page of the Oracle Universal Installer*

Once you have set the fields in the File Locations page as necessary, click Next to continue. After loading the necessary information from the CD-ROM, the installer will display the UNIX Group Name page, as shown in Figure 2-3.

The UNIX Group Name field on this page lets you specify the UNIX group to designate as the owner of the Oracle installation. Specify the oinstall group that you created earlier in this chapter, and then click Next to continue. Subsequently, the installer prompts you to run a shell script named /usr/oracle/orainstRoot.sh (or $ORACLE_HOME/orainstRoot.sh) *as the root user* before continuing with the installation as shown in Figure 2-4.

At this point, start a new terminal window, and then enter the following commands to run the requested script *as the root user*:

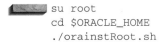

```
su root
cd $ORACLE_HOME
./orainstRoot.sh
```

After running the script, you should see results similar to the following:

```
Creating Oracle Inventory pointer file (/etc/oraInst.loc)
Changing groupname of /usr/oraInventory/oraInventory to oinstall.
```

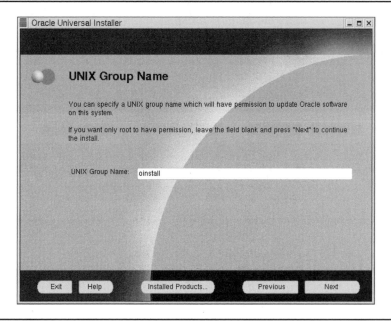

FIGURE 2-3.   *The UNIX Group Name page of the Oracle Universal Installer*

FIGURE 2-4. *When prompted, run the requested shell script as the root user during installation*

NOTE
You can leave the terminal window open—you'll need it again later in the installation process.

Next, return to the dialog box that prompted you to run the orainstRoot.sh script and click Retry to continue. The next page that the installer displays is the Available Products page, as shown in Figure 2-5.

In this exercise, you are installing Oracle8i Enterprise Edition. Therefore, select Oracle8i Enterprise Edition 8.1.6.1.0 and click Next to continue to the Installation Types page, as shown in Figure 2-6.

The Installation Types page lets you choose to proceed with a Typical, Minimal, or Custom installation from this point forward. Unless you have some special requirements for your system, you should choose Typical to make the installation process as simple as possible.

NOTE
The software products installed when you choose Typical are necessary to complete the exercises in subsequent chapters of this book.

Once you choose your installation type, click Next to continue to the Privileged Operating System Groups page, as shown in Figure 2-7.

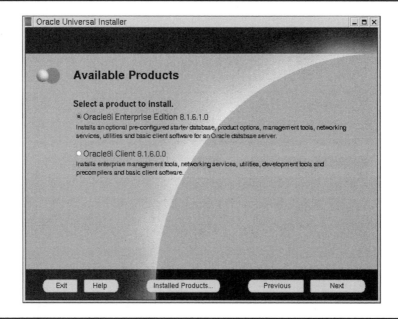

FIGURE 2-5. *The Available Products page of the Oracle Universal Installer*

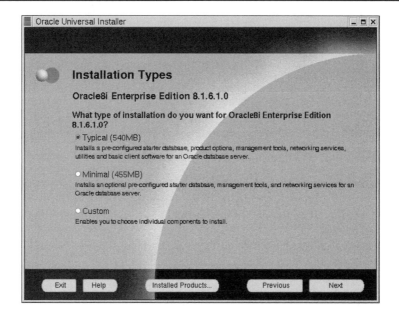

FIGURE 2-6. *The Installation Types page of the Oracle Universal Installer*

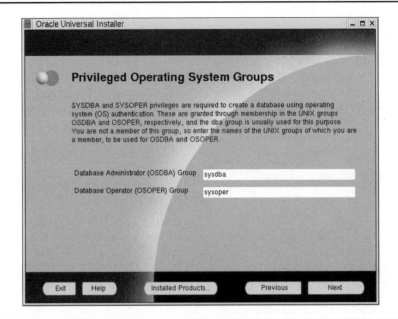

FIGURE 2-7. *The Privileged Operating System Groups page of the Oracle Universal Installer*

Use the fields of the Privileged Operating System Groups page to specify the Linux groups that you created earlier in this chapter—specify sysdba in the Database Administrator Group field and sysoper in the Database Operator Group field, and then click Next to continue to the Database Identification page, as shown in Figure 2-8.

The Database Identification page lets you specify information about the starter (or seed) database that the installer creates on your Linux computer, including the starter database's global database name and SID:

■ An *Oracle System Identifier* (SID) is a unique identifier that you can use to refer to an instance of the database that is available on your system (Chapter 1 introduces the term "database instance"). Earlier in this chapter, you set the $ORACLE_SID environment variable, which you should also specify in the SID field to indicate a unique identifier for the default instance that will correspond to the starter database—*oralin* is the SID that I have chosen for the example installation.

■ A database's *global database name* is the complete name of the database, including the database's encompassing network domain. Use standard dot notation to specify your starter database's global database name, such as *db_name.domain_name*. The *db_name* portion of a global database name must be 8 characters or less and consist of alphanumeric characters, and it can contain the special characters _, #, and $. The *domain_name* portion of a global database name must be 128 characters or less. For example, in Figure 2-8, I chose to use *oralin.animatedlearning.com* because the database's default SID will be *oralin* and my company's domain name is *animatedlearning.com*.

Once you enter your database's global database name and SID, click Next to continue and display the Database File Location page, as shown in Figure 2-9. The Database File Location page lets you indicate where the installer should create the database files (data files, log files, and control files) that comprise the starter database. In this exercise, I'm assuming that you only have one disk with which to work—in this case, just specify your Oracle home directory location (for example, /usr/oracle), and then click Next to continue.

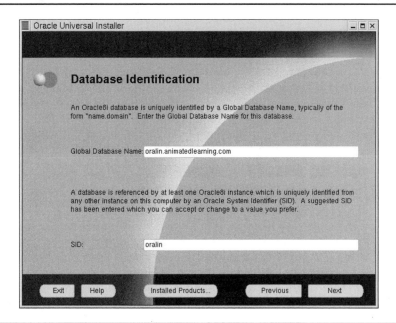

FIGURE 2-8. *The Database Identification page of the Oracle Universal Installer*

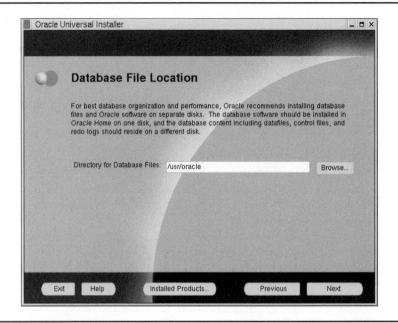

FIGURE 2-9. *The Database File Location page of the Oracle Universal Installer*

Finally, the installer presents the Summary page. The Summary page lets you review a tree list of the options that you have selected for this installation of Oracle8i. Take a close look at each option in the list to make sure that you did not make any incorrect choices when moving through the pages of the installer.

TIP
If you hold your mouse pointer over an option in the list, the installer displays a quick Help bubble.

After confirming the installation options in the list, click Install to display the Install page, as shown in Figure 2-10, and start the installation process. The progress bar of the Install page shows the status of the installation as it proceeds, as well as the location of the installer log file for this installation session.

Be patient as the installer goes about its business—depending on your computer's CPU, CD-ROM drive, and hard drive, it might take quite some time for the installer to install the software and then link various software executables. Eventually, the installer will present the Setup Privileges message box as shown in Figure 2-11.

FIGURE 2-10.   *The Install page for the Oracle Universal Installer*

The Setup Privileges message box prompts you to run another shell script *as the root user.* Switch to the terminal window that you used earlier, which should already have a session established *as root* and the current working directory set as $ORACLE_HOME. Next, execute the following command:

 `./root.sh`

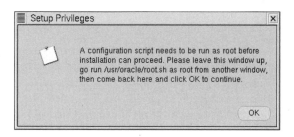

FIGURE 2-11.   *When prompted, run the requested shell script as the root user during installation*

After you run the script and indicate the path to your local bin directory, you should see output similar to the following:

```
Running Oracle8 root.sh script...
The following environment variables are set as:
    ORACLE_OWNER= oracle
    ORACLE_HOME=  /usr/oracle
    ORACLE_SID=   oralin

Enter the full pathname of the local bin directory: [/usr/local/bin]:
 /usr/local/bin
Creating /etc/oratab file...
Entry will be added to the /etc/oratab file by
Database Configuration Assistant when a database is created
Finished running generic part of root.sh script.
Now product-specific root actions will be performed.
IMPORTANT NOTE: Please delete any log and trace files previously
               created by the Oracle Enterprise Manager Intelligent
               Agent. These files may be found in the directories
               you use for storing other Net8 log and trace files.
               If such files exist, the OEM IA may not restart.
```

Once you run the root.sh shell script, exit your root session and the terminal window—you will not need it during the remainder of the installation process. Next, return to the message box that prompted you to run the script, and click OK to continue. Subsequently, the installer runs several configuration tools to configure Oracle's networking product (Net8) and a starter database on your machine. When the Database Configuration Assistant completes configuring the starter database, it displays an alert box similar to that shown in Figure 2-12. Record the information in this message box before dismissing it, because the alert box displays the SID and global database name for the starter database, as well as the default administration accounts and passwords for the starter database. Make a note of this information for the future.

The final page of the installer is the End of Installation page, shown in Figure 2-13. Assuming that your installation was successful, you can click Exit to exit the installer.

EXERCISE 2.4: Troubleshooting Installation Errors

If you have problems installing Oracle8i, make note of the messages and alerts provided by the installer as it installs Oracle8i. After you exit the installer, you can also check the installer log file to look at the actions carried out by the installer during your installation session. On Linux, the Oracle Universal Installer log file is $ORACLE_BASE/oraInventory/logs/installActions.log. Also, review the release

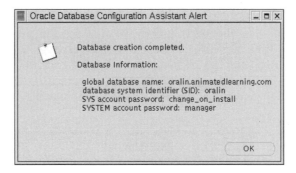

FIGURE 2-12. *The Database Configuration Assistant displays an alert box after configuring the starter database so that you can note the database's SID and global database name, as well as the passwords for the SYS and SYSTEM accounts*

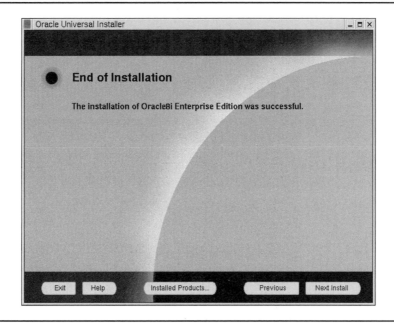

FIGURE 2-13. *The End of Installation page of the Oracle Universal Installer*

notes for your version of Oracle (see the "Oracle8i Documentation" section, earlier in this chapter).

If you need additional support with the version of Oracle8i Enterprise Edition for Linux, consider using Oracle Corporation's online technical support Web site, called OracleINSTALL, which is located at the following URL:

http://www.oracle.com/support/oracleinstall/dbserver/oracle8i.html

NOTE
As you might imagine, Oracle Corp. frequently updates the addresses of Web pages at their site. Consequently, if the preceding URL does not work, try going to Oracle Corp.'s primary Web site (http://www.oracle.com) and navigating to the location of the site that provides free technical support for software products, specifically Oracle8i Enterprise Edition for Linux.

Support Files for This Book's Hands-On Exercises

All subsequent chapters in this book contain hands-on exercises that provide you with invaluable experience using Oracle8i. At the beginning of most chapters, a section called "Chapter Prerequisites" explains the steps necessary to prepare for the chapter's exercises. Typically, you'll be asked to use Oracle's SQL*Plus utility to run a SQL command script that builds a practice schema for the chapter, complete with a set of tables and other supporting database objects. Most scripts also set up custom display formats for the SQL*Plus session, so that the results produced by the chapter's exercises are easy to read.

NOTE
Several Java source files are also available to support the exercises in Chapter 6.

The support files for this book are not present on the CD-ROM distributed with this book. Instead, you can download the latest support files for this book as a zip archive from the Osborne/McGraw-Hill Web site. The archive is located at the following URL:

http://www.osborne.com/

To install the practice scripts, complete the following steps:

1. Start a session as the oracle user.

2. Create a temporary directory to organize the practice scripts (for example, /tmp/8istarterkit):

```
cd /tmp
mkdir 8istarterkit
cd 8istarterkit
```

3. Download the archive into the temporary directory using your Web browser.

4. Extract the scripts from the archive using the following unzip command:

```
unzip 8istarterkit.zip
```

The file will extract and create the following directory structure, assuming that you downloaded the file in /tmp/8istarterkit and expanded it in the same directory.

- The doc directory contains a single file, readme.txt, that contains the latest information about the support files for this book.

- The Java directory contains several Java source files that support the exercises in Chapter 6.

- The scripts directory contains some shell scripts to support the exercises in Chapter 3.

- The SQL directory contains several SQL command scripts, named by chapter number, that support the corresponding chapters in this book.

When you start a new chapter, follow the directions in the "Chapter Prerequisites" section to prepare for the chapter's exercises. Also note that certain exercises in the book contain additional instructions for using specific support files.

CAUTION

Unless otherwise indicated, after you successfully run a chapter's supporting SQL command script using SQL*Plus, do not exit the SQL*Plus session. You should use the SQL*Plus session to complete the exercises in the chapter, starting with the first exercise in the chapter, all the way through to the final exercise in the chapter. If you do not have time to complete all exercises in the chapter during one sitting, leave your computer running and the SQL*Plus session open so that you can pick up where you left off when you have more time. If you must shut down your computer, the next time that you start SQL*Plus you must rerun the chapter's SQL command script (to refresh the necessary data and SQL*Plus display settings) and then repeat all exercises in the chapter, starting with the first exercise again.

CHAPTER
3

Configuring Oracle8*i*
for Access

racle is a sophisticated DBMS that manages access to almost any size of database that you can imagine. Hundreds, thousands, or even tens of thousands of concurrent users can connect to a single database server, locally or across a computer network. To accomplish these extraordinary tasks efficiently and reliably, Oracle creates and uses numerous software structures. This chapter explains these structures, including:

- Database servers and instances

- Oracle server processes and threads

- Net8, Oracle's networking software for distributed-processing environments

Oracle Database Instances

As you learned in Chapter 1, a *database instance* is the collection of server-side processes and memory areas that Oracle uses for managing access to a database. Figure 3-1 is a basic illustration that shows you the shape of an Oracle database instance's processes and memory areas.

NOTE
Chapter 12 provides more information about the memory structures in an Oracle instance.

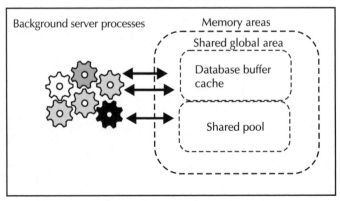

FIGURE 3-1. *An Oracle database instance*

Connecting to Oracle8i

After an Oracle instance is up and running, you (and other database users) can establish a connection to the server and perform database work. Behind the scenes, the mechanisms of the database instance work to complete the requests of all users. At the same time, the database instance automatically protects the work of all transactions while preserving the integrity of the shared database. The next three exercises show you how to connect to and disconnect from Oracle8i using SQL*Plus.

NOTE
The next two exercises in this chapter assume that your Oracle database is running and available for general use. If it is not, Oracle will return errors when you attempt the exercises in this section. In this case, you can read the exercises in this section for your information and then move to the exercises in the next section to learn more about database startup.

EXERCISE 3.1: Starting SQL*Plus and Establishing a Database Session

To begin interacting with Oracle, you can start SQL*Plus and establish a database session. To start SQL*Plus, *establish a Linux session as the oracle user,* and then enter the following command from a shell prompt:

```
sqlplus
```

SQL*Plus will then display a message similar to the following:

```
SQL*Plus: Release 8.1.6.0.0 - Production on Sat Jun 3 15:02:21 2000

(c) Copyright 1999 Oracle Corporation.  All rights reserved.

Enter user-name:
```

Notice that after SQL*Plus starts, it prompts you for *credentials* (a username and password) that it can use to establish a new database session. Your starter database has several default user accounts that you can use to get started with Oracle8i. For example, try using the default database administration account with the username SYSTEM and the password MANAGER.

```
Enter user-name: SYSTEM
Enter password:
```

NOTE
For security, SQL*Plus does not echo a password as you enter it after the "Enter password:" prompt. Also, usernames and passwords are not case-sensitive with Oracle.

If an instance is currently available, you should see a series of messages similar to the following:

```
Connected to:
Oracle8i Enterprise Edition Release 8.1.6.1.0 - Production
With the Partitioning option
JServer Release 8.1.6.0.0 - Production

SQL>
```

The blinking cursor after the "SQL>" in the last line of the display is SQL*Plus's default command prompt. Here, you can interactively type SQL and SQL*Plus commands to perform work. Later in this chapter, you'll see how to enter some simple SQL commands. The next chapter will provide you with a more thorough introduction to SQL.

If you start SQL*Plus and attempt to establish a normal database session when an instance is not currently running, you will see the following error message:

```
ERROR:
ORA-01034: ORACLE not available
```

In this case, you need to start an instance before you can access Oracle8i. See Exercises 3.5 and 3.6 later in this chapter for more information about performing database startup.

EXERCISE 3.2: Establishing a Different SQL*Plus Session

If you are already running SQL*Plus and would like to establish a different connection to your Oracle database, you can use the SQL*Plus command CONNECT, with the following syntax:

```
CONNECT username/password[@service] ;
```

NOTE
The @service string is optional if you are running SQL*Plus on the same computer that is running Oracle, but required if you are connecting to a database on a remote machine. You'll learn more about service names later in this chapter when you learn more about Net8 configuration.

For example, your starter database has several demonstration tables owned by the user account SCOTT that has the password TIGER. Enter the following command to disconnect as SYSTEM and establish a new database session as the user SCOTT.

 `CONNECT scott/tiger;`

EXERCISE 3.3: Disconnecting from Oracle and Exiting SQL*Plus

After you are finished using SQL*Plus, you can disconnect from Oracle and exit SQL*Plus by entering the EXIT command (type **EXIT**) at the SQL*Plus prompt.

Server Startup and Shutdown

Before anyone can work with an Oracle database, someone must *start up* the database server. This process includes *starting* a database instance, *mounting* (associating) the database to the instance, and *opening* the database. After a server startup, the database is generally available for use with applications.

Conversely, you can make a database unavailable by performing a database server *shutdown*. A server shutdown is the reverse of a server startup: you *close* the database, *dismount* it from the instance, and then *shut down* the instance. After a server shutdown, users cannot access the database until after you restart the server.

Server Crashes

A *server crash* is an abnormal server shutdown. For example, an unfortunate operating system operation or problem could unexpectedly kill one or more of a server's background processes. Consequently, the database server might crash. Oracle has built-in features that protect the work of all committed transactions, and it automatically performs the necessary recovery from an instance that crashes. See Chapter 11 for more information about Oracle's database-protection mechanisms.

Oracle's Parallel Server Option and High Availability

Many sites use Oracle to support mission-critical applications. A mission-critical application, by definition, has stringent high-availability requirements. Such sites can tolerate little or no downtime due to a server crash. In such circumstances, Oracle's *Parallel Server* option can help.

In a parallel server configuration, multiple database instances running on different nodes of a loosely coupled computer mount and open the same Oracle database in parallel. Users can work with the database through any instance that is mounted to the database. If an isolated system failure causes one of the instances to crash, other servers remain available so that users can continue work uninterrupted. This book does not discuss Oracle's Parallel Server option in any detail, but mentions this option in the context of certain discussions.

Controlling Server Startup and Shutdown

Now that you have a basic understanding of database availability, the following exercises teach you how to check the status of and control the availability of Oracle8i on Linux.

EXERCISE 3.4: Checking the Status of Oracle8i on Linux

Perhaps the quickest way to check if a database instance is up and running is to use a simple operating system command. First, establish a Linux session as the oracle user, and then execute the following command from a shell prompt:

```
ps -ax | grep -e ora_
```

The *ps command* with the *a* and *x* switches reveals a snapshot of information about the current processes running under Linux. The output of the ps command is piped to the grep command to display listings for processes that contain the string "ora_". If an Oracle8i instance is running, the output from the previous command should look similar to the following.

```
537 ?        S       0:00 ora_pmon_oralin
539 ?        S       0:00 ora_dbw0_oralin
541 ?        S       0:00 ora_lgwr_oralin
543 ?        S       0:00 ora_ckpt_oralin
545 ?        S       0:01 ora_smon_oralin
547 ?        S       0:00 ora_reco_oralin
549 ?        S       0:00 ora_snp0_oralin
551 ?        S       0:00 ora_snp1_oralin
553 ?        S       0:00 ora_snp2_oralin
555 ?        S       0:00 ora_snp3_oralin
557 ?        S       0:00 ora_s000_oralin
559 ?        S       0:00 ora_d000_oralin
837 pts/0    S       0:00 grep -e ora_
```

This output reveals the background processes running as part of an Oracle8i instance. You'll learn more about background processes later in this chapter. For now, you can use the information in this exercise to understand simply whether Oracle8i is available (whether an instance is running) or not. If the instance's background processes are running, then an Oracle8i instance is more than likely available to provide access to the starter database on your computer. However, if the ps command does not display any background processes that correspond to an Oracle8i instance, an instance is not running and the starter database is not accessible.

EXERCISE 3.5: Establishing a Privileged Administrator Database Session

Before you can complete certain database administrator tasks, such as server startup and shutdown, you'll need to establish a privileged administrator session with SQL*Plus. A *privileged administrator session* is a session that has access to either the SYSDBA and/or SYSOPER Oracle database privileges.

- Using a session with the *SYSOPER privilege*, you can start up and shut down an Oracle database server; mount, open, close, back up, and recover a database; and manage a database's transaction log structure.

- Using a session with the *SYSDBA privilege*, you can perform any database operation and, in turn, can grant any system privilege to other database users. Therefore, it is extremely important to restrict which users have the SYSDBA system privilege.

NOTE

You control access to the SYSDBA and SYSOPER privileges for local Linux sessions using the corresponding Linux groups that you created during Oracle8i installation. You control access to the SYSDBA and SYSOPER privileges for network connections to Oracle using the ORAPWD utility, an administrator password file, and the SQL commands GRANT and REVOKE. As this book is intended for users just getting started with Oracle8i, it does not discuss how to add other administrators to the administrator password file, change the administrator password, and other operations involving the ORAPWD utility. See your Oracle documentation for more information about administrator security and the ORAPWD utility if you are curious.

By default, the SYS account in your starter database is registered in the administrator password file, and the default administrator password is ORACLE. To establish a SYSDBA privileged administrator SQL*Plus session to your starter database's instance using the SYS account, *establish a Linux session as the oracle* *user,* and then start SQL*Plus. At the "Enter user-name:" prompt, enter the following to establish a privileged administration session:

 `sys/oracle as sysdba`

When an instance is not currently running, SQL*Plus will display the following message:

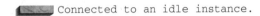 `Connected to an idle instance.`

 NOTE
Whether or not an instance is currently available, at this point you have established a privileged administrator session with all privileges, and you can complete powerful system-wide operations, such as server startup and shutdown.

EXERCISE 3.6: Starting Oracle8*i*

If an Oracle instance is not currently running, you can use the special DBA command *STARTUP* to make the starter database available for access. An abbreviated syntax listing of the STARTUP command is as follows:

 `STARTUP [NOMOUNT|MOUNT|OPEN] [pfile=filename] ;`

 NOTE
For a complete syntax listing of the STARTUP command, see your Oracle documentation.

- The *NOMOUNT option* starts a database instance, but does not mount or open the database.

- The *MOUNT option* starts an instance and mounts the database, but does not open the database for general use.

- The *OPEN option* completes all phases of database startup so that users can access the database for general use.

The *pfile parameter* indicates the name of an initialization file. An *initialization file* (also called an *init.ora file* or *parameter file*) is a configuration file for an Oracle database instance. A server's initialization file is essentially a list of parameters. You can add, delete, and adjust the settings for various instance parameters to configure and tune the operation of an Oracle database before starting a new instance for the database.

NOTE

To complete this exercise, all that you need to know about your database's initialization file is its name and location—Exercise 3.10 will teach you more about initialization files and parameters.

The installer automatically creates an initialization file for your starter database. The location of this file depends on two things that you specified during Oracle8*i* installation: the setting of the $ORACLE_SID environment variable and the setting for the $ORACLE_BASE environment variable in effect during the installation. Assuming that you followed the steps in Chapter 2 exactly, the full path and name of the initialization file for your starter database should be

/usr/oraInventory/admin/oralin/initoralin.ora

The installer also creates a handy symbolic link for your starter database's initialization file in the $ORACLE_HOME/dbs directory. Assuming that you followed the steps in Chapter 2 exactly, the full path and name of the symbolic link to the starter database's initialization file should be

/usr/oracle/dbs/initoralin.ora

To start up your database, enter the following STARTUP command, which references the link to the database's initialization file:

STARTUP OPEN PFILE=$ORACLE_HOME/dbs/initoralin.ora;

After you issue the STARTUP command, SQL*Plus should display the following messages to indicate that a new database instance is now started and mounted to the starter database, and that the database is open for user access:

ORACLE instance started.

```
Total System Global Area    56012784 bytes
Fixed Size                     69616 bytes
Variable Size               38993920 bytes
Database Buffers            16777216 bytes
Redo Buffers                  172032 bytes
Database mounted.
Database opened.
```

NOTE
If you attempt to start up Oracle when an instance is already running, Oracle returns a corresponding error message.

EXERCISE 3.7: Stopping Oracle8i

The process of database shutdown is the reverse of server startup. When an Oracle instance is running with a database open, you can shut down the instance and make the starter database unavailable by using the special DBA command SHUTDOWN. An abbreviated syntax listing of the SHUTDOWN command follows:

```
SHUTDOWN [NORMAL|IMMEDIATE|TRANSACTIONAL|ABORT] ;
```

- The *NORMAL* option (the default option) prohibits new database connections and shuts down the database after all users have disconnected.

- The *IMMEDIATE* option prohibits new database connections, rolls back all current transactions, immediately disconnects all users, and shuts down the database.

- The *TRANSACTIONAL* option prohibits new database connections, prohibits new transactions from beginning, allows current transactions to complete, disconnects all users, and shuts down the database.

- The *ABORT* option should be your last resort, such as after other types of database shutdown hang. The ABORT option shuts down the database without rolling back current transactions, disconnecting users, or writing modified database information in server memory back to the database's data files. Consequently, Oracle must perform crash recovery during the subsequent database startup.

For example, enter the following command to close and dismount the database, and then shut down the current running instance of Oracle8i on your Linux computer.

```
SHUTDOWN IMMEDIATE;
```

If an instance was currently running, you should see messages similar to the following that indicate a successful database shutdown:

```
Database closed.
Database dismounted.
ORACLE instance shut down.
```

NOTE
After completing this exercise and before continuing with Exercise 3.8, you will need to repeat Exercise 3.6 to make Oracle8i available for general use again.

Oracle Processing Architectures

Now that you know how to get an Oracle instance up and running and connect to the server with SQL*Plus, it is time to learn more about the software architecture of an Oracle database instance and how to investigate it further. These topics are discussed in the following sections.

Server-Side Background Processes

Every Oracle database instance on Linux executes as several background processes. Each background server process performs a specialized system function. Figure 3-2 and the following sections explain the most common background processes that you'll find in any Oracle database instance.

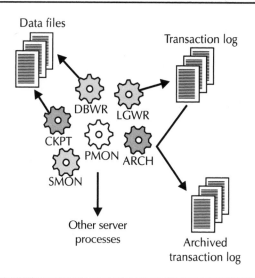

FIGURE 3-2. *The background processes of an Oracle database instance*

The Database Writer (DBW*n*)

When you modify some database data (for example, insert, update, or delete a row in a database table), Oracle does not simply modify the data on disk. This type of processing would be extremely inefficient in a large multiuser system because the system would constantly be reading data from and writing data back to the database's data files. Instead, a server process working on behalf of your session reads one or more data blocks from a data file into the server's memory. Oracle then makes the change that you request in the server's memory. Eventually, the *database writer* (DBWR) background process writes modified data blocks from memory back to the database's data files. To consolidate disk accesses, reduce unnecessary overhead, and make Oracle perform optimally, an instance's DBWR writes modified data blocks from memory to disk only in certain situations: when DBWR sits idle for several seconds, when a user process wants to read a new data block into memory but no free space is available, or when the system performs a checkpoint. The section "The Checkpoint Process (CKPT)," later in the chapter, explains checkpoints.

NOTE
Every Oracle instance has at least one DBWR process. Systems that must support high-volume transaction throughput can operate better with two or more DBWR processes (DBW0, DBW1, DBW2, and so on).

The Log Writer (LGWR)

The *log writer* (LGWR) background process records information about the changes made by all transactions that commit. Oracle performs transaction logging as follows:

1. As you carry out a transaction, Oracle creates small records called *redo entries* that contain just enough information to regenerate the changes made by the transaction.

2. Oracle temporarily stores your transaction's redo entries in the server's redo log buffer. The server's *redo log buffer* is a small memory area that temporarily caches transaction redo entries for all system transactions.

3. When you ask Oracle to commit your transaction, LGWR reads the corresponding redo entries from the redo log buffer and writes them to the database's transaction log. The database's *transaction log* or *online redo log* is a set of files dedicated to logging the redo entries created by all system transactions. Chapter 11 discusses the transaction log and other database-protection mechanisms.

NOTE

Oracle does not consider a transaction to be committed until LGWR successfully writes your transaction's redo entries and a commit record to the transaction log.

The Archiver (ARCH)

The *archiver* (ARCH) background process automatically backs up the transaction log files after LGWR fills them with redo entries. The sequential set of archived transaction log files that ARCH creates is collectively called the database's *archived transaction log* or *offline redo log*. If a database experiences a serious failure (for example, a disk failure), Oracle uses the database backups and the archived transaction log to recover the database and all committed transactions. Chapter 11 explains more about Oracle's protective mechanisms, including database backups and the archived transaction log.

NOTE

Automatic transaction log archiving is an optional feature of Oracle. Therefore, ARCH is present only when you use this feature.

The Checkpoint Process (CKPT)

Periodically, DBWR performs a checkpoint. During a *checkpoint*, DBWR writes all modified data blocks in memory back to the database's data files. The purpose of a checkpoint is to establish mileposts of transaction consistency on disk. After performing a checkpoint, the changes made by all committed transactions have been written to the database's data files. Therefore, a checkpoint indicates how much of the transaction log's redo entries Oracle must apply if a server crash occurs and database recovery is necessary.

During a checkpoint, the special *checkpoint* (CKPT) background process updates the headers in all of the database's data files to indicate the checkpoint.

NOTE

CKPT is always present in an Oracle8i instance. However, with earlier releases of Oracle, CKPT was an optional server process whose responsibilities would otherwise be performed by LGWR.

The System Monitor (SMON)

During database processing, an Oracle instance's *system monitor* (SMON) background process performs many internal operations, some of which you might never even realize. For example, SMON periodically coalesces the free space in a database for more efficient space allocation. SMON does its work quietly in the background during times of low activity, or when certain operations are required.

The Process Monitor (PMON)

Occasionally, user connections do not end gracefully. For example, a network error might unexpectedly disconnect your database session before you can disconnect from Oracle. An instance's *process monitor* (PMON) background process notices when user connections have been broken. PMON cleans up after orphaned connections by rolling back a dead session's transaction and releasing any of the session's resources that might otherwise block other users from performing database work.

The Recoverer (RECO)

Oracle can support distributed database systems and distributed transactions. A *distributed database* is a collection of individual databases that appears to applications and end users as a single database. A *distributed transaction* is a transaction that updates the data in multiple databases. To protect the integrity of data throughout a distributed database, Oracle has special transaction-protection mechanisms that ensure a consistent outcome (commit or rollback) of a distributed transaction at all participating sites.

For example, an untimely network failure might interrupt the commit of a distributed transaction. In this case, the outcome of the transaction might be complete at some databases while being left in doubt at others. To automatically resolve in-doubt distributed transactions, every Oracle instance has a *recoverer* (RECO) background process. RECO automatically wakes up to resolve all in-doubt distributed transactions as they happen. RECO resolves the local outcome of an in-doubt distributed transaction so that it matches the outcome of the transaction at other nodes.

NOTE

This book does not discuss Oracle's distributed database features in any detail, because multiple database configurations are necessary to test and perform most distributed database operations.

Job Queue (SNP*n*) and Advanced Queue Time Managers (QMN*n*)

Oracle also supports two different job queue facilities. A *job* is a task or operation that Oracle executes asynchronously at a scheduled time. Database applications

can use either Oracle's *job queue* facility, or its *advanced queuing* (AQ) facility
to create and schedule jobs that carry out work. To run scheduled jobs, Oracle
database instances can start one or more *job queue* (SNP*n*) background processes.
To support jobs scheduled with the advanced queuing facility, an Oracle instance
can start one or more *advanced queue manager* (QMN*n*) background processes.

EXERCISE 3.8: Checking the Status of Background Processes

After connecting to the starter database using the steps in Exercise 3.1, use SQL*Plus
to submit the following SELECT statement to display the background processes
currently at work in your Oracle instance:

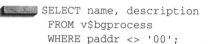
```
SELECT name, description
  FROM v$bgprocess
 WHERE paddr <> '00';
```

NOTE
*Don't concentrate on understanding the specifics
of the SQL commands used in the practice exercises
for this chapter. Instead, focus on the output
produced by each command. The next chapter
teaches you the basics of SQL.*

The results of your query should look something like the following output:

```
NAME    DESCRIPTION
-----   -----------------------
PMON    process cleanup
DBW0    db writer process 0
LGWR    Redo etc.
CKPT    checkpoint
SMON    System Monitor Process
RECO    distributed recovery
SNP0    Job Queue Process 0
SNP1    Job Queue Process 1
SNP2    Job Queue Process 2
SNP3    Job Queue Process 3

10 rows selected.
```

Notice that the SELECT statement reveals the name and description of all
background processes that have a process address (PADDR) not equal to "00". In
the preceding results, the instance has the following background processes: PMON,
DBW0, LGWR, CKPT, SMON, RECO, SNP0, SNP1, SNP2, and SNP3.

Processes That Support User Connections

An Oracle instance creates and uses a separate set of processes to support database user sessions that connect to the server. Oracle can support user connections to an Oracle instance in any type of computing environment. For example, Oracle can support users that connect to an Oracle database server across a network using a PC or network computer. Oracle can also support users that start a host session and connect to an Oracle instance on the same computer. The following sections explain the different processing architectures that Oracle uses to support user connections in different types of computing environments.

Client/Server Process Architectures

A *client/server* application is a type of *distributed processing* application. In a distributed processing application, the tasks performed by the application are "distributed" across two or more distinct processing components. In a client/server application, there are three components—the client, the server, and a network that connects the client and the server. Figure 3-3 illustrates a typical client/server configuration.

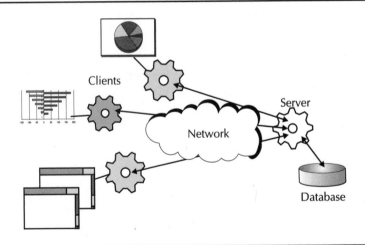

FIGURE 3-3. *A typical client/server configuration*

The following sections explain each component of a client/server system.

The Client

The *client* is the front end of the application that you use to perform work. The client is typically in charge of the following types of operations:

- Presenting a user interface with which you can interact, such as a form for data entry

- Validating data entry, such as checking that you enter a valid date in a date field

- Requesting information from a database server, such as customer records or sales orders

- Processing information returned from a database server, such as filling a form with data, calculating field totals on a report, or creating graphs and charts

The Server

The *server* is the back end of the application. Behind the scenes, a database server works to manage a database among all the users and applications that use it to store and retrieve data. The server is responsible for the following operations:

- Opening a database and making it accessible to applications

- Preventing unauthorized database access by having tight security controls

- Preventing destructive interference among concurrent transactions accessing the same data sets

- Protecting a database with bulletproof database backup and recovery features

- Maintaining data integrity and consistency as many users perform work

The Network

Typically, the client and server components of an application execute on different computers that communicate with each other across a *network*. In order to converse, the clients and servers in a network must all employ communication software that lets them speak the same lingo. Later in this chapter, you'll learn more about Oracle's Net8, the networking software that lets clients and servers communicate in an Oracle client/server network.

Oracle-Specific Processing Architectures

Now that you have a general understanding of distributed processing, let's take a look at the specific processing architectures that Oracle uses to support client connections.

Dedicated Servers

The simplest architecture that Oracle can use to support client connections is the *dedicated server architecture*. Figure 3-4 shows a dedicated server architecture.

In a dedicated server configuration, Oracle starts a dedicated *foreground server process* for each client that connects to the instance. A client's foreground server process performs database work for its client only. For example, when you send an UPDATE statement to Oracle, your foreground server process checks the server memory for the necessary data blocks; if they are not already in memory, your server process reads the blocks from disk into server memory; finally, your server process updates the data blocks in server memory.

The dedicated server configuration is not particularly efficient for large user populations. That's because each dedicated server process performs work for only

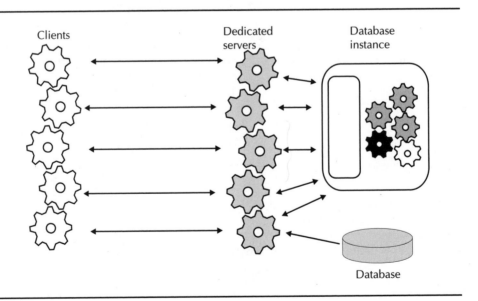

FIGURE 3-4. *A dedicated server architecture*

one user session. If a dedicated server process sits idle a large percentage of the time (for example, as a salesperson talks to a customer and fills out a form), the inactive server process unnecessarily consumes server resources. Multiply this by hundreds or thousands of users, and the processes necessary to support user connections quickly deplete a server's resources. Considering these drawbacks, dedicated server connections are typically used only for intensive batch operations that keep the server process busy a large percentage of the time. Dedicated server connections are also required to execute certain administrative tasks (for example, server startup, shutdown, and database recovery). Instead, most client/server configurations use a multithreaded server configuration.

NOTE

When you read your Oracle documentation or other books about Oracle, you might also see the terms two-task client and shadow process. These terms are synonyms for the terms dedicated server architecture and foreground server process, respectively.

Multithreaded Servers (MTS)

The typical process architecture that Oracle uses to support client connections is the *multithreaded server* (MTS) architecture. Figure 3-5 illustrates a multithreaded server configuration.

A multithreaded server configuration is a small collection of server-side processes that, together, can efficiently support large user populations. The components in a multithreaded server configuration include dispatchers, shared servers, and queues.

- A *dispatcher* process receives client requests and places them in the server's *request queue*. A dispatcher also returns the results for requests back to the appropriate client. An Oracle database instance must start at least one dispatcher for every network protocol that it plans to support (for example, TCP/IP, IPX/SPX, DecNet).

- A *shared server* process executes the requests that it finds in the server's request queue and returns corresponding results to the server's *response queue*. An Oracle instance can start one or more shared servers. After instance startup, Oracle automatically adjusts the number of shared servers as the transaction load on the system fluctuates. When there are many requests waiting for execution in the request queue, Oracle starts additional shared servers to handle the load. Conversely, when the requests in the queue are cleared, Oracle can stop unnecessary shared servers to reduce the overhead on the host computer.

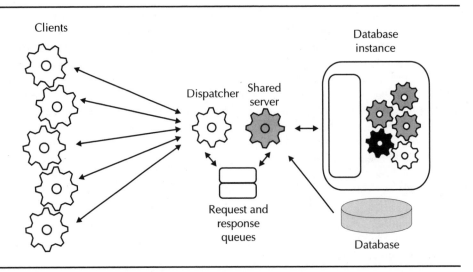

FIGURE 3-5.   *A multithreaded server (MTS) architecture*

A multithreaded server configuration is very efficient for typical application environments because a small number of shared servers perform the work for many connected clients. Consequently, very little overhead is necessary in order to support large user populations, and the host computer running Oracle can perform better.

NOTE
MTS connections are not possible unless you specifically configure an instance with the necessary processes (a dispatcher and one shared server). Subsequent sections of this chapter explain how to configure MTS for an instance.

Configuring an Instance for MTS Connections

Now that you have a good understanding of Oracle's processing architectures, the following hands-on exercises teach you how to perform the following related tasks:

- Check your current type of connection

- Configure your database instance for MTS connections by editing your server's initialization file

- Test that an MTS configuration is working properly

EXERCISE 3.9: Checking Your Current Type of Network Connection

Now that you understand the different types of user connections that are possible, let's investigate what type of connection you are currently using. *As the oracle user,* start SQL*Plus and connect to Oracle using the SYSTEM account using the following command line parameters:

```
sqlplus system/manager@oralin
```

Notice that when you start SQL*Plus, the command line parameters establish a network connection to the database as SYSTEM using the service name oralin (your starter database). After you connect to Oracle using SQL*Plus with the steps in Exercise 3.1, enter the following query to list the type of connection you currently have to the starter database.

```
SELECT server
  FROM v$session
  WHERE audsid = USERENV('SESSIONID');
```

Unless you have done some prior configuration work with your starter database, the output of your query should be as follows:

```
SERVER
---------
DEDICATED
```

The example output for this query indicates that the current connection to Oracle uses a dedicated server configuration. A dedicated server connection is the default type of client/server (two-task) connection if you install Oracle8*i* for Linux using the Typical installation option. The next section shows how to configure an instance so that MTS connections are the default type of client/server connection.

EXERCISE 3.10: Configuring Your Instance for MTS Connections

When you install Oracle8*i* for Linux using the Typical installation option, the installer does not configure the starter database's instance with the dispatcher that client/server connections use to establish MTS connections. To support MTS connections, you need to make some configuration changes to your instance by editing your initialization parameter file.

To start this exercise, establish a session as the oracle user, and then open your database's initialization file with a text editor, such as vi. Recall that your starter database's initialization file can be accessed by this handy symbolic link:

```
$ORACLE_HOME/dbs/initoralin.ora
```

Once you open the initialization file in a text editor, you will notice that the file header (the top part of the file) is a series of *comments* (lines that begin with the # symbol) that explain the purpose of the file. Following the file header are the parameters and related comments for each parameter. The parameter names in init.ora are not case-sensitive—you can specify them using any case of letters. Two basic parameters to look for and examine are the following:

■ The *DB_NAME* parameter indicates the name of the database that you plan to mount to the instance. If you do not set the parameter correctly, Oracle will not be able to start the instance or open the database. If you followed the instructions in Chapter 2 to the letter, your starter database's DB_NAME will be set to oralin.

■ The *DB_DOMAIN* parameter specifies the second half of your database's name by indicating the network domain that encompasses the location of the database. For example, the starter database on the test computer at my company, Animated Learning, is located in the animatedlearning.com network domain. Therefore, DB_DOMAIN is set to animatedlearning.com, and the starter database's complete global name is oralin.animatedlearning.com.

Subsequent chapters of this book explain several other parameters that you can adjust to configure and tune Oracle's operation. For the remainder of this exercise, let's focus on the following parameters that you need to add to the starter database's initialization file to configure the instance to accept MTS connections.

■ The *MTS_DISPATCHERS* parameter is a string that specifies how many dispatchers should start for a given network protocol.

■ The *MTS_SERVERS* parameter determines the initial number of shared servers that will be created during instance startup, as well as the minimum number of shared servers possible in the MTS configuration. When you expect many concurrent database requests via MTS connections, you can improve response times by increasing the value of MTS_SERVERS.

■ The *MTS_MAX_SERVERS* parameter limits how many shared servers an MTS can start. The setting for MTS_MAX_SERVERS prevents Oracle from starting too many shared servers during times of peak demand.

In your text editor session, move to the last line of the file, and then add the following three parameters as new lines so that when you start a new instance, Oracle will start a dispatcher process along with a single shared server process:

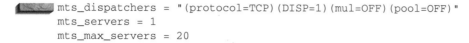

```
mts_dispatchers = "(protocol=TCP)(DISP=1)(mul=OFF)(pool=OFF)"
mts_servers = 1
mts_max_servers = 20
```

The specification for the MTS_DISPATCHERS parameter establishes one dispatcher (DISP=1) for the TCP/IP network protocol (PROTOCOL=TCP), with multiplexing disabled (MUL=OFF) and connection pooling disabled (POOL=OFF). You'll learn more about the multiplexing and connection pooling features of Net8 later in this chapter.

To complete this exercise, save your changes to the initialization file and close it.

NOTE
Oracle8i has more than 200 documented parameters (and many other undocumented parameters) that you can explicitly specify in an initialization file. Even when an initialization file doesn't include a specific parameter, Oracle uses the parameter's default value. When a parameter file explicitly specifies a parameter, the setting for the parameter overrides the default parameter value that is embedded within the Oracle software. For a complete description of all Oracle8i initialization parameters and their default values, see the Oracle8i Reference, which is part of your Oracle online documentation set.

Bug Alert
If you do not want to manually edit your initialization file to configure a database instance for MTS connections, you can also use the *Database Configuration Assistant*, a utility that ships with Oracle8i. Unfortunately, the version of Oracle8i that ships with this book installs a buggy Database Configuration Assistant that does not let you modify the configuration for a database instance. To keep current with the latest versions of Oracle8i for Linux and potential patches that fix bugs such as this one, regularly visit the Oracle Technology Web site at http://technet.oracle.com.

EXERCISE 3.11: Testing Your New MTS Configuration

You will not see the effects of your configuration changes in the previous exercise until you restart your server and reconnect to the starter database. To see the results of your labor, complete the following steps:

1. If you currently have an open SQL*Plus session, disconnect from Oracle and exit SQL*Plus by completing the steps in Exercise 3.3.

2. Shut down the current database instance by completing the steps in Exercise 3.7.

3. Start up a new instance by completing the steps in Exercise 3.6.

Once you have a new instance running, *establish a session as the oracle user*, and then start a new SQL*Plus session using the SYSTEM account. Be sure to specify the starter database's default Net8 service name, oralin, so that your connection uses a network connection rather than an IPC (inter-process communication) connection. For example, at your shell prompt, enter the following command:

```
sqlplus system/manager@oralin
```

Next, list the type of connection that you currently have to the starter database by executing the query listed in Exercise 3.9. The results from the query should appear as follows:

```
SELECT server
  FROM v$session
  WHERE audsid = USERENV('SESSIONID');

SERVER
---------
SHARED
```

If your server is listed as SHARED, you've successfully configured your instance so that client/server (two-task) connections automatically use the instance's MTS processing architecture.

Oracle Networking and Net8

Computer applications typically operate using a client/server system that incorporates a network of computers. To transmit data between the clients and servers in your Oracle environment, you must use Oracle's network communication software. *Net8*, known as *SQL*Net* in previous versions of Oracle, is networking software that makes it possible for Oracle clients and servers to communicate across a network. Executing on both the clients and servers of the system, Net8 makes the presence of the network in a client/server system transparent—an application developer does not have to code low-level application logic (for example, network protocol calls) to access Oracle data across a network. Instead, a client application uses standard SQL statements to request data from a remote Oracle server as if the database were on the same machine as the client. The following sections explain the fundamental concepts of Net8.

Basic Net8 Architecture

The Net8 software that executes on both clients and servers in an Oracle network includes several different layers of functionality that work to hide the complexities of network communication in a distributed processing application. On the client side, Net8 permits an application to locate and access a remote database using SQL as if the database resided on the same computer. On the server side, Net8 permits the database server to receive and send data in response to client SQL requests as though the client were running on the same machine as the server.

The *Transparent Network Substrate* (TNS) layer of Net8 is software that provides Oracle clients and servers with a common application programming interface (API) to all industry-standard network protocols. By plugging network protocol adapters into TNS, clients and servers can communicate using any network protocol. Net8 supports all common network protocols, including TCP/IP, IPX/SPX, DecNet, LU6.2, and more.

Figure 3-6 illustrates a network communication via Net8 between a client application and an Oracle database server. When a client application executes a

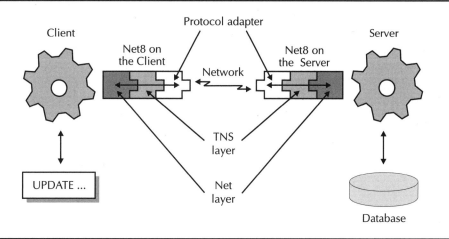

FIGURE 3-6. *Net8 hides the network between the clients and servers of an application*

SQL statement, the statement passes through each layer of Net8 running on the client, which packages the request and sends it across the network. At the server end, Net8 opens the network package, passes the request through the various Net8 layers in reverse order, and finally feeds the SQL statement to the database server as though it were issued by a local application. After statement processing, the server returns the results in the reverse order through Net8 and the network, back to the client.

TNS Connections

A *TNS* connection is a communication pathway between two nodes in an Oracle network. A TNS connection is a persistent pathway that transmits data between two TNS components. In every TNS connection, one node is the initiator and the other is the destination. Typically, the initiator of a TNS connection is a client application, and the destination is an Oracle database server. However, servers can also communicate with one another in an Oracle distributed database system using TNS connections. This book does not discuss distributed database systems in any detail.

Connection Pooling

Typical database connections support applications that sit idle a large percentage of the time. For example, when using a typical order-entry application, the salesperson does not actually send or receive any database information across the TNS connection while filling out a screen form with order information.

To limit the number of physical network connections and make more efficient use of network resources, Net8 can *pool* a preset number of TNS connections. With connection pooling, a database session that sits idle can temporarily allow another session to use its physical TNS connection to the database server, and later reclaim its connection when the session needs to communicate with the server. Consequently, connection pooling allows many sessions to communicate with a database server by sharing a predetermined number of available TNS connections. Fewer network resources are needed to support typical applications, and less server overhead typically translates to better server performance. Figure 3-7 illustrates the basics of connection pooling.

The server does not begin pooling TNS connections until after the preset number of physical network connections are open. To open a subsequent TNS connection, the database server must first locate an idle session and then logically reassign the idle session's connection to the new connection. The preset limit of physical network connections is a limit that you can set as a configuration parameter before server startup.

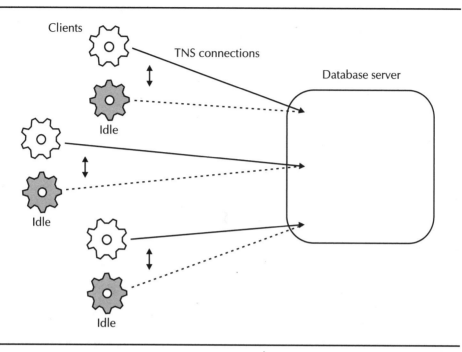

FIGURE 3-7. *Connection pooling allows database sessions to use a set number of physical TNS connections and reduce network overhead*

Multiplexing

To further reduce the overhead of systems that must support many network connections, Net8 can *multiplex* many network connections into a single physical network transport. Figure 3-8 illustrates Net8 multiplexing.

The objective of multiplexing is to reduce the operating system overhead (on the host computer) that is necessary to support many network connections. By concentrating many network connections into a single network transport, you reduce the number of processes and open network sockets needed on the server computer to support large user populations.

The TNS Listener

A *TNS listener* is necessary to establish TNS network connections. A TNS listener is a process that receives the connection request of an initiator, resolves the given address to the network address of the destination, and establishes a TNS connection

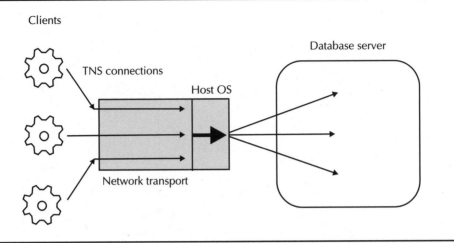

FIGURE 3-8. *Multiplexing many network connections into a single physical network transport reduces the operating system overhead*

to the destination. For example, when you start an application and request a connection to the database named ORACLE, your connection request is forwarded to the network's TNS listener, which then resolves the address of ORACLE to the computer that is running an instance for the associated database. The TNS listener then requests the instance to establish a TNS connection between your client application and the instance's multithreaded server configuration (or a dedicated server).

TNS Addressing

All computer networks use an addressing scheme that uniquely identifies the location of each computer and service on the network. Network configuration files typically establish network names that users can use to identify specific services on the network. For example, on a TCP/IP computer, there is typically a small file called *hosts* that identifies the IP addresses of computers that are accessible on the network. On Linux, the hosts file is found in the /etc directory, and looks similar to the following:

```
127.0.0.1      localhost
128.126.50.100 linux1.animatedlearning.com  linux1
```

TNS Configuration Files
Oracle TNS networks also require address mappings that describe where TNS services can be found on the network, such as TNS listeners and Oracle database

servers. One way to accomplish TNS addressing is to create and distribute *TNS configuration files* to each client and server in the network. Then, when a client initiates a TNS connection, it can use the local copy of the appropriate configuration file to resolve the TNS service address.

When your network uses configuration files to set up a TNS network, the most common TNS configuration files that you will have are as follows:

Filename	Description
tnsnames.ora	The *tnsnames.ora* configuration file resides on both clients and servers in an Oracle network. tnsnames.ora contains address information that Net8 running on a client or server uses to establish connections with other Oracle services in a network.
sqlnet.ora	The *sqlnet.ora* configuration file resides on both clients and servers in an Oracle network. sqlnet.ora contains special configuration parameters that configure a connection from a client or server to another Oracle service in a network.
listener.ora	The *listener.ora* configuration file resides only on servers that run a TNS listener process. listener.ora configures one or more TNS listener processes. The file describes the names, addresses, and databases that correspond to one or more listener processes.

When using Oracle8i for Linux, the default directory location for all TNS configuration files is $ORACLE_HOME/network/admin.

Oracle Names

Configuring and maintaining large Oracle networks can be a challenging administrative task. When you use TNS configuration files for network addressing, each client and server must have the most recent copy of the configuration files or else applications might not work properly. Distributing files to the nodes in the system can be particularly difficult when the network contains hundreds or thousands of clients that need access to network services. Putting configuration files in a shared, central network location does not work well, because the files become hot spots that can create bottlenecks.

To solve many network management problems in an Oracle network, you can employ an optional TNS service component called Oracle Names. *Oracle Names* is name-server software that an Oracle client/server system can use to centrally manage network names and corresponding addresses. Rather than use configuration files, a client contacts an Oracle Names server to resolve the address to a network service in the Oracle network. The Oracle Names server replies with the network address of the requested service, which the client then uses to establish a connection with the service. You can start redundant Oracle Names servers in the same network to distribute loads and prevent single points of failure from making the network unavailable. And, if the network changes in some way, all that's necessary is a quick change to the names servers in the system, and all clients will see new address information automatically.

Configuring Net8

Net8 configuration is accomplished using the *Net8 Assistant*, a simple utility that makes it easy to create and maintain Oracle networks. Fortunately, the Oracle8*i* installer automatically installs and configures Net8, including a TNS listener service and the necessary TNS configuration files that facilitate access to the starter database. The following exercises show you how to use the Net8 Assistant to investigate the configuration of your system.

EXERCISE 3.12: Starting the Net8 Assistant

In this exercise, you'll learn how to examine your current Net8 configuration using the Net8 Assistant. To start the Net8 Assistant, establish an X-Windows session *as the oracle user*, and then enter the following command at a shell prompt:

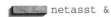 `netasst &`

Figure 3-9 shows the Net8 Assistant. The Net8 Assistant is a dual-paned window that you can use to display the properties of the components in your network. The left pane is an expandable tree of folders. When you select a specific component, the right pane of the Net8 Assistant window shows a property sheet with one or more pages.

The four components that you can configure in an Oracle network using the Net8 Assistant are the following:

- Profiles
- Network service names
- TNS listeners
- Oracle Names servers

The following exercises will teach you more about these components.

EXERCISE 3.13: Exploring a Profile

In the context of Net8, a *profile* is a set of preferences that you can use to configure how clients and servers use Net8. The Net8 Assistant stores the preferences that you set for a profile in the sqlnet.ora configuration file.

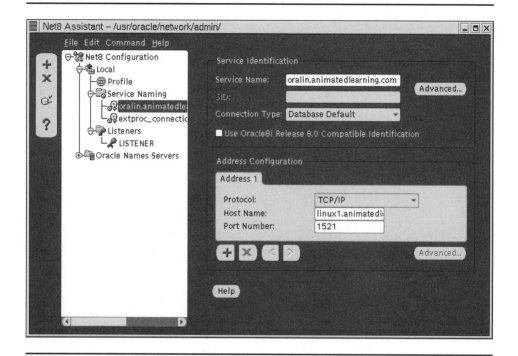

FIGURE 3-9. *The Net8 Assistant*

To display the properties of the current profile, click the Profile icon in the network tree of Net8 Assistant. Figure 3-10 shows the Naming properties of the current profile, specifically the methods that Net8 uses to resolve connection requests to network services.

Notice that in the Selected Methods list, the profile is configured to resolve network connection requests in the following order:

1. Resolve a name using TNSNAMES—the local tnsnames.ora configuration file.

2. If the name cannot be resolved using TNSNAMES, resolve the name using ONAMES—an Oracle Names server.

3. If the name cannot be resolved using TNSNAMES or ONAMES, resolve a host name using HOSTNAME—a TCP/IP address translation mechanism, such as a hosts file.

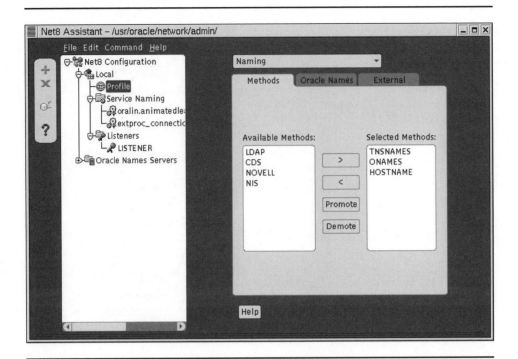

FIGURE 3-10. *Use Net8 Assistant to display and edit the properties of a profile*

Feel free to examine the other properties of your default Net8 profile and use the tool's Help system to learn more about various preferences that you can enable and configure.

EXERCISE 3.14: Examining Existing Network Services

To display the names and properties of network services currently in your network, open the Service Naming folder in the Net8 Assistant, and then click a specific service name. Figure 3-9 shows the properties of the oralin database service that was automatically configured by the installer for the starter database. In this example, notice that the service's network protocol is TCP/IP, the name of the host server computer is linux1.animatedlearning.com, the port number is 1521, and the service name is oralin.animatedlearning.com.

NOTE
The settings that you see will most likely be different based on your computer's network name.

When you add or delete a network service or modify an existing network service using the Net8 Assistant, the tool saves your changes in the tnsnames.ora configuration file.

TIP
Before you make any changes to your network services, you might want to create a backup of the existing tnsnames.ora configuration file—the Net8 Assistant does not ask you to confirm changes before overwriting the existing tnsnames.ora file.

EXERCISE 3.15: Displaying the Listener's Properties

To display the properties of the network addresses for your network's TNS listener, open the Listeners folder in the Net8 Assistant, and then click on a specific listener.

Figure 3-11 shows the properties of an address of the default listener named LISTENER that was automatically configured by the installer. In this example, notice that the address is specifically for Net8 Clients that want to establish TCP/IP connections.

When you add or delete an address for a listener or modify an existing listener address using the Net8 Assistant, the tool saves your changes in the listener.ora configuration file.

EXERCISE 3.16: Starting and Stopping the Listener

The Oracle installer automatically configures the default listener for your Oracle system. You can check the status of the TNS listener using a command line utility called the Listener Control utility, which is found at $ORACLE_HOME/bin/lsnrctl. This utility displays a simple command prompt that accepts commands such as START, STOP, and STATUS to start, stop, and check the current status of a TNS listener. You can also enter utility commands as command line parameters rather than start the utility in interactive mode. For example, to display the status of your default listener, *establish a Linux session as the oracle user*, and then issue the following command:

```
lsnrctl STATUS
```

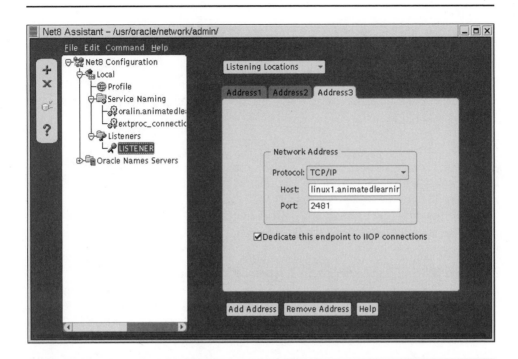

FIGURE 3-11. *The properties of a TNS listener address*

By default, Linux does not start your listener during system startup. When your default listener is not running, you will see error messages similar to the following after running the previous command.

```
LSNRCTL for Linux: Version 8.1.6.0.0 - Production on 06-JUN-2000 10:15:16

(c) Copyright 1998, 1999, Oracle Corporation.  All rights reserved.

Connecting to (DESCRIPTION=(ADDRESS=(PROTOCOL=IPC)(KEY=EXTPROC)))
TNS-01103: Protocol specific component of the address is incorrectly
specified
 TNS-12541: TNS:no listener
  TNS-12560: TNS:protocol adapter error
   TNS-00511: No listener
    Linux Error: 2: No such file or directory
```

To start the default listener on your system, *establish a Linux session as the oracle user*, and then issue the following command:

 lsnrctl START

After starting the listener, the Listener Control utility will return messages similar to the following:

```
LSNRCTL for Linux: Version 8.1.6.0.0 - Production on 06-JUN-2000 10:16:04

(c) Copyright 1998, 1999, Oracle Corporation.  All rights reserved.

Starting /usr/oracle/bin/tnslsnr: please wait...

TNSLSNR for Linux: Version 8.1.6.0.0 - Production
System parameter file is /usr/oracle/network/admin/listener.ora
Log messages written to /usr/oracle/network/log/listener.log
Listening on: (DESCRIPTION=(ADDRESS=(PROTOCOL=ipc)(KEY=EXTPROC)))
Listening on: (DESCRIPTION=(ADDRESS=(PROTOCOL=tcp)
(HOST=linux1.animatedlearning.com)(PORT=1521)))
Listening on: (DESCRIPTION=(ADDRESS=(PROTOCOL=tcp)
(HOST=linux1.animatedlearning.com)(PORT=2481))
(PROTOCOL_STACK=(PRESENTATION=GIOP)(SESSION=RAW)))

Connecting to (DESCRIPTION=(ADDRESS=(PROTOCOL=IPC)(KEY=EXTPROC)))
STATUS of the LISTENER
-----------------------
Alias                   LISTENER
Version                 TNSLSNR for Linux: Version 8.1.6.0.0 - Production
Start Date              06-JUN-2000 10:16:04
Uptime                  0 days 0 hr. 0 min. 0 sec
Trace Level             off
Security                OFF
SNMP                    OFF
Listener Parameter File /usr/oracle/network/admin/listener.ora
Listener Log File       /usr/oracle/network/log/listener.log
Services Summary...
  PLSExtProc      has 1 service handler(s)
  oralin          has 1 service handler(s)
The command completed successfully
```

Likewise, to stop the default listener on your system, enter the following command:

 lsnrctl STOP

TIP
To display a list of Help topics for the Listener Control utility, use the HELP command.

This concludes your preliminary investigation of the default Net8 configuration for your starter database. Should you ever need to update the Net8 configuration for your system, you can use the Net8 Assistant. To complete this exercise, exit the Net8 Assistant without saving any changes.

Final Configuration Steps for Oracle8i on Linux

The previous sections of this chapter explain the essential configuration steps for running Oracle8i on Linux. The next two exercises identify two additional steps that you should perform to complete the configuration of Oracle8i on your Linux.

EXERCISE 3.17: Configuring Linux to Automatically Start Up and Shut Down a Database and Listener

By default, the installer does not configure your Linux computer to automatically start up and shut down the Oracle database and TNS listener when Linux starts and shuts down, respectively. To do this, you need to perform the following steps:

1. Edit the /etc/oratab file.

2. Create the database startup/shutdown script /etc/rc.d/init.d/dbora.

3. Create symbolic links for database startup and shutdown.

To get started, *establish a Linux session as the root user*. Next, open the /etc/oratab file in a text editor, such as vi. By default, the installer places a line for the starter database in the /etc/oratab file, as follows:

```
oralin:/usr/oracle:N
```

Notice that the line has the syntax

```
$ORACLE_SID:$ORACLE_HOME:{Y|N}
```

Edit this line so that the *N* flag is set to *Y* for yes, as follows:

```
oralin:/usr/oracle:Y
```

Once you complete your edit, save and close the /etc/oratab file.

Next, you need to create a shell script named /etc/rc.d/init.d/dbora that your Linux computer's init program can run during system startup and shutdown. The dbora script can contain the following functionality:

■ To start up an Oracle database, the script must establish a session as the oracle user, and then run the $ORACLE_HOME/bin/dbstart script.

- To shut down an Oracle database, the script must establish a session as the oracle user, and then run the $ORACLE_HOME/bin/dbshut script.

- To start up a TNS listener, the script must establish a session as the oracle user, and then run the listener control utility with the START command.

- To shut down a TNS listener, the script must establish a session as the oracle user, and then run the listener control utility with the STOP command.

The Oracle documentation contains an example dbora script without the functionality to start up and shut down a listener; however, here's another more functional example of a dbora shell script that I use on my system:

```
#!/bin/bash
#######################################################################
# Description: Script to startup and shutdown Oracle and listener    #
# File: /etc/rc.d/init.d/dbora                                       #
#######################################################################
# Setup environment for script execution
. /usr/oracle/.bash_profile

# Determine and execute action based on command line parameter

case "$1" in
  start)
      echo "Starting Oracle database(s) listed in /etc/oratab ..."
      sleep 2
      su - oracle -c "$ORACLE_HOME/bin/dbstart"
      echo "Starting TNS listener ..."
      sleep 2
      su - oracle -c "$ORACLE_HOME/bin/lsnrctl start"
      touch /var/lock/subsys/dbora
      ;;
  stop)
      echo "Shutting down TNS listener ..."
      sleep 2
      su - oracle -c "$ORACLE_HOME/bin/lsnrctl stop"
      echo "Shutting down Oracle database(s) listed in /etc/oratab ..."
      sleep 2
      su - oracle -c "$ORACLE_HOME/bin/dbshut"
      rm -f /var/lock/subsys/dbora
      ;;
  status)
      ps -ax | grep -e ora_ -e tnslsnr
      ;;
  *)
```

```
        echo "Usage: dbora {start|stop|status}"
        exit 1
esac

exit 0
```

For your convenience, a copy of my dbora shell script is in the 8istarterkit/scripts directory created by this book's archive. After *establishing a session as root*, copy the dbora script to the /etc/rc.d/init.d directory, and then set the ownership and permissions using the following commands:

```
chown root.root /etc/rc.d/init.d/dbora
chmod 750 /etc/rc.d/init.d/dbora
```

At this point, you might want to test your script to make sure that everything works properly. For example, to reveal the status of your Oracle instance and listener (that is, whether they are running or not), *establish a session as root*, and then enter the following command:

```
/etc/rc.d/init.d/dbora status
```

If the database and listener are running, you'll see an output similar to that in Exercise 3.4. Depending on the current status, you can then try the start and stop options of the dbora script to start up and shut down your Oracle system.

```
/etc/rc.d/init.d/dbora start

/etc/rc.d/init.d/dbora stop
```

The first command will produce output indicating both database and listener startup. The second command will produce output indicating both database and listener shutdown.

Bug Alert and Solution
The version of Oracle8i that ships with this book installs a dbstart script with a bug that does not let you start up an Oracle8i database. The 8istarterkit/scripts directory in your practice archive contains a functioning version of the dbstart script. *Establish a session as the oracle user*, and then copy the updated version of the dbstart script from the 8istarterkit/scripts directory to the $ORACLE_HOME/bin directory. Then set the ownership and permissions for the script using the following commands:

```
chown oracle.oinstall $ORACLE_HOME/bin/dbstart
chmod 755 $ORACLE_HOME/bin/dbstart
```

After you confirm that your dbora script works as designed, you need to configure your Linux computer's init program to automatically start up and shut down your Oracle database server and TNS listener. Assuming that your Linux system uses the Unix System V-ish style of init, you can accomplish this task by creating symbolic links in the various /etc/rc.d directories of your system. After *establishing a session as root,* create the following links for system startup, reboot, and shutdown:

```
ln -s /etc/rc.d/init.d/dbora /etc/rc.d/rc0.d/K05dbora
ln -s /etc/rc.d/init.d/dbora /etc/rc.d/rc2.d/S95dbora
ln -s /etc/rc.d/init.d/dbora /etc/rc.d/rc3.d/S95dbora
ln -s /etc/rc.d/init.d/dbora /etc/rc.d/rc5.d/S95dbora
ln -s /etc/rc.d/init.d/dbora /etc/rc.d/rc6.d/K05dbora
```

NOTE
Depending on your version of Linux, you might need to configure the init process differently. See your Linux documentation for more details.

After you configure the links for the init process, you can test your work by shutting down and restarting the system:

```
shutdown -r now
```

During system shutdown and startup, you should see output consistent with the output produced when you ran the dbora stop and dbora start commands earlier in this exercise.

EXERCISE 3.18: Configuring Other Linux Accounts to Access Oracle

Before installing Oracle8i on your Linux computer, steps in Chapter 2 showed you how to configure the environment for the oracle user so that the installation ran smoothly. After installation, you'll no doubt need to set up other Linux user accounts that will be using Oracle so that they also have the proper environment settings.

To illustrate this process, let's create a new Linux account specifically for the purpose of database administration. In general, Oracle Corp. recommends that you not use the oracle user account other than for Oracle software installation and updates. Therefore, let's create a new Linux account called oradba1 that we can use to perform database administration tasks.

First, establish a Linux session as the root user. Then enter the following commands at a shell prompt to create the new oradba1 account:

```
useradd oradba1 -d /usr/oradba1 -g sysdba
passwd oradba1
```

Notice that the -g parameter in the useradd command sets the new oradba1 account's default group as sysdba, the group necessary for all-powerful Oracle database administrators. If you were creating a new Linux account for an end user or an application developer, you would not set the user's default group to sysdba or sysoper, but to some other appropriate Linux group.

Next, modify the oracle user account's login file to initialize a common Oracle environment for all users. To accomplish this task, use your root session to open the oracle account's login file (for example, /usr/oracle/.bash_profile) in a text editor, such as vi. At the end of the file, add the following two lines:

```
ORAENV_ASK=NO; export ORAENV_ASK
. /usr/local/bin/oraenv
```

NOTE

Substitute appropriate environment variable syntax if the oracle user account uses the C shell, and call the /usr/local/bin/coraenv script rather than /usr/local/bin/oraenv.

After you save your changes, establish a new Linux session as the oracle user to initialize the common Oracle environment, and then terminate the session.

Now it's time to configure the new oradba1 account so that corresponding sessions have the proper environment settings ($ORACLE_HOME, $ORACLE_SID, $PATH, and so on) as configured by the oracle user account. To make this convenient, all that you have to do is edit the account's login file (for example, /usr/oradba1/.bash_profile) and add the following line to the end of the file:

```
. /usr/local/bin/oraenv
```

NOTE

If the user account uses the C shell, call the /usr/local/bin/coraenv script rather than /usr/local/bin/oraenv.

After you save the oradba1 account's login file, establish a new Linux session as the oradba1 user to test your work. Immediately after login, you should see the following prompt:

```
ORACLE_SID = [oradba1] ?
```

At this prompt, set the current $ORACLE_SID to *oralin* (or whatever you chose for your instance). Next, use the env command to display a list of your session's environment settings:

```
env | more
```

If you completed the previous steps in this exercise properly, you should see settings similar to the following within the environment settings:

```
ORACLE_SID=oralin
ORACLE_HOME=/usr/oracle
PATH=/usr/local/bin:/bin:/usr/bin:/usr/oracle/bin
```

Finally, you can test that the configuration works properly by attempting to start SQL*Plus from your oradba1 session. If everything is set up correctly, your configuration for the new account is complete. If you receive permission errors when trying to run SQL*Plus, the two most likely reasons are:

- You did not set the correct permissions for $ORACLE_HOME directory as instructed in Chapter 2.

- You did not run the root.sh script when prompted during the installation process, or did not run the root.sh script as the root user.

Chapter Summary

This chapter has explained several of the software components that you will configure and work with when you use Oracle8i.

- An Oracle instance is a set of operating system processes and memory structures that, once started, provide for application access to a database.

- Oracle uses a number of background server processes (for example, DBWR, LGWR, ARCH, CKPT, SMON, and PMON) to perform specialized internal functions.

- Oracle can use either dedicated or multithreaded server configurations to support user connections to a database instance.

- When an Oracle database server must support user connections across a network, clients and servers in the system must run Net8, Oracle's networking software.

- To configure Net8, you can use the graphical administration tools Net8 Assistant and Net8 Configuration Assistant.

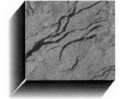

PART II

Fundamentals of Application Development

CHAPTER

4

Basic Database Access with SQL

o get work done, applications must communicate with Oracle8i to enter and retrieve data, and do so in a way that protects the integrity of the database's data. This chapter introduces the basic concepts of how applications use SQL statements and encompassing transactions to interact with an Oracle8i database system.

Chapter Prerequisites

To practice the hands-on exercises in this chapter, you need to start a Linux session as the user oracle, start SQL*Plus, and run the following command script

   location/8istarterkit/SQL/chap04.sql

where *location* is the file directory where you expanded the support archive that accompanies this book. For example, after starting SQL*Plus and connecting as SCOTT, you can run this chapter's SQL command script using the SQL*Plus command @, as in the following example (assuming that your chap04.sql file is in /tmp/8istarterkit/SQL):

```
SQL> /tmp/8istarterkit/SQL/chap04.sql;
```

Once the script completes successfully, leave the current SQL*Plus session open and use it to perform this chapter's exercises in the order in which they appear.

What Is SQL?

To accomplish work with Oracle8i, applications must use *Structured Query Language* (SQL) commands. SQL (pronounced either as "sequel" or "ess-que-ell") is a relatively simple command language that database administrators, developers, and application users use to

- Retrieve, enter, update, and delete database data
- Create, alter, and drop database objects
- Restrict access to database data and system operations

The only way that an application can interact with an Oracle database server is to issue a SQL command. Sophisticated graphical user interfaces might hide SQL commands from users and developers, but under the covers, an application always communicates with Oracle using SQL.

Types of SQL Commands

The four primary categories of SQL commands are DML, transaction control, DDL, and DCL commands.

- *Data manipulation* or *data modification language* (DML) commands are SQL commands that retrieve, insert, update, and delete table rows in an Oracle database. The four basic DML commands are SELECT, INSERT, UPDATE, and DELETE. Subsequent sections of this chapter provide you with a thorough introduction to these four commands.

- Applications that use SQL and relational databases perform work by using transactions. A *database transaction* is a unit of work accomplished by one or more related SQL statements. To preserve the integrity of information in a database, relational databases such as Oracle ensure that all work within each transaction either commits or rolls back. An application uses the *transaction control* SQL commands COMMIT and ROLLBACK to control the outcome of a database transaction. Subsequent sections of this chapter explain how to design transactions and use transaction control SQL commands.

- *Data definition language* (DDL) commands create, alter, and drop database objects. Most types of database objects have corresponding CREATE, ALTER, and DROP commands. See Chapter 7 for more information about, and examples of, several DDL commands.

- An administrative application uses *data control language* (DCL) commands to control user access to an Oracle database. The three most commonly used DCL commands are the GRANT, REVOKE, and SET ROLE commands. See Chapter 9 for more information about, and examples of, these DCL commands.

Application Portability and the ANSI/ISO SQL Standard

The *ANSI/ISO SQL standard* defines a generic specification for SQL. Most commercial relational database systems, including Oracle8i, support ANSI/ISO standard SQL. When a database supports the SQL standard and an application uses only standard SQL commands, the application is said to be *portable*. In other words, if you decide to substitute another database that supports the ANSI/ISO SQL standard, the application continues to function unmodified.

The ANSI/ISO SQL-92 standard has four different levels of compliance: Entry, Transitional, Intermediate, and Full. Oracle8i complies with the SQL-92 Entry level, and has many features that conform to the Transitional, Intermediate, and Full levels. Oracle also has many features that comply with the SQL3 standard, including its new object-oriented database features, discussed in Chapter 8.

Oracle8i also supports many extensions to the ANSI/ISO SQL-92 standard. Such extensions enhance the capabilities of Oracle. *SQL extensions* can take the form of nonstandard SQL commands or just nonstandard options for standard SQL commands. However, understand that when an application makes use of proprietary Oracle8i SQL extensions, the application is no longer portable—you would likely need to modify and recompile the application before it will work with other database systems.

Now that you have a general understanding of SQL, the remaining sections in this chapter introduce you to the SQL commands that you will most often use to access an Oracle database: SELECT, INSERT, UPDATE, DELETE, COMMIT, and ROLLBACK.

Retrieving Data with Queries

The most basic SQL statement is a query. A *query* is a SQL statement that uses the SELECT command to retrieve information from a database. A query's *result set* is the set of columns and rows that the query requests from a database server. For example, the following query retrieves all rows and columns from the ORDERS table:

```
SELECT * FROM orders;

       ID      C_ID ORDERDATE SHIPDATE  PAIDDATE  STATUS
--------- --------- --------- --------- --------- ------
        1         1 18-JUN-99 18-JUN-99 30-JUN-99 F
        2         2 18-JUN-99                     B
        3         3 18-JUN-99 18-JUN-99 21-JUN-99 F
        4         4 19-JUN-99 21-JUN-99 21-JUN-99 F
        5         5 19-JUN-99 19-JUN-99 28-JUN-99 F
        6         6 19-JUN-99 19-JUN-99           F
        7         7 19-JUN-99                     B
        8         8 20-JUN-99 20-JUN-99 20-JUN-99 F
        9         9 21-JUN-99                     B
       10         2 21-JUN-99 22-JUN-99 22-JUN-99 F
       11         4 22-JUN-99 22-JUN-99           F
       12         7 22-JUN-99 23-JUN-99 30-JUN-99 F
       13         4 22-JUN-99                     B
       14         1 23-JUN-99 25-JUN-99           F

14 rows selected.
```

The Structure of a Query

Although the structure of a SELECT statement can vary, all queries have two basic components: a SELECT clause and a FROM clause.

A query's *SELECT clause* specifies a *column list* that identifies the columns that must appear in the query's result set. Each column in the SELECT clause must correspond to one of the tables in the query's FROM clause. A SELECT clause can also contain *expressions* that derive information from columns using functions or operators that manipulate table data. Subsequent sections of this chapter explain how to build expressions in a query's SELECT clause.

A query's *FROM clause* specifies the rows for the query to target. The FROM clause of a typical query specifies a list of one or more tables. Simple queries target just one table, while more advanced queries join information by targeting multiple related tables. Alternatively, a FROM clause in a query can specify a *subquery* (a *nested* or *inner query*) to build a specific set of rows as the target for the main (or *outer*) query. When you use a subquery in a query's FROM clause, SELECT clause expressions in the outer query must refer to columns in the result set of the subquery.

Building Basic Queries

The following set of hands-on exercises teaches you how to build basic queries and several related functions, including the following:

- How to retrieve all columns and rows from a table

- How to retrieve specific columns of all rows in a table

- How to "describe" the structure of a table

- How to specify an alias for a column in a query

EXERCISE 4.1: Retrieving All Columns and Rows from a Table

Using SQL*Plus, enter the following query to retrieve all columns and rows from the ORDERS table.

```
SELECT * FROM orders;
```

The results of the query should be identical to the following:

```
       ID      C_ID ORDERDATE SHIPDATE  PAIDDATE  STATUS
--------- --------- --------- --------- --------- ------
        1         1 18-JUN-99 18-JUN-99 30-JUN-99 F
```

```
    2        2 18-JUN-99                         B
    3        3 18-JUN-99 18-JUN-99 21-JUN-99 F
    4        4 19-JUN-99 21-JUN-99 21-JUN-99 F
    5        5 19-JUN-99 19-JUN-99 28-JUN-99 F
    6        6 19-JUN-99 19-JUN-99             F
    7        7 19-JUN-99                         B
    8        8 20-JUN-99 20-JUN-99 20-JUN-99 F
    9        9 21-JUN-99                         B
   10        2 21-JUN-99 22-JUN-99 22-JUN-99 F
   11        4 22-JUN-99 22-JUN-99             F
   12        7 22-JUN-99 23-JUN-99 30-JUN-99 F
   13        4 22-JUN-99                         B
   14        1 23-JUN-99 25-JUN-99             F

14 rows selected.
```

The wildcard asterisk character (*) in the SELECT clause indicates that the query should retrieve all columns from the target table.

EXERCISE 4.2: Retrieving Specific Columns from a Table

To retrieve specific columns from all rows in a table, a query's SELECT clause must explicitly specify the name of each column to retrieve. For example, enter the following statement to retrieve just the ID and ORDERDATE columns for all rows in the ORDERS table.

```
SELECT id, orderdate FROM orders;
```

The result set is as follows:

```
       ID ORDERDATE
--------- ---------
        1 18-JUN-99
        2 18-JUN-99
        3 18-JUN-99
        4 19-JUN-99
        5 19-JUN-99
        6 19-JUN-99
        7 19-JUN-99
        8 20-JUN-99
        9 21-JUN-99
       10 21-JUN-99
       11 22-JUN-99
       12 22-JUN-99
       13 22-JUN-99
       14 23-JUN-99

14 rows selected.
```

EXERCISE 4.3: Using the SQL*Plus DESCRIBE Command

If you are using SQL*Plus and you do not know the names of the columns in a table that you would like to query, use the special SQL*Plus command *DESCRIBE* to output the structure of the table. Enter the following DESCRIBE statement to display the column names of the ORDERS table (as well as additional information for each column).

 DESCRIBE orders;

The results of the previous command should be similar to the following:

```
Name                                            Null?    Type
----------------------------------------------- -------- ----------
ID                                              NOT NULL NUMBER(38)
C_ID                                            NOT NULL NUMBER(38)
ORDERDATE                                       NOT NULL DATE
SHIPDATE                                                 DATE
PAIDDATE                                                 DATE
STATUS                                                   CHAR(1)
```

EXERCISE 4.4: Specifying an Alias for a Column

To customize the names of the columns in a query's result set, you have the option of specifying an *alias* (an alternate name) for each column (or expression) in the query's SELECT clause. To rename a column or expression in the SELECT clause, just specify an alias after the list item.

> **NOTE**
> *You must delimit the alias with double quotes if you want to specify the case, spacing, or include special characters in an alias.*

To use a column alias, enter the following query, which specifies an alias for the ONHAND column of the PARTS table.

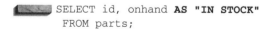 SELECT id, onhand **AS "IN STOCK"**
   FROM parts;

The result set is as follows:

```
    ID IN STOCK
--------- ---------
     1      277
     2      143
     3     7631
     4     5903
     5      490
```

As this example demonstrates, you can precede a column alias with the optional keyword AS to make the alias specification more readable.

Building Expressions in a Query's SELECT Clause

In addition to simple column specifications, the SELECT clause of a query can also include expressions. An *expression* is a SQL construct that derives a character string, date, or numeric value. There are several different types of constructs that you can use to build expressions in a query's SELECT clause and return the resulting data in the query's result set, including operators, SQL functions, and decoded expressions. The next few sections provide a brief introduction to SELECT clause expressions.

EXERCISE 4.5: Building SELECT Clause Expressions with the Concatenation String Operator

An *operator* is a symbol that transforms a column value or combines it somehow with another column value or *literal* (an explicit value). For example, a simple way to build an expression in a SELECT clause is to use the *concatenation operator*—two solid vertical bars (||)—to concatenate character columns and/or string literals.

Enter the following query, which includes a simple SELECT clause expression. For each record in the CUSTOMERS table, the expression concatenates the LASTNAME field with a comma and a blank space (delimited by single quotes), and then the resulting string with the FIRSTNAME field. The expression also has a column alias to make its column heading in the result set more readable.

```
SELECT lastname || ', ' || firstname AS name
  FROM customers;
```

The result set is as follows:

```
NAME
--------------------
Joy, Harold
Musial, Bill
Sams, Danielle
Elias, Juan
Foss, Betty
Schaub, Greg
Wiersbicki, Joseph
Ayers, Jack
```

```
Clay, Dorothy
Haagensen, Dave

10 rows selected.
```

NOTE

The expressions on which an operator acts are called operands. The concatenation operator is an example of a binary operator—an operator that takes two operands and creates a new result. An operand that creates a value from a single operand is called a unary operator.

EXERCISE 4.6: Building SELECT Clause Expressions with Arithmetic Operators

Oracle's unary and binary arithmetic operators are listed in Table 4-1. An *arithmetic operator* accepts one or more numeric operands and produces a single numeric result.

Let's try a query that contains a SELECT clause expression that uses a binary arithmetic operator. Enter the following query, which determines how many of each part remains in inventory above the corresponding part's reorder threshold.

```
SELECT id, onhand - reorder AS threshold
  FROM parts;
```

Arithmetic Operator	Description
+x (unary)	Indicates that *x* is positive
-x (unary)	Indicates that *x* is negative
x || y (binary)	Concatenates *x* and *y*
x + y (binary)	Adds *x* and *y*
x - y (binary)	Subtracts *y* from *x*
x * y (binary)	Multiplies *x* by *y*
x / y (binary)	Divides *x* by *y*

TABLE 4-1. *The Arithmetic Operators Supported by Oracle8i*

The result set is as follows:

```
       ID THRESHOLD
--------- ---------
        1       227
        2       118
        3      6631
        4      4903
        5       290
```

EXERCISE 4.7: Building SELECT Clause Expressions with SQL Functions

You can also build an expression in a query's SELECT clause by using one or more of SQL's built-in functions. A *function* takes zero, one, or multiple arguments and returns a single value. There are two general types of SQL functions that you can use with queries: single-row functions and group functions.

A *single-row* (or *scalar*) *function* returns a value for every row that is part of a query's result set. Oracle8i supports many different categories of single-row SQL functions, including character, date, numeric, and conversion functions. For example, enter the following query, which uses the SQL functions *UPPER* and *LOWER* in SELECT clause expressions to display the company name in uppercase letters for each customer record and the last name of each customer record in lowercase letters.

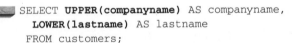

```
SELECT UPPER(companyname) AS companyname,
    LOWER(lastname) AS lastname
 FROM customers;
```

The result set is as follows:

```
COMPANYNAME                     LASTNAME
------------------------------- ---------------
MCDONALD CO.                    joy
CAR AUDIO CENTER                musial
WISE TRUCKING                   sams
ROSE GARDEN INN                 elias
FOSS PHOTOGRAPHY                foss
PAMPERED PETS                   schaub
KEY LOCKSMITH                   wiersbicki
PARK VIEW INSURANCE             ayers
KENSER CORP.                    clay
DAVE'S TREE SERVICE             haagensen

10 rows selected.
```

Now enter the following query, which uses two numeric single-row SQL functions in SELECT clause expressions, *SQRT* and *LN*, to display the square root of 49 and the natural logarithm of 10, respectively.

```
SELECT SQRT(49), LN(10)
  FROM DUAL;
```

The result set is as follows:

```
 SQRT(49)    LN(10)
--------- ---------
        7 2.3025851
```

NOTE
The previous query targets a special table called DUAL that is present in every Oracle database. DUAL is an empty table, consisting of one column and one row, that you can use to satisfy the requirement for a table in a query's FROM clause. DUAL is useful for queries that just perform arithmetic or use a SQL function to return a value.

A *group* (or *aggregate*) *function* returns an aggregate value for all rows that are part of a query's result set. For example, enter the following query, which uses the group SQL functions *COUNT, MAX, MIN,* and *AVG* to return the number of records in the PARTS table, as well as the maximum, minimum, and average UNITPRICE for records in the PARTS table, respectively.

```
SELECT COUNT(id) AS count,
  MAX(unitprice) AS max_price,
  MIN(unitprice) AS min_price,
  AVG(unitprice) AS ave_price
  FROM parts;
```

The result set is as follows:

```
    COUNT MAX_PRICE MIN_PRICE AVE_PRICE
--------- --------- --------- ---------
        5      4895        99    1718.6
```

The example queries in this section have introduced just a few of the many SQL functions that are available with Oracle8i. See your Oracle documentation for a complete list of the SQL functions that you can use when building SQL statements.

EXERCISE 4.8: Working with Nulls in SELECT Clause Expressions

A *null* indicates the absence of a value. For example, the SHIPDATE field of a sales record in the ORDERS table will be null until the order ships, after which you can replace the null with an actual date value. When building SELECT clause expressions for queries, you must pay special attention to the possibility of nulls; otherwise you might obtain inaccurate or nonsense query results. In most cases, an expression that includes a null evaluates to null.

To explicitly handle nulls in SELECT clause expressions, you can use the special scalar SQL function *NVL* to return a value of your choice when a column is null. For example, enter the following query that substitutes the string literal "UNKNOWN" when the FAX field of a record in the CUSTOMERS table is null.

```
SELECT id, NVL(fax, 'UNKNOWN') AS fax
 FROM customers;
```

The result set is as follows:

```
    ID FAX
--------- ----------------------
     1 UNKNOWN
     2 775-859-2121
     3 203-955-9532
     4 214-907-3188
     5 215-543-9800
     6 602-617-7321
     7 718-445-8799
     8 UNKNOWN
     9 916-672-8753
    10 UNKNOWN
```

10 rows selected.

EXERCISE 4.9: Using Decoded SELECT Clause Expressions

A *decoded expression* is a special type of SELECT clause expression that you use to translate codes or symbols in a column. For example, enter the following query, which includes a decoded SELECT clause expression to convert the codes F and B of the STATUS column in the ORDERS table to the corresponding string literals FILLED and BACKORDERED.

```
SELECT id,
   DECODE (
    status,
    'F','FILLED', 'B','BACKORDERED',
```

```
   'OTHER' ) AS status
FROM orders;
```

The result set is as follows:

```
        ID STATUS
--------- ---------------
         1 FILLED
         2 BACKORDERED
         3 FILLED
         4 FILLED
         5 FILLED
         6 FILLED
         7 BACKORDERED
         8 FILLED
         9 BACKORDERED
        10 FILLED
        11 FILLED
        12 FILLED
        13 BACKORDERED
        14 FILLED
```

```
14 rows selected.
```

This example demonstrates that to specify a decoded expression in a SELECT clause, you use the *DECODE( ) keyword* and several parameters. The first parameter is the expression to be evaluated, which can be as simple as a column in a table. The second parameter is a comma-separated list of value pairs. For each possible value of the expression in the first parameter, specify a corresponding display value. The final parameter, which is optional, is a default display value for all expression values that are not specified in the list of value pairs. In the example here, the default display value is the string literal "OTHER".

Retrieving Specific Rows from Tables

So far, all of the example queries in this chapter show how to retrieve every row from a table. Optionally, a query can limit the result set to those rows in the target table that satisfy a *WHERE clause* condition. If the Boolean condition of the WHERE clause evaluates to TRUE for a particular row, Oracle includes the row in the query's result set. For example, the following query includes a WHERE clause condition that limits the result set to only those records in the ORDERS table that have a STATUS code equal to B.

```
SELECT id AS backorders
  FROM orders
 WHERE status = 'B';
```

The result set is as follows:

```
BACKORDERS
----------
         2
         7
         9
        13
```

NOTE
*If you submit a query and omit a WHERE clause,
Oracle selects all rows from the targets specified in
the query's FROM clause.*

The next three exercises explain how to build WHERE clause conditions with
relational operators, subqueries, and logical operators.

EXERCISE 4.10: Building WHERE Clause Conditions with Relational Operators

Oracle supports several relational operators that you can use to build WHERE clause
conditions. A *relational* (or *comparison*) *operator* compares two operands to determine
whether they are equal, or if one operand is greater than the other. A condition that
uses a relational operator produces a Boolean value of TRUE or FALSE; however, if a
null is involved in the condition, some relational operators produce an UNKNOWN
result. Table 4-2 lists the relational operators that Oracle8*i* supports.

Relational Operator	Description
$x = y$	Determines if x equals y.*
$x \mathrel{!=} y$ $x \mathrel{\char94=} y$ $x <> y$	Determines if x is not equal to y.*
$x > y$	Determines if x is greater than y.*
$x < y$	Determines if x is less than y.*
$x >= y$	Determines if x is greater than or equal to y.*
	*If y is a subquery, it must return a single row.

TABLE 4-2.   *The Relational Operators Supported by Oracle8i*

Relational Operator	Description
x <= *y*	Determines if *x* is less than or equal to *y*.
x IN (*list|subquery*)	Determines if the operand *x* is present in the list of values specified or returned by a subquery.
x NOT IN (*list|subquery*)	Determines if the operand *x* is not present in the list of values specified or returned by a subquery. The evaluation is FALSE when a list member is null.
x {=|!=|>|<|>=|<=} {ANY|SOME} (*list|subquery*)	Compares the operand *x* to the list of values specified or returned by a subquery. The evaluation is FALSE when a subquery does not return any rows. The keywords ANY and SOME are equivalent.
x {=|!=|>|<|>=|<=} ALL (*list|subquery*)	Compares the operand *x* to the list of values specified or returned by a subquery. The evaluation is TRUE when a subquery does not return any rows.
x BETWEEN *y* AND *z*	Determines if *x* falls within the inclusive range of *y* and *z*.
x NOT BETWEEN *y* AND *z*	Determines if *x* does not fall within the inclusive range of *y* and *z*.
EXISTS (*subquery*)	Determines if the subquery returns rows. The evaluation is TRUE when the subquery returns one or more rows, and FALSE when the subquery does not return any rows.
x LIKE *y* [ESCAPE *z*]	Determines if *x* matches the pattern *y*. *y* can include the wildcard characters % and _. % matches any string of zero or more characters, except null. _ matches any single character. Use the optional ESCAPE parameter only when you want Oracle to interpret literally a wildcard character within *y*—specify the wildcard character as the escape character.

TABLE 4-2.   *The Relational Operators Supported by Oracle8i (continued)*

Relational Operator	Description
x NOT LIKE *y* [ESCAPE *z*]	Determines if *x* does not match the pattern *y*. *y* can include the wildcard characters % and _ , and you can include the optional ESCAPE parameter (explained above).
x IS NULL	Determines if *x* is null.
x IS NOT NULL	Determines if *x* is not null.

TABLE 4-2. *The Relational Operators Supported by Oracle8i* (continued)

Let's try a couple of queries that use relational operators to build WHERE clause conditions. First, enter the following query to display the ID and ORDERDATE of all records in the ORDERS tables that have an ORDERDATE greater than June 21, 1999.

```
SELECT id, orderdate
 FROM orders
WHERE orderdate > '21-JUN-99';
```

The result set is as follows:

```
     ID ORDERDATE
--------- ---------
     11 22-JUN-99
     12 22-JUN-99
     13 22-JUN-99
     14 23-JUN-99
```

Next, enter the following query to list the ID and LASTNAME of all customer records that do not have a FAX number. Notice that the WHERE clause condition uses the special IS NULL relational operator to test for the presence of a null in each record.

```
SELECT id, lastname
 FROM customers
WHERE fax IS NULL;
```

The result set is as follows:

```
     ID LASTNAME
--------- --------------
      1 Joy
      8 Ayers
     10 Haagensen
```

EXERCISE 4.11: Building WHERE Clause Conditions with Subqueries

Some queries need to retrieve the answers based on multiple-part questions. For example, how would you build a query that reports the IDs of all orders placed by customers of a particular sales representative? This is really a two-part question, because the ORDERS table does not contain a field to record the sales representative that made the sale. However, the ORDERS table does include a field for the customer that made the purchase, and the CUSTOMERS table uses the S_ID column to indicate the sales representative for each customer record. Therefore, you can answer the original question by first building a list of customers that correspond to the sales representative, and then using the list to retrieve the IDs of the orders that correspond to just those customers.

To answer a multiple-part question in SQL with just one query, the query can use a WHERE clause condition with a subquery. A *subquery* is a technique that you can use to build an operand for the right side of a WHERE clause condition that uses a relational operator. When a WHERE clause condition uses a subquery, Oracle evaluates the subquery (or *inner, nested query*) first to return a value or list of values to the relational operator before evaluating the *main* (or *outer*) *query*.

Let's try a query that uses a subquery to answer the question asked at the beginning of this exercise. Enter the following query, which uses a WHERE clause condition with the relational operator IN and a subquery to report the ID and ORDERDATE of all orders placed by customers of sales representative number 2.

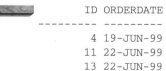

```
SELECT id, orderdate
  FROM orders
 WHERE c_id IN (
   SELECT id FROM customers
    WHERE s_id = 2 );
```

The result set is as follows:

```
        ID ORDERDATE
--------- ---------
         4 19-JUN-99
        11 22-JUN-99
        13 22-JUN-99
```

Now consider what you would do if you needed to answer the previous question, but you did not know the ID of the sales representative with the last name "Jonah."

In this case, you would need to answer a three-part question with a single query. First, you would need to get the ID of the sales representative named Jonah, then get a list of Jonah's customers, and then list the ID and ORDERDATE that correspond to those customers only. To accomplish this feat with a single query, the subquery of the main query must use a subquery itself. Enter the following query to try this out for yourself.

```
SELECT id, orderdate
 FROM orders
 WHERE c_id IN (
   SELECT id FROM customers
    WHERE s_id = (
     SELECT id FROM salesreps
      WHERE lastname = 'Jonah') );
```

The result set is as follows:

```
       ID ORDERDATE
--------- ---------
        4 19-JUN-99
       11 22-JUN-99
       13 22-JUN-99
```

Notice that the innermost subquery uses the equals relational operator (=) and a subquery to determine the ID of the sales representative with the last name "Jonah." Oracle supports the use of a subquery with many relational operators—see Table 4-2 for a complete list of all relational operators that support subqueries, and their corresponding descriptions.

EXERCISE 4.12: Building Composite WHERE Clause Conditions with Logical Operators

Oracle also supports the use of the logical operators AND and OR to build a composite WHERE clause condition—a condition that includes two or more conditions.

■ The AND operator combines the results of two conditions. The entire condition evaluates to TRUE only when both conditions on either side of the AND operator are TRUE. It evaluates to FALSE when either or both conditions are FALSE, and it evaluates to UNKNOWN when both conditions are null, or when either condition is TRUE and the other is null.

■ The OR operator combines the results of two conditions. The entire condition evaluates to FALSE only when both conditions on either side of the OR operator are FALSE. It evaluates to TRUE when either or both conditions are TRUE, and it evaluates to UNKNOWN when both conditions are null, or when either condition is FALSE and the other is null.

Enter the following query, which uses the AND logical operator to build a composite WHERE clause condition that reports the ID and ORDERDATE of records in the ORDERS table that were ordered on or after June 21, 1999, and have a STATUS equal to B (on back order).

```
SELECT id, orderdate
  FROM orders
 WHERE orderdate >= '21-JUN-99' AND status = 'B';
```

The result set is as follows:

```
       ID ORDERDATE
--------- ---------
        9 21-JUN-99
       13 22-JUN-99
```

NOTE
Oracle also supports the logical operator NOT so that you can build a query with a WHERE clause condition that tests for records that contradict a condition.

Grouping and Sorting Data Within a Query's Result Set

The previous exercises in this chapter teach you how to include specific columns and rows in a query's result set. The next two sections explain how to format the output of a query's result set by grouping and sorting the records.

EXERCISE 4.13: Grouping Records in a Query's Result Set

Many queries need to answer questions based on *aggregates* or *summaries* of information rather than the details of individual records in a table. To group data in a query's result set, the query must include a *GROUP BY clause*. The list of columns in the GROUP BY clause specify how to aggregate the rows in the result set. A GROUP BY clause can list any column name in the table that appears in the query's FROM clause; however, a GROUP BY clause cannot reference aliases defined in the SELECT clause.

When you build the SELECT clause of a query that includes a GROUP BY clause, you can include an expression that uses a group function, including the functions AVG, COUNT, MAX, MIN, STDDEV, SUM, and VARIANCE. You can also include an unaggregated column or expression in the SELECT clause, but the same column or expression must be one of the columns or expressions in the GROUP BY clause.

Let's try grouping some data in a query's result set by entering the following query, which uses the group SQL function COUNT and a GROUP BY clause to display the number of orders placed by each customer.

```
SELECT c_id AS customer,
   COUNT(id) AS orders_placed
 FROM orders
 GROUP BY c_id;
```

The result set is as follows:

```
CUSTOMER ORDERS_PLACED
--------- -------------
        1             2
        2             2
        3             1
        4             3
        5             1
        6             1
        7             2
        8             1
        9             1
```

9 rows selected.

To eliminate selected groups from a query's result set, you can add a *HAVING clause* to the query's GROUP BY clause. Much like a WHERE clause condition, Oracle includes only those groups in a query's result set that evaluate to TRUE for the HAVING clause condition. For example, enter the following query, which displays the ID and number of orders placed by customers that have placed more than one order.

```
SELECT c_id AS customer,
   COUNT(id) AS orders_placed
 FROM orders
 GROUP BY c_id
 HAVING COUNT(id) > 1;
```

The result set is as follows:

```
CUSTOMER ORDERS_PLACED
--------- -------------
        1             2
        2             2
        4             3
        7             2
```

NOTE
A query can use both a WHERE clause and the HAVING clause of a GROUP BY clause to eliminate data from the query's result set. Before forming groups, Oracle first removes all rows from the query's result set that do not satisfy the condition of the WHERE clause. Next, Oracle uses the expressions in the GROUP BY clause to form summary groups. Finally, Oracle removes the groups in the result set that do not satisfy the condition of the HAVING clause.

EXERCISE 4.14: Ordering Records in a Query's Result Set

A query can sort the rows in its result set in ascending or descending order by including an *ORDER BY clause.* You can sort rows by any number of columns and expressions that are in the query's SELECT clause, or by any column in the target table even if it is not included in the SELECT clause. In the ORDER BY clause, specify a comma-separated list of the columns and expressions to sort on, either by name, by their position in the SELECT clause, or by their alias in the SELECT list, and indicate whether you want ascending (ASC) or descending (DESC) order for each item. The default sort order for all columns and expressions in an ORDER BY clause is ascending order.

Enter the following query, which displays each customer record's ID, LASTNAME, and ZIPCODE, sorted in ascending order by the record's ZIPCODE.

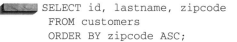

```
SELECT id, lastname, zipcode
  FROM customers
  ORDER BY zipcode ASC;
```

The result set is as follows:

```
    ID LASTNAME                        ZIPCODE
--------- ------------------------------- -------
     3 Sams                            06103
     7 Wiersbicki                      11220
     5 Foss                            19144
     1 Joy                             21209
    10 Haagensen                       44124
     8 Ayers                           66604
     4 Elias                           75252
     6 Schaub                          85023
     2 Musial                          89501
     9 Clay                            95821

10 rows selected.
```

NOTE
When you order a query's result set by an expression that returns nulls, Oracle places the rows with nulls last in the result set when you order in ascending order; when you order in descending order, Oracle places the rows with nulls first in the result set.

Joining Data in Related Tables

The previous examples in this chapter are all queries that target data from only one table. A query can also *join* information from multiple related tables. When you want to join information from *N* number of tables, include a comma-separated list of the tables to join in the query's FROM clause. The query's WHERE clause should have *N*–1 join conditions that explain how to relate the data in the tables. The join query's SELECT clause can contain columns and expressions that refer to some or all of the columns in the target tables; however, when two columns in different tables have identical names, you must qualify references to these columns throughout the query with a table name to avoid ambiguity. The following two exercises contain examples of these syntax rules and explain two specific types of join queries: inner joins and outer joins.

EXERCISE 4.15: Building an Inner Join of Two Tables

An *inner join* combines the rows of two related tables based on a common column (or combination of common columns). The result set of an inner join does not include rows in either table that do not have a match in the other table.

To specify an inner-join operation, use a WHERE clause condition that relates the common columns in each table as operands on either side of the equality operator. For example, enter the following query that performs an inner join of the CUSTOMERS and ORDERS table.

```
SELECT c.id AS customer_id,
  o.id AS order_id
 FROM customers c, orders o
 WHERE c.id = o.c_id
 ORDER BY c.id;
```

The result set is as follows:

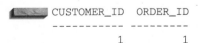

```
CUSTOMER_ID  ORDER_ID
-----------  ---------
          1          1
```

```
1          14
2           2
2          10
3           3
4           4
4          11
4          13
5           5
6           6
7           7
7          12
8           8
9           9
```

`14 rows selected.`

This example of an inner join retrieves a cross-product of all rows in the CUSTOMERS table that have placed orders. Notice that the result set of this query does not include any row for the customer with an ID of 10, because that customer has not placed any orders.

The previous example also shows how to declare aliases for tables in a query's FROM clause, and to use the aliases to qualify column names in other clauses of the query. The qualification of a column name with its table name is necessary when the two tables in the join have columns with the same name.

NOTE
When a join uses the equality comparison operator in the join condition, the query is commonly referred to as an equi join.

EXERCISE 4.16: Building an Outer Join of Two Tables

Similar to an inner join, an *outer join* also combines the rows of two related tables, based on a common column (or combination of common columns). However, the result set of an outer join includes rows from one of the tables even when there are not any matching rows in the other table.

The WHERE clause condition of an outer join is similar to that of an inner, equi join with one exception—you must place the outer-join operator, a plus sign delimited by parentheses (+), after one of the columns in the join condition. Specifically, the outer-join operator follows the column in the join condition that corresponds to the table for which you expect no matching rows. For example, enter the following query, which performs an outer join of the CUSTOMERS and ORDERS tables, and includes all customers even when a customer does not have any matching orders.

```
SELECT c.id AS customer_id,
    o.id AS order_id
  FROM customers c, orders o
  WHERE c.id = o.c_id(+)
  ORDER BY c.id;
```

The result set is as follows:

```
CUSTOMER_ID  ORDER_ID
-----------  ---------
          1          1
          1         14
          2          2
          2         10
          3          3
          4          4
          4         11
          4         13
          5          5
          6          6
          7          7
          7         12
          8          8
          9          9
         10
```

15 rows selected.

Notice that the result set includes a row for the record in the CUSTOMERS table with an ID of 10, even though the customer has not placed any orders. Oracle returns nulls for all columns that have no match in an outer join's result set.

Inserting, Updating, and Deleting Rows in Tables

All of the previous examples in this chapter show you how to retrieve data from tables in an Oracle database using various queries (SELECT commands). Now let's take a look at how to input, modify, and delete table data using the SQL commands INSERT, UPDATE, and DELETE.

EXERCISE 4.17: Inserting New Rows into a Table

To insert a new row into a table, you use the SQL command *INSERT*. For example, enter the following statement, which inserts a new part into the PARTS table.

```
INSERT INTO parts
   (id, description, unitprice, onhand, reorder)
   VALUES (6, 'Mouse', 49, 1200, 500);
```

This example statement demonstrates how to use the most common clauses and parameters of the INSERT command.

■ Use the INTO parameter to specify the target table.

■ To insert a single row into the target table, use a VALUES clause that contains a comma-separated list of values for various columns in the table.

■ Optionally, a comma-separated list of column names specifies the columns that correspond to the values in the VALUES clause. The number of columns in the list of column names must match the values in the VALUES clause. When you omit a column list altogether, the VALUES clause must specify values for every column in the target table in the order that the columns appear in the table.

EXERCISE 4.18: Updating Rows in a Table

To update column values in one or more rows of a table, use the SQL command *UPDATE*. For example, enter the following UPDATE statement, which updates the UNITPRICE value for a part in the PARTS table.

```
UPDATE parts
   SET unitprice = 55, onhand = 1100
   WHERE id = 6;
```

Notice that the SET clause of the example UPDATE statement updates the UNITPRICE and ONHAND values of a specific record in the PARTS table—the record identified by the condition of the WHERE clause. Be careful—when an UPDATE statement omits selection criteria (in other words, a WHERE clause), the UPDATE statement updates all rows in the target table.

EXERCISE 4.19: Deleting Rows from a Table

To delete one or more rows from a table, you use the SQL command *DELETE*. For example, enter the following DELETE statement, which deletes a specific record from the PARTS table.

```
DELETE FROM parts
   WHERE id = 6 AND description = 'Mouse';
```

As this example demonstrates, a DELETE statement should always include a WHERE clause with a condition that targets specific rows in a table, unless you want to delete *all* rows in the table.

Committing and Rolling Back Transactions

As you learned earlier in this chapter, a database *transaction* is a unit of work performed by one or more closely related SQL statements. The following hands-on exercise teaches you how to commit or roll back a transaction.

EXERCISE 4.20: Committing and Rolling Back Transactions

Enter the following series of related SQL statements, which together form a transaction that inserts a new order into the ORDERS table and two associated line items into the ITEMS table.

```
INSERT INTO orders
    VALUES (15, 3, '23-JUN-99', '23-JUN-99', NULL, 'F');
INSERT INTO items
    VALUES (15, 1, 4, 1);
INSERT INTO items
    VALUES (15, 2, 5, 1);
```

To permanently *commit* the work of the transaction to the database, use the SQL command *COMMIT* (with or without the optional keyword *WORK*).

```
COMMIT WORK;
```

Alternatively, to undo or *roll back* the work of a transaction's SQL statements, use the SQL command *ROLLBACK* (with or without the optional keyword *WORK*).

```
ROLLBACK WORK;
```

NOTE

After you commit a transaction, Oracle automatically starts the next transaction. Therefore, you cannot roll back a transaction after you commit it.

A fundamental principle that you must clearly understand is that a transaction is a unit of work. That is, although a transaction might be made up of several SQL statements, they all commit or roll back as a single operation. For example, when an application commits a transaction, Oracle permanently records the changes made by *all* SQL statements in the transaction. If for some reason Oracle cannot commit the work of any statement in a transaction, Oracle automatically rolls back the effects of all statements in the transaction.

When you start a database application and establish a connection to a database, Oracle implicitly starts a new transaction for your session. After you commit or roll back a transaction, Oracle again implicitly starts a new transaction for your session.

Transaction Design

The design of application transactions is very important, because a transaction's design can directly affect database integrity and the performance of applications. The following sections discuss several issues to consider when designing a database application's transactions.

Units of Work

Remember that a transaction is meant to encompass many closely related SQL statements that, together, perform a single unit of work. More specifically, a transaction should not encompass multiple units of work, nor should it encompass a partial unit of work. The following example demonstrates bad transaction design.

```
INSERT INTO customers ... ;
INSERT INTO parts ... ;
INSERT INTO orders ... ;
INSERT INTO items ... ;
INSERT INTO items ... ;
COMMIT WORK ;
```

In this example, the bad transaction design encompasses three separate units of work.

1. The transaction inserts a new customer record.

2. The transaction inserts a new part record.

3. The transaction inserts the records for a new sales order.

Technically, each unit of work in the transaction has nothing to do with the others. When a transaction encompasses more than a single unit of work, Oracle must maintain internal system information on behalf of the transaction for a longer period of time. Quite possibly, this can detract from system performance, especially when many transactions burden Oracle with the same type of bad transaction design.

To contrast the previous type of bad transaction design, consider another example:

```
INSERT INTO orders ... ;
COMMIT WORK ;
INSERT INTO items ... ;
COMMIT WORK ;
INSERT INTO items ... ;
COMMIT WORK ;
```

This example does the opposite of the previous example—there are three transactions to input the records for a single sales order. The overhead of many unnecessary small transaction commits can also detract from server performance. More important, partial transactions can risk the integrity of a database's data. For example, consider what would happen if you use the above transaction design to insert a new sales order, but before you can commit the insert of all line items for the new sales order, your session abnormally disconnects from the database server. At this point, the database contains a partial sales order, at least until you reconnect to finish the sales order. In the interim, a shipping transaction might look at the partial sales order and not realize that it is working with incomplete information. As a result, the shipping department might unknowingly send a partial product shipment to a customer and mark it as complete. The irate customer calls days later demanding to know why she didn't receive the other ordered products. When the shipping clerk looks at the order in the database, he sees the missing line items, but he cannot explain why the order did not contain the products and was marked as complete.

Read-Write Transactions

By default, when Oracle starts a new transaction for your session, the transaction is read-write. A *read-write transaction* can include any type of SQL statement, including DML statements that query, insert, update, and delete table rows. To explicitly declare a transaction as a read-write transaction, you can begin the transaction with the SQL command *SET TRANSACTION* and the *READ WRITE* option.

 `SET TRANSACTION READ WRITE;`

Read-Only Transactions

A *read-only transaction* includes queries only. In other words, a read-only transaction does not modify the database in any way. Certain reporting applications might want to explicitly declare a transaction as read-only with the READ ONLY option of the SET TRANSACTION command.

 `SET TRANSACTION READ ONLY;`

When you declare an explicit read-only transaction, Oracle guarantees *transaction-level read consistency* for the transaction. This means that the result sets of all queries in the transaction reflect the database's data as it existed at the beginning of the transaction, even though other transactions modify and commit work to the database. Reporting applications commonly use an explicit read-only transaction to encompass several queries and produce a report with consistent data.

Chapter Summary

This chapter has provided you with a broad overview of SQL and a tutorial for using the most common SQL commands.

- To accomplish work with Oracle8i, applications must use SQL commands.

- Use the SQL command SELECT to build queries that retrieve data from database tables. A query's FROM clause specifies the table(s) to target. A query's SELECT clause determines what columns to include in the query's result set—the SELECT clause can contain simple column names as well as expressions that use operators, literals, or SQL functions to derive data. A query's optional WHERE clause condition determines which rows to include in the query's result set. You can use the optional ORDER BY clause to sort the records in a query's result set. Use the optional GROUP BY clause to summarize or aggregate data in a query's result set.

- Use the SQL command INSERT to insert a row into a table. An INSERT statement's INTO parameter specifies the target table, and the VALUES clause contains a list of values for the various columns in the table. You can also include an optional list of column names before the VALUES clause to specify target columns in the table for the values in the VALUES clause.

- Use the SQL command UPDATE to update rows in a table. Use the SET clause to identify the column values to change, and a WHERE clause to target specific rows in the table that you want to update.

- Use the SQL command DELETE to delete rows from a table. A DELETE statement should always include a WHERE clause with a condition that targets specific rows in a table, unless you want to delete all rows in the table.

- Use the SQL commands COMMIT and ROLLBACK to control the outcome of your session's current transaction. A COMMIT statement permanently commits the changes made by all SQL statements in the transaction. A ROLLBACK statement undoes the effects of all SQL statements in the transaction. Oracle automatically starts a new transaction after you commit or roll back your current transaction.

CHAPTER
5

Writing Database
Access Programs with
PL/SQL

QL is nothing more than a data access language that allows applications to put data into and get data out of an Oracle database. In other words, SQL by itself is not a full-featured programming language that you can use to develop powerful database applications. To build a database application, you must use a procedural language that encompasses SQL to interact with an Oracle database. This chapter explains Oracle's very own procedural language, PL/SQL, which you can use to program an Oracle database server and associated applications. The following topics will be covered:

- PL/SQL coding basics

- Anonymous PL/SQL blocks

- Stored procedures, functions, and packages

- Database triggers

NOTE

By no means is this chapter a complete guide to PL/SQL. However, this chapter does provide an intermediate-level tutorial of PL/SQL's capabilities, so that you can get started programming an Oracle database server.

Chapter Prerequisites

To practice the hands-on exercises in this chapter, you need to start a Linux session as the user oracle, then start SQL*Plus and run the following command script

location/8istarterkit/SQL/chap05.sql

where *location* is the file directory where you expanded the support archive that accompanies this book. For example, after starting SQL*Plus and connecting as SCOTT, you can run this chapter's SQL command script using the SQL*Plus command @, as in the following example (assuming that your chap05.sql file is in /tmp/8istarterkit/SQL).

```
SQL> @/tmp/8istarterkit/SQL/chap05.sql;
```

Once the script completes successfully, leave the current SQL*Plus session open and use it to perform this chapter's exercises in the order that they appear.

What Is PL/SQL?

PL/SQL is a procedural programming language that's built into most Oracle products. With PL/SQL, you can build programs to process information by combining PL/SQL procedural statements that control program flow with SQL statements that access an Oracle database. For example, the following is a very simple PL/SQL program that updates a part's UNITPRICE, given the part's ID number.

```
CREATE OR REPLACE PROCEDURE updatePartPrice (
  partId IN INTEGER,
  newPrice IN NUMBER )
IS
  invalidPart EXCEPTION;
BEGIN
-- HERE'S AN UPDATE STATEMENT TO UPDATE A DATABASE RECORD
  UPDATE parts
    SET unitprice = newPrice
    WHERE id = partId;
-- HERE'S AN ERROR-CHECKING STATEMENT
  IF SQL%NOTFOUND THEN
    RAISE invalidPart;
  END IF;
EXCEPTION
-- HERE'S AN ERROR-HANDLING ROUTINE
  WHEN invalidPart THEN
    raise_application_error(-20000, 'Invalid Part ID');
END updatePartPrice;
```

This example program is a procedure that is stored as a program unit in a database. Using PL/SQL, you can build many types of database access program units, including anonymous PL/SQL blocks, procedures, functions, and packages. All of the sections in this chapter include examples of PL/SQL programs. But before learning about full-blown PL/SQL programs, you need to understand the basic programmatic constructs and commands that the PL/SQL language offers.

NOTE
PL/SQL is a procedural language that's very similar to Ada. PL/SQL has statements that allow you to declare variables and constants, control program flow, assign and manipulate data, and more.

PL/SQL Blocks

A PL/SQL program is structured using distinct *blocks* that group related declarations and statements. Each block in a PL/SQL program has a specific task and solves a particular problem. Consequently, you can organize a PL/SQL program so that it is easy to understand.

A PL/SQL block can include three sections as the following pseudo-code illustrates: program declarations, the main program body, and exception handlers.

```
DECLARE
-- program declarations are optional
BEGIN
-- program body is required
EXCEPTION
-- exception handlers are optional
END;
```

Most of the examples in this chapter ask you to use SQL*Plus and interactively type and execute anonymous PL/SQL blocks while learning the fundamentals of PL/SQL. An *anonymous PL/SQL* block has no name and is not stored permanently as a file or in an Oracle database. An application, such as SQL*Plus, simply sends the PL/SQL block to the database server for processing at run time. Once Oracle executes an anonymous PL/SQL block, the block ceases to exist.

Program Declarations

The *declaration section* of a PL/SQL block is where the block declares all variables, constants, exceptions, and so on, that are then accessible to all other parts of the same block. The declarative section of a PL/SQL block starts with the DECLARE keyword and implicitly ends with the BEGIN keyword of the program body. If the program does not need to make any declarations, the declaration section is not necessary.

The Program Body

The main program *body* of a PL/SQL block contains the executable statements for the block. In other words, the body is where the PL/SQL block defines its functionality. The body of a PL/SQL block begins with the BEGIN keyword and ends with the EXCEPTION keyword that starts the exception handling section of the block; if the block does not include any exception handlers, the program body ends with the END keyword that ends the block altogether.

Exception Handlers

The optional *exception handling section* of a PL/SQL block contains the *exception handlers* (error handling routines) for the block. When a statement in the block's body *raises an exception* (detects an error), it transfers program control to a corresponding exception handler in the exception section for further processing. The exception handling section of a PL/SQL block begins with the EXCEPTION keyword and ends with the END keyword. If a program does not need to define any exception handlers, the exception handling section of the block is not necessary.

Program Comments

All blocks of a PL/SQL program should include *comments* that document program declarations and functionality. Comments clarify the purpose of specific programs and code segments.

PL/SQL supports two different styles for comments, as the following code segment shows.

```
-- PRECEDE A SINGLE-LINE COMMENT WITH A DOUBLE-HYPHEN.
/* DELIMIT A MULTI-LINE COMMENT WITH "/*" AS A PREFIX AND "*/" AS
   A SUFFIX. A MULTI-LINE COMMENT CAN CONTAIN ANY NUMBER OF LINES. */
```

The examples in the remainder of this chapter often use comments to help explain the functionality of code listings.

The Fundamentals of PL/SQL Coding

All procedural languages, such as PL/SQL, have fundamental language elements and functionality that you need to learn about before you can build programs using the language. The following sections introduce the basic elements of PL/SQL, including the following:

- ■ How to declare program variables and assign them values

- ■ How to control program flow with loops and conditional logic

- ■ How to embed SQL statements and interact with Oracle databases

- ■ How to declare and use subprograms (procedures and functions) within PL/SQL blocks

- ■ How to declare user-defined types, such as records and nested tables

- ■ How to declare and use cursors to process queries that return multiple rows

- ■ How to use exception handlers to handle error conditions

Working with Program Variables

All procedural programs typically declare one or more program variables and use them to hold temporary information for program processing. The next two exercises teach you how to declare program variables (and constants), initialize them, and assign them values in the body of a PL/SQL program.

EXERCISE 5.1: Declaring Variables and Constants with Basic Datatypes

The declaration section of a PL/SQL program can include *variable* and *constant* declarations. The general syntax that you use to declare a scalar variable or constant is as follows:

```
variable [CONSTANT] datatype [[NOT NULL] {DEFAULT|:=} expression];
```

NOTE
To declare a constant rather than a variable, include the CONSTANT keyword in the declaration. You must initialize a constant, after which the constant's value cannot change.

When you declare a variable, you can choose to initialize it immediately or wait until later in the body of the program; however, if you include the not null constraint, you must initialize the variable as part of its declaration. By default, PL/SQL initializes a variable as null unless the program explicitly initializes the variable.

A program can declare a variable or constant using any Oracle or ANSI/ISO datatype or subtype listed in Table 5-1.

Datatype	Subtype	Description
BINARY_INTEGER	NATURAL, NATURALN, POSITIVE, POSITIVEN, SIGNTYPE	Stores signed integers in the range -2,147,483,647 to 2,147,483,647. Uses library arithmetic. NATURAL and NATURALN store only nonnegative integers; the latter disallows nulls. POSITIVE and POSITIVEN store only positive integers; the latter disallows nulls. SIGNTYPE stores only -1, 0, and 1.

TABLE 5-1. *PL/SQL Scalar Datatypes and Related Subtypes*

Datatype	Subtype	Description
NUMBER (*precision,scale*)	DEC, DECIMAL, DOUBLE PRECISION, FLOAT (*precision*), INTEGER, INT, NUMERIC, REAL, SMALLINT	Stores fixed or floating-point numbers in the range 1^{-130} to 10^{125}. Uses library arithmetic.
PLS_INTEGER		Stores signed integers in the range -2,147,483,647 to 2,147,483,647. Uses machine arithmetic for fast calculations.
CHAR (*size*)	CHARACTER (*size*)	Stores fixed-length character strings. Maximum size is 32,767 bytes; however, database maximum CHAR is 2,000 bytes.
VARCHAR2 (*size*)	VARCHAR (*size*), STRING	Stores variable-length character strings. Maximum size is 32,767 bytes; however, database maximum VARCHAR2 is 4,000 bytes.
DATE		Stores time-related information, including dates, hours, minutes, and seconds.
BOOLEAN		Stores logical values (TRUE, FALSE, and NULL).
ROWID		Stores the physical row address of a row in a database table.
UROWID		Stores the physical, logical, or foreign (non-Oracle) address of a row in a database table.
CLOB		Stores large, single-byte character objects.
BLOB		Stores large binary objects.
BFILE		Stores file pointers to LOBs managed by file systems external to the database.

TABLE 5-1. *PL/SQL Scalar Datatypes and Related Subtypes* (continued)

NOTE

A subtype is a constrained version of its base type.

For the first hands-on exercise in this chapter, use SQL*Plus to enter the following anonymous PL/SQL block that declares and initializes several variables of different datatypes and then outputs their current values to standard output.

```
DECLARE
  outputString VARCHAR2(20) := 'Hello World';
  todaysDate DATE := SYSDATE;
  pi CONSTANT NUMBER := 3.14159265359;
BEGIN
  DBMS_OUTPUT.PUT_LINE(outputString);
  DBMS_OUTPUT.PUT_LINE(todaysDate);
  DBMS_OUTPUT.PUT_LINE(pi);
END;
/
```

NOTE

*To end a PL/SQL program in SQL*Plus, you must terminate the code with a line that includes only the slash (/) character.*

The output of the program should be similar to the following:

```
Hello World
16-MAY-00
3.14159265359

PL/SQL procedure successfully completed.
```

There are a couple of subtle points to understand about this first example PL/SQL program.

- When a program declares a variable using a datatype that requires a constraint specification (such as VARCHAR2), the declaration must specify the constraint.

- The body of the example program uses the *DBMS_OUTPUT. PUT_LINE procedure* to direct output to the standard output. The DBMS_OUTPUT.PUT_LINE procedure is analogous in functionality to the println procedure in C, and the System.out.println method of Java. However, you will not see the output of a call to DBMS_OUTPUT.PUT_LINE when using SQL*Plus unless you enable the SQL*Plus environment setting SERVEROUTPUT. The prerequisite command script for this chapter executes a SET SERVEROUTPUT ON statement for you.

EXERCISE 5.2: Assigning Values to Variables

Value assignment is one of the most common operations within any type of procedural program. The general syntax that you use to assign a value to a variable is as follows:

```
variable := expression
```

An *assignment statement* in a PL/SQL program assigns the value that results from an expression to a PL/SQL construct, such as a variable, using the *assignment operator* (:=). For example, enter the following PL/SQL block, which declares some variables, assigns them values in the program body, and then uses the DBMS_OUTPUT.PUT_LINE procedure to output their current values to standard output.

```
DECLARE
  outputString VARCHAR2(20);
  todaysDate DATE;
  tomorrowsDate DATE;
  lastDayOfTheMonth DATE;
BEGIN
  outputString := 'Hello ' || 'World';
  todaysDate := SYSDATE;
  tomorrowsDate := SYSDATE + 1;
  lastDayOfTheMonth := LAST_DAY(SYSDATE);
  DBMS_OUTPUT.PUT_LINE(outputString);
  DBMS_OUTPUT.PUT_LINE(todaysDate);
  DBMS_OUTPUT.PUT_LINE(tomorrowsDate);
  DBMS_OUTPUT.PUT_LINE(lastDayOfTheMonth);
END;
/
```

The program output should be similar to the following:

```
Hello World
16-MAY-00
17-MAY-00
31-MAY-00

PL/SQL procedure successfully completed.
```

Notice that the assignment statements in the body of the program use different types of expressions that build values to assign to variables. Several sections in the previous chapter teach you how to build expressions for a query's SELECT clause using literals, operators, and SQL functions. Similarly, you can build expressions for the right side of an assignment statement in a PL/SQL program. For example, the expressions in the example program use literals, the concatenation and addition operators (|| and +), and the LAST_DAY and SYSDATE functions.

NOTE

Most SQL functions are also built-in and supported in PL/SQL statements.

Controlling Program Flow

Typical procedural programs have flow. That is, a program uses some sort of logic to control whether and when the program executes given statements. PL/SQL programs can control program flow using iterative logic (loops), conditional logic (if-then-else), and sequential logic (goto). The following exercises teach you how to use the different program flow control statements that PL/SQL offers.

EXERCISE 5.3: Using PL/SQL Loops

A PL/SQL program can use a *loop* to iterate the execution of a series of statements a certain number of times. Enter the following anonymous PL/SQL block, which teaches you how to use a *basic loop*. The beginning of a basic loop starts with a LOOP statement and ends with an END LOOP statement.

```
DECLARE
  loopCounter INTEGER := 0;
BEGIN
  LOOP
   DBMS_OUTPUT.PUT(loopCounter || ' ');
   loopCounter := loopCounter + 1;
   EXIT WHEN loopCounter = 10;
  END LOOP;
  DBMS_OUTPUT.PUT_LINE('Loop Exited.');
END;
/
```

The program output should look like the following:

```
0 1 2 3 4 5 6 7 8 9 Loop Exited.

PL/SQL procedure successfully completed.
```

It is important to understand that every basic loop definition should use either an *EXIT WHEN* or *EXIT* statement to terminate the loop—otherwise the loop executes infinitely!

NOTE
The preceding example uses the DBMS_OUTPUT.PUT procedure to place display output in a temporary buffer. The subsequent call to DBMS_OUTPUT.PUT_LINE prints the entire contents of the session's display buffer.

Next, enter the following anonymous PL/SQL block, which teaches you how to use a different type of loop, a *WHILE loop*. The LOOP statement of a WHILE loop begins with a WHILE condition and ends with an END LOOP statement.

```
DECLARE
  loopCounter INTEGER := 0;
BEGIN
  WHILE loopCounter < 10 LOOP
    DBMS_OUTPUT.PUT(loopCounter || ' ');
    loopCounter := loopCounter + 1;
  END LOOP;
  DBMS_OUTPUT.PUT_LINE('Loop Exited.');
END;
/
```

The program output should look like the following:

```
0 1 2 3 4 5 6 7 8 9 Loop Exited.

PL/SQL procedure successfully completed.
```

Notice that the definition of a WHILE loop requires that you specify a condition to describe how the loop terminates.

Finally, enter the following anonymous PL/SQL block, which teaches you how to use a third type of loop, a *FOR loop*. The LOOP statement of a FOR loop begins with a FOR clause and ends with an END LOOP statement.

```
BEGIN
  <<outer_loop>>
  FOR outerLoopCounter IN 0 .. 25 LOOP
    DBMS_OUTPUT.PUT_LINE('Outer Loop: ' || outerLoopCounter);
    DBMS_OUTPUT.PUT(' Inner Loop: ');
    <<inner_loop>>
    FOR innerLoopCounter IN REVERSE 1 .. 3 LOOP
      DBMS_OUTPUT.PUT(innerLoopCounter || ' ');
      EXIT inner_loop
        WHEN ((outerLoopCounter = 2) AND (innerLoopCounter = 3));
      EXIT outer_loop
        WHEN ((outerLoopCounter = 5) AND (innerLoopCounter = 2));
    END LOOP inner_loop;
```

```
    DBMS_OUTPUT.PUT_LINE('Inner Loop Exited.');
    DBMS_OUTPUT.PUT_LINE('------------------');
  END LOOP outer_loop;
  DBMS_OUTPUT.PUT_LINE('Outer Loop Exited.');
END;
/
```

The program output should look like the following:

```
Outer Loop: 0
Inner Loop: 3 2 1 Inner Loop Exited.
------------------
Outer Loop: 1
Inner Loop: 3 2 1 Inner Loop Exited.
------------------
Outer Loop: 2
Inner Loop: 3 Inner Loop Exited.
------------------
Outer Loop: 3
Inner Loop: 3 2 1 Inner Loop Exited.
------------------
Outer Loop: 4
Inner Loop: 3 2 1 Inner Loop Exited.
------------------
Outer Loop: 5
Inner Loop: 3 2 Outer Loop Exited.

PL/SQL procedure successfully completed.
```

The preceding example includes several important points that you should understand about FOR loops and loops in general:

- You can nest loops within loops.

- You can use loop labels to name loops, and then reference specific loops by name in EXIT and END LOOP statements.

- A FOR loop can declare its integer counter variable as part of the FOR ... LOOP statement.

- A FOR loop automatically increments or decrements its counter variable so that you do not have to explicitly do so in the body of the loop.

EXERCISE 5.4: Using the PL/SQL Command IF ... ELSIF ... ELSE

An *IF* statement in a PL/SQL program evaluates a Boolean condition, and if the condition is TRUE executes one or more statements. You can also use the optional

ELSIF and ELSE clauses to enter subsequent conditions to be evaluated if the first condition is not TRUE. Enter the following anonymous PL/SQL block, which teaches you how to use the PL/SQL command IF ... ELSIF ... ELSE for conditions.

```
BEGIN
  FOR i IN 1 .. 20 LOOP
   IF ((i mod 3 = 0) AND (i mod 5 = 0)) THEN
    DBMS_OUTPUT.PUT('multipleOfBoth');
   ELSIF i mod 3 = 0 THEN
    DBMS_OUTPUT.PUT('multipleOf3');
   ELSIF i mod 5 = 0 THEN
    DBMS_OUTPUT.PUT('multipleOf5');
   ELSE
    DBMS_OUTPUT.PUT(i);
   END IF;
   DBMS_OUTPUT.PUT(' ');
  END LOOP;
  DBMS_OUTPUT.PUT_LINE(' ');
END;
/
```

The program output should look like the following:

```
1 2 multipleOf3 4 multipleOf5 multipleOf3 7 8 multipleOf3
multipleOf5 11 multipleOf3 13 14 multipleOfBoth 16 17
multipleOf3 19 multipleOf5

PL/SQL procedure successfully completed.
```

EXERCISE 5.5: Using the PL/SQL Command GOTO

Unlike conditional and iterative flow control, sequential control or branching is rarely necessary in PL/SQL programs; however, PL/SQL provides the *GOTO* command should the need arise. For example, enter the following anonymous PL/SQL block, which teaches you how to use a GOTO statement to branch to a program label that precedes an executable statement in a PL/SQL program.

```
BEGIN
  -- set the loop to iterate 10 times
  FOR i IN 1 .. 10 LOOP
   DBMS_OUTPUT.PUT(i || ' ');
   IF i = 5 THEN
    GOTO message1;
   END IF;
  END LOOP;
```

```
DBMS_OUTPUT.PUT_LINE('All loop iterations printed.');

<<message1>>
DBMS_OUTPUT.PUT_LINE('Only 5 loop iterations printed.');
END;
/
```

The program output is as follows:

```
1 2 3 4 5 Only 5 loop iterations printed.

PL/SQL procedure successfully completed.
```

Interacting with Databases

The previous example exercises are PL/SQL programs that generate simple output to demonstrate some basics of PL/SQL. However, the primary reason for using PL/SQL is to create database access programs. A PL/SQL program can interact with an Oracle database only through the use of SQL. The following exercises show you how a PL/SQL program can manipulate database information using standard SQL DML statements and cursors.

EXERCISE 5.6: Manipulating Table Data with DML Statements

PL/SQL programs can include any valid INSERT, UPDATE, or DELETE statement to modify the rows in a database table. For example, enter the following anonymous PL/SQL block, which inserts a new record into the PARTS table.

```
DECLARE
 newId INTEGER := 6;
 newDesc VARCHAR2(250) := 'Mouse';
BEGIN
 INSERT INTO parts
  VALUES (newId, newDesc, 49, 1200, 500);
END;
/
```

The output produced by this program is simply the following line:

```
PL/SQL procedure successfully completed.
```

A variable or constant in a PL/SQL block can satisfy the requirement for an expression in a DML statement. For example, the previous example program uses program variables to supply the first two values in the VALUES clause of the INSERT statement.

Now, query the PARTS table to see the new record.

```
SELECT * FROM parts
  WHERE id = 6;
```

The result set is as follows:

```
        ID DESCRIPTION      UNITPRICE    ONHAND REORDER
--------- --------------- --------- --------- -------
         6 Mouse                  49      1200 500
```

All data modifications made by INSERT, UPDATE, and DELETE statements inside of a PL/SQL block are part of your session's current transaction. Although you can include COMMIT and ROLLBACK statements inside many types of PL/SQL blocks, transaction control is typically controlled outside of PL/SQL blocks, so that transaction boundaries are clearly visible to those using your PL/SQL programs.

EXERCISE 5.7: Assigning a Value to a Variable with a Query

PL/SQL programs often use the *INTO clause* of the SQL command SELECT to assign a specific database value to a program variable. Oracle supports the use of a *SELECT ... INTO* statement only inside PL/SQL programs. Try out this type of assignment statement by entering the following anonymous PL/SQL block, which uses a SELECT ... INTO statement to assign a value to a program variable.

```
DECLARE
  partDesc VARCHAR2(250);
BEGIN
  SELECT description INTO partDesc
   FROM parts
   WHERE id = 3;
  DBMS_OUTPUT.PUT_LINE('Part 3 is a ' || partDesc);
END;
/
```

The program output is as follows:

```
Part 3 is a Laptop PC

PL/SQL procedure successfully completed.
```

A SELECT ... INTO command must have a result set with only one row—if the result set of a SELECT ... INTO statement contains more than one row, Oracle raises the TOO_MANY_ROWS exception. To process a query that returns more than one row, a PL/SQL program must use a cursor. You'll learn more about cursors later in this chapter.

Declaring and Using Subprograms: Procedures and Functions

The declarative section of a PL/SQL block can declare a common subtask as a named *subprogram* (or *subroutine*). Subsequent statements in the main program body can then *call* (execute) the subprogram to perform work whenever necessary.

PL/SQL supports two types of subprograms: procedures and functions. A *procedure* is a subprogram that performs an operation. A *function* is a subprogram that computes a value and returns it to the program that called the function.

EXERCISE 5.8: Declaring and Using a Procedure

The general syntax for declaring a procedure is as follows:

```
PROCEDURE procedure
  [(parameter [IN|OUT|IN OUT] datatype [{DEFAULT|:=} expression]
  [,...] )]
  declarations ...
{IS|AS}
 BEGIN
  statements ...
 END [procedure];
```

When you declare a subprogram, such as a procedure, you can pass values into and out of the subprogram using *parameters.* Typically, a calling program passes one or more variables as parameters to a subprogram.

For each parameter, you must specify a datatype in an unconstrained form. Furthermore, you should indicate the mode of each parameter as IN, OUT, or IN OUT:

- An *IN parameter* passes a value into a subprogram, but a subprogram cannot change the value of the external variable that corresponds to an IN parameter.

- An *OUT parameter* cannot pass a value into a subprogram, but a subprogram can manipulate an OUT parameter to change the value of the corresponding variable in the outside calling environment.

- An *IN OUT parameter* combines the capabilities of IN and OUT parameters.

Enter the following anonymous PL/SQL block, which declares a procedure to print horizontal lines of a specified width.

```
DECLARE
  PROCEDURE printLine(width IN INTEGER, chr IN CHAR DEFAULT '-') IS
  BEGIN
```

```
  FOR i IN 1 .. width LOOP
    DBMS_OUTPUT.PUT(chr);
  END LOOP;
  DBMS_OUTPUT.PUT_LINE('');
END printLine;
BEGIN
printLine(40, '*');                    -- print a line of 40 *s
printLine(width => 20, chr => '=');    -- print a line of 20 =s
printLine(10);                         -- print a line of 10 -s
END;
/
```

The program output is as follows:

```
****************************************
====================
----------

PL/SQL procedure successfully completed.
```

The body of the example in this exercise calls the printLine procedure three times:

- The first procedure call provides values for both parameters of the procedure using *positional notation*—each parameter value that you specify in a procedure call corresponds to the procedure parameter declared in the same position.

- The second procedure call provides values for both parameters of the procedure using *named notation*—the name of a parameter and the *association operator* (=>) precedes a parameter value.

- The third procedure call demonstrates that you must provide values for all procedure parameters without default values, but can optionally omit values for parameters with a default value.

EXERCISE 5.9: Declaring and Using a Function

The general syntax for declaring a function is as follows:

```
FUNCTION function
  [(parameter [IN|OUT|IN OUT] datatype [{DEFAULT|:=} expression]
  [,...] )]
  RETURN datatype
  declarations ...
{IS|AS}
  BEGIN
  statements ...
  END [function];
```

Notice that a function differs from a procedure in that it returns a value to its calling environment. The specification of a function declares the type of the *return value*. Furthermore, the body of a function must include one or more *RETURN statements* to return a value to the calling environment.

Enter the following anonymous PL/SQL block, which declares and uses a function.

```
DECLARE
 tempTotal NUMBER;
 FUNCTION orderTotal(orderId IN INTEGER)
  RETURN NUMBER
 IS
  orderTotal NUMBER;
  tempTotal NUMBER;
 BEGIN
  SELECT SUM(i.quantity * p.unitprice) INTO orderTotal
   FROM items i, parts p
   WHERE i.o_id = orderId
   AND i.p_id = p.id
   GROUP BY i.o_id;
  RETURN orderTotal;
 END orderTotal;
BEGIN
 DBMS_OUTPUT.PUT_LINE('Order 1 Total: ' || orderTotal(1));
 tempTotal := orderTotal(2);
 DBMS_OUTPUT.PUT_LINE('Order 2 Total: ' || tempTotal);
END;
/
```

The program output is as follows:

```
Order 1 Total: 7094
Order 2 Total: 3196

PL/SQL procedure successfully completed.
```

The main program body of the PL/SQL block calls the orderTotal function twice. A program can call a function anywhere an expression is valid—for example, as a parameter for a procedure call or on the right side of an assignment statement. A SQL statement can also reference a user-defined function in the condition of a WHERE clause.

Working with Record Types

So far in this chapter, you've seen how to declare simple scalar variables and constants based on Oracle datatypes (for example, NUMBER) and subtypes of the base datatypes (for example, INTEGER). A block in a PL/SQL program can also declare *user-defined types* and then use the user-defined types to declare corresponding program variables. This section teaches you how to declare and use an elementary user-defined type, a record type. A *record type* consists of a group of one or more related fields, each of which has its own name and datatype. Typically, PL/SQL programs use a record type to create variables that match the structure of a record in a table. For example, you might declare a record type called partRecord and then use the type to create a record variable that holds a part's ID, DESCRIPTION, UNITPRICE, ONHAND, and REORDER fields. After you declare a record variable, you can manipulate the individual fields of the record or pass the entire record to subprograms as a unit.

The general syntax for declaring a record type is as follows:

```
TYPE recordType IS RECORD
(   field datatype [NOT NULL] {DEFAULT|:=} expression ]
 [, field ...]
)
```

The specification of an individual field in a record type is similar to declaring a scalar variable—you must specify the field's datatype, and you can specify an optional not null constraint, as well as initialize the field.

EXERCISE 5.10: Declaring and Using Record Types

Enter the following anonymous PL/SQL block, which demonstrates how to declare and use a record type. The declaration section of the block declares a user-defined record type to match the attributes of the PARTS table, and then declares two record variables using the new type. The body of the program demonstrates how to do the following:

- Reference individual fields of record variables using dot notation

- Assign values to the fields of a record variable

- Pass a record variable as a parameter to a procedure call

- Copy the field values of one record variable to the fields of another variable of the same record type

- Use the fields of a record variable as expressions in an INSERT statement

```
DECLARE
  TYPE partRecord IS RECORD (
   id INTEGER,
   description VARCHAR2(250),
```

```
  unitprice NUMBER(10,2),
  onhand INTEGER,
  reorder INTEGER
 );
 selectedPart partRecord;
 copiedPart partRecord;
 PROCEDURE printPart (title IN VARCHAR2, thisPart IN partRecord) IS
 BEGIN
  FOR i IN 1 .. 50 LOOP
   DBMS_OUTPUT.PUT('-');
  END LOOP;
  DBMS_OUTPUT.PUT_LINE('');
  DBMS_OUTPUT.PUT_LINE(title || ': ID: ' || thisPart.id ||
   ' DESCRIPTION: ' || thisPart.description);
 END printPart;
BEGIN
/* Assign values to the fields of a record variable
|| using a SELECT .. INTO statement.
*/
 SELECT id, description, unitprice , onhand, reorder INTO selectedPart
  FROM parts WHERE id = 3;
 printPart('selectedPart Info', selectedPart);

/* Assign the field values of one record variable to
|| the corresponding fields in another record
|| variable of the same type. Then assign new
|| values to the fields of original record variable
|| to demonstrate that record copies are not by reference.
*/
 copiedPart := selectedPart;

 selectedPart.id := 7;
 selectedPart.description := 'Laser Printer';
 selectedPart.unitprice := 399;
 selectedPart.onhand := 780;
 selectedPart.reorder := 500;

 printPart('newPart Info', selectedPart);
 printPart('copiedPart Info', copiedPart);

/* Use the fields of a record variable as expressions
|| in the VALUES clause of an INSERT statement.
*/
 INSERT INTO parts
  VALUES (selectedPart.id, selectedPart.description,
   selectedPart.unitprice, selectedPart.onhand, selectedPart.reorder);
END;
/
```

The program output is as follows:

```
--------------------------------------------------
selectedPart Info: ID: 3 DESCRIPTION: Laptop PC
--------------------------------------------------
newPart Info: ID: 7 DESCRIPTION: Laser Printer
--------------------------------------------------
copiedPart Info: ID: 3 DESCRIPTION: Laptop PC

PL/SQL procedure successfully completed.
```

NOTE
As an additional exercise, build a query of the PARTS table to view the new part inserted by the example program.

Using the %TYPE and %ROWTYPE Attributes

A PL/SQL program can use the *%TYPE* and *%ROWTYPE attributes* to declare variables, constants, individual fields in records, and record variables that match the properties of database columns and tables or other program constructs. Not only do attributes simplify the declaration of program constructs, but their use also makes programs flexible for database modifications. For example, after an administrator modifies the PARTS table to add a new column, a record variable declared using the %ROWTYPE attribute automatically adjusts to account for the new column at run time, without any modification of the program.

EXERCISE 5.11: Using the %TYPE Attribute

The declaration of a PL/SQL variable, constant, or field in a record variable can use the *%TYPE attribute* to capture the datatype of another program construct or column in a database table at run time. For example, enter the following anonymous PL/SQL block, which uses the %TYPE attribute to reference the columns in the PARTS table when declaring the partRecord type.

```
DECLARE
  TYPE partRecord IS RECORD (
    id parts.id%TYPE,
    description parts.description%TYPE,
    unitprice parts.unitprice%TYPE,
    onhand parts.onhand%TYPE,
    reorder parts.reorder%TYPE
  );
  selectedPart partRecord;
```

```
BEGIN
 SELECT id, description, unitprice , onhand, reorder INTO selectedPart
  FROM parts WHERE id = 3;
 DBMS_OUTPUT.PUT_LINE('ID: ' || selectedPart.id);
 DBMS_OUTPUT.PUT_LINE('DESCRIPTION: ' || selectedPart.description);
 DBMS_OUTPUT.PUT_LINE('UNIT PRICE: ' || selectedPart.unitprice);
 DBMS_OUTPUT.PUT_LINE('CURRENTLY ONHAND: ' || selectedPart.onhand);
 DBMS_OUTPUT.PUT_LINE('REORDER AT: ' || selectedPart.reorder);
END;
/
```

The program output is as follows:

```
ID: 3
DESCRIPTION: Laptop PC
UNIT PRICE: 2100
CURRENTLY ONHAND: 7631
REORDER AT: 1000

PL/SQL procedure successfully completed.
```

EXERCISE 5.12: Using the %ROWTYPE Attribute

A PL/SQL program can use the *%ROWTYPE attribute* to easily declare record variables and other constructs at run time. For example, enter the following anonymous PL/SQL block, which shows how to use the %ROWTYPE attribute to simplify the declaration of a record variable that corresponds to the fields in the PARTS table.

```
DECLARE
 selectedPart parts%ROWTYPE;
BEGIN
 SELECT id, description, unitprice , onhand, reorder INTO selectedPart
  FROM parts WHERE id = 3;
 DBMS_OUTPUT.PUT_LINE('ID: ' || selectedPart.id);
 DBMS_OUTPUT.PUT_LINE('DESCRIPTION: ' || selectedPart.description);
 DBMS_OUTPUT.PUT_LINE('UNIT PRICE: ' || selectedPart.unitprice);
 DBMS_OUTPUT.PUT_LINE('CURRENTLY ONHAND: ' || selectedPart.onhand);
 DBMS_OUTPUT.PUT_LINE('REORDER AT: ' || selectedPart.reorder);
END;
/
```

The program output is as follows:

```
ID: 3
DESCRIPTION: Laptop PC
UNIT PRICE: 2100
CURRENTLY ONHAND: 7631
```

```
REORDER AT: 1000

PL/SQL procedure successfully completed.
```

Notice that a record variable that you declare using the %ROWTYPE attribute automatically has field names that correspond to the fields in the referenced table.

Working with Cursors

Whenever an application submits a SQL statement to Oracle, the server opens at least one cursor to process the statement. A *cursor* is essentially a work area for a SQL statement. When a PL/SQL program (or any other application) submits an INSERT, UPDATE, or DELETE statement, Oracle automatically opens a cursor to process the statement. Oracle also can automatically process SELECT statements that return just one row. However, database access programs frequently must process a query that returns a set of database records, rather than just one row. To process the rows of a query that correspond to a multirow result set, a PL/SQL program must explicitly declare a cursor with a name, and then reference the cursor by its name to process rows one at a time. The steps for using cursors inside PL/SQL programs include the following:

1. Declare the cursor. You use a query to define the columns and rows of a cursor.

2. Open the cursor. You use the PL/SQL command *OPEN* to open a declared cursor.

3. Fetch rows from the cursor. You use the PL/SQL command *FETCH* to fetch rows, one-by-one, from an open cursor.

4. Close the cursor. You use the PL/SQL command *CLOSE* to close an open cursor.

EXERCISE 5.13: Declaring and Using a Simple Cursor

To familiarize yourself with the steps necessary to declare and use a cursor, enter the following anonymous PL/SQL block, which declares and uses a very simple cursor to print out selected columns in all the rows of the PARTS table.

```
DECLARE
  -- Step 1: Declare the cursor.
  CURSOR nextPartsRow IS
    SELECT * FROM parts
    ORDER BY id;

  currentPart parts%ROWTYPE; -- record variable that matches the cursor
```

```
BEGIN
 -- Step 2. Open the cursor.
 OPEN nextPartsRow;

 FETCH nextPartsRow INTO currentPart;
-- Step 3. Using a WHILE loop, fetch individual rows from the cursor.
 WHILE nextPartsRow%FOUND LOOP
  DBMS_OUTPUT.PUT_LINE(currentPart.id||' '||currentPart.description);
  FETCH nextPartsRow INTO currentPart;
 END LOOP;

 -- Step 4. Close the cursor.
 CLOSE nextPartsRow;
END;
/
```

The program output is as follows:

```
1 Fax Machine
2 Copy Machine
3 Laptop PC
4 Desktop PC
5 Scanner
6 Mouse
7 Laser Printer

PL/SQL procedure successfully completed.
```

Notice that after fetching the first row from the cursor, the program uses a WHILE loop to fetch subsequent rows from the open cursor, one-by-one. A PL/SQL program can use a *cursor attribute* to make decisions when processing cursors. The condition of the WHILE loop in the example program uses the %FOUND cursor attribute to detect when the last row of the cursor has been fetched. Table 5-2 lists the cursor attributes available with PL/SQL.

EXERCISE 5.14: Using Cursor FOR Loops

Because cursors are designed to process queries with multiple-row result sets, programs almost always process cursors using loops. To simplify the steps necessary to set up and process a cursor, a PL/SQL program can use a cursor FOR loop. A *cursor FOR loop* automatically declares a variable or record capable of receiving the rows in the cursor, opens the cursor, fetches rows from the cursor, and closes the cursor when the last row is fetched from the cursor. Enter the following anonymous PL/SQL block, which is a revision of the block in the previous exercise, and notice how a cursor FOR loop can simplify the steps necessary to process a cursor.

```
DECLARE
  CURSOR partsRows IS
    SELECT * FROM parts
      ORDER BY id;
BEGIN
  FOR currentPart IN partsRows LOOP
    DBMS_OUTPUT.PUT_LINE(currentPart.id||' '||currentPart.description);
  END LOOP;
END;
/
```

The program output is as follows:

```
1 Fax Machine
2 Copy Machine
3 Laptop PC
4 Desktop PC
5 Scanner
6 Mouse
7 Laser Printer

PL/SQL procedure successfully completed.
```

Explicit Cursor Attribute	Description
cursor%FOUND	The %FOUND attribute evaluates to TRUE when the preceding FETCH statement corresponds to at least one row in a database; otherwise, %FOUND evaluates to FALSE.
cursor%NOTFOUND	The %NOTFOUND attribute evaluates to TRUE when the preceding FETCH statement does not correspond to at least one row in a database; otherwise, %NOTFOUND evaluates to FALSE.
cursor%ISOPEN	The %ISOPEN attribute evaluates to TRUE when the target cursor is open; otherwise, %ISOPEN evaluates to FALSE.
cursor%ROWCOUNT	The %ROWCOUNT attribute reveals the number of rows fetched so far for an explicitly declared cursor.

TABLE 5-2. *Attributes of Explicitly Declared Cursors*

EXERCISE 5.15: Declaring Cursors with Parameters

When you declare a cursor, you can also declare one or more cursor parameters that the PL/SQL program uses to define the cursor's record selection criteria at run time. When a program opens a cursor that has a cursor parameter, the program can indicate a value for each cursor parameter. To learn how to declare and use a cursor that has a cursor parameter, enter the following anonymous PL/SQL block.

```
DECLARE
  CURSOR customersRows (salesRepId INTEGER) IS
    SELECT id, firstname ||' ' || lastname AS name
      FROM customers
      WHERE s_id = salesRepId;
BEGIN
  DBMS_OUTPUT.PUT_LINE('Sales Rep #1''s Customers');
  FOR currentCustomer IN customersRows (1) LOOP
    DBMS_OUTPUT.PUT_LINE('ID: ' || currentCustomer.id ||
      ', NAME: ' || currentCustomer.name);
  END LOOP;
END;
/
```

The program output is as follows:

```
Sales Rep #1's Customers
   ID: 2, NAME: Bill Musial
   ID: 3, NAME: Danielle Sams
   ID: 7, NAME: Joseph Wiersbicki
   ID: 9, NAME: Dorothy Clay
   ID: 10, NAME: Dave Haagensen

PL/SQL procedure successfully completed.
```

EXERCISE 5.16: Manipulating a Cursor's Current Row

As a program fetches individual rows from a cursor's result set, it is accessing the cursor's *current row*. A PL/SQL program can take advantage of the special *CURRENT OF clause* in the WHERE condition of an UPDATE or DELETE statement that must process the current row of a cursor. Enter the following anonymous PL/SQL block, which teaches you how to use the CURRENT OF clause in the WHERE condition of a DELETE statement. This block deletes the two new records inserted into the PARTS table by previous example programs in this chapter.

```
DECLARE
  CURSOR partsRows (partId INTEGER) IS
    SELECT * FROM parts
```

```
        WHERE id >= partId
        FOR UPDATE;
BEGIN
  FOR currentPart IN partsRows (6) LOOP -- selects parts 6 and 7
    DELETE FROM parts
      WHERE CURRENT OF partsRows;
    DBMS_OUTPUT.PUT_LINE('Deleted part ' || currentPart.id || ', ' ||
      currentPart.description);
  END LOOP;
END;
/
```

Assuming that your PARTS table has rows for parts 6 and 7 (a Mouse and a Laser Printer, respectively), which were inserted by earlier exercises in this chapter, the program output should be as follows:

```
Deleted part 6, Mouse
Deleted part 7, Laser Printer

PL/SQL procedure successfully completed.
```

Notice in the declaration of the cursor in the example program that when you declare a cursor with the intention of updating or deleting rows fetched by the cursor, you must declare the cursor's defining query with the FOR UPDATE keywords. This requirement forces Oracle to lock the rows in the cursor's result set, which prevents other transactions from updating or deleting the same rows until your transaction commits or rolls back.

Working with Collections

PL/SQL blocks can also declare and use collections. A *collection* in a PL/SQL program is a variable that is made up of an ordered set of like elements. To create a collection, you must first declare either a nested table type or a varray (varying array) type, and then declare a variable of the collection type. The next few sections explain more about nested tables and varrays.

> **NOTE**
> *Oracle8i's PL/SQL also supports a third collection type, PL/SQL tables (index-by tables), for backward compatibility with previous versions of Oracle. However, you should use nested tables rather than PL/SQL tables when developing new applications, to gain additional functionality. This chapter does not explain PL/SQL table types further.*

Nested Tables

A PL/SQL program can use a *nested table type* to create variables that have one or more columns and an *unlimited* number of rows, just like tables in a database. The general syntax for declaring a nested table type is as follows:

```
TYPE tableType IS TABLE OF
{ datatype | {variable|table.column}%TYPE | table%ROWTYPE }
  [NOT NULL] ;
```

The following exercises teach you how to declare, use, and manipulate nested tables.

EXERCISE 5.17: Declaring and Initializing a Nested Table

Enter the following anonymous PL/SQL block, which demonstrates how to declare a nested table type and then use the type to declare a new collection variable. The following example also demonstrates how to initialize a collection with its constructor method and then reference specific elements in the nested table collection by subscript.

```
DECLARE
-- declare a nested table type of INTEGERs
 TYPE integerTable IS TABLE OF INTEGER;
-- declare and initialize a collection with its constructor
 tempIntegers integerTable := integerTable(1, 202, 451);
BEGIN
 FOR i IN 1 .. 3 LOOP
  DBMS_OUTPUT.PUT_LINE('Element #' || i || ' is ' || tempIntegers(i));
 END LOOP;
END;
/
```

The program output is as follows:

```
Element #1 is 1
Element #2 is 202
Element #3 is 451

PL/SQL procedure successfully completed.
```

This very simple example demonstrates a few fundamental points you will need to understand about nested tables:

- Before you can use a collection, such as a nested table, you must initialize it using the type's corresponding *constructor*. PL/SQL automatically provides a constructor with the same name as the collection type. When you call a constructor to initialize a collection variable, you can specify a comma-separated list of initial elements for the collection, or a set of empty parentheses to initialize the collection as NULL.

- A nested table collection can have any number of rows. The size of a table can increase or decrease dynamically, as necessary. The next practice exercise will show how to add and delete elements in a nested table.

- Nested tables are initially *dense*, because at first, all elements have consecutive subscripts.

EXERCISE 5.18: Using Collection Methods with a Nested Table

PL/SQL supports several different *collection methods* that you can use to manipulate collections. To use a collection method, an expression in a PL/SQL program names the collection with the collection method as a suffix, using dot notation. Table 5-3 lists the collection methods that are available in PL/SQL.

Collection Method	Description
COUNT	Returns the number of elements currently in the collection.
DELETE[(x[,y] ...)]	Deletes some or all of the collection's elements without deallocating the space used by the elements.
EXISTS(x)	Returns TRUE if the xth element in the collection exists. Otherwise, the method returns FALSE.
EXTEND[(x[,y])]	Appends x copies of the yth element to the tail end of the collection. If y is omitted, appends x null elements to the collection. If both x and y are omitted, appends a single null element to the collection.
FIRST	Returns the index number of the first element in the collection.
LAST	Returns the index number of the last element in the collection.
LIMIT	Returns the maximum number of elements that a varray's collection can contain.

TABLE 5-3. *Collection Methods*

Collection Method	Description
NEXT(*x*)	Returns the index number of the element after the xth element of the collection.
PRIOR(*x*)	Returns the index number of the element before the xth element of the collection.
TRIM(*x*)	Trims *x* elements from the end of the collection.

TABLE 5-3. *Collection Methods* (continued)

Enter the following anonymous PL/SQL block, which demonstrates how to use several collection methods with a nested table of records.

```
DECLARE
  -- declare a nested table type of PARTS
  TYPE partsTable IS TABLE OF parts%ROWTYPE;
  -- declare and initialize a collection with its constructor
  tempParts partsTable := partsTable();
  -- cursor to fetch rows from PARTS table
  CURSOR nextPartsRow IS
    SELECT * FROM parts ORDER BY id;
  currentElement INTEGER;

BEGIN
/* ADD ELEMENTS TO COLLECTION
|| Create 10 new elements (rows) in the collection
|| using the collection's EXTEND method.
*/
  tempParts.EXTEND(10);

/* POPULATE COLLECTION
|| Use a cursor to populate every even-numbered element
|| in the tempParts nested table collection with the
|| five rows in the PARTS table.
*/
  FOR currentPart IN nextPartsRow LOOP
    tempParts(nextPartsRow%ROWCOUNT * 2) := currentPart;
  END LOOP;

/* OUTPUT COLLECTION ELEMENT FIELDS
|| Output the ID and DESCRIPTION fields of all elements
```

```
|| in the tempParts nested table collection; if the
|| element is NULL, indicate this.
*/
 DBMS_OUTPUT.PUT_LINE(
  'Densely populated tempParts elements: ' || tempParts.COUNT);
 currentElement := tempParts.FIRST;
 FOR i IN 1 .. tempParts.COUNT LOOP
  DBMS_OUTPUT.PUT('Element #' || currentElement || ' is ');
  IF tempParts(currentElement).id IS NULL THEN
   DBMS_OUTPUT.PUT_LINE('an empty element.');
  ELSE
   DBMS_OUTPUT.PUT_LINE('ID: '|| tempParts(currentElement).id ||
    ', ' || 'DESCRIPTION: ' || tempParts(currentElement).description);
  END IF;
  currentElement := tempParts.NEXT(currentElement);
 END LOOP;

/* DELETE EMPTY COLLECTION ELEMENTS
|| Use the collection's DELETE method to delete the
|| empty elements (rows) from the nested table.
*/
 FOR i IN 1 .. tempParts.COUNT LOOP
  IF tempParts(i).id IS NULL THEN
   tempParts.DELETE(i);
  END IF;
 END LOOP;

/* OUTPUT SPARSE VERSION OF THE COLLECTION
|| Print out ID and DESCRIPTIONS of the elements in
|| the sparse version of the nested table.
*/
 DBMS_OUTPUT.PUT_LINE(
  'Sparsely populated tempParts elements: ' || tempParts.COUNT);
 currentElement := tempParts.FIRST;
 FOR i IN 1 .. tempParts.COUNT LOOP
  DBMS_OUTPUT.PUT('Element #' || currentElement || ' is ');
  IF tempParts(currentElement).id IS NULL THEN
   DBMS_OUTPUT.PUT_LINE('an empty element.');
  ELSE
   DBMS_OUTPUT.PUT_LINE('ID: '|| tempParts(currentElement).id ||
    ', ' || 'DESCRIPTION: ' || tempParts(currentElement).description);
  END IF;
  currentElement := tempParts.NEXT(currentElement);
 END LOOP;
END;
/
```

The program output is as follows:

```
Densely populated tempParts elements: 10
Element #1 is an empty element.
Element #2 is ID: 1, DESCRIPTION: Fax Machine
Element #3 is an empty element.
Element #4 is ID: 2, DESCRIPTION: Copy Machine
Element #5 is an empty element.
Element #6 is ID: 3, DESCRIPTION: Laptop PC
Element #7 is an empty element.
Element #8 is ID: 4, DESCRIPTION: Desktop PC
Element #9 is an empty element.
Element #10 is ID: 5, DESCRIPTION: Scanner
Sparsely populated tempParts elements: 5
Element #2 is ID: 1, DESCRIPTION: Fax Machine
Element #4 is ID: 2, DESCRIPTION: Copy Machine
Element #6 is ID: 3, DESCRIPTION: Laptop PC
Element #8 is ID: 4, DESCRIPTION: Desktop PC
Element #10 is ID: 5, DESCRIPTION: Scanner

PL/SQL procedure successfully completed.
```

Besides demonstrating how to use the EXTEND, COUNT, FIRST, NEXT, and DELETE collection methods, this example shows that while nested tables are initially dense (elements have consecutive subscripts), they can later become *sparse* (elements can have nonconsecutive subscripts) if the program deletes elements from the collection. With this possibility in mind, the loops that output elements in the example program do not rely on the loop's counter variable to reference collection elements.

Varying Arrays

A program can also declare a *varying array (varray) type* to create table-like variables that have one or more columns and a *limited* number of rows. The general syntax for declaring a varray type is as follows:

```
TYPE varrayType IS {VARRAY | VARYING ARRAY} (size) OF
{ datatype | {variable|table.column}%TYPE | table%ROWTYPE }
   [NOT NULL] ;
```

For the most part, varray collections are similar to nested table collections, with the following important differences:

■ When you declare a varray type, you must declare the number of elements in the varray, which remains constant.

■ Varrays must remain *dense*. A program must insert members into a varray using consecutive subscripts, and cannot delete elements from a varray.

Handling Program Exceptions

A program is not complete unless it contains routines to process the errors that can occur during program execution. Rather than embed error-handling routines into the body of a program, a PL/SQL program addresses error-handling requirements using exceptions and associated exception handlers. An *exception* is a named error condition. A PL/SQL program *raises* a named exception when it detects an error, and then it passes control to an associated *exception handler* routine that is separate from the main program body. The next two exercises teach you more about exceptions and exception handling, including predefined and user-defined exceptions.

EXERCISE 5.19: Handling Predefined Exceptions

PL/SQL includes many *predefined exceptions* that correspond to several common Oracle errors. When a program encounters a predefined exception, it automatically transfers program control to the associated exception handler—a program does not have to explicitly perform checks for predefined exceptions.

PL/SQL identifies almost 20 predefined exceptions, including the NO_DATA_FOUND and TOO_MANY_ROWS predefined PL/SQL exceptions:

■ A PL/SQL program automatically raises the NO_DATA_FOUND exception when a SELECT INTO statement has a result set with no rows.

■ A PL/SQL program automatically raises the TOO_MANY_ROWS exception when a SELECT INTO statement has a result set with more than one row.

NOTE
*For a complete list of predefined exceptions, see
your Oracle documentation.*

Enter the following anonymous PL/SQL block, which includes exception handlers to handle the NO_DATA_FOUND and TOO_MANY_ROWS predefined PL/SQL exceptions.

```
DECLARE
  PROCEDURE printOrder (thisOrderDate IN DATE) IS
    thisId INTEGER;
  BEGIN
```

```
   SELECT id INTO thisId FROM orders
    WHERE orderdate = thisOrderDate;
   DBMS_OUTPUT.PUT_LINE('Order ID ' || thisId
    || ' on ' || thisOrderDate);
  EXCEPTION
   WHEN no_data_found THEN
    DBMS_OUTPUT.PUT_LINE('No data found for SELECT .. INTO');
  END printOrder;
BEGIN
 printOrder('23-JUN-99');
 printOrder('24-JUN-99');
 printOrder('18-JUN-99');
 printOrder('19-JUN-99');
EXCEPTION
 WHEN too_many_rows THEN
  DBMS_OUTPUT.PUT_LINE('Too many rows found for SELECT .. INTO');
END;
/
```

The program output is as follows:

```
Order ID 14 on 23-JUN-99
No data found for SELECT .. INTO
Too many rows found for SELECT .. INTO

PL/SQL procedure successfully completed.
```

There are several important points that this example demonstrates about exception handling in general:

- You can include an exception-handling section in any PL/SQL block—both the anonymous PL/SQL block and its subprogram (the printOrder procedure) have their own exception-handling sections.

- The first call to the printOrder procedure does not raise any exceptions and prints the ID of the only order placed on 23-Jun-99.

- The second call to the printOrder procedure raises the predefined exception NO_DATA_FOUND, because the SELECT ... INTO statement in the procedure does not retrieve any rows. The NO_DATA_FOUND exception handler local to the procedure handles the exception by printing a message, and then returns control to the calling program, the anonymous PL/SQL block, which then calls the printOrder procedure a third time.

- The third call to the printOrder procedure raises the predefined exception TOO_MANY_ROWS, because the SELECT ... INTO statement in the procedure returns more than one row. The procedure's exception-handling section does not handle the TOO_MANY_ROWS exception locally, so the exception propagates to the calling program, the anonymous PL/SQL block, which does have an exception handler for TOO_MANY_ROWS. The exception handler prints a message, and then passes control to the calling program, which in this case, is SQL*Plus. Execution of the anonymous PL/SQL block stops, and the fourth call to the printOrder procedure never executes.

NOTE

If a statement in a PL/SQL block raises an exception and the block does not have an associated exception handler, the program stops execution and returns the error number and message that correspond to the exception to the calling program.

EXERCISE 5.20: Declaring and Handling User-Defined Exceptions

A program can also declare *user-defined exceptions* in the declarative section of a block. However, a program must perform explicit checks for a user-defined exception that then raise the exception. Enter the following anonymous PL/SQL block, which demonstrates the use of user-defined exceptions and corresponding exception handlers.

```
DECLARE
  partNum INTEGER := 10;
  errNum INTEGER;
  errMsg VARCHAR2(2000);
  invalidPart EXCEPTION;
BEGIN
 UPDATE parts
  SET description = 'Test'
   WHERE id = partNum;
-- Explicitly check for the user-defined exception
 IF SQL%NOTFOUND THEN
   RAISE invalidPart;
 END IF;
 DBMS_OUTPUT.PUT_LINE('Part updated.');
EXCEPTION
 WHEN invalidPart THEN
   raise_application_error(-20003, 'Invalid Part ID #' || partNum);
 WHEN OTHERS THEN
  errNum := SQLCODE;
  errMsg := SUBSTR(SQLERRM, 1, 100);
```

```
    raise_application_error(-20000, errNum ||' '||errMsg);
END;
/
```

The program output is as follows:

```
DECLARE
*
ERROR at line 1:
ORA-20003: Invalid Part ID #10
ORA-06512: at line 17
```

The example in this section introduces several interesting points about exception handling:

■ You declare a user-defined exception in the declarative section of a PL/SQL block with the *EXCEPTION* keyword.

■ You raise a user-defined exception with the PL/SQL command *RAISE.*

■ A PL/SQL program can use the *RAISE_APPLICATION_ERROR* procedure to return a user-defined error number and message to the calling environment. All user-defined error messages must be in the range –20000 to –20999.

■ A PL/SQL program can use the *WHEN OTHERS* exception handler to handle all exceptions that do not have a specific handler.

■ A PL/SQL program can use the special *SQLCODE* and *SQLERRM* functions to return the most recent Oracle error number and message.

Types of PL/SQL Programs

Now that you understand the basics of the PL/SQL language, it's time to learn more about the different types of programs you can create with PL/SQL, including anonymous PL/SQL blocks, procedures, functions, packages, and database triggers.

Anonymous PL/SQL Blocks

The previous examples in this chapter are all anonymous PL/SQL blocks. An *anonymous block* is a PL/SQL block that appears within your application. An anonymous PL/SQL block has no name and is not stored for subsequent reuse. The application simply sends the block of code to the database server for processing at run time. Once the server executes an anonymous block, the block ceases to exist.

Stored Procedures and Functions

Several exercises in this chapter taught you how to declare and use PL/SQL subprograms (procedures and functions) within PL/SQL blocks to encapsulate frequently used tasks. A *subprogram* is a named PL/SQL program that can take parameters and be called again and again to perform work. You can also store procedures and functions as compiled bits of application logic inside an Oracle database as named schema objects. By centralizing common procedures and functions in the database, any application can make use of them to perform work. Judicious use of stored procedures and functions can increase developer productivity and simplify application development. The next two practice exercises demonstrate how to create stored procedures and functions in an Oracle database.

EXERCISE 5.21: Creating and Using Stored Procedures

To create a stored procedure in an Oracle database, use the SQL command *CREATE PROCEDURE*. Specification of a stored PL/SQL subprogram is basically the same as when you declare a subprogram in the declarative section of a PL/SQL block. However, when you declare a stored procedure, you can use the AUTHID CURRENT_USER or AUTHID DEFINER options to indicate the privilege domain that Oracle uses when executing the procedure:

- If you create the procedure with the *AUTHID CURRENT_USER* option, Oracle executes the procedure (when called) using the privilege domain of the user calling the procedure. To execute the procedure successfully, the caller must have the privileges necessary to access all database objects referenced in the body of the stored procedure.

- If you create the procedure with the default *AUTHID DEFINER* option, Oracle executes the procedure using the privilege domain of the owner of the procedure. To execute the procedure successfully, the procedure owner must have the privileges necessary to access all database objects referenced in the body of the stored procedure. To simplify privilege management for application users, the default AUTHID DEFINER option should be your typical choice when creating a stored procedure—this way, you do not have to grant privileges to all the users that need to call the procedure.

NOTE
For more information about database access privileges, see Chapter 9.

Enter the following example, which demonstrates how to create and store the familiar printLine procedure in an Oracle database.

```
CREATE OR REPLACE PROCEDURE printLine(
   width IN INTEGER,
   chr IN CHAR DEFAULT '-')
AUTHID DEFINER
IS
BEGIN
 FOR i IN 1 .. width LOOP
  DBMS_OUTPUT.PUT(chr);
 END LOOP;
 DBMS_OUTPUT.PUT_LINE('');
END printLine;
/
```

Now, you can use the printLine procedure in any other PL/SQL program just by calling the stored procedure in the database. For example, try entering the following anonymous PL/SQL blocks, which use the printLine stored procedure.

```
BEGIN
 printLine(40, '*');                    -- print a line of 40 *s
END;
/
BEGIN
 printLine(width => 20, chr => '=');  -- print a line of 20 =s
END;
/
BEGIN
 printLine(10);                         -- print a line of 10 -s
END;
/
```

The program outputs are as follows:

```
****************************************

PL/SQL procedure successfully completed.

====================

PL/SQL procedure successfully completed.
----------

PL/SQL procedure successfully completed.
```

EXERCISE 5.22: Creating and Using Stored Functions

To create a stored function in an Oracle database, use the SQL command *CREATE FUNCTION*. Specify a function just as you would in the declarative section of a PL/SQL block—do not forget to declare the function's return type and to use one or more RETURN statements in the body of the function to return the function's return value. Enter the following example, which demonstrates how to create and store the orderTotal function in an Oracle database.

```
CREATE OR REPLACE FUNCTION orderTotal(orderId IN INTEGER)
   RETURN NUMBER
IS
 orderTotal NUMBER;
 tempTotal NUMBER;
BEGIN
 SELECT SUM(i.quantity * p.unitprice) INTO orderTotal
  FROM items i, parts p
  WHERE i.o_id = orderId
  AND i.p_id = p.id
  GROUP BY i.o_id;
 RETURN orderTotal;
END orderTotal;
/
```

Now, enter the following query, which uses the orderTotal function to return the IDs and order dates of all orders that total more than $5,000.

```
SELECT id, orderdate
  FROM orders
  WHERE orderTotal(id) > 5000;
```

The results are as follows:

```
       ID ORDERDATE
--------- ---------
        1 18-JUN-99
        5 19-JUN-99
       10 21-JUN-99
       11 22-JUN-99
```

Packages

A package is a group of procedures, functions, and other PL/SQL constructs, all stored together in a database as a unit. Packages are especially useful for organizing a number of PL/SQL procedures and functions that relate to a particular database application.

A package has two parts, a specification and a body:

- A *package specification* defines the interface to the package. In a package specification, you declare all package variables, constants, cursors, procedures, functions, and other constructs that you want to make available to programs outside the package. In other words, everything that you declare in a package's specification is *public*. You declare a package specification with the SQL command *CREATE PACKAGE*.

- A *package body* defines all public procedures and functions declared in the package specification. Additionally, a package body can include other construct definitions not in the specification; such package constructs are *private* (available only to programs within the package). You declare a package body with the SQL command *CREATE PACKAGE BODY*.

All variables, constants, and cursors declared in either a package specification or body outside of a subprogram are considered *global*. Unlike private variables, constants, and cursors declared within specific procedures and functions, global constructs are available to all package procedures and functions and have a state that persists independent of any particular package subprogram on a per-session basis.

EXERCISE 5.23: Declaring and Using a Package

Enter the following example to create a very simple package called *partMgmt*, which demonstrates some of the functionality available with PL/SQL packages.

```
CREATE OR REPLACE PACKAGE partMgmt IS
-- Public subprograms
 PROCEDURE insertPart (partRecord IN parts%ROWTYPE);
 PROCEDURE updatePart (partRecord IN parts%ROWTYPE);
 PROCEDURE deletePart (partId IN INTEGER);
 PROCEDURE printPartsProcessed;
END partMgmt;
/

CREATE OR REPLACE PACKAGE BODY partMgmt AS
-- Private global variable
 rowsProcessed INTEGER := 0;

-- Public subprograms
 PROCEDURE insertPart (partRecord IN parts%ROWTYPE) IS
 BEGIN
  INSERT INTO parts
   VALUES (partRecord.id, partRecord.description,
    partRecord.unitprice, partRecord.onhand,
```

```
      partRecord.reorder);
   rowsProcessed := rowsProcessed + 1;
 END insertPart;

 PROCEDURE updatePart (partRecord IN parts%ROWTYPE) IS
 BEGIN
  UPDATE parts
   SET description = partRecord.description,
        unitprice = partRecord.unitprice,
        onhand = partRecord.onhand,
        reorder = partRecord.reorder
    WHERE id = partRecord.id;
   rowsProcessed := rowsProcessed + 1;
 END updatePart;

 PROCEDURE deletePart (partId IN INTEGER) IS
 BEGIN
  DELETE FROM parts
    WHERE id = partId;
   rowsProcessed := rowsProcessed + 1;
 END deletePart;

 PROCEDURE printPartsProcessed IS
 BEGIN
  DBMS_OUTPUT.PUT_LINE(
   'Parts processed this session: ' || rowsProcessed);
 END printPartsProcessed;

END partMgmt;
/
```

Now, enter the following anonymous PL/SQL block, which uses the insertPart procedure of the partMgmt package to insert a new part in the PARTS table.

```
DECLARE
 newPart parts%ROWTYPE;
BEGIN
 newPart.id := 6;
 newPart.description := 'Mouse';
 newPart.unitprice := 49;
 newPart.onhand := 1200;
 newPart.reorder := 500;

 partMgmt.insertPart(newPart);
END;
/
```

Notice that when you reference a package object (for example, a global variable or subprogram), you must use dot notation to qualify the package object with its package name. Now, enter the following anonymous PL/SQL block to update the new part's ONHAND quantity using the updatePart procedure in the partMgmt package.

```
DECLARE
  aPart parts%ROWTYPE;
BEGIN
  SELECT * INTO aPart FROM parts
   WHERE id = 6;
  aPart.onhand := 1123;

  partMgmt.updatePart(aPart);
END;
/
```

Now use the SQL*Plus command *EXECUTE* to execute the deletePart procedure of the partMgmt package to delete the newest part. The EXECUTE command is equivalent to surrounding a procedure call with the BEGIN and END keywords that delimit the start and end of an anonymous PL/SQL block.

```
EXECUTE partMgmt.deletePart(6);
```

Finally, enter the following EXECUTE command to output the number of rows in the PARTS table processed by the current session using the partMgmt package.

```
EXECUTE partMgmt.printPartsProcessed;
```

The program output is as follows:

```
Parts processed this session: 3

PL/SQL procedure successfully completed.
```

The printPartsProcessed procedure demonstrates that the rowsProcessed global variable retains its state, independent of calls to individual package subprograms.

Prebuilt Utility Packages

Oracle includes several prebuilt utility packages that provide additional functionality not available with SQL or PL/SQL. Table 5-4 lists several of the prebuilt packages available with Oracle8i.

Package Name	Description
DBMS_ALERT	Procedures and functions that allow applications to name and signal alert conditions without polling
DBMS_AQ DBMS_AQADM	Procedures and functions to queue the execution of transactions and administer queuing mechanisms
DBMS_DDL DBMS_UTILITY	Procedures that provide access to a limited number of DDL statements inside PL/SQL programs
DBMS_DESCRIBE	Procedures that describe the API for stored procedures and functions
DBMS_JOB	Procedures and functions to manage a database's job queuing mechanisms
DBMS_LOB	Procedures and functions to manipulate BLOBs, CLOBs, NCLOBs, and BFILEs
DBMS_LOCK	Procedures and functions that allow applications to coordinate access to shared resources
DBMS_OUTPUT	Procedures and functions that allow a PL/SQL program to generate terminal output
DBMS_PIPE	Procedures and functions that allow database sessions to communicate using pipes (communication channels)
DBMS_ROWID	Procedures and functions that allow applications to easily interpret a base-64 character external ROWID
DBMS_SESSION	Procedures and functions to control an application user's session
DBMS_SQL	Procedures and functions to perform dynamic SQL from within a PL/SQL program
DBMS_TRANSACTION	Procedures to perform a limited amount of transaction control
UTL_FILE	Procedures and functions that allow a PL/SQL program to read and write text files to the server's file system

TABLE 5-4. *Some of the Many Prebuilt Packages Available with Oracle8i*

NOTE
See your Oracle documentation for complete information about the APIs for all prebuilt packages and examples of their use.

Database Triggers

A *database trigger* is a stored procedure that you associate with a specific table. When applications target the table with a SQL DML statement that meets the trigger's execution conditions, Oracle automatically *fires* (executes) the trigger to perform work. Therefore, you can use triggers to customize an Oracle database server's reaction to application events.

To create a database trigger, you use the SQL command *CREATE TRIGGER*. The simplified syntax (not complete) for the CREATE TRIGGER command is as follows:

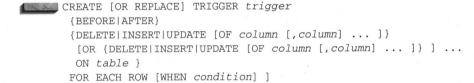

```
CREATE [OR REPLACE] TRIGGER trigger
  {BEFORE|AFTER}
  {DELETE|INSERT|UPDATE [OF column [,column] ... ]}
   [OR {DELETE|INSERT|UPDATE [OF column [,column] ... ]} ] ...
   ON table }
  FOR EACH ROW [WHEN condition] ]
  ... PL/SQL block ...
  END [trigger]
```

A trigger definition includes the following unique parts:

- A trigger's definition includes a list of *trigger statements*, including INSERT, UPDATE, and/or DELETE, that fire the trigger. A trigger is associated with one, and only one, table.

- A trigger can be set to fire before or after the trigger statement to provide specific application logic.

- A trigger's definition indicates whether the trigger is a statement trigger or a row trigger. A *statement trigger* fires only once, no matter how many rows the trigger statement affects.

EXERCISE 5.24: Creating and Using Database Triggers

Enter the following CREATE TRIGGER statement to create a trigger that automatically logs some basic information about the DML changes made to the PARTS table. The logPartChanges trigger is an after-statement trigger that fires once after the triggering statement, no matter how many rows the trigger statement affects.

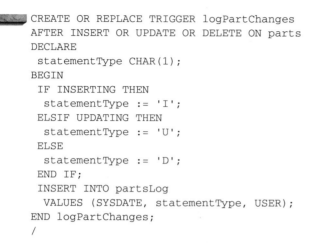

```
CREATE OR REPLACE TRIGGER logPartChanges
AFTER INSERT OR UPDATE OR DELETE ON parts
DECLARE
 statementType CHAR(1);
BEGIN
 IF INSERTING THEN
  statementType := 'I';
 ELSIF UPDATING THEN
  statementType := 'U';
 ELSE
  statementType := 'D';
 END IF;
 INSERT INTO partsLog
  VALUES (SYSDATE, statementType, USER);
END logPartChanges;
/
```

Notice in the logPartChanges trigger that when a trigger allows different types of statements to fire the trigger, the *INSERTING, UPDATING,* and *DELETING predicates* allow conditional statements to identify the type of statement that actually fired the trigger.

Now create the logDetailedPartChanges trigger, which is a before-row trigger that logs more detailed information about DML modifications that target the PARTS table.

```
CREATE OR REPLACE TRIGGER logDetailedPartChanges
BEFORE INSERT OR UPDATE OR DELETE ON parts
FOR EACH ROW
BEGIN
 INSERT INTO detailedpartslog
  VALUES (SYSDATE, USER,
   :new.id, :new.description, :new.unitprice,
   :new.onhand, :new.reorder,
   :old.id, :old.description, :old.unitprice,
   :old.onhand, :old.reorder
   );
END logDetailedPartChanges;
/
```

NOTE
Optionally, a row trigger can include a trigger restriction—a Boolean condition that determines when to fire the trigger.

Notice in the logDetailedPartChanges trigger that *:new* and *:old correlation values* allow a row trigger to access new and old field values of the current row. When a trigger statement is an INSERT statement, all old field values are null. Similarly, when a trigger statement is a DELETE statement, all new field values are null.

Finally, let's test out our new triggers and see what they actually do. Enter the following SQL statements that insert, update, and delete rows in the PARTS table, and then query the PARTSLOG and DETAILEDPARTSLOG tables.

```
INSERT INTO parts
  VALUES (6, 'Mouse', 49, 1200, 500);
UPDATE parts
  SET onhand = onhand - 10;
DELETE FROM parts
  WHERE id = 6;
SELECT * FROM partsLog;
SELECT newid, newonhand, oldid, oldonhand FROM detailedpartslog;
```

The result sets for the queries should be similar to the following:

```
CHANGEDATE C USERID
---------- - ----------
19-MAY-00  I PRACTICE05
19-MAY-00  U PRACTICE05
19-MAY-00  D PRACTICE05


    NEWID NEWONHAND     OLDID OLDONHAND
--------- --------- --------- ---------
        6      1200
        1       267         1       277
        2       133         2       143
        3      7621         3      7631
        4      5893         4      5903
        5       480         5       490
        6      1190         6      1200
                            6      1190
```

An important point to understand about database triggers is that triggers execute within the context of the current transaction. Therefore, if you were to roll back the current transaction, you would get the "no rows selected" message when you subsequently queried the PARTSLOG and DETAILEDPARTSLOG tables.

Chapter Summary

This chapter has provided you with a broad overview of the extended capabilities that PL/SQL offers for creating powerful database access programs. You've learned about the basics of the language itself, as well as how to create PL/SQL programs using stored procedures, functions, packages, and database triggers.

CHAPTER
6

Using Java with Oracle8i

ava is a relatively new technology, which simplifies the development of distributed applications operating in a network environment. This chapter explains how to use Java along with Oracle8i to develop all parts of a database application, including:

- How to build Java applications that access an Oracle8i database using JDBC and SQLJ

- How to build stored procedures and other database-stored application components using Java

What This Chapter Is, and What This Chapter Is Not

This chapter assumes that you currently have a good working knowledge of Java and simply would like to learn about the basics of using Java with Oracle8i for application development. If you do not understand the fundamentals of using Java and its object-oriented approach to application development, you should read another book, such as *Teach Yourself Java*, by Joseph O'Neil (Osborne/McGraw-Hill, 1998), before continuing with this chapter.

Chapter Prerequisites

To practice the hands-on exercises in this chapter, you need to start a Linux session as the user oracle, then start SQL*Plus and run the following command script

location/8istarterkit/SQL/chap06.sql

where *location* is the file directory where you expanded the support archive that accompanies this book. For example, after starting SQL*Plus and connecting as SCOTT, you could run this chapter's SQL command script using the SQL*Plus command @, as in the following example (assuming that your chap06.sql file is in /tmp/8istarterkit/SQL).

 `SQL> @/tmp/8istarterkit/SQL/chap06.sql;`

Once the script completes successfully, leave the current SQL*Plus session open, and use it to perform this chapter's exercises in the order that they appear.

NOTE
You should also have JDK 1.1.6 installed and configured for use on your Linux computer. To download a copy of this software for Linux, please visit http://www.blackdown.org and use the accompanying installation and configuration instructions. Also note that although other releases of 8.1.6 on other platforms support JDK 1.2 for JDBC application development, the 8.1.6.1.0 release of Oracle8i for Linux does not ship with the classes necessary to support JDK 1.2 development.

Overview of Oracle8i Database Access and Java

In general, there are two techniques that you can use to build Java programs so that they can access information in an Oracle8i database: JDBC and SQLJ. The following sections explain more about both topics.

JDBC

JDBC stands for *Java Database Connectivity.* JDBC is an industry standard based on the X/Open SQL Command Level Interface (CLI), which provides application developers a database-independent application programming interface (API) for building database applications. In other words, a Java application that uses JDBC to access one database system will access another database without modification, as long as the new database system also supports JDBC.

In general, there are two primary layers of interface to understand when learning about the JDBC API: the driver layer and the application layer. The *driver layer* handles all of the underlying details of communication with a specific database system. Each database vendor (such as Oracle Corp.) is responsible for the implementation of a JDBC driver that developers can then use to interact with their specific database system. On the other hand, the *application layer* is the part of JDBC that you'll be using most. The application layer is implemented as the java.sql.* classes in the Java Developer's Kit (JDK). Calls to the java.sql.* classes and their methods allow Java programs to interact with databases via SQL.

Besides database independence, another key strength of JDBC is its support for database applications that construct SQL statements at run time, otherwise known as *dynamic SQL*. The design of JDBC can support dynamic SQL because Java does not perform any syntax checking or semantics checking of SQL statements when you compile classes that make calls to the JDBC API. A notable side effect of using dynamic SQL, however, is that any errors that originate from incorrect SQL syntax, insufficient database access privileges, or other types of SQL errors will not be evident until run time.

SQLJ

SQLJ is a preprocessor (or precompiler) that you can use to build Java applications that embed SQL statements and other database operations into the Java application itself. When you compile a SQLJ input file, an extra step is necessary to translate the embedded SQL statements in the source file to JDBC-compliant calls before building an associated class file.

As long as you know the SQL that you want to use for an application when you are building it, you will probably find SQLJ easier to use than JDBC. Furthermore, SQLJ provides for SQL syntax and semantics checking when you compile your Java classes so that you can eliminate otherwise embarrassing errors from appearing during application run time.

Oracle8i's JVM

Accessing an Oracle database with stand-alone Java applications and applets that use JDBC or SQLJ is just one area of application development in which you can use Java. Oracle8i also includes a *Java Virtual Machine* (JVM) so that you can load and execute classes from within the database server itself. Oracle8i's JVM (also known as the *Aurora JVM*) supports the Java language specification so that, among other things, you can build server-side stored procedures and functions using Java.

Developing Java Database Applications Using JDBC

The following sections explain how to configure and build Java applications that access an Oracle database using JDBC. The examples assume that you have already installed JDK 1.1.6, have tested its functionality, and understand how to use the Java programming language.

JDBC Configuration Steps

Before you can begin writing Java-based Oracle database programs with JDBC, you must make sure that your computer is properly configured to do so. Unfortunately, the default installation of Oracle8i for Linux does not complete all the necessary configuration steps. The exercises in this section explain how to configure your computer for writing Java-based applications that rely on Oracle's implementation of JDBC.

EXERCISE 6.1: Setting the CLASSPATH and LD_LIBRARY_PATH Environment Variables for JDBC

To build Java classes that use Oracle's JDBC classes, you must configure the CLASSPATH and LD_LIBRARY_PATH environment variables for your Linux environment.

- The CLASSPATH environment variable is a colon-separated list of directories and archives that contain commonly referenced Java classes. To use Oracle's JDBC classes, you must add $ORACLE_HOME/jdbc/lib/classes111.zip to the CLASSPATH environment variable setting. The CLASSPATH environment variable setting should also include a period (.) so that the Java compiler can locate classes in the current working directory. If you are not familiar with the CLASSPATH environment variable for JDK 1.1.6, please read your JDK documentation.

- To use Oracle's JDBC OCI driver on Linux, you must also set the LD_LIBRARY_PATH environment variable to $ORACLE_HOME/lib.

For example, establish a new Linux session as the oracle user. Assuming that this account uses the /bin/bash shell, edit the .bash_profile login file in the oracle account's home directory and append the following lines to set the CLASSPATH and PATH environment variables:

```
CLASSPATH=.:$ORACLE_HOME/jdbc/lib/classes111.zip; export CLASSPATH
LD_LIBRARY_PATH=$ORACLE_HOME/lib; export LD_LIBRARY_PATH
```

Next, either log out and log in again as the oracle user, or use the following command to rerun the account's login script and set the new environment variables:

```
. $HOME/.bash_profile
```

NOTE
If the oracle account uses a shell other than /bin/bash, modify the code examples above for the shell.

At this point, Linux sessions established via the oracle user account should now be able to compile Java classes that require the Oracle JDBC classes.

EXERCISE 6.2: Testing JDBC Access to Oracle8i

Once you configure an account for using Oracle's JDBC classes and JDBC driver, you should test the configuration to make sure things work correctly. After establishing a session as the oracle user account, from the shell command prompt, change your current working directory to the location *8iStarterKit_Home*/Java, where *8iStarterKit_Home* is the location where you expanded the self-extracting archive that supports this book. Next, compile the Prompt.java and JdbcConnect.java source files with JDK 1.1.6 using the following commands:

```
javac Prompt.java
javac JdbcConnect.java
```

NOTE
If these files do not compile successfully, make sure that you have completed the steps in Exercise 6.1.

Next, run the compiled JdbcConnect application as follows:

```
java JdbcConnect
```

The program will display a sequence of prompts that you can use to enter a username, password, and database connect string to establish a connection to the starter database. Try connecting to the starter database on your Linux computer with the username "practice06" and the password "password". The output of the program might look as follows:

```
Username: practice06
Password: password
Host:

Connecting ...  successful connection, JDBC configured properly.
```

If you receive the final message that indicates a successful connection, everything is ready to go; otherwise, review Exercise 6.1 again and check your Oracle documentation for additional configuration help.

The Essentials of JDBC

Figure 6-1 illustrates the fundamental steps that a Java application uses to access a database with the JDBC API. The following sections explain more about the sequence of steps in Figure 6-1.

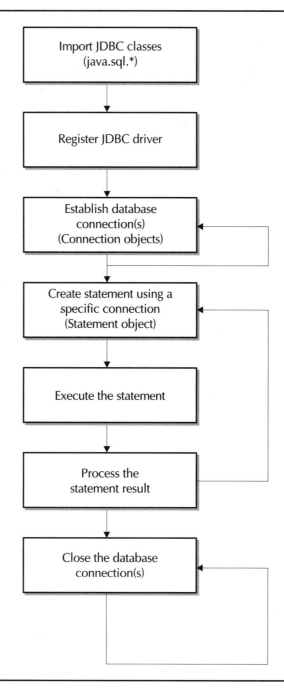

FIGURE 6-1. *Fundamental steps necessary for JDBC database access*

Access to JDBC Classes and a JDBC Driver

JDBC is an interface implemented as the *java.sql* classes—to use JDBC, a Java class must first import these classes. The java.sql classes throw the *SQLException* class, a subclass of the Exception class. All Java programs that use JDBC calls must catch SQLException objects.

Once a class has access to JDBC classes, it must then register a JDBC driver. A *JDBC driver* is an implementation of the *java.sql.DriverManager* class. When using JDBC, a Java program must register the driver that will be used by calling the *DriverManager.registerDriver* method.

Connection Objects

A *Connection* object maintains the state of a database session. Once a Java program starts a Connection with a call to the *DriverManager.getConnection* method, the program can execute SQL statements and process their results within the context of the Connection. By default, a Connection object starts with its *auto-commit state* set to TRUE—a mode whereby each statement executes within its own transaction. To control this functionality, a Java program can call the Connection's *setAutoCommit* method. Before exiting, a program should close an open connection with a call to the Connection's *close* method.

Statement Objects

A Java program uses a *Statement* object to execute a SQL statement and process the results of executing the statement. The declaration of a Statement object typically initializes the Statement by making a call to a Connection's *createStatement* method to set the Statement's context.

A Java program executes a Statement object by making a call to the Statement's *execute, executeUpdate,* or *executeQuery* method—different methods are available for different types of SQL statements. The ExecuteDML example program in the following exercise uses the executeUpdate method, which returns an integer to indicate the number of rows processed by an INSERT, UPDATE, or DELETE statement.

Using JDBC to Access Oracle8i

Now that you understand the general concepts of using JDBC, the following exercise demonstrates how to use Connection and Statement objects to access your Oracle8i starter database.

NOTE

For complete reference information about JDBC, please see the API reference in your JDK documentation for the java.sql package.

EXERCISE 6.3: The ExecuteDML Class

To illustrate the JDBC fundamentals that the previous section describes, as well as some of the power of JDBC, examine the following Java application, ExecuteDML. Calls to JDBC classes and methods are highlighted for your convenience.

The ExecuteDML class is a Java application that lets you connect to an Oracle8 or Oracle8i database and submit valid DML statements (INSERT, UPDATE, or DELETE) or transaction-control commands (COMMIT, ROLLBACK). Rather than explain the functionality of the program in the context of the surrounding paragraphs of this exercise, the program contains extensive comments that explain each section of code so that you can follow along and learn the basic steps for using JDBC. To quickly identify the steps that the previous section explains, look first for the comments in all capital letters.

```java
// This class provides a command-line interpreter for
// one-line DML statements. Acceptable commands are
// INSERT, UPDATE, DELETE, COMMIT, and ROLLBACK.
// To end the program, enter EXIT at the DML prompt.

// IMPORT JDBC CLASSES
import java.sql.*;

public class ExecuteDML {

  public static void main(String[] args) {

    // Declare a null Connection first so that you can
    // reference it throughout the method.
    Connection conn = null;

    try {

      // DRIVER REGISTRATION
      // Register the Oracle JDBC driver for the application.
      DriverManager.registerDriver(new oracle.jdbc.driver.OracleDriver());

      // OPEN DATABASE CONNECTION
      // 1. Use the custom-built DbConnect constructor to prompt the user for
      //    all information necessary to build a connect string.
      DbConnect mydb = new DbConnect(8);
      // 2. Get a connection using the connect string just built.
      conn = DriverManager.getConnection(mydb.myConnection);
      // 3. Set the connection's AutoCommit property to false; otherwise
      //    every DML statement will automatically commit.
      conn.setAutoCommit(false);
      // 4. Display some information about the database connection.
      DatabaseMetaData md = conn.getMetaData();
      System.out.println(md.getDatabaseProductVersion());
```

```java
        System.out.println(md.getDriverName() + " " + md.getDriverVersion() + "\n");

        // BUILD SQL STATEMENTS
        // 1. Variables necessary for statement processing.
        int rowsProcessed;
        String sql = "";
        // 2. Create statement object.
        Statement s = conn.createStatement();
        // 3. Loop forever, reading one-line DML statements and executing them.
        while(true) {
          // Prompt for new DML statement.
          sql = Prompt.read("DML> ");
          // Evaluate conditions for loop termination.
          if (sql == null || sql.equalsIgnoreCase("EXIT") ) break;
          // Ignore blank lines.
          if (sql.length() == 0) continue;
          // Do not accept statements that end with a semicolon.
          if (sql.endsWith(";")) {
            System.out.println("\n Do not end commands with \";\".\n");
            continue;
          }
          try {
            // Check for acceptable statements.
            if (sql.toUpperCase().startsWith("INSERT") |
                sql.toUpperCase().startsWith("UPDATE") |
                sql.toUpperCase().startsWith("DELETE") |
                sql.toUpperCase().startsWith("COMMIT") |
                sql.toUpperCase().startsWith("ROLLBACK") ) {
              // Execute statement, capture and print rows processed.
              rowsProcessed = s.executeUpdate(sql);
              System.out.println("\n" + rowsProcessed + " rows processed.\n");
            }
            else
              System.out.println("\nError: Invalid DML statement.\n" +
                "Enter INSERT ..., UPDATE ..., DELETE ..., COMMIT, or ROLLBACK.\n");
          }
          catch (SQLException e) {System.err.println("Error: " + e.getMessage());}
        }
      }
      catch (Exception e) {System.err.println(e);}
      finally {
        System.out.println("\nEnd of program.");
        // CLOSE THE DATABASE CONNECTION
        try {conn.close();} catch (Exception e) {}
      }
    }
}
```

NOTE

The ExecuteDML application uses the custom DbConnect and Prompt classes. If you are interested, you can explore the functionality of the custom DbConnect and Prompt classes by examining the corresponding source files in your 8iStarterKit_Home/Java directory.

To compile the ExecuteDML application, use your current Linux session established via the oracle user account to enter the following commands from a shell prompt (with the current working directory set as *8iStarterKit_Home*/Java).

```
javac DbConnect.java
javac ExecuteDML.java
```

TIP

A better way to learn JDBC is to use a text editor or your Java integrated development environment (IDE) to type the lines of all source code yourself, rather than just compiling the source code distributed with this book. In other words, the best way to learn about something is to do it yourself!

Next, run the compiled ExecuteDML application as follows:

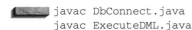
```
java ExecuteDML
```

The program displays a sequence of prompts that you can use to enter a username, password, and database connect string to establish a connection to the starter database. Try connecting with the account practice06/password that is in place to support this chapter. Once you connect, the program reveals some information about the connection and then provides you with a simple DML command prompt:

```
DML> _
```

At the DML prompt, you can enter an INSERT, UPDATE, DELETE, COMMIT, or ROLLBACK statement, provided that it is on one line and does not end with a semicolon. You can also enter EXIT to end the program. After you compile ExecuteDML, run the program and try to duplicate the following session:

```
Username: practice06
Password: password
Host:

Oracle8i Enterprise Edition Release 8.1.6.1.0 - Production
With the Partitioning option
JServer Release 8.1.6.0.0 - Production
Oracle JDBC driver 8.1.6.0.0

DML> CREATE TABLE foo (a CHAR(1))

Error: Invalid DML statement.
Enter INSERT ..., UPDATE ..., DELETE ..., COMMIT, or ROLLBACK.

DML> INSERT INTO salesreps VALUES (4, 'Slague', 'Richard', 5);

 Do not end commands with ";".

DML> INSERT INTO salesreps VALUES (4, 'Slague', 'Richard', 5)

1 rows processed.

DML> UPDATE salesreps SET commission = 10 WHERE id = 4

1 rows processed.

DML> COMMIT

0 rows processed.

DML> INSERT INTO salesreps VALUES (4, 'Wilson', 'Jack', 5)
Error: ORA-00001: unique constraint (PRACTICE06.S_ID) violated

DML> EXIT

End of program.
```

Notice from the output of the previous example ExecuteDML session that the ExecuteDML Java class is able to process DML SQL statements that you enter interactively—this is called dynamic SQL processing because the SQL is not embedded and compiled as part of your program. Dynamic SQL processing, as stated earlier in this chapter, is one of the primary reasons to choose JDBC when developing Java applications. For more detailed information about JDBC, please consult *The Complete Guide to Java Database Programming JDBC, ODBC, and SQL* by Matthew D. Siple (Computing McGraw-Hill, 1997).

Developing Java Database Applications Using SQLJ

Now that you understand the general steps necessary to develop Java/JDBC applications, the following sections will teach you a slightly different approach— how to build Java applications that access an Oracle database using SQLJ. Again, the examples assume that you have already installed JDK 1.1.6, have tested its functionality, and understand how to use the Java programming language.

SQLJ Configuration Steps

Before you can use SQLJ, you must make sure that your computer is properly configured to do so. First of all, make sure that you have completed the steps in Exercise 6.1 and tested JDBC with the steps in Exercise 6.2. Then, complete the following two exercises to configure SQLJ and test that it is working properly.

EXERCISE 6.4: Setting the CLASSPATH Environment Variable for SQLJ

Just as in Exercise 6.1, you may need to adjust the setting of the oracle user account's CLASSPATH environment variable—if you are not familiar with the steps necessary to edit a Linux account's environment variable settings, please review Exercise 6.1 now. To support SQLJ, you must adjust the CLASSPATH environment variable so that it includes $ORACLE_HOME/sqlj/lib/translator.zip (enter this on one line):

```
CLASSPATH=.:$ORACLE_HOME/jdbc/lib/classes111.zip:
    $ORACLE_HOME/sqlj/lib/translator.zip; export CLASSPATH
```

Next, either log out and log in again as the oracle user, or use the following command to rerun the account's login script and set the new environment variables:

```
. $HOME/.bash_profile
```

NOTE
If you use a shell other than /bin/bash, modify the preceding code examples for your shell.

Once you complete this configuration step, you should be able to compile Java classes that require the SQLJ classes.

EXERCISE 6.5: Testing SQLJ Configuration and Access to Oracle8i

Once you complete Exercise 6.4, you should test your computer's configuration to make sure that you can use SQLJ. Using a shell session established via the oracle user account that has the updated CLASSPATH and PATH environment variable settings, change your current working directory to the location *8iStarterKit_Home/*Java, where *8iStarterKit_Home* is the location where you expanded the self-extracting archive that supports this book.

Next, compile the SqljConnect.java source file with JDK 1.1.6 using the following command:

```
javac SqljConnect.java
```

NOTE
If the file does not compile successfully, make sure that you have completed the steps in Exercises 6.1 and 6.4.

Next, run the compiled SqljConnect application as follows:

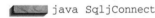

```
java SqljConnect
```

Just as with the JdbcConnect program in Exercise 6.2, the SqljConnect program displays a sequence of prompts that you can use to enter a username, password, and database connect string to establish a connection to the starter database. For example, try connecting with the practice06/password account, and the output of the program should appear as follows:

```
Username: practice06
Password: password
Host:

Connecting ...  successful connection, SQLJ configured properly.
```

If you receive a message that indicates a successful connection, everything is ready to go; otherwise, review Exercises 6.1 and 6.4 again, and check your Oracle documentation for additional configuration help.

The Essentials of SQLJ

Figure 6-2 illustrates the fundamental steps that a Java application uses to access a database with SQLJ. The following sections explain more about each step in Figure 6-2.

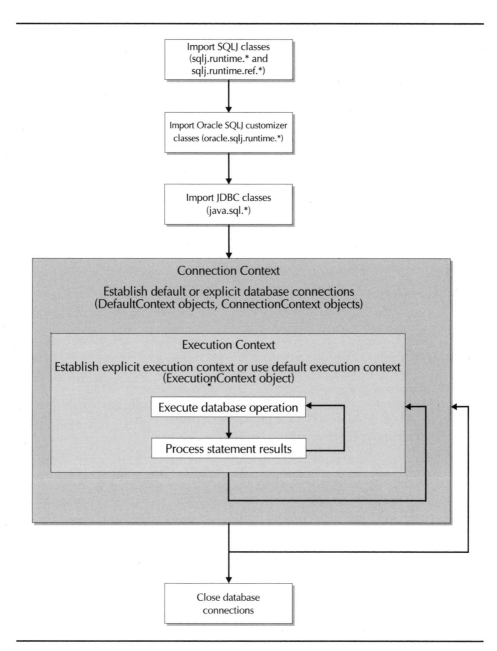

FIGURE 6-2. *Fundamental steps necessary for SQLJ database access*

ConnectionContext and DefaultContext Objects

A *ConnectionContext* object maintains an underlying instance of a JDBC Connection object. Within the context of a ConnectionContext, a Java program that uses SQLJ can execute SQL statements and other database operations. A Java program can open one or more ConnectionContext objects (that is, one or more connections) and execute database operations using specific ConnectionContext objects.

DefaultContext is a subclass of ConnectionContext. A *DefaultContext* object provides a database connection that a Java program can use to execute database operations without having to specify a ConnectionContext. Unless you plan to establish multiple database connections in a Java program, simplify the program by using the DefaultContext object. You can access the attributes and methods of the underlying JDBC Connection of a ConnectionContext (or DefaultContext) object by calling the object's *getConnection* method. For example, a program might want to access the underlying JDBC Connection object of a ConnectionContext to change the connection's auto-commit state.

ExecutionContext Objects

Within the context of a ConnectionContext (or DefaultContext) object, there exists one or more *ExecutionContext* objects (see Figure 6-2). All database operations that you execute using a ConnectionContext happen within the inner context of an ExecutionContext object. Each ConnectionContext has a default ExecutionContext that you can use to execute database operations.

An ExecutionContext object maintains state for the execution of the most recent database operation. If necessary, a program can explicitly declare the default ExecutionContext object for a ConnectionContext so that it can access the ExecutionContext object's methods and variables.

Embedded SQL Statements and Database Operations

SQLJ is a precompiler that lets you *embed* complete SQL statements and other database operations, such as calls, to database stored procedures and functions inside a Java class definition. A Java program that contains embedded database operations is often called the *host program*. The embedded statements are also called *SQLJ executable statements*.

To embed a SQL statement, procedure call, or function call (referred to from this point forward as a *database operation*), a host Java program uses the following syntax:

```
#sql [connection_context[,] execution_context] [result = ] {database operation}
```

The required parts of an embedded database operation include the following two parts:

■   The specification of a database operation always begins with the *#sql* token, which serves as a flag to the SQLJ preprocessor.

■   The database operation itself follows the #sql token and is delimited with curly braces. It is important to realize that in the previous syntax listing, the curly braces are required syntax.

Optionally, a database operation embedded in a host Java program can include the following syntax:

■   You can specify a ConnectionContext and ExecutionContext for the database operation. If you do not indicate a ConnectionContext or ExecutionContext, Java assumes that you want to use the current default contexts.

■   If the database operation returns a value, such as when executing a stored function, the operation must assign its return value to a *result expression*.

Host Expressions

Embedded SQL statements and other database operations can reference variables and other structures of the host program if necessary—altogether, you can refer to these types of references as *host expressions*. You indicate a host expression inside an executable database operation, such as a SQL statement, using the following syntax:

 `:[IN|OUT|INOUT][ ]{variable|(expression)}`

Notice the following features:

■   All references to host expressions begin with a colon.

■   In its simplest form, the specification of a host expression is the name of a *host variable*—a variable that the Java program can access. Otherwise, the specification of a host expression must be delimited with parentheses.

■   Optionally, you can specify the mode for a host expression as IN, OUT, or INOUT. If you set the mode of a host variable to OUT or INOUT, the variable must be assignable.

SQLJ Source Files

Unlike normal Java source code files, Java source code files that include SQLJ executable statements (referred to as *SQLJ source code files*) have some special requirements. For example, a SQLJ source code file must have the *.sqlj* extension. Furthermore, a SQLJ source file can declare a maximum of one public class, and the filename must match the name of this class.

Oracle's SQLJ Translator

You cannot compile SQLJ source code files using a normal call to the javac compiler. Instead, you must call Oracle's *SQLJ Translator*. On Linux, Oracle's SQLJ Translator is the *sqlj* utility in the $ORACLE_HOME/bin directory—this directory should be in your system path if you followed the steps in Chapters 2 and 3. The translator itself is a precompiler that performs many steps.

Figure 6-3 illustrates the basic steps that the SQLJ Translator performs when you translate a SQLJ source code file. While an in-depth discussion of the SQLJ Translator's functionality is beyond the scope of this book, the following sections explain some of the more important points to know about the translator so that you understand the output produced in subsequent exercises of this chapter.

SQL Syntax and Semantics Checking   One of the true powers of SQLJ is its ability to perform SQL syntax- and semantics-checking during the compilation of your Java classes, rather than at run time (as is the case with Java programs that use JDBC). The SQLJ Translator performs the following steps:

■   The translator parses the SQLJ source code to check for proper SQLJ syntax and identify any type mismatches between SQL datatypes and associated Java host variables.

■   The translator checks the semantics of embedded SQL statements and other database operations. With online semantics-checking, the translator connects to the database and validates access to the tables, stored procedures, and stored functions that the Java program uses.

SQLJ Profiles, Profile-Keys, and the Customizer   When the translator processes a SQLJ source code file, it generates a SQLJ profile for each instance of the ConnectionContext or DefaultContext class in the source code. A *SQLJ profile* contains information necessary to execute the embedded SQL statements in the SQLJ source code. When you execute a compiled SQLJ application, the SQLJ run-time reads the profiles to retrieve the embedded SQL operations and hand them off to the underlying JDBC driver for execution. By default, the translator stores profiles in resource files with the *.ser* extension. However, because certain browsers do not support .ser files, you can specify an option when running the translator that converts the .ser files to .class files.

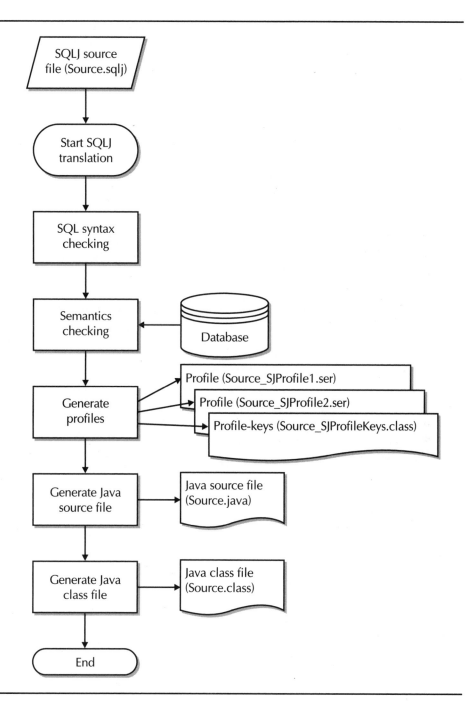

FIGURE 6-3.   *The basic steps performed by the SQLJ Translator*

Along with SQLJ profiles, the translator also generates a *profile-keys* .class file. The SQLJ run-time uses the profile-keys class to map calls in the translated SQLJ .class file to the associated profiles.

NOTE
The translator generates profiles and the profile-keys .class file only when a SQLJ source code file includes SQLJ executable statements.

By default, the translator automatically customizes each profile for a SQLJ source code file so that the embedded SQL operations are customized for use with a particular database. When you use Oracle's SQLJ Translator, it automatically optimizes each SQLJ profile using the Oracle customizer.

.java and .class Files   As the translator works with a SQLJ source code file, it converts embedded SQL operations to SQLJ run-time calls (calls to the classes in the sqlj.runtime and sqlj.runtime.ref classes), and then generates a corresponding .java source code file, as well as .class files for each class in the SQLJ source code file.

Using SQLJ to Access Oracle8i

Now that you understand the general concepts of using SQLJ and the SQLJ Translator, the next exercise demonstrates the use of DefaultContext and ExecutionContext objects, SQLJ executable statements, and host expressions inside a Java class.

EXERCISE 6.6: The ManageSalesReps and SalesRep Classes

To illustrate each of the steps necessary for using SQLJ, examine the following Java classes: ManageSalesReps and SalesRep. For clarity, all calls to SQLJ classes and methods are highlighted. The paragraphs that follow each class listing and the comments within each class explain more about each class's functionality. First, here is the ManageSalesReps class.

```
// IMPORT SQLJ Classes
import sqlj.runtime.*;
import sqlj.runtime.ref.*;

// IMPORT ORACLE'S SQLJ CUSTOMIZER
import oracle.sqlj.runtime.*;

/ IMPORT UNDERLYING JDBC Classes
import java.sql.*;

public class ManageSalesReps {

    // Several methods of ManageSalesReps encapsulate repetitive
```

```java
// operations, including clrscr, PromptSalesRep,
// PrintSalesRep, and PromptAction.

public static void main(String[] args) {
  SalesRep sr;

try {

  // ESTABLISH A CONNECTION AND GET A HANDLE
  // FOR THE DEFAULT CONNECTION CONTEXT
  DbConnect myDb = new DbConnect(8);
  DefaultContext defaultConnection = Oracle.connect(myDb.myConnection);
  // The following are JDBC calls to access the underlying Connection
  Connection conn = defaultConnection.getConnection();
  DatabaseMetaData md = conn.getMetaData();
  System.out.println(md.getDatabaseProductVersion());
  System.out.println(md.getDriverName() + " " + md.getDriverVersion() + "\n");
  conn.setAutoCommit(true);

  // GET A HANDLE FOR THE DEFAULT EXECUTION CONTEXT OF THE
  // DEFAULT CONNECTION CONTEXT
  ExecutionContext defExecution = defaultConnection.getExecutionContext();

  // USER INTERFACE FOR MANAGING SALES REPRESENTATIVES
  // The remainder of main builds a simple interface
  // that prompts the user to manage sales representatives.

  // declare some necessary variables for user responses
  int action = 0;
  String confirm;

  // clear screen
  confirm = Prompt.read("Press RETURN to continue ...");
  clrscr(25);

  // loop forever asking what action to take
  while(true) {
    action = PromptAction();
    if (action == 4) break;
    if (action > 4 | action < 1) continue;<R      sr = PromptSalesRep();
    PrintSalesRep(sr);
    try {
      switch (action) {
      case 1:  // insert
        confirm = Prompt.read("\n Insert this sales representative? (y/n): ");
        if (confirm.equalsIgnoreCase("Y")) {
          sr.insert();
          System.out.println("\n " + defExecution.getUpdateCount() + " row(s) inserted.");
        } else System.out.println("\n Insert aborted.");
        break;
      case 2:  // update
        confirm = Prompt.read("\n Update this sales representative? (y/n): ");
        if (confirm.equalsIgnoreCase("Y")) {
          sr.update();
          System.out.println("\n " + defExecution.getUpdateCount() + " row(s) updated.");
        } else System.out.println("\n Update aborted.");
        break;
      case 3:  // delete
```

```
          confirm = Prompt.read("\n Delete this sales representative? (y/n): ");
          if (confirm.equalsIgnoreCase("Y")) {
            sr.delete();
            System.out.println("\n " + defExecution.getUpdateCount() + " row(s) deleted.");
          } else System.out.println("\n Delete aborted.");
          break;
        default:
          continue;
        }
      }
      catch (SQLException e) {
        System.err.println("\n Error: " + e.getMessage());
      }
      confirm = Prompt.read("\n Press RETURN to continue ...");
    }
    System.out.println("\n End of Program.");
    conn.close();
  }
  catch (SQLException e) {System.err.println("\n Error: " + e.getMessage());}
}

public static SalesRep PromptSalesRep () {
  int id, commission;
  String lastName, firstName;

  clrscr(25);
  System.out.println(" ENTER SALES REPRESENTATIVE INFORMATION\n"+
                     " ====================================");
  // loop forever until an integer is entered
  while(true) {
    try {
        id = Integer.parseInt(Prompt.read(" Enter ID (integer): "));
        break;
      }
    catch (NumberFormatException e) {
      System.out.println("\n Illegal integer!\n");
    }
  }
  lastName = Prompt.read(" Enter Last Name:  ");
  firstName = Prompt.read(" Enter First Name: ");
  // loop forever until an integer is entered
  while(true) {
    try {
      commission = Integer.parseInt(Prompt.read(" Enter Commission Rate: "));
      break;
    }
    catch (NumberFormatException e) {
      System.out.println("\n Illegal integer!\n");
    }
  }
  SalesRep sr = new SalesRep(id, lastName, firstName, commission);
  return sr;
}

public static void PrintSalesRep (SalesRep sr) {
  clrscr(25);
  System.out.println("\n CURRENT SALES REPRESENTATIVE INFORMATION" +
                     "\n =======================================\n");
```

```
      System.out.println(" Id:            " + sr.id);
      System.out.println(" Last Name:     " + sr.lastName);
      System.out.println(" First Name:    " + sr.firstName);
      System.out.println(" Commission %: " + sr.commission);
    }

  public static int PromptAction () {
    int action;
    clrscr(25);
    System.out.println(" MANAGE SALES REPRESENTATIVES\n" +
                       " =============================\n");
    System.out.println(" 1. Insert New Sales Representative");
    System.out.println(" 2. Update a Sales Representative");
    System.out.println(" 3. Delete a Sales Representative");
    System.out.println(" 4. Exit\n\n\n");
    try {
      action = Integer.parseInt(Prompt.read(" Enter Choice (1,2,3,4): "));
    }
    catch (NumberFormatException e) {action = 0;}
    return action;
  }

  public static void clrscr (int lines) {
    for (int i = 0; i < lines; i++) System.out.println(""); )
}
```

The purpose of the ManageSalesReps class is to establish a database connection and then provide a very simple interface that prompts the user to manage sales representatives. Once the ManageSalesReps class establishes the necessary ConnectionContext (actually, an instance of DefaultContext) and ExecutionContext, it calls the methods of the SalesRep class, which encapsulate the SQL operations necessary to insert, update, and delete records specifically from the PRACTICE06.SALESREPS table. The source code for the SalesRep class follows.

NOTE

ManageSalesReps also relies on the custom DbConnect and Prompt classes that should already be compiled in your 8iStarterKit_Home/Java directory from previous exercises in this chapter.

```
// IMPORT SQLJ Classes
import sqlj.runtime.*;
import sqlj.runtime.ref.*;

// IMPORT ORACLE'S SQLJ CUSTOMIZER
import oracle.sqlj.runtime.Oracle;

// IMPORT UNDERLYING JDBC Classes
import java.sql.*;

public class SalesRep {
  int id;
```

```
  String lastName, firstName;
  int commission;

  // constructor
  public SalesRep(int id, String lastName, String firstName, int commission) {
    this.id = id;
    this.lastName = lastName;
    this.firstName = firstName;
    this.commission = commission;
  }

  // METHODS TO INSERT, UPDATE, AND DELETE SALESREPS IN
  // THE DATABASE POINTED TO BY THE DEFAULT OR CURRENT
  // CONTEXT OF THE CALLING PROGRAM.

  public void insert () throws SQLException {
    int id = this.id;
    String lastName = this.lastName;
    String firstName = this.firstName;
    int commission = this.commission;
    #sql { INSERT INTO practice06.salesreps
           VALUES (:id, :lastName, :firstName, :commission) };
  }

  public void update () throws SQLException {
    int id = this.id;
    String lastName = this.lastName;
    String firstName = this.firstName;
    int commission = this.commission;
    #sql { UPDATE practice06.salesreps
           SET lastname = :lastName,
               firstname = :firstName,
               commission = :commission
           WHERE id = :id };
  }

  public void delete () throws SQLException {
    int id = this.id;
    String lastName = this.lastName;
    String firstName = this.firstName;
    int commission = this.commission;
    #sql { DELETE FROM practice06.salesreps
           WHERE id = :id };
  }
}
```

An important point to notice is that the SQLJ executable statements in the methods of the SalesRep class do not explicitly manage a ConnectionContext, DefaultContext, or ExecutionContext—they implicitly use the default contexts from the calling program.

To better understand the ManageSalesReps and SalesRep classes and the steps necessary for using SQLJ, I highly recommend that you build these source files yourself using your favorite text editor or Java IDE. Otherwise, you can simply compile the source code distributed with this book for both classes—the source

Considering Datatype Conversion Between SQL and Java Types

As you build Java classes that use SQL to modify database information, carefully consider the type declarations inside Java classes and methods and keep in mind the following important points:

- The Java scalar types (for example, int and float) are not considered "database-friendly" because they do not represent a null as the absence of value—instead, they represent a null as the value 0, which can lead to incorrect interpretations of database information. Therefore, use Java scalar types for declarations only when nulls are not possible for the corresponding database values.

- On the other hand, the Java object types (for example, Integer and Float) and JDBC SQL types (java.sql.Types.*) represent nulls correctly, and can avoid the problem mentioned in the previous point.

- The conversion of data between SQL datatypes and Java types (scalar or object) might result in a loss of precision.

When using Oracle8i, one way to avoid all of the sticky issues related to type conversion between SQL and Java types is to use the special oracle.sql.* classes when declaring Java constructs rather than using native Java scalar types, Java object types (java.lang.*), or JDBC SQL types (java.sql.Types.*). Besides guaranteeing the safe conversion of data between Java and SQL, the oracle.sql.* classes are extremely efficient at representing SQL data.

code files are in the *8iStarterKit_Home*/Java directory. Make sure to use a Linux session via the oracle user account that has been configured for JDBC and SQLJ use.

To compile the SalesRep.sqlj source file with online semantics-checking, enter the following command using the current Command Prompt window (with the current working directory set as *8iStarterKit_Home*/Java).

```
sqlj -user practice06/password SalesRep.sqlj
```

After the SalesRep class compiles, take a look at the files that the translator created in the working directory, which will include files for a corresponding profile, profile-keys, Java source, and Java class file.

Next, compile the ManageSalesReps.java source file. Because the ManageSalesReps class does not contain any SQLJ executable statements, the translator is not necessary and you can use the normal javac compiler.

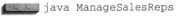

```
javac ManageSalesReps.java
```

Once ManageSalesReps compiles successfully, run the ManageSalesReps application with the following command:

```
java ManageSalesReps
```

The program displays a very simple menu interface that continually prompts you to insert, update, or delete sales representatives. Try out each available operation to witness the behavior of the program. You should also try entering unexpected values at the various prompts (for example, a character or string when an integer is expected) to see how the program traps and handles exceptions. For more detailed information on SQLJ, please consult *Oracle8i SQLJ Programming*, by Nirva Morisseau-Leroy, Gerald P. Momplaisir, and Martin K. Solomon (Osborne/McGraw-Hill, 1999).

Building and Using Java Stored Procedures

The previous sections in this chapter describe the steps necessary for building stand-alone Java applications, external to Oracle itself, that use either JDBC or SQLJ to access data in an Oracle8i database. However, developing Java database programs outside the database is really just half of the picture. When building Oracle database applications using any type of application development environment, you should take advantage of Oracle's capability to centralize common segments of code as database stored procedures and functions. The good news for Java programmers is that, starting with Oracle8i, you can now build stored procedures, functions, database triggers, and object type methods (see Chapter 8) using Java. In this section, you'll learn about the steps for building basic stored procedures and functions using Java.

NOTE
If you are not familiar with the concepts and benefits of stored procedures and functions, review Chapter 5.

The Essentials of Java Stored Procedures

Oracle8i supports several different techniques for building Java stored procedures and functions. Discussing every available option and the details of associated steps is beyond the scope of this book. However, Figure 6-4 illustrates one of the most straightforward and concise methodologies that you can use to build and use Java database stored procedures and functions.

The following sections explain more about the steps in the development methodology shown in Figure 6-4.

NOTE
From this point forward, the sections of this chapter will use the term "stored procedure" to refer collectively to stored procedures, functions, and other types of database-stored application logic.

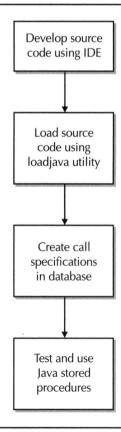

FIGURE 6-4. *Fundamental steps for developing Java stored procedures in Oracle8i*

Developing Source Code for Java Stored Procedures

The first step necessary to develop Java stored procedures for your Oracle8i database is to build the underlying classes and their methods that will, in turn, serve as the stored procedures. To make things simple, stick with your Java IDE or favorite text editor to build the Java source files.

Java classes that will serve as database stored procedures will most likely use SQL to modify database information. Therefore, when building the source files for Java stored procedures, remember to carefully consider the type declarations inside Java classes and methods—see the "Considering Datatype Conversion Between SQL and Java Types" sidebar, earlier in this chapter, for more background about this important topic.

Another important choice to make when building the source files for Java stored procedures is whether they will use JDBC or SQLJ to access the database. When Java stored procedures include static embedded SQL statements or procedure calls, you'll find it very easy to use SQLJ. For example, Java classes and methods that serve as stored procedures do not need to consider database connections, connection contexts, and so on, because the server-side SQLJ Translator automatically executes all SQLJ statements using the current database connection of the user that is calling the stored procedure. And don't forget about the added benefits of performing the compile-time syntax- and semantics-checking that only SQLJ provides. Alternatively, if you need the flexibility of dynamic SQL, JDBC is the correct choice.

No matter whether you choose SQLJ or JDBC for server-side Java classes, there are a couple of important restrictions to consider. For one, while Oracle's JVM can execute multithreaded Java applications, there are no concurrency or performance benefits to gain by developing multithreaded server-side Java classes for Oracle. Furthermore, you should not expect server-side Java classes to be able to support classes that carry out GUI functions, such as those provided by the java.awt.* classes.

Loading Java Classes into the Database

Once you build the Java classes that you plan to use as stored procedures, the next step is to load either the Java source code or compiled Java classes into a database schema. Oracle provides several different options for loading Java into the database that can support the needs of almost any new or existing development environment. In general, the easiest way to load Java classes into the database is to use the loadjava command-line utility that is installed with Oracle8i. The *loadjava* utility can load Java classes into a database schema from Java source files (.java, .sqlj), compiled Java class files (.class), resource files (.ser), and Java classes stored in uncompressed JAR or ZIP archives. The loadjava utility loads (and compiles, if necessary) a Java class into a database schema and stores it as a schema object—if you load a Java source file, the source and compiled class are both stored as separate schema objects.

TIP
If you choose to load Java source code into the database and then allow Oracle's JVM to compile the source code, it will be difficult to debug source code that is riddled with errors. Instead, it's a good idea to first compile and debug the source code outside the database using your friendly Java IDE or the Java compiler, and then load the source code once you are sure that it is bug-free.

The syntax for the loadjava utility is as follows:

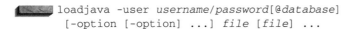

```
loadjava -user username/password[@database]
    [-option [-option] ...] file [file] ...
```

Although discussing the details of every feature and option of the loadjava utility is beyond the scope of this book, here are some of the more important things to know for the purposes of understanding the subsequent exercise in this chapter.

- You must enter the -user option and the information necessary to establish a database connection to the target database schema that the loadjava utility will use to store the Java classes that you are loading.

- Several loadjava options (-resolver, -resolve, -andresolve, -oracleresolver) are available to instruct the server-side JVM how and when to resolve classes referenced by the class being loaded into the database (similar in function to the CLASSPATH environment variable for Java classes external to Oracle). As long as you build self-contained classes for stored procedures (that is, classes that do not reference other classes), you can ignore loadjava's resolution mechanisms. Otherwise, refer to your Oracle documentation for more information about the class options of loadjava.

- Just as you can specify whether PL/SQL stored procedures will execute with the privileges of the current user (invoker) or owner (definer) of the stored procedure (see Chapter 5), you can also control this setting for Java stored procedures as you load the underlying class files into the database. By default, loadjava loads Java classes into the database with invoker rights, to allow for reusability among various schemas and databases. To override the default, specify the -definer command line option.

The next exercise in this chapter demonstrates the use of the loadjava utility.

NOTE
To unload Java classes loaded into a database schema with loadjava, you can use the companion utility dropjava, which supports similar syntax. See your Oracle documentation for more information about loadjava and dropjava.

Writing Call Specifications for Java Classes

After you load Java classes into your database schema, the next step is to *publish* their availability by creating *call specifications* for each Java method that you plan to call using SQL or PL/SQL. A call specification provides a safe mapping from a Java method's parameter types (and function's return type) to SQL and PL/SQL types.

NOTE
For stored procedures and functions, you can declare call specifications for public static methods in a Java class.

A call specification and its associated Java method must be in the same database schema. Depending on the type of Java method you are publishing, you can define a call specification as an individual stored procedure or function, as a packaged procedure or function, or as a member method in an object type (see Chapter 8). For example, the call specification for a Java method that does not return a value (a void method) can be a stored procedure or packaged procedure; alternatively, the call specification for a Java method that returns a value should be a stored function or packaged function.

In any case, the body of a procedure or function that serves as a call specification for a Java method uses the special LANGUAGE JAVA clause of the SQL commands CREATE PROCEDURE, CREATE FUNCTION, and CREATE PACKAGE BODY. The LANGUAGE JAVA clause specifies mapping information that Oracle uses to map the parameter types (and the return type for a function) to the corresponding parameters of the associated Java method. A subsequent exercise in this chapter demonstrates the use of the LANGUAGE JAVA clause in several CREATE PROCEDURE statements.

When building call specifications for Java methods, remember to consider the conversion of SQL types to Java types. See the "Considering Datatype Conversion Between SQL and Java Types" sidebar, earlier in this chapter, for more background about this important topic.

Testing and Using Java Stored Procedures

Once you load and publish Java stored procedures, make sure you thoroughly test and validate their functionality. When using SQL*Plus, you can use the special SQL*Plus command *CALL* (similar to EXECUTE) to call Java stored procedures.

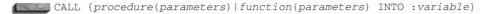

```
CALL {procedure(parameters)|function(parameters) INTO :variable}
```

Developing Java Stored Procedures for Oracle8*i*

Now that you have a general idea of the steps necessary for building stored procedures and functions in an Oracle8i database using Java, the following exercise takes you through each step with a simple example.

EXERCISE 6.7: The Part Class and Associated Database Stored Procedures

This exercise teaches you how to build a Java class and associated stored procedures that you can use to insert, update, and delete rows in the PARTS table of this chapter's practice schema (practice06).

The first step is to build the Java class. Using your Java IDE or favorite text editor, create the following SQLJ source code file that defines the Part class.

```
// IMPORT NECESSARY Classes
import sqlj.runtime.*;
import sqlj.runtime.ref.*;
import java.sql.*;

public class Part {

  // METHODS TO INSERT, UPDATE, AND DELETE PARTS

  public static void insert (
     oracle.sql.NUMBER id,
     oracle.sql.CHAR description,
     oracle.sql.NUMBER unitPrice,
     oracle.sql.NUMBER onHand,
     oracle.sql.NUMBER reorder ) throws SQLException {
    try {
      #sql {
        INSERT INTO practice06.parts
          VALUES (:id, :description, :unitPrice, :onHand, :reorder) };
    } catch (SQLException e) {System.err.println(e.getMessage());}
```

```
    }

    public static void update (
        oracle.sql.NUMBER id,
        oracle.sql.CHAR description,
        oracle.sql.NUMBER unitPrice,
        oracle.sql.NUMBER onHand,
        oracle.sql.NUMBER reorder ) throws SQLException {
      try {
        #sql {
          UPDATE practice06.parts
            SET description = :description,
                unitprice = :unitPrice,
                onhand = :onHand,
                reorder = :reorder
            WHERE id = :id };
      } catch (SQLException e) {System.err.println(e.getMessage());}
    }

    public static void delete (oracle.sql.NUMBER id) throws SQLException {
      try {
        #sql {DELETE FROM practice06.parts WHERE id = :id };
      } catch (SQLException e) {System.err.println(e.getMessage());}
    }
}
```

There are several important points to notice about the Part class:

■ The Part class contains three simple methods: insert, update, and delete. Each method accomplishes the corresponding DML operation for rows in the PRACTICE06.PARTS table.

■ Each method of the class uses a SQLJ executable statement to perform DML access to the PRACTICE06.PARTS table.

■ The methods of the Part class do not explicitly create ConnectionContext, DefaultContext, or ExecutionContext objects. Instead, the SQLJ executable statements in the methods of the Part class will implicitly use the invoker's database connection and default execution context to access the database.

■ The parameters of the methods use the oracle.sql wrapper type specifications (oracle.sql.NUMBER and oracle.sql.CHAR), rather than Java scalar types, Java object types, or JDBC SQL types, to avoid problems associated with nulls and loss of data precision.

Once you build the SQLJ source code file for the Part class, make sure to save it with the .sqlj extension. If you do not want to build the source file yourself, you can use the Part.sqlj source file that is in your *8iStarterKit_Home*/Java directory.

Before you load the Part class into the database, you should compile the source code using your IDE or the SQLJ Translator to make sure that the class compiles correctly. For example, enter the following command using a Command Prompt window (with the current working directory set as *8iStarterKit_Home*/Java) to compile the source code file provided with this book.

```
sqlj -user practice06/password Part.sqlj
```

Assuming that the class compiles successfully, you can now turn your attention to loading the class into the database with the loadjava utility. Because we know the Part class compiles without error, load the class into the database by loading the source file with the following command:

```
. loadjava -u practice06/password@oralin -v Part.sqlj
```

The output that the loadjava utility produces should be as follows:

```
initialization complete
loading  : Part
creating : Part
```

If you are curious, you might want to see some of the work that the loadjava utility has performed. Using your current SQL*Plus session while connected to the starter database as practice06/password, enter the following query to display information in the USER_OBJECTS data dictionary view about the Part class:

```
SELECT object_name, object_type
  FROM user_objects
  WHERE object_name LIKE 'Part%';
```

The results of this query should be as follows:

```
OBJECT_NAME          OBJECT_TYPE
-------------------- ------------------
Part                 JAVA CLASS
Part                 JAVA SOURCE
Part_SJProfileKeys   JAVA CLASS
```

Notice that the starter database contains source and class files for the Part class. And because the Part class uses SQLJ executable statements, the database also contains a profile-keys class file for the Part class.

Once you load the Part class into the starter database, you cannot actually use the methods of the class as stored procedures until you build the call specifications for the methods. This example demonstrates how to create top-level call specifications with stored procedure definitions. Using your current SQL*Plus session, while connected to the database as practice06/password, enter the following three CREATE PROCEDURE statements.

```
CREATE OR REPLACE PROCEDURE insertPart (
    id NUMBER,
    description VARCHAR2,
    unitprice NUMBER,
    onhand NUMBER,
    reorder NUMBER)
    AS
    LANGUAGE JAVA
    NAME 'Part.insert(
     oracle.sql.NUMBER,
     oracle.sql.CHAR,
     oracle.sql.NUMBER,
     oracle.sql.NUMBER,
     oracle.sql.NUMBER)';
    /

CREATE OR REPLACE PROCEDURE updatePart (
    id NUMBER,
    description VARCHAR2,
    unitprice NUMBER,
    onhand NUMBER,
    reorder NUMBER)
    AS
    LANGUAGE JAVA
    NAME 'Part.update(
     oracle.sql.NUMBER,
     oracle.sql.CHAR,
     oracle.sql.NUMBER,
     oracle.sql.NUMBER,
     oracle.sql.NUMBER)';
    /

CREATE OR REPLACE PROCEDURE deletePart (id NUMBER)
    AS
    LANGUAGE JAVA
    NAME 'Part.delete(oracle.sql.NUMBER)';
    /
```

Notice that the call specifications map the following:

■ The name of a database stored procedure to a method in the Part class.

■ The parameters of each stored procedure to the parameters of a method in the Part class. The types specified for a method's parameters match those in the underlying method.

Once you publish the availability of the Java stored procedures, you can use your current SQL*Plus session to test their functionality. Before actually calling the procedures, enter the following commands to configure the SQL*Plus session so that it displays the output of all calls to the System.out and System.err methods in the Java methods.

```
SET SERVEROUTPUT ON SIZE 5000
CALL dbms_java.set_output(5000);
COMMIT;
```

NOTE
*If you do not direct output of System.out and System.err calls to the SQL*Plus display buffer, Oracle8i records this output in the session's trace file. By default, you can find session trace files for your database in the $ORACLE_HOME/admin/ oralin/udump directory.*

Finally, use a mix of queries and the SQL*Plus command CALL to call and test the functionality of your new Java stored procedures. For example, see if you can duplicate the following sequence of statements and results that test the insertPart, updatePart, and deletePart Java stored procedures.

```
SQL> SELECT * FROM parts;

        ID DESCRIPTION          UNITPRICE    ONHAND    REORDER
--------- -------------------- --------- --------- ---------
         1 Fax Machine               299       277         50
         2 Copy Machine             4895       143         25
         3 Laptop PC                2100      7631       1000
         4 Desktop PC               1200      5903       1000
         5 Scanner                    99       490        200

SQL> CALL insertPart(6,'Test Part 1',100, 100, 100);

Call completed.

SQL> CALL insertPart(7,'Test Part 2',100, 100, 100);

Call completed.

SQL> CALL insertPart(8,'Test Part 1',100, 100, 100);
```

```
ORA-00001: unique constraint (PRACTICE06.PAR_DESCRIPTION) violated

Call completed.

SQL> SELECT * FROM parts;

      ID DESCRIPTION          UNITPRICE    ONHAND   REORDER
--------- -------------------- --------- --------- ---------
       1 Fax Machine                299       277        50
       2 Copy Machine              4895       143        25
       3 Laptop PC                 2100      7631      1000
       4 Desktop PC                1200      5903      1000
       5 Scanner                     99       490       200
       6 Test Part 1                100       100       100
       7 Test Part 2                100       100       100

7 rows selected.

SQL> CALL updatePart(7,'Test Part 2', 500, 500, 500);

Call completed.

SQL> SELECT * FROM parts;

      ID DESCRIPTION          UNITPRICE    ONHAND   REORDER
--------- -------------------- --------- --------- ---------
       1 Fax Machine                299       277        50
       2 Copy Machine              4895       143        25
       3 Laptop PC                 2100      7631      1000
       4 Desktop PC                1200      5903      1000
       5 Scanner                     99       490       200
       6 Test Part 1                100       100       100
       7 Test Part 2                500       500       500

7 rows selected.

SQL> CALL deletePart(6);

Call completed.

SQL> CALL deletePart(7);
```

```
Call completed.

SQL> CALL deletePart(1);
ORA-02292: integrity constraint (PRACTICE06.PARTS_FK) violated
 - child record found

Call completed.

SQL> SELECT * FROM parts;

       ID DESCRIPTION           UNITPRICE    ONHAND    REORDER
--------- -------------------- ---------- --------- ---------
        1 Fax Machine                 299       277        50
        2 Copy Machine               4895       143        25
        3 Laptop PC                  2100      7631      1000
        4 Desktop PC                 1200      5903      1000
        5 Scanner                      99       490       200
```

Notice that several statements are included in the example session to demonstrate that actions performed by the Java stored procedures are bound by the restrictions enforced by the integrity constraints placed on the PARTS table (see the next chapter for more information about integrity constraints).

Chapter Summary

Although the information and exercises in this chapter by no means qualify you as an expert with Oracle8i's support for Java, you should now have a solid foundation of skills upon which you can build, should you be interested in learning more about combining the power of the Oracle8i database server with the Java application development language. This chapter has taught you the fundamental concepts and steps involved in deploying the following:

- Stand-alone Java applications that access an Oracle8i database using JDBC

- Stand-alone Java applications that access an Oracle8i database using SQLJ

- Stored procedures in an Oracle8i database using Java

CHAPTER
7

Building a Basic
Relational Schema

Every database application is built upon a set of related database objects that store the application's data and allow the application to function. This chapter introduces Oracle8i database objects, such as tables, and discusses the logical concepts of database objects. Discussions of data storage (storage parameters, partitioning, and so on) will come in subsequent chapters of this book. This chapter's topics include:

- Schemas

- Tables

- Integrity constraints

- Views

- Sequences

- Synonyms

- Indexes

- The data dictionary

Chapter Prerequisites

To practice the hands-on exercises in this chapter, you need to start a Linux session as the user oracle, then start SQL*Plus and run the following command script:

location/8istarterkit/SQL/chap07.sql

where *location* is the file directory where you expanded the support archive that accompanies this book. For example, after starting SQL*Plus and connecting as SCOTT, you can run this chapter's SQL command script using the SQL*Plus command @, as in the following example (assuming that your chap07.sql file is in /tmp/8istarterkit/SQL).

```
SQL> @/tmp/8istarterkit/SQL/chap07.sql;
```

Once the script completes successfully, leave the current SQL*Plus session open and use it to perform this chapter's exercises in the order that they appear.

Schemas

It is easier to solve most problems in life when you are organized and have a well-designed plan to achieve your goal. If you are unorganized, you will most certainly realize your goals less efficiently, if at all. Designing an information management system that uses Oracle is no different.

Databases organize related objects within a database *schema*. For example, it's typical to organize within a single database schema all of the tables and other database objects necessary to support an application. This way, it's clear that the purpose of a certain table or other database object is to support the corresponding application system. Figure 7-1 illustrates the idea of an application schema.

Schemas, an Entirely Logical Concept

It's important to understand that schemas do not physically organize the storage of objects. Rather, schemas *logically* organize related database objects. In other words, the logical organization of database objects within schemas is purely for the benefit

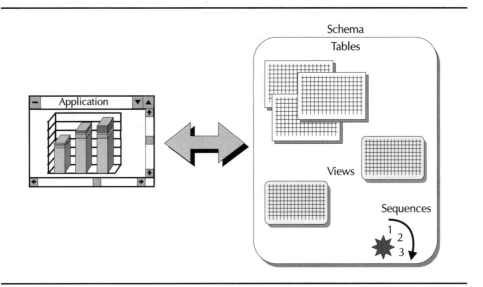

FIGURE 7-1.   *A schema is a logical organization of related database objects*

of organization and has absolutely nothing to do with the physical storage of database objects.

The logical organization that schemas offer can have practical benefits. For example, consider an Oracle database with two schemas, S1 and S2. Each schema can have a table called T1. Even though the two tables share the same name, they are uniquely identifiable because they are within different database schemas. Using standard dot notation, the complete names for the different tables would be S1.T1 and S2.T1.

If the idea of logical versus physical organization is confusing to you, consider how operating systems organize files on disk. The layout of directories and files in a graphical file management utility, such as the GNU Midnight Commander, does not necessarily correspond to the physical location of the directories and files on a particular disk drive. Directories represent the logical organization of operating system files. The underlying operating system decides where to physically store the blocks for each operating system file, independent of the logical organization of encompassing directories.

Subsequent chapters of this book explain more about how Oracle can physically organize the storage of database objects using physical storage structures.

The Correlation of Schemas and Database User Accounts

With Oracle, the concept of a database schema is directly tied to the concept of a database user. That is, a schema in an Oracle database has a one-to-one correspondence with a user account, such that a user and the associated schema have the same name. As a result, people who work with Oracle often blur the distinction between users and schemas, commonly saying things like "the user SCOTT owns the EMP and DEPT tables" rather than "the schema SCOTT contains the EMP and DEPT tables." Although these two sentences are more or less equivalent, understand that there might be a clear distinction between users and schemas with relational database implementations other than Oracle. Therefore, while the separation between users and schemas might seem trivial for Oracle, the distinction can be very important if you plan to work with other database systems.

NOTE
The scripts that you executed to support the practice exercises of this chapter and previous chapters create new database users/schemas (practice03, practice04, and so on) that contain similar sets of tables and other database objects (PARTS, CUSTOMERS, and so on).

Database Tables

Tables are the basic data structure in any relational database. A *table* is nothing more than an organized collection of *records*, or *rows*, that all have the same *attributes*, or *columns*. Figure 7-2 illustrates a typical CUSTOMERS table in a relational database. Each customer record in the example CUSTOMERS table has the same attributes, including an ID, a company name, a last name, a first name, and so on.

When you create tables, the two primary things that you must consider are the following:

- The table's columns, which describe the table's structure

- The table's integrity constraints, which describe the data that is acceptable within the table

The following sections explain more about columns and integrity constraints.

Columns and Datatypes

When you create a table for an Oracle database, you establish the structure of the table by identifying the columns that describe the table's attributes. Furthermore, every column in a table has a *datatype*, which describes the basic type of data that is acceptable in the column, much like when you declare the datatype of a variable in a PL/SQL or Java program. For example, the ID column in the CUSTOMERS table uses the basic Oracle datatype NUMBER because the column stores ID numbers.

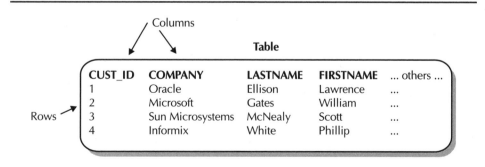

FIGURE 7-2. *A table is a set of records with the same attributes*

Oracle supports many fundamental datatypes that you can use when creating a relational database table and its columns. Table 7-1 and the following sections describe the most commonly used Oracle datatypes.

CHAR and VARCHAR2: Oracle's Character Datatypes

Oracle's CHAR and VARCHAR2 are the datatypes most commonly used for columns that store character strings. The Oracle datatype *CHAR* is appropriate for columns that store fixed-length character strings, such as two-letter USA state codes. Alternatively, the Oracle datatype *VARCHAR2* is useful for columns that store variable-length character strings, such as names and addresses. The primary difference between these character datatypes relates to how Oracle stores strings shorter than the maximum length of a column:

■ When a string in a CHAR column is less than the column's size, Oracle pads (appends) the end of the string with blank spaces to create a string that matches the column's size.

■ When a string in a VARCHAR2 column is less than the column's maximum size, Oracle stores only the string and does not pad the string with blanks.

Thus, when the strings in a column vary in length, Oracle can store them more efficiently in a VARCHAR2 column than in a CHAR column. Oracle also uses different techniques for comparing CHAR and VARCHAR2 strings to one another so that comparison expressions evaluate as expected.

Datatype	Description
CHAR(*size*)	Stores fixed-length character strings up to 2,000 bytes
VARCHAR2(*size*)	Stores fixed-length character strings up to 4,000 bytes
NUMBER(*precision, scale*)	Stores any type of number
DATE	Stores dates and times
CLOB	Stores single-byte character large objects (CLOBs) up to 4 gigabytes
BLOB	Stores binary large objects (BLOBs) up to 4 gigabytes

TABLE 7-1. *The Most Commonly Used Oracle Datatypes*

NUMBER: Oracle's Numeric Datatype

To declare columns that accept numbers, you can use Oracle's *NUMBER* datatype. Rather than have several numeric datatypes, Oracle's NUMBER datatype supports the storage of all types of numbers, including integers, floating-point numbers, real numbers, and so on. You can limit the domain of acceptable numbers in a column by specifying a *precision* and a *scale* for a NUMBER column.

DATE: Oracle's Time-Related Datatype

When you declare a table column with the *DATE* datatype, the column can store all types of time-related information, including dates and associated times.

CLOBs, BLOBs, and More: Oracle's Multimedia Datatypes

Because databases are secure, fast, and safe storage areas for data, they are often employed as data repositories for multimedia applications. To support such content-rich applications, Oracle8i supports several different *large object* (LOB) datatypes that can store unstructured information, such as text documents, static images, video, audio, and more.

- A *CLOB* column stores character objects, such as documents.

- A *BLOB* column stores large binary objects, such as graphics, video clips, or sound files.

- A *BFILE* column stores file pointers to LOBs managed by file systems external to the database. For example, a BFILE column might be a list of filename references for photos stored on a CD-ROM.

The following section explains several other important LOB characteristics, comparing LOBs with some older Oracle large object datatypes.

Contrasting LOBs with Older Oracle Large Object Datatypes

For backward compatibility, Oracle8i continues to support older Oracle datatypes designed for large objects, such as *LONG* and *LONG RAW*. However, Oracle8i's newer LOB datatypes have several advantages over the older Oracle large datatypes:

- A table can have multiple CLOB, BLOB, and BFILE columns. In contrast, a table can have only one LONG or LONG RAW column.

- A table stores only small *locators* (pointers) for the LOBs in a column, rather than the actual large objects themselves. In contrast, a table stores data for a LONG column within the table itself.

■ A LOB column can have storage characteristics independent from those of the encompassing table, making it easier to address the large disk requirements typically associated with LOBs. For example, it's possible to separate the storage of primary table data and related LOBs in different physical locations (for example, disk drives). In contrast, a table physically stores the data for a LONG column in the same storage area that contains all other table data.

■ Applications can efficiently access and manipulate pieces of a LOB. In contrast, applications must access an entire LONG field as an atomic (indivisible) piece of data.

Before migrating or designing new multimedia applications for Oracle, consider the advantages of Oracle8*i*'s newer LOB datatypes versus older large object datatypes.

Oracle's National Language Support Character Datatypes

Oracle's *National Language Support* (NLS) features allow databases to store and manipulate character data in many languages. Some languages have character sets that require several bytes for each character. The special Oracle datatypes *NCHAR*, *NVARCHAR2*, and *NCLOB* are datatypes that are counterparts to the CHAR, VARCHAR2, and CLOB datatypes, respectively.

ANSI Datatypes and Others

Oracle8*i* also supports the specification of Oracle datatypes using other standard datatypes. For example, Table 7-2 lists the ANSI/ISO (American National Standards Institute/International Organization for Standardization) standard datatypes that Oracle supports.

Default Column Values

When you declare a column for a table, you can also declare a corresponding *default column value*. Oracle uses the default value of a column when an application inserts a new row into the table but omits a value for the column. For example, you might indicate that the default value for the ORDERDATE column of the ORDERS table be the current system time when an application creates a new order.

This ANSI/ISO datatype ...	... converts to this Oracle datatype
CHARACTER CHAR	CHAR
CHARACTER VARYING CHAR VARYING	VARCHAR2
NATIONAL CHARACTER NATIONAL CHAR NCHAR	NCHAR
NATIONAL CHARACTER VARYING NATIONAL CHAR VARYING NCHAR VARYING	NVARCHAR2
NUMERIC DECIMAL INTEGER INT SMALLINT FLOAT DOUBLE PRECISION REAL	NUMBER

TABLE 7-2. *Oracle Supports the Specification of Oracle Datatypes Using ANSI/ISO Standard Datatypes*

NOTE
Unless you indicate otherwise, the initial default value for a column is null (an absence of value).

Creating and Managing Tables

Now that you understand that the structure of a table is defined by its columns and that each column in a table has a datatype, it's time to learn the basics of creating and managing the structure of tables in an Oracle database. The following practice exercises introduce the SQL commands CREATE TABLE and ALTER TABLE.

EXERCISE 7.1: Creating a Table

You create a table using the SQL command *CREATE TABLE*. For the purposes of this simple exercise, the basic syntax for creating a relational database table with the CREATE TABLE command is as follows:

```
CREATE TABLE [schema.]table
(  column datatype [DEFAULT expression]
[, column datatype [DEFAULT expression] ]
[ ... other columns ... ]
)
```

Using your current SQL*Plus session, enter the following command to create the familiar PARTS table in this lesson's practice schema.

```
CREATE TABLE parts (
  id  INTEGER,
  description  VARCHAR2(250),
  unitprice  NUMBER(10, 2),
  onhand  INTEGER,
  reorder  INTEGER
);
```

Your current schema (practice07) now has a new table, PARTS, that you can query, insert records into, and so on. Notice that the PARTS table has five columns:

- The statement declares the ID, ONHAND, and REORDER columns with the ANSI/ISO datatype INTEGER, which Oracle automatically converts to the Oracle datatype NUMBER with 38 digits of precision.

- The statement declares the DESCRIPTION column with the Oracle datatype VARCHAR2 to accept variable length strings up to 250 bytes in length.

- The statement declares the UNITPRICE column with the Oracle datatype NUMBER to hold numbers up to ten digits of precision and to round numbers after two digits to the right of the decimal place.

Before continuing, create the familiar CUSTOMERS table using the following CREATE TABLE statement:

```
CREATE TABLE customers (
  id  INTEGER,
  lastname  VARCHAR2(100),
  firstname  VARCHAR2(50),
  companyname  VARCHAR2(100),
```

```
street  VARCHAR2(100),
city  VARCHAR2(100),
state  VARCHAR2(50),
zipcode  NUMBER(10),
phone  VARCHAR2(30),
fax  VARCHAR2(30),
email  VARCHAR2(100)
);
```

When you are designing the tables in a database schema, sometimes it can be tricky to choose the correct datatype for a column. For example, consider the ZIPCODE column in the CUSTOMERS table of the previous example, declared with the NUMBER datatype. Consider what will happen when you insert a customer record with the ZIPCODE "01003"—Oracle is going to store this number as "1003", certainly not what you intended. Furthermore, consider what would happen if you insert a customer record with a ZIP code and an extension such as "91222-0299"— Oracle is going to evaluate this numeric expression and store the resulting number "90923". These two simple examples illustrate that the selection of a column's datatype is certainly an important consideration, and is not to be taken lightly. In the next practice exercise, you'll learn how to change the datatype of the ZIPCODE column to store postal codes correctly.

To complete this exercise, create the SALESREPS table with the following CREATE TABLE statement.

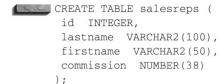
```
CREATE TABLE salesreps (
  id  INTEGER,
  lastname  VARCHAR2(100),
  firstname  VARCHAR2(50),
  commission  NUMBER(38)
);
```

NOTE
The examples in this section introduce the basics of the CREATE TABLE command. Subsequent exercises in this and other chapters demonstrate more advanced clauses and parameters of the CREATE TABLE command.

EXERCISE 7.2: Altering and Adding Columns in a Table

After you create a table, you can alter its structure using the SQL command *ALTER TABLE*. For example, you might want to change the datatype of a column, change a column's default column value, or add an entirely new column altogether. For the purposes of this simple exercise, the basic syntax of the ALTER TABLE command for adding or modifying a column in a relational database table is as follows:

```
ALTER TABLE [schema.]table
[ ADD column datatype [DEFAULT expression] ]
[ MODIFY column [datatype] [DEFAULT expression] ]
```

For example, enter the following ALTER TABLE statement, which modifies the datatype of the ZIPCODE column in the CUSTOMERS table that you created in Exercise 7.1.

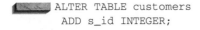

```
ALTER TABLE customers
  MODIFY zipcode VARCHAR2(50);
```

NOTE
You can change the datatype of a column, the precision or scale of a NUMBER column, or the size of a CHAR or VARCHAR2 column only when the table does not contain any rows, or when the target column is null for every record in the table.

Suppose you realize that the CUSTOMERS table must be able to track each customer's sales representative. Enter the following ALTER TABLE statement, which adds the column S_ID to record the ID of a customer's sales representative.

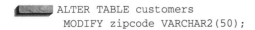

```
ALTER TABLE customers
  ADD s_id INTEGER;
```

NOTE
The examples in this section introduce the basics of the ALTER TABLE command. Subsequent exercises in this chapter and others demonstrate more advanced clauses and parameters of the ALTER TABLE command.

Data Integrity and Integrity Constraints

Data integrity is a fundamental principle of the relational database model. Saying that a database has integrity is another way of saying that the database contains only accurate and acceptable information. For obvious reasons, data integrity is a desirable attribute for a database.

To a small degree, a column's datatype establishes a more limited domain of acceptable values for the column—it limits the type of data that the column can store. For example, a DATE column can contain valid dates and times, but not numbers or character strings. But while simple column datatypes are useful for enforcing a basic level of data integrity, there are typically more complex integrity rules that must be enforced in a relational database. In fact, the relational database model, itself, outlines several inherent data integrity rules that a relational database management system (RDBMS) must uphold. The next few sections describe these common integrity rules and related issues.

Domain Integrity, Nulls, and Complex Domains

Domain integrity defines the domain of acceptable values for a column. For example, you might have a rule that a customer record is not valid unless the customer's state abbreviation code is one of the fifty or so USA state codes.

Besides using column datatypes, Oracle supports two types of integrity constraints that allow you to further limit the domain of a column:

- A column can have a *not null constraint* to eliminate the possibility of nulls (absent values) in the column.

- You can use a *check constraint* to declare a complex domain integrity rule as part of a table. A check constraint commonly contains an explicit list of the acceptable values for a column. For example, "M" and "F" in a column that contains gender information; "AL", "AK", ... "WY" in a column that contains USA state codes; and so on.

Entity Integrity, Primary Keys, and Alternate Keys

Entity integrity ensures that every row in a table is unique. As a result, entity integrity eliminates the possibility of duplicate records in the table and makes every row in the table uniquely identifiable.

The primary key of a table ensures its entity integrity. A *primary key* is a column that uniquely identifies each row in a table. Typically, tables in a relational database use ID-type columns as primary keys. For example, a customer table might include an ID column to uniquely identify the customer records within. This way, even if two customers, say John Smith and his son John Smith (Jr.), have the same name, address, phone number, and so on, they have distinct ID numbers that make them different.

A table's primary key is sometimes a *composite key*; that is, it is composed of more than one column. For example, the primary key in a typical line-item table of an order-entry system might have a composite primary key that consists of the ORDER_ID and ITEM_ID columns. In this example of a composite primary key, many line-item records can have the same line-item ID (1, 2, 3, ...), but no two line-item records can have the same order ID and line-item ID combination (order ID 1, line-item IDs 1,2,3, ...; order ID 2, line-item IDs 1,2,3, ...; and so on).

■ Optionally, a table might require secondary levels of entity integrity. *Alternate keys* are columns or sets of columns that do not contain duplicate values within them. For example, the EMAIL column in an employee table might be made an alternate key to guarantee that all employees have unique e-mail addresses.

Referential Integrity, Foreign Keys, and Referential Actions

Referential integrity, sometimes called *relation integrity*, establishes the relationships among different columns and tables in a database. Referential integrity ensures that each column value in a *foreign key* of a *child* (or *detail*) *table* matches a value in the primary or an alternate key of a related *parent* (or *master*) *table*. For example, a row in the CUSTOMERS (child) table is not valid unless the customer's S_ID field refers to a valid sales representative ID in the SALESREPS (parent) table. When the parent and child table are the same, this is called s*elf-referential integrity*. Figure 7-3 illustrates the terminology and concepts related to referential integrity.

Referential Actions   Referential integrity ensures that each value in a foreign key always has a matching parent key value. To guarantee referential integrity, an RDBMS must also be able to address database operations that manipulate parent keys. For example, when a user deletes a sales order, what happens to the dependent line items for that order? *Referential actions* describe what will be done in cases where an application updates or deletes a parent key that has dependent child records.

The relational database model describes several referential actions:

■ **Update/Delete Restrict**   The RDBMS does not allow an application to update a parent key or delete a parent row that has one or more dependent child records. For example, you cannot delete a sales order from the ORDERS table if it has associated line items in the ITEMS table.

■ **Delete Cascade**   When an application deletes a row from the parent table, the RDBMS cascades the delete by deleting all dependent records in a child table. For example, when you delete an order from the ORDERS table, the RDBMS automatically removes all corresponding line items from the ITEMS table.

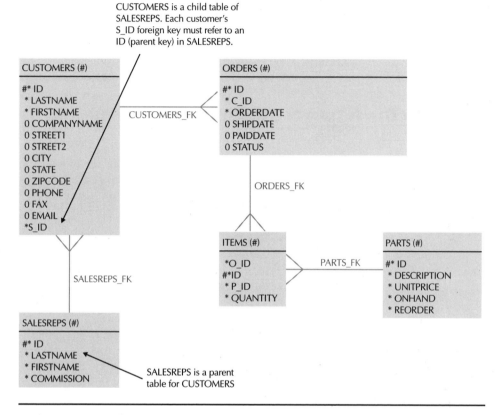

FIGURE 7-3. *Referential integrity describes the relationships among columns and tables in a relational database*

- **Update Cascade**   When an application updates a parent key, the RDBMS cascades the update to the dependent foreign keys. For example, when you change an order's ID in the ORDERS table, the RDBMS would automatically update the order ID of all corresponding line-item records in the ITEMS table. This referential action is rarely useful, because applications typically do not allow users to update key values.

- **Update/Delete Set Null**   When an application updates or deletes a parent key, all dependent keys are set to null.

- **Update/Delete Set Default** When an application updates or deletes a parent key, all dependent keys are set to a meaningful default value.

By default, Oracle8i enforces the Update/Delete Restrict referential actions for all referential integrity constraints. Optionally, Oracle can perform the Delete Cascade or Delete Set Null referential action for a referential integrity constraint.

When Does Oracle Enforce Integrity Constraint Rules?

Oracle can enforce an integrity constraint at two different times:

- By default, Oracle enforces all integrity constraints immediately after an application submits a SQL statement to insert, update, or delete rows in a table. When a statement causes a data integrity violation, Oracle automatically rolls back the effects of the statement.

- Optionally, Oracle can delay the enforcement of a *deferrable integrity constraint* until just before the commit of a transaction. When you commit a transaction and the transaction has modified table data such that it does not conform to all integrity constraints, Oracle automatically rolls back the entire transaction (that is, the effects of all statements in the transaction).

Typical database applications should choose to immediately check data integrity as each SQL statement is executed. However, certain applications, such as large data loads, might need to update many tables and temporarily violate integrity rules until just before the end of the transaction.

Creating and Managing Integrity Constraints

You can create integrity constraints for a table when you create the table, or subsequently by altering the table. The next few practice exercises teach you how to use the SQL commands CREATE TABLE and ALTER TABLE to create not null, check, primary key, unique, and referential integrity constraints.

EXERCISE 7.3: Creating a Table with Integrity Constraints

One way to declare integrity constraints for a table is to do so when you create the table. To create a table with integrity constraints, use the *CONSTRAINT* clause of the CREATE TABLE command. The following syntax listing is a partial list of the options available with the CONSTRAINT clause of the CREATE TABLE command.

```
CREATE TABLE [schema.]table (
 { column datatype [DEFAULT expression]
```

```
    [CONSTRAINT constraint]
    { [NOT] NULL
    | {UNIQUE|PRIMARY KEY}
    | REFERENCES [schema.]table [(column)] [ON DELETE CASCADE]
    | CHECK (condition) }
    [ another constraint specification ]
| [CONSTRAINT constraint]
    { {UNIQUE|PRIMARY KEY} (column [, column] ... )
    | FOREIGN KEY (column [, column] ... )
      REFERENCES [schema.]table [(column [, column] ... )]
        [ON DELETE {CASCADE|SET NULL}]
    | CHECK (condition)    }
[ , ... other columns/constraints or constraints ]
)
```

Notice that you can declare an integrity constraint along with a column, or you can declare an integrity constraint separate from a specific column declaration. In general, you can always choose either option to create a constraint, except in the following situations:

- To declare a column with a not null constraint, you must do so as part of the column declaration.

- To declare a composite primary key, unique, or referential integrity constraint, you must declare the constraint separate from a specific column declaration.

Enter the following CREATE TABLE statement to create the familiar ORDERS table with some integrity constraints.

```
CREATE TABLE orders (
  id  INTEGER
    CONSTRAINT orders_pk PRIMARY KEY,
  orderdate DATE DEFAULT SYSDATE
    NOT NULL,
  shipdate DATE,
  paiddate DATE,
  status CHAR(1) DEFAULT 'F'
    CONSTRAINT status_ck
    CHECK (status IN ('F','B'))
);
```

This statement creates the ORDERS table and declares three integrity constraints as part of column declarations (see the bold CONSTRAINT clauses above).

■ The ID column is the ORDERS table's primary key—every record must have an ID (a null is implicitly disallowed) that is unique from all others. The statement names the primary key constraint ORDERS_PK.

■ The statement declares the ORDERDATE column as not null. Because the statement does not explicitly name the not null constraint, Oracle generates a unique name for the constraint. Later in this chapter, you'll learn how to reveal information about schema objects and integrity constraints, including generated constraint names.

■ The STATUS_CK check constraint ensures that the STATUS field value is *F* or *B* for every record in the ORDERS table. Because the statement does not declare the STATUS column with a not null constraint, the STATUS column can also contain nulls.

The next section provides more examples of integrity constraint declarations with the ALTER TABLE command, including how to declare unique and referential integrity constraints.

EXERCISE 7.4: Adding a Not Null Constraint to an Existing Column

After you create a table, you might need to add (or remove) a not null integrity constraint to (or from) an existing column—you can do so by using the following syntax of the ALTER TABLE command:

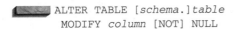

```
ALTER TABLE [schema.]table
  MODIFY column [NOT] NULL
```

For example, enter the following command to add a not null integrity constraint to the DESCRIPTION column of the PARTS table:

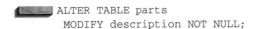

```
ALTER TABLE parts
  MODIFY description NOT NULL;
```

NOTE
To subsequently remove the not null constraint from the STATUS column, you would use the previous statement but omit the NOT keyword.

EXERCISE 7.5: Adding Primary Key and Unique Constraints to a Table

You can also declare an integrity constraint after you create a table using the ALTER TABLE command, as follows:

```
ALTER TABLE [schema.]table
  ADD [CONSTRAINT constraint]
    { {UNIQUE|PRIMARY KEY} (column [, column] ... )
    | FOREIGN KEY (column [, column] ... )
        REFERENCES [schema.]table [(column [, column] ... )]
        [ON DELETE {CASCADE|SET NULL}]
    | CHECK (condition)  }
```

For example, the PARTS and CUSTOMERS tables that you created in Exercise 7.1 do not have primary keys—enter the following commands to add primary key constraints for these tables.

```
ALTER TABLE parts
  ADD CONSTRAINT parts_pk PRIMARY KEY (id);

ALTER TABLE customers
  ADD CONSTRAINT customers_pk PRIMARY KEY (id);
```

Enter the following command to add a composite unique constraint to the CUSTOMERS table that prevents duplicate LASTNAME/FIRSTNAME combinations. Because the statement does not explicitly name the unique constraint, Oracle generates a unique system identifier for the new constraint.

```
ALTER TABLE customers
  ADD UNIQUE (lastname, firstname);
```

EXERCISE 7.6: Adding Referential Constraints to a Table

You can also use the syntax of the ALTER TABLE command in the previous exercise to add a referential integrity constraint to a table. For example, enter the following statement to add a referential integrity constraint to the CUSTOMERS table that ensures each customer record's S_ID refers to an ID in the SALESREPS table.

```
ALTER TABLE customers
  ADD CONSTRAINT salesreps_fk
  FOREIGN KEY (s_id) REFERENCES salesreps (id);
```

The previous statement should return the following error number and message:

```
ORA-02270: no matching unique or primary key for this column-list
```

Why? Remember that when you declare a referential integrity constraint for a table, the foreign key must refer to a primary key or unique key in a table. Because the SALESREPS table does not have a primary key, the preceding statement returns an error.

To remedy this situation, first add the primary key to the SALESREPS table, and then reissue the previous statement to add the referential integrity constraint to the CUSTOMERS table.

```
ALTER TABLE salesreps
  ADD CONSTRAINT salesreps_pk PRIMARY KEY (id);

ALTER TABLE customers
  ADD CONSTRAINT salesreps_fk
    FOREIGN KEY (s_id) REFERENCES salesreps (id);
```

Notice that the specification of the SALESREPS_FK referential integrity constraint does not specify a referential action for deletes. By this omission, the referential integrity constraint enforces the delete restrict referential action. A subsequent exercise in this chapter demonstrates how to declare a referential integrity constraint with the delete cascade referential action.

EXERCISE 7.7: Adding a Column with Constraints

When you add a column to a table, you can also add a constraint to the table at the same time, using the following syntax of the ALTER TABLE command:

```
ALTER TABLE [schema.]table
  ADD (
  column [datatype] [DEFAULT expression]
  [ [CONSTRAINT constraint]
    { NOT NULL
    | {UNIQUE|PRIMARY KEY}
    | REFERENCES table [(column)]
      [ON DELETE {CASCADE|SET NULL}]
    | CHECK (condition) } ]
    [ another constraint specification ]
  [, other columns and their constraints ...]
  )
```

For example, each record in the ORDERS table needs a field to keep track of the ID of the customer that places the order. To add this column, enter the following statement, which adds the C_ID column to the ORDERS table, along with a not null and referential integrity constraint.

```
ALTER TABLE orders
  ADD c_id INTEGER
    CONSTRAINT c_id_nn NOT NULL
    CONSTRAINT customers_fk
      REFERENCES customers (id);
```

The combination of the not null and referential integrity constraints in this exercise ensure that each record in the ORDERS table must have a C_ID (customer ID) that refers to an ID in the CUSTOMERS table.

EXERCISE 7.8: Declaring a Referential Constraint with a Delete Action

We need one more table to complete the table specifications in our very simple practice schema—enter the following CREATE TABLE statement, which builds the ITEMS table, along with several integrity constraints (highlighted in bold).

```
CREATE TABLE items (
  o_id  INTEGER
   CONSTRAINT orders_fk
    REFERENCES orders ON DELETE CASCADE,
  id  INTEGER,
  p_id  INTEGER
   CONSTRAINT parts_fk
    REFERENCES parts,
  quantity  INTEGER DEFAULT 1
   CONSTRAINT quantity_nn NOT NULL,
  CONSTRAINT items_pk
   PRIMARY KEY (o_id, id)
);
```

The following list describes the integrity constraints declared for the ITEMS table:

- The ORDERS_FK referential integrity constraint ensures that the O_ID field of each record in the ITEMS table refers to an ID in the ORDERS table. This referential integrity constraint also specifies the delete cascade referential action—whenever a transaction deletes a record in the ORDERS table, Oracle will automatically cascade the delete by deleting the associated records in the ITEMS table.

- The QUANTITY_NN not null constraint prevents nulls from being entered in the QUANTITY column.

- The PARTS_FK referential integrity constraint ensures that the P_ID field of each record in the ITEMS table refers to an ID in the PARTS table.

- The ITEMS_PK primary key constraint is a composite primary key. This constraint ensures that neither the O_ID nor ID columns contain nulls, and that each record's O_ID/ID combination is unique among all others in the ITEMS table.

EXERCISE 7.9: Testing an Integrity Constraint

At this point, we've got all of our tables built. The statements in this exercise have you insert some rows into various tables to confirm that the integrity constraints we created in the previous exercises actually enforce our business rules.

First, observe what happens when you enter the following statements, which insert three new sales representatives into the SALESREPS table.

```
INSERT INTO salesreps
   (id, lastname, firstname, commission)
   VALUES (1,'Pratt','Nick',5);

INSERT INTO salesreps
   (id, lastname, firstname, commission)
   VALUES (2,'Jonah','Suzanne',5);

INSERT INTO salesreps
   (id, lastname, firstname, commission)
   VALUES (2,'Greenberg','Bara',5);
```

The first and second INSERT statements should execute without error. However, when you attempt the third INSERT statement, Oracle will return the following error number and message:

```
ORA-00001: unique constraint (PRACTICE07.SALESREPS_PK) violated
```

The primary key constraint of the SALESREPS table prohibits two records from having the same ID. In this example, the third INSERT statement attempts to insert a new record with an ID number of 2, which is already in use by another record. If you rewrite the third INSERT statement with a different ID, the row will insert without error.

```
INSERT INTO salesreps
   (id, lastname, firstname, commission)
   VALUES (3,'Greenberg','Bara',5);
```

You can permanently commit your current transaction by issuing a COMMIT statement.

```
COMMIT;
```

Now, let's test a referential integrity constraint and see what happens. Enter the following statements, which insert some records into the CUSTOMERS table.

```
INSERT INTO customers
   ( id, lastname, firstname, companyname, street,
```

```
      city, state, zipcode, phone, fax, email, s_id)
    VALUES (1,'Joy','Harold','McDonald Co.',
      '4458 Stafford St.','Baltimore','MD','21209',
      '410-983-5789',NULL,'harold_joy@mcdonald.com',3);

    INSERT INTO customers
     ( id, lastname, firstname, companyname, street,
       city, state, zipcode, phone, fax, email, s_id)
    VALUES (2,'Musial','Bill','Car Audio Center',
      '12 Donna Lane','Reno','NV','89501','775-859-2121',
      '775-859-2121','musial@car-audio.net',5);
```

The first INSERT statement should execute without error, provided that you successfully executed the previous INSERT statement in this exercise (inserting the record for the sales representative with an ID of 3). However, when you attempt to execute the second INSERT statement, Oracle will return the following error number and message.

```
ORA-02291: integrity constraint (PRACTICE07.SALESREPS_FK) violated
- parent key not found
```

The SALESREPS_FK referential integrity constraint in the CUSTOMERS table does not permit a customer record with an S_ID that fails to match an ID in the SALESREPS table. In this case, the INSERT statement attempts to insert a record that refers to a sales representative with an ID of 5, which does not exist. The following rewrite of the second INSERT statement should succeed without error:

```
INSERT INTO customers
    ( id, lastname, firstname, companyname, street,
      city, state, zipcode, phone, fax, email, s_id)
    VALUES (2,'Musial','Bill','Car Audio Center',
      '12 Donna Lane','Reno','NV','89501','775-859-2121',
      '775-859-2121','musial@car-audio.net',1);

COMMIT;
```

EXERCISE 7.10: Declaring and Using a Deferrable Constraint

All of the constraints that you specified in Exercises 7.3 through 7.8 are immediately enforced as each SQL statement is executed. The previous exercise demonstrates this immediate constraint enforcement—when you attempt to insert a row that does not have a unique primary key value into the PARTS table, Oracle immediately enforces the constraint by rolling back the INSERT statement and returning an error.

You can also create a deferrable constraint, if your application logic requires (for example, during a bulk data load). If you do so, upon beginning a new transaction, you can instruct Oracle to defer the enforcement of selected or all deferrable constraints until you commit the transaction. To create a deferrable constraint, include the optional keyword DEFERRABLE when you specify the constraint.

To demonstrate deferrable constraints, let's make the STATUS_CK check constraint of the ORDERS table a deferrable constraint. This would permit a sales representative to defer the decision as to whether a new order should be backordered because of a lack of inventory for a particular part being ordered. First, you have to drop the existing check constraint, as follows:

```
ALTER TABLE orders
  DROP CONSTRAINT status_ck;
```

Next, enter the following command to recreate the STATUS_CK check constraint as a deferrable constraint:

```
ALTER TABLE orders
  ADD CONSTRAINT status_ck
    CHECK (status IN ('F','B')) DEFERRABLE;
```

Now let's test the deferrable constraint. To defer the enforcement of a deferrable constraint, you start a transaction with the SQL command *SET CONSTRAINTS*, which has the following syntax:

```
SET CONSTRAINT[S]
{ [schema.]constraint [,[schema.]constraint] ...
| ALL }
{ IMMEDIATE | DEFERRED }
```

Notice that the SET CONSTRAINTS command lets you explicitly set the enforcement of specific or all constraints. To defer the enforcement of our STATUS_CK constraint, start the new transaction with the following statement:

```
SET CONSTRAINTS status_ck DEFERRED;
```

Next, enter the following statement to insert a record into the ORDERS table that does not meet the condition of the STATUS_CK check constraint—the STATUS code for the order is "U" rather than "B" or "F".

```
INSERT INTO orders
  (id, c_id, orderdate, shipdate, paiddate, status)
  VALUES (1,1,'18-JUN-99','18-JUN-99','30-JUN-99','U');
```

Now, commit the transaction with a COMMIT statement, to see what happens. Oracle should return the following error messages:

```
COMMIT;
```

```
ORA-02091: transaction rolled back
ORA-02290: check constraint (PRACTICE07.STATUS_CK) violated
```

When you commit the transaction, Oracle enforces the rule of the STATUS_CK deferrable constraint and notices that the new row in the ORDERS table does not comply with the associated business rule. Therefore, Oracle rolls back all of the statements in the current transaction.

Views

Once you define the tables in a database, you can start to focus on other things that enhance the usability of the application schema. You can start by defining views of the tables in your schema. A *view* is a database object that presents table data. Why and how would you use views to present table data?

- You can use a simple view to expose all rows and columns in a table, but hide the name of the underlying table for security purposes. For example, you might create a view called CUST that presents all customer records in the CUSTOMERS table.

- You can use a view to protect the security of specific table data by exposing only a subset of the rows and/or columns in a table. For example, you might create a view called CUST_CA that presents only the LASTNAME, FIRSTNAME, and PHONE columns in the CUSTOMERS table for customers that reside in the state of California.

- You can use a view to simplify application coding. A complex view might join the data of related parent and child tables to make it appear as though a different table exists in the database. For example, you might create a view called ORDER_ITEMS that joins related records in the ORDERS and ITEMS tables.

- You can use a view to present derived data that is not actually stored in a table. For example, you might create a view of the ITEMS table with a column called TOTAL that calculates the line total for each record.

As you can see from this list, views provide a flexible means of presenting the table data in a database. In fact, you can create a view of any data that you can represent with a SQL query. That's because a view is really just a query that Oracle stores as a schema object. When an application uses a view to do something, Oracle derives the data of the view based on the view's *defining query*. For example, when an application queries the CUST_CA view described in the previous list, Oracle processes the query against the data described by the view's defining query.

Creating Views

To create a view, you use the SQL command *CREATE VIEW*. The following is an abbreviated syntax listing of the CREATE VIEW command:

```
CREATE [OR REPLACE] VIEW [schema.]view
 AS subquery
 [WITH READ ONLY]
```

The next few sections and practice exercises explain more about the specific types of views that Oracle8i supports, and provide you with examples of using the various clauses, parameters, and options of the CREATE VIEW command.

Read-Only Views

One type of view that Oracle8i supports is a *read-only view*. As you might expect, database applications can use a read-only view to retrieve corresponding table data, but cannot insert, update, or delete table data through a read-only view.

EXERCISE 7.11: Creating a Read-Only View

Enter the following statement to create a read-only view of the ORDERS table that corresponds to the orders that are currently on backlog.

```
CREATE VIEW backlogged_orders
 AS SELECT * FROM orders WHERE status = 'B'
 WITH READ ONLY;
```

Notice the following points about this first example of the CREATE VIEW command:

■ The AS clause of the CREATE VIEW command specifies the view's defining query. The result set of a view's defining query determines the view's structure (columns and rows).

■ To create a read-only view, you must specify the WITH READ ONLY option of the CREATE VIEW command to explicitly declare that the view is read-only; otherwise, Oracle creates the view as an updateable view.

Updateable Views

Oracle8i also allows you to define *updateable views* that an application can use to insert, update, and delete table data or query data.

EXERCISE 7.12: Creating an Updateable View

To create a view as an updateable view, simply omit the WITH READ ONLY option of the CREATE VIEW command when you create the view. For example, enter the following CREATE VIEW statement, which creates an updateable join view of the ORDERS and PARTS tables.

```
CREATE VIEW orders_items
 AS
  SELECT o.id AS orderid,
   o.orderdate AS orderdate,
   o.c_id AS customerid,
   i.id AS itemid,
   i.quantity AS quantity,
   i.p_id AS partid
  FROM orders o, items i
  WHERE o.id = i.o_id;
```

Even though you declare a view as updateable, Oracle doesn't automatically support INSERT, UPDATE, and DELETE statements for the view unless the view's definition complies with the materialized view principle. Briefly stated, the *materialized view principle* ensures that the server can correctly map an insert, update, or delete operation through a view to the underlying table data of the view.

The ORDERS_ITEMS view is an example of a view that does not comply with the materialized view principle because the view joins data from two tables. Therefore, even though you created the ORDERS_ITEMS view as updateable, Oracle does not support INSERT, UPDATE, and DELETE statements with the view until you create one or more INSTEAD OF triggers for the updateable view.

INSTEAD OF Triggers and Updateable Views

Even when a view's attributes violate the materialized view principle, you can make the view updateable if you define INSTEAD OF triggers for the view. An *INSTEAD OF* trigger is a special type of row trigger that you define for a view. An INSTEAD OF trigger explains what should happen when INSERT, UPDATE, or DELETE statements target the view that would otherwise not be updateable.

EXERCISE 7.13: Creating an INSTEAD OF Trigger for an Updateable View

To create an INSTEAD OF trigger, use the following syntax of the CREATE TRIGGER command:

```
CREATE [OR REPLACE] TRIGGER trigger
 INSTEAD OF
 {DELETE|INSERT|UPDATE [OF column [,column] ... ]}
```

```
[OR {DELETE|INSERT|UPDATE [OF column [,column] ... ]} ] ...
ON table|view }
... PL/SQL block ...
END [trigger]
```

For example, enter the following statement, which creates an INSTEAD OF trigger that defines the logic for handling an INSERT statement that targets the ORDERS_ITEMS view.

```
CREATE OR REPLACE TRIGGER orders_items_insert
INSTEAD OF INSERT ON orders_items
DECLARE
 currentOrderId INTEGER;
 currentOrderDate DATE;
BEGIN
-- Determine if the order already exists.
 SELECT id, orderdate
   INTO currentOrderId, currentOrderDate
  FROM orders
  WHERE id = :new.orderid;
-- If the NO_DATA_FOUND exception is not raised,
-- insert a new item into the ITEMS table.
 INSERT INTO items
  (o_id, id, quantity, p_id)
  VALUES (:new.orderid, :new.itemid,
   :new.quantity, :new.partid);
EXCEPTION
 WHEN no_data_found THEN
  INSERT INTO orders
   (id, orderdate, c_id)
   VALUES (:new.orderid, :new.orderdate,
    :new.customerid);
  INSERT INTO items
   (o_id, id, quantity, p_id)
   VALUES (:new.orderid, :new.itemid,
    :new.quantity, :new.partid);
END orders_items_insert;
/
```

Now, when an INSERT statement targets the ORDERS_ITEMS view, Oracle will translate the statement using the logic of the ORDERS_ITEMS_INSERT trigger to insert rows into the underlying ORDERS and ITEMS tables. For example, enter the following INSERT statement:

```
INSERT INTO orders_items
 ( orderid, orderdate, customerid, itemid, quantity)
 VALUES (1, '18-JUN-99', 1, 1, 1);
```

Now, query the ORDERS and ITEMS tables to see that the trigger worked as planned.

```
SELECT * FROM orders;

       ID ORDERDATE SHIPDATE  PAIDDATE  S     C_ID
--------- --------- --------- --------- - ---------
        1 18-JUN-99                     F        1

SELECT * FROM items;

     O_ID        ID      P_ID  QUANTITY
--------- --------- --------- ---------
        1         1                   1
```

Sequences

An OLTP application, such as an airline reservation system, typically supports a large number of concurrent users. As each user's transaction inserts one or more new rows into various database tables, coordinating the generation of unique primary keys among multiple, concurrent transactions can be a significant challenge for the application.

Fortunately, Oracle8i has a feature that makes the generation of unique values a trivial matter. A *sequence* is a schema object that generates a series of unique integers, and it is appropriate only for tables that use simple, numerical columns as keys, such as the ID columns used in all tables of our practice schema. When an application inserts a new row into a table, the application simply requests a database sequence to provide the next available value in the sequence for the new row's primary key value. What's more, the application can subsequently reuse a generated sequence number to coordinate the foreign key values in related child rows. Oracle manages sequence generation with an insignificant amount of overhead, allowing even the most demanding of online transaction processing (OLTP) applications to perform well.

Creating and Managing Sequences

To create a sequence, you use the SQL command *CREATE SEQUENCE*.

```
CREATE SEQUENCE [schema.]sequence
  [START WITH integer]
  [INCREMENT BY integer]
  [MAXVALUE integer|NOMAXVALUE]
  [MINVALUE integer|NOMINVALUE]
  [CYCLE|NOCYCLE]
  [CACHE integer|NOCACHE]
  [ORDER|NOORDER]
```

Notice that when you create a sequence, you can customize it to suit an application's particular needs; for example, an Oracle sequence can ascend or descend by one or more integers, have a maximum or minimum value, and more.

If need be, you can subsequently alter the properties of a sequence using the SQL command *ALTER SEQUENCE*. The ALTER SEQUENCE command supports the same options and parameters as the CREATE SEQUENCE command, with the exception of the START WITH parameter.

EXERCISE 7.14: Creating a Sequence

Enter the following CREATE SEQUENCE statement to create a sequence for sales order IDs.

```
CREATE SEQUENCE order_ids
  START WITH 2
  INCREMENT BY 1
  NOMAXVALUE;
```

The ORDER_IDS sequence starts with the integer 2 (remember, we already have a record in the ORDERS table with an ID set to 1), increments every sequence generation by 1, and has no maximum value.

EXERCISE 7.15: Using and Reusing a Sequence Number

To generate a new sequence number for your user session, a SQL statement must reference the sequence and its NEXTVAL pseudocolumn. Enter the following INSERT statement to insert a new sales order and use the ORDER_IDS sequence to generate a unique order ID.

NOTE
A pseudocolumn is similar to a column in a table. SQL statements can reference pseudocolumns to retrieve data, but cannot insert, update, or delete data by referencing a pseudocolumn.

```
INSERT INTO orders
  (id, c_id, orderdate, status)
  VALUES (order_ids.NEXTVAL,2,'18-JUN-99','B');
```

NOTE
Once your session generates a new sequence number, only your session can reuse the sequence number—other sessions generating sequence numbers with the same sequence receive subsequent sequence numbers of their own.

To reuse the current sequence number assigned to your session, a SQL statement must reference the sequence and its CURRVAL pseudocolumn. Using the CURRVAL pseudocolumn, your session can reuse the current sequence number any number of times, even after a transaction commits or rolls back. For example, enter the following INSERT statements to insert several new line items into the ITEMS table for the current order, and then commit the transaction.

```
INSERT INTO items
  (o_id, id, quantity)
  VALUES (order_ids.CURRVAL,1,1);

INSERT INTO items
  (o_id, id, quantity)
  VALUES (order_ids.CURRVAL,2,4);

INSERT INTO items
  (o_id, id, quantity)
  VALUES (order_ids.CURRVAL,3,5);

COMMIT;
```

Synonyms

When developers build a database application, it's prudent to avoid having application logic directly reference tables, views, and other database objects. Otherwise, applications must be updated and recompiled after an administrator makes a simple modification to an object, such as a name change or structural change.

To help make applications less dependent on database objects, you can create synonyms for database objects. A *synonym* is an alias for a table, view, sequence, or other schema object that you store in the database. Because a synonym is just an alternate name for an object, it requires no storage other than its definition. When an application uses a synonym, Oracle forwards the request to the synonym's underlying base object.

Private and Public Synonyms

Oracle allows you to create both public and private synonyms. A *public synonym* is an object alias (another name) that is available to every user in a database. A *private synonym* is a synonym within the schema of a specific user who has control over its use by others.

Creating Synonyms

To create a synonym, use the SQL command *CREATE SYNONYM*.

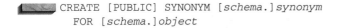
```
CREATE [PUBLIC] SYNONYM [schema.]synonym
   FOR [schema.]object
```

If you include the optional PUBLIC keyword, Oracle creates a synonym as a public synonym; otherwise, Oracle creates a synonym as a private synonym.

EXERCISE 7.16: Creating a Synonym

Enter the following statement to create the private synonym CUST in the current schema. The private synonym is an alias for the CUSTOMERS table in the same schema.

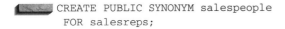
```
CREATE SYNONYM cust
   FOR customers;
```

Next, enter the following statement to create a public synonym for the SALESREPS table of the current schema.

```
CREATE PUBLIC SYNONYM salespeople
   FOR salesreps;
```

EXERCISE 7.17: Using a Synonym

The use of a synonym is transparent—just reference the synonym anywhere you would its underlying object. For example, enter the following query that uses the new CUST synonym.

```
SELECT id, lastname FROM cust;
```

The result set is as follows:

```
        ID LASTNAME
--------- ---------------
         1 Joy
         2 Musial
```

Indexes

The performance of an application is always critical. That's because the productivity of an application user directly relates to the amount of time that the user must sit idle while the application tries to complete work. With database applications, performance depends greatly on how quickly an application can access table data. Typically, disk I/O is the primary performance determining factor for table access—the less disk I/O that's necessary to access table data, the better the dependent applications will perform. In general, it's best to try to minimize the amount of disk access that applications must perform when working with database tables.

NOTE
This section introduces indexes to support subsequent sections of this book. For complete information about the various types of indexes that Oracle supports and other performance-related topics, see Chapter 12.

The judicious use of table indexes is the principal method of reducing disk I/O and improving the performance of table access. Just like an index in a book, an *index* of a table column (or set of columns) allows Oracle to quickly find specific table records. When an application queries a table and uses an indexed column in its selection criteria, Oracle automatically uses the index to quickly find the target rows with minimal disk I/O. Without an index, Oracle has to read the entire table from disk to locate rows that match a selection criteria.

The presence of an index for a table is entirely optional and transparent to users and developers of database applications. For example:

■   Applications can access table data with or without associated indexes.

■   When an index is present and it will help the performance of an application request, Oracle automatically uses the index; otherwise, Oracle ignores the index.

■   Oracle automatically updates an index to keep it in synch with its table.

Although indexes can dramatically improve the performance of application requests, it's unwise to index every column in a table. Indexes are meaningful only for the key columns that application requests specifically use to find rows of interest. Furthermore, index maintenance generates overhead—unnecessary indexes can actually slow down your system rather than improve its performance.

Oracle8i supports several different types of indexes to satisfy many types of application requirements. The most frequently used type of index in an Oracle database is a B-tree index, sometimes referred to in the Oracle documentation set as a normal index. The following sections explain more about B-tree indexes, which you can create for a table's columns.

B-Tree Indexes

The default and most common type of index for a table column is a B-tree index. A *B-tree index*, or *normal index*, is an ordered tree of index nodes, each of which contains one or more index entries. Each *index entry* corresponds to a row in the table, and contains two elements:

■   The indexed column value (or set of values) for the row

■   The ROWID (or physical disk location) of the row

A B-tree index contains an entry for every row in the table, unless the index entry for a row is null. Figure 7-4 illustrates a typical B-tree index.

When using a B-tree index, Oracle descends the tree of index nodes looking for index values that match the selection criteria of the query. When it finds a match, Oracle uses the corresponding ROWID to locate and read the associated table row data from disk.

Using B-Tree Indexes Appropriately

B-tree indexes are not appropriate for all types of applications and all types of columns in a table. In general, B-tree indexes are the best choice for OLTP applications where data is constantly being inserted, updated, and deleted. In such environments, B-tree indexes work best for key columns that contain many distinct values relative to the total number of key values in the column. The primary and alternate keys in a table are perfect examples of columns that should have B-tree indexes. Conveniently, Oracle8i automatically creates B-tree indexes for all primary key and unique integrity constraints of a table.

Creating B-Tree Indexes

To create an index, you use the SQL command *CREATE INDEX*. The following is an abbreviated version of the syntax listing for the CREATE INDEX command that focuses solely on the parts of that command that pertain to B-tree (normal) indexes.

```
CREATE [UNIQUE] INDEX [schema.]index
  ON { [schema.]table
  ( column [ASC|DESC] [, column [ASC|DESC]] ... )
```

Notice the following points about the CREATE INDEX command:

■ By including the optional keyword UNIQUE, you can prevent duplicate values in the index. However, rather than creating a unique index, Oracle Corp. recommends that you declare a unique constraint for a table so that the integrity constraint is visible along with other integrity constraints in the database.

■ You must specify one or more columns to be indexed. For each index, you can specify that you want the index to store values in ascending or descending order.

NOTE
Versions of Oracle previous to Oracle8i supported the DESC keyword when creating a B-tree index, but always created ascending indexes. Oracle8i now supports descending indexes.

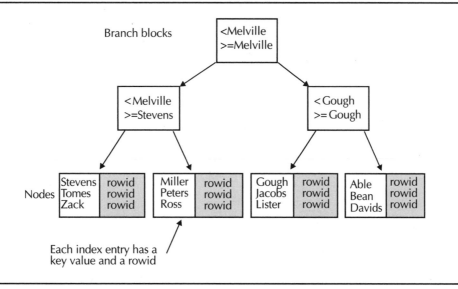

Branch blocks

<Melville
>=Melville

<Melville
>=Stevens

<Gough
>= Gough

Nodes

Stevens Tomes Zack	rowid rowid rowid
Miller Peters Ross	rowid rowid rowid
Gough Jacobs Lister	rowid rowid rowid
Able Bean Davids	rowid rowid rowid

Each index entry has a
key value and a rowid

FIGURE 7-4. *A B-tree index*

EXERCISE 7.18: Creating a B-Tree Index

To facilitate faster joins between the ITEMS and PARTS tables, enter the following command, which creates a B-tree index for the columns in the PARTS_FK foreign key column of the ITEMS table.

```
CREATE INDEX items_p_id
  ON items (p_id ASC);
```

The Data Dictionary: A Unique Schema

Every Oracle database uses a number of system tables and views to keep track of *metadata*—data about the data in a database. This collection of system objects is called the Oracle database's *data dictionary* or *system catalog*. Oracle organizes a database's data dictionary within the *SYS* schema.

As you create and manage schemas in an Oracle database, you can reveal information about associated schema objects by querying the tables and views of the data dictionary. For example, Table 7-3 provides a list of the several data dictionary views that correspond to the schema objects introduced in this chapter.

Type of Schema Object	Data Dictionary Views of Interest
Tables and columns	DBA_TABLES, ALL_TABLES, and USER_TABLES display general information about database tables.
	DBA_TAB_COLUMNS, ALL_TAB_COLUMNS, and USER_TAB_COLUMNS display information about the columns in each database table.
	Note: DBA_OBJECTS, ALL_OBJECTS, and USER_OBJECTS display information about schema objects, including tables.
Integrity constraints	DBA_CONSTRAINTS, ALL_CONSTRAINTS, and USER_CONSTRAINTS display general information about constraints.
	DBA_CONS_COLUMNS, ALL_CONS_COLUMNS, and USER_CONS_COLUMNS display information about columns and associated constraints.
Views	DBA_VIEWS, ALL_VIEWS, and USER_VIEWS.
	Note: DBA_OBJECTS, ALL_OBJECTS, and USER_OBJECTS also display information about schema objects, including views.
Sequences	DBA_SEQUENCES, ALL_SEQUENCES, and USER_SEQUENCES.
	Note: DBA_OBJECTS, ALL_OBJECTS, and USER_OBJECTS display information about schema objects, including sequences.
Synonyms	DBA_SYNONYMS, ALL_SYNONYMS, and USER_SYNONYMS.
	Note: DBA_OBJECTS, ALL_OBJECTS, and USER_OBJECTS display information about schema objects, including synonyms.
Indexes	DBA_INDEXES, ALL_INDEXES, USER_INDEXES, DBA_IND_COLUMNS, ALL_IND_COLUMNS, and USER_IND_COLUMNS.

TABLE 7-3. *The Data Dictionary Views that Correspond to Tables, Columns, Constraints, Views, Sequences, Synonyms, and Indexes*

Categories of Data Dictionary Views

Oracle's data dictionary contains several different categories of data dictionary views:

- Views that begin with the prefix "DBA_" present all information in the corresponding data dictionary base tables. Because the DBA views are comprehensive, they are accessible only to users that have the SELECT ANY TABLE system privilege. (See Chapter 9 for more information about privileges and database security.)

- Views that begin with the prefix "ALL_" are available to all users and show things specific to the privilege domain of the current user.

- Views that begin with the prefix "USER_" are available to all users and show things specific to the current user.

EXERCISE 7.19: Querying the Data Dictionary

In this final practice exercise of this chapter, let's query the data dictionary to reveal information about the integrity constraints created in the previous exercises in this chapter. For this query, we need to target the USER_CONSTRAINTS data dictionary view. First, enter the following DESCRIBE command to reveal the columns available in the USER_CONSTRAINTS view.

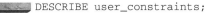DESCRIBE user_constraints;

```
Name                        Null?      Type
-------------------------   --------   ------------
OWNER                       NOT NULL   VARCHAR2(30)
CONSTRAINT_NAME             NOT NULL   VARCHAR2(30)
CONSTRAINT_TYPE                        VARCHAR2(1)
TABLE_NAME                  NOT NULL   VARCHAR2(30)
SEARCH_CONDITION                       LONG
R_OWNER                                VARCHAR2(30)
R_CONSTRAINT_NAME                      VARCHAR2(30)
DELETE_RULE                            VARCHAR2(9)
STATUS                                 VARCHAR2(8)
DEFERRABLE                             VARCHAR2(14)
DEFERRED                               VARCHAR2(9)
VALIDATED                              VARCHAR2(13)
GENERATED                              VARCHAR2(14)
BAD                                    VARCHAR2(3)
RELY                                   VARCHAR2(4)
LAST_CHANGE                            DATE
```

As you can see, the USER_CONSTRAINTS view contains many columns for recording the properties of integrity constraints. For this exercise, enter the following query to display the name of each constraint, the table that it is associated with, the type of constraint, and whether the constraint is deferrable.

```
SELECT constraint_name, table_name,
   DECODE(constraint_type,
     'C','CHECK',
     'P','PRIMARY KEY',
     'U','UNIQUE',
     'R','REFERENTIAL',
     'O','VIEW WITH READ ONLY',
     'OTHER') constraint_type,
   deferrable
 FROM user_constraints;
```

If you completed the previous exercises in this chapter, the result set of the query should be as follows:

```
CONSTRAINT_NAME  TABLE_NAME        CONSTRAINT_TYPE       DEFERRABLE
---------------  ----------------  --------------------  --------------
SYS_C002892      BACKLOGGED_ORDERS VIEW WITH READ ONLY   NOT DEFERRABLE
CUSTOMERS_PK     CUSTOMERS         PRIMARY KEY           NOT DEFERRABLE
SYS_C002882      CUSTOMERS         UNIQUE                NOT DEFERRABLE
SALESREPS_FK     CUSTOMERS         REFERENTIAL           NOT DEFERRABLE
QUANTITY_NN      ITEMS             CHECK                 NOT DEFERRABLE
ITEMS_PK         ITEMS             PRIMARY KEY           NOT DEFERRABLE
ORDERS_FK        ITEMS             REFERENTIAL           NOT DEFERRABLE
PARTS_FK         ITEMS             REFERENTIAL           NOT DEFERRABLE
SYS_C002876      ORDERS            CHECK                 NOT DEFERRABLE
STATUS_CK        ORDERS            CHECK                 DEFERRABLE
ORDERS_PK        ORDERS            PRIMARY KEY           NOT DEFERRABLE
C_ID_NN          ORDERS            CHECK                 NOT DEFERRABLE
CUSTOMERS_FK     ORDERS            REFERENTIAL           NOT DEFERRABLE
SYS_C002879      PARTS             CHECK                 NOT DEFERRABLE
PARTS_PK         PARTS             PRIMARY KEY           NOT DEFERRABLE
SALESREPS_PK     SALESREPS         PRIMARY KEY           NOT DEFERRABLE

16 rows selected.
```

Notice that Oracle generated unique names starting with the prefix "SYS_" for all of the constraints that you did not explicitly name. The DECODE expression in the query's SELECT clause translates codes in the CONSTRAINT_TYPE column to readable information.

Chapter Summary

This chapter has introduced many different types of objects that you can create in a basic relational database schema.

- Tables are the basic data structure in any relational database. A table is nothing more than an organized collection of rows that all have the same columns. A column's datatype describes the basic type of data that is acceptable in the column. To create and alter a table's structure, you use the SQL commands CREATE TABLE and ALTER TABLE.

■ To enforce business rules that describe the acceptable data for columns in a table, you can declare integrity constraints along with a table. You can use domain integrity constraints, such as not null constraints and check constraints, to explicitly define the domain of acceptable values for a column. You can use entity integrity constraints, such as primary key and unique constraints, to prevent duplicate rows in a table. And finally, you can use referential integrity constraints to establish and enforce the relationships among different columns and tables in a database. You can declare all types of integrity constraints when you create a table with the CREATE TABLE command, or after table creation with the ALTER TABLE command.

■ A view is a schema object that presents data from one or more tables. A view is nothing more than a query that Oracle stores in a database's data dictionary as a schema object. When you use a view to do something, Oracle derives the data of the view from the view's defining query. To create a view, you use the SQL command CREATE VIEW.

■ A sequence is a schema object that generates a series of unique integers. Sequences are most often used to generate unique primary keys for ID-type columns. When an application inserts a new row into a table, the application can request a database sequence to generate the next available value in the sequence for the new row's primary key value. The application can subsequently reuse a generated sequence number to coordinate the foreign key values in related child rows. To create a sequence, use the SQL command CREATE SEQUENCE. To generate and then reuse a sequence number, reference the sequence's NEXTVAL and CURRVAL pseudocolumns, respectively.

■ To help make applications less dependent on tables and other schema objects, you can create synonyms for schema objects. A synonym is an alias for a table, view, sequence, or other schema object that you store in the database. You create synonyms with the SQL command CREATE SYNONYM.

■ To improve the performance of table access, you can create an index for one or more columns in the table. Use the SQL command CREATE INDEX to create an index.

CHAPTER
8

Extending Oracle
with Objects

The previous chapters of this book explain many of the basic relational database features of Oracle8i, including how you can use SQL and PL/SQL to work with relational database objects, such as tables and views. In this chapter, you'll learn how to use Oracle8i's object-oriented database features to build next-generation database systems that take advantage of the object-oriented development paradigm. You'll also learn about other Oracle8i features that let you integrate existing relational databases with newer object-oriented databases so that applications can operate with both types of systems seamlessly. This chapter covers the following topics:

- The basics of object-oriented technology, including classes, instances, subclasses, inheritance, polymorphism, and encapsulation

- Objects and object types

- Object attributes and methods

- Object views

Chapter Prerequisites

To practice the hands-on exercises in this chapter, start a Linux session as the user oracle, start SQL*Plus, and run the following command script:

location/8istarterkit/SQL/chap08.sql

where *location* is the file directory where you expanded the support archive that accompanies this book. For example, after starting SQL*Plus and connecting as SCOTT, you can run this chapter's SQL command script using the SQL*Plus command @, as in the following example (assuming that your chap08.sql file is in /tmp/8istarterkit/SQL).

```
SQL> @/tmp/8istarterkit/SQL/chap08.sql;
```

Once the script completes successfully, leave the current SQL*Plus session open and use it to perform this chapter's exercises in the order that they appear.

Oriented Toward Objects

Have you ever thought about how a standard light bulb works? I'm not 100 percent sure, but I know that there are positive and negative electrical feeds, a glass bulb that encapsulates what I think is an air-free cavity, a lighting filament, and probably a few other things that I have never seen. What I do know for sure is that when I screw a light bulb into a socket and then turn on the lamp, the room fills with light. Simple, right? I don't concern myself with how the light bulb works, just with making sure it works after I screw it into a socket and flip on a switch.

The goal of object-oriented programming is to use software objects as simply as we use light bulbs. For the same reason people shouldn't have to obtain a Ph.D. in electrical engineering to use a light bulb, programmers should not have to program the low-level internal system calls necessary to create a simple window or a scroll bar when designing every new GUI application interface. And in the world of database applications, all developers should not have to be relational database modeling experts or SQL gurus just to write queries that access database information. The object-oriented approach to software development is advantageous because it can reduce the effort necessary to build applications. An object is a reusable application component, and developers simply need to know how to use it, not how it works.

Oracle8i and Object-Oriented Databases

To support object-oriented database application development, Oracle8i lets you create and use object types in your database designs. Implemented to closely follow the ANSI/ISO SQL3 standard, object types let you define complex datatypes that more closely resemble real-world things, and then you can tightly couple operations (behaviors) with each type.

For example, you might define an object type called orderType that represents the attributes of a typical sales order placed in your company's order-entry system. Furthermore, you could define an orderTotal method with the orderType to make it easy for applications to calculate the total value of a sales order's line items.

This simple example illustrates just a few of the benefits of using objects in an Oracle database. However, before learning more about how to create an Oracle database that uses objects, you must first understand some basic terminology related to object-oriented database extensions.

Object-Oriented Database Terms and Concepts

If you are new to object-oriented programming and database design, there are many general terms and terms specific to Oracle that you need to learn before you begin to understand how to work with objects. The following sections explain several concepts related to object-oriented databases.

Object Types, Classes, and Objects

In simple terms, an *object* is a collection of related data. For example, an object in an Oracle database typically represents a real-world thing, such as a person, place, or thing. Each object is an *instance* of a *class* or *object type*. For example, each instance of the orderType class shown in Figure 8-1 would represent a particular sales order in a typical order-entry application. (In relational terms, you might think of objects as rows in a table.)

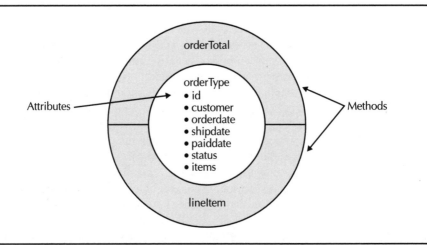

FIGURE 8-1. *An object type (a class) has attributes to describe the corresponding object, as well as methods that allow applications to work with objects of the class*

Attributes and Methods

An object type's *attributes* describe the data elements in corresponding objects. For example, every order has an ID, customer, order date, and so on. (In relational terms, you might think of object type attributes as column definitions in a table.)

An object type's *methods* (or *predefined behaviors*) encapsulate or describe the interface that applications use to work with objects of the type. As a result, application developers do not need to know the complicated details about objects to manipulate them; they simply code applications to access object data using the methods that are available for the type. For example, an application that works with orders can calculate the total value of an order's line items by simply calling the orderTotal method associated with the appropriate orderType object. (In relational terms, you might think of an object type's methods as the package of procedures and functions that provide an interface to work with a table's data.)

Subclasses, Inheritance, and Polymorphism

A *subclass* is a specialized class of an object type. In traditional object-oriented systems, a subclass *inherits* the attributes and methods of its parent class, and can have additional attributes and methods that are specific to the subclass. However, Oracle8i does *not* support inheritance of either attributes or methods (that is, subclasses are not supported in Oracle8i).

NOTE
When future releases of Oracle8i support the inheritance of methods, the concept of polymorphism will also be important. When a subclass inherits the methods of its parent class, inherited methods can behave exactly as they do in the parent class, or they can behave differently (they can be polymorphic). Polymorphism happens when a method behaves differently and has varying effects for classes in an object hierarchy.

How Will You Use Objects?

Now that you have a basic understanding of objects and object types, how will you decide to use them, if at all? In general, there are three ways to use object types in Oracle database designs:

- To implement user-defined datatypes that enhance the creation of relational database models

- To create nested tables inside relational database tables

- To create object tables that implement an object-oriented database design rather than a relational database design

As you can see, there are varying degrees to which you can commit to Oracle8i's object-oriented database extensions—you can use object types simply to enhance a relational database design or take the leap and implement tables defined by object types. As with any important decision, consider the specific requirements that you face, and determine the best choice for your system. Later sections of this chapter show you how to accomplish each type of implementation.

Do I Have to Use Object Types?

Another important choice not mentioned in the previous section is that you can ignore object types completely and stick with pure relational database designs. In addition to the fact that many respected relational database purists emotionally argue that objects are not meant for the database side of an application, there are some practical reasons to avoid using object types in an Oracle database. For example, you might want to wait until Oracle8i's object technology matures with subsequent releases, and becomes more robust, and offers such features as subclass inheritance, polymorphism, and type versioning—until then, you might choose to use object types only in prototype systems. Or, you just might not have the time or nerve to convert existing applications to take advantage of new object-oriented database extensions. Whatever your reasons, it's entirely up to you whether you use object types to some degree or not at all.

Object Types

Now you are ready to learn the basics of creating and using objects in an Oracle database. The following sections explain how to create some simple object types and then how to use them to build other schema objects.

Designing Object Types

Before you start creating object types in a database, it's a good idea to understand what you want to achieve by using them. In general, you will create an object type to build a complex, user-defined datatype that more closely matches a real-world thing. Then you and other developers can use this object type to declare and work with tables and other schema objects more easily.

For example, suppose you notice that the specification of an "address" varies across a business's database applications. Some implementations of an address are better than others—for example, poor implementations might not allow enough room for an unusually long street address or might not offer a field for a country specification. One way to ensure the consistency of addresses throughout database applications is to write and distribute standard development guidelines to all corporate developers. However, that would require the developers to actually read, understand, and most importantly, adhere to the guidelines. An easier way to ensure consistent addresses in your system is to create a new address datatype that developers can use in their database designs.

A more advanced use of an object type is to create a nested table type that you can use to embed the data of what would otherwise be a child table into its parent table. For example, rather than create distinct ORDERS and ITEMS tables, you can create a collection datatype that you then nest in the ORDERS table. Using this design, each ORDER record can have a nested table of associated ITEMS. Rather than performing a join to retrieve an order and its line items, a simple query gets all of the nested table's information at once. Nested tables hide the relationship of two tables (in other words, the data model) from applications and put it with the data itself, and they can reduce the complexity of subsequent application development.

Creating and Using Object Types

When you want to create a new object type, you can declare two separate parts—the type's *specification* and its *body*:

■ Similar to PL/SQL packages, an object type's *specification* is the public interface that developers use to work with the type when building applications. To create an object type's specification, you use the SQL command *CREATE TYPE*.

■ An object type's *body* is the private implementation of the type's methods; it's only necessary to create a body for an object type when the type's specification declares one or more methods. To create an object type's body, you use the SQL command *CREATE TYPE BODY.*

NOTE
When an object type specification includes neither attributes nor method specifications, the object type is an incomplete object type. Sometimes it's necessary to declare incomplete object types before you know what you want them to look like, so that you can build other dependent objects.

EXERCISE 8.1: Creating an Abstract Datatype

The most straightforward use of object types is for the creation of an *abstract datatype (ADT)*, or *user-defined datatype,* that you can then use to build other kinds of objects more easily. For example, enter the following statement to create a new object type for addresses.

```
CREATE OR REPLACE TYPE addressType AS OBJECT (
  street VARCHAR2(100),
  city VARCHAR2(100),
  state VARCHAR2(50),
  zipcode VARCHAR2(50),
  MAP MEMBER FUNCTION compare RETURN VARCHAR2 );
/
```

NOTE
Ignore the MAP MEMBER clause in the preceding statement for now. A subsequent exercise in this chapter will explain object type methods.

EXERCISE 8.2: Using an Abstract Datatype

After you declare a user-defined datatype as an object type, you can then use it to build other kinds of objects in database schemas. For example, enter the following

CREATE TABLE statement to declare the structure of an address in a relational database table using the new addressType.

```
CREATE TABLE customers (
  id INTEGER PRIMARY KEY,
  lastname VARCHAR2(100) NOT NULL,
  firstname VARCHAR2(50) NOT NULL,
  companyname VARCHAR2(100),
  address addressType,
  phone VARCHAR2(30),
  fax VARCHAR2(30),
  email VARCHAR2(100),
  s_id INTEGER NOT NULL
);
```

Likewise, when you must declare address parameters for a stored procedure, it's easy with the new addressType. (You do not have to enter the following statement—it's here just to demonstrate the concept of using the new object type when declaring a procedure's parameters.)

```
CREATE OR REPLACE PROCEDURE new_customer (
  custId IN INTEGER,
  custLastName IN VARCHAR2,
  custFirstName IN VARCHAR2,
  custCompanyName IN VARCHAR2,
  custAddress IN addressType,
  custPhone IN VARCHAR2,
  custFax IN VARCHAR2,
  custEmail IN VARCHAR2,
  custSalesRepId IN INTEGER )
IS
BEGIN
  NULL;
END;
/
```

To complete this exercise, drop the CUSTOMERS table so that we can recreate it in a subsequent lesson.

```
DROP TABLE customers;
```

EXERCISE 8.3: Creating an Object Type and a Simple Object Table

Exercise 8.1 showed you how to create an object type simply to enhance the creation of relational database objects, such as tables and stored procedures. When you want to go all the way to an object-oriented database design, you can use object types to create object tables. An *object table* is a database table that you define using an object type only, not relational columns and their datatypes. When you create an object table, the table's columns correspond to the attributes of the object type that you use to create the table.

The rows in an object table are *objects* of the table's underlying object type. Each object in an object table has a unique *object identifier* (*OID*), which Oracle automatically indexes and guarantees to be unique among all other OIDs. Oracle uses OIDs of object tables to define the relationships among various object tables in a database. You will learn more about OIDs in subsequent exercises in this chapter.

Enter the following statement to create an object type that you can use to create a PARTS table in the current schema.

```
CREATE OR REPLACE TYPE partType AS OBJECT (
 id INTEGER,
 description VARCHAR2(250),
 unitprice NUMBER(10,2),
 onhand INTEGER,
 reorder INTEGER
);
/
```

Notice that you do not declare integrity constraints, such as a primary key, when creating an object type that you will subsequently use as the basis for an object table.

Now enter the following CREATE TABLE statement to create the PARTS table. Rather than specifying relational columns and datatypes, use the *OF* clause of the SQL command CREATE TABLE to create the table using the new partType object type. The CREATE TABLE command is also where you can include constraint declarations, just as you would in a normal CREATE TABLE statement.

```
CREATE TABLE parts OF partType
 (id PRIMARY KEY);
```

Finally, enter a DESCRIBE command to confirm that Oracle8i creates the columns of the PARTS object table using the attributes of the partType object type.

```
DESCRIBE parts;
```

The results of the DESCRIBE command should be as follows:

```
Name               Null?     Type
-----------------  --------  -------------
ID                 NOT NULL  NUMBER(38)
DESCRIPTION                  VARCHAR2(250)
UNITPRICE                    NUMBER(10,2)
ONHAND                       NUMBER(38)
REORDER                      NUMBER(38)
```

EXERCISE 8.4: Creating an Object Type and a Table with ObjectReferences

Object tables can maintain relationships among related objects using *object references* (*REFs*), which are references to OIDs. When you specify a new object type, an attribute can indicate a pointer to related objects by using a *REF type modifier*. Subsequently, when you create objects in an object table, each object's REF must point to a persistent object of the specified object type.

For example, enter the following statements to create two new object types and associated object tables. Notice that the customerType uses the addressType, as well as a REF type modifier to refer to salesRepType objects.

```
CREATE OR REPLACE TYPE salesRepType AS OBJECT (
  id INTEGER,
  lastname VARCHAR2(100),
  firstname VARCHAR2(50),
  commission INTEGER
);
/

CREATE OR REPLACE TYPE customerType AS OBJECT (
  id INTEGER,
  lastname VARCHAR2(100),
  firstname VARCHAR2(50),
  companyname VARCHAR2(100),
  address addressType,
  phone VARCHAR2(30),
  fax VARCHAR2(30),
  email VARCHAR2(100),
  salesRep REF salesRepType
);
/

CREATE TABLE salesReps OF salesRepType
  (id PRIMARY KEY);

CREATE TABLE customers OF customerType
  (id PRIMARY KEY);
```

In the next section of this chapter, you'll learn how to insert and manipulate objects in a table using SQL and PL/SQL, including objects that contain REFs. For now, understand that in some ways, a REF in an object table is like a foreign key in a relational database table, but there are also some important differences:

- Oracle8i does not automatically prevent the deletion of an object, even when other objects reference it. Consequently, you can be left with *dangling REFs* in an object table. In Chapter 7, you learned that with foreign keys, the default delete restrict referential action prevents the deletion of a parent record when dependent child records exist.

■ Oracle does not cascade the deletion of an object to objects that reference it. In Chapter 7, you learned that with foreign keys, you can define a foreign key with the delete cascade referential action, which cascades the deletion of a parent record to dependent child records.

EXERCISE 8.5: Creating Collections in a Database

In Chapter 5, you learned how to create PL/SQL programs with collections based on nested table types and varray types. Oracle8i also permits you to create collections in a database table using an object type. For example, when you nest a child table inside its parent table, Oracle automatically manages the built-in relationships among each row of the parent table and the associated nested table rows. Nested tables in the database remove the complexity of relational joins from applications and can make some areas of subsequent application development easier.

Collections such as nested tables are appropriate in database tables for master-detail relationships in which detail rows store unique information. For example, consider the typical ORDERS and ITEMS tables in a relational order-entry database. Each line item is a unique collection of data that corresponds to a particular order. This is the kind of master-detail relationship that is the perfect candidate for a nested table.

Let's try creating a nested ITEMS table in an ORDERS table, using our practice schema. To accomplish this task, we need to create the following object types in sequence.

1. To describe the attributes of an order item, create an object type called itemType.

2. Next, create a nested table type called itemListType based on the itemType.

3. Finally, create the orderType, and use the itemListType to declare a nested table attribute.

To complete these steps, enter the following statements:

```
CREATE OR REPLACE TYPE itemType AS OBJECT (
 id INTEGER,
 part REF partType,
 quantity INTEGER
 );
/

CREATE OR REPLACE TYPE itemListType
 AS TABLE OF itemType;
```

```
/

CREATE OR REPLACE TYPE orderType AS OBJECT (
 id INTEGER,
 customer REF customerType,
 orderdate DATE,
 shipdate DATE,
 paiddate DATE,
 status CHAR(1),
 items itemListType,
 MEMBER FUNCTION orderTotal RETURN NUMBER,
 MEMBER FUNCTION lineItem (
   quantity IN INTEGER,
   partId IN INTEGER)
  RETURN itemListType
);
/
```

NOTE

For the moment, ignore the declaration of the methods for the orderType. A subsequent exercise in this chapter will explain these object type methods.

Now, you can use the orderType to create the ORDERS object table. When you nest one table inside a database table, Oracle stores the data within one physical data segment (see Chapter 10 for information about segments), but creates two logical tables in the data dictionary. Therefore, when you create the ORDERS table using the orderType, which contains a nested table attribute, you must use the *NESTED TABLE* clause of the SQL command CREATE TABLE to name the nested table. For example, enter the following CREATE TABLE statement to create the ORDERS object table:

```
CREATE TABLE orders OF orderType
  (id PRIMARY KEY)
 NESTED TABLE items STORE AS items (
  (PRIMARY KEY(NESTED_TABLE_ID, id)));
```

The NESTED TABLE clause can also specify other properties for a nested table, such as constraint specifications, storage parameters, and more. For example, the NESTED TABLE clause of the previous CREATE TABLE statement declares a composite primary key constraint for the nested table using the hidden column NESTED_TABLE_ID and ID attribute (within each line item).

Although the nested table inside the ORDERS table has a name, you must always refer to the data in the nested table indirectly, using the corresponding attribute of the outer table. The practice exercises in the next section of this chapter explain how to insert and manipulate persistent object data using extensions to SQL and PL/SQL, including how to access data in a nested table attribute of a database table.

EXERCISE 8.6: Revealing Object Type Dependencies

The previous examples show how you can use object types to build other schema objects, such as tables and stored procedures. When you do so, understand that you establish a tree of dependencies among schema objects and object types that must remain intact. In fact, Oracle keeps track of dependencies and will not let you pull the rug out from under anything. You can query the data dictionary at any time to display the dependencies of objects. For example, execute the following query to reveal the tables in your current schema (PRACTICE08) that are dependent on one or more object types.

```
SELECT name, type, referenced_name, referenced_type
  FROM user_dependencies
 WHERE type = 'TABLE'
   AND referenced_type = 'TYPE'
 ORDER BY name, type;
```

The result set is as follows:

```
NAME                TYPE           REFERENCED_NAME  REFERENCED_TYPE
---------------     ----------     ---------------  ---------------
CUSTOMERS           TABLE          CUSTOMERTYPE     TYPE
CUSTOMERS           TABLE          ADDRESSTYPE      TYPE
CUSTOMERS           TABLE          SALESREPTYPE     TYPE
ITEMS               TABLE          ITEMTYPE         TYPE
ITEMS               TABLE          PARTTYPE         TYPE
ORDERS              TABLE          ORDERTYPE        TYPE
ORDERS              TABLE          CUSTOMERTYPE     TYPE
ORDERS              TABLE          ITEMLISTTYPE     TYPE
PARTS               TABLE          PARTTYPE         TYPE
SALESREPS           TABLE          SALESREPTYPE     TYPE

10 rows selected.
```

Dependencies are okay when you never need to change things. In the real world, however, *schema evolution* is inevitable. That's when the dependencies that object types establish can become a nightmare. For example, suppose you want to expand the customerType with a new attribute for PHOTO. Because the CUSTOMERS table depends on customerType, you cannot change the definition of customerType without first dropping the CUSTOMERS table. In summary, carefully plan the object types for your database so that you get things right the first time. Then keep your fingers crossed and hope that things do not change once you have everything up and running.

NOTE

A great way to work around the limitations of Oracle8i's support for schema evolution is to implement relational tables and provide object abstractions for the tables using object views. The "Objects and Views" section of this chapter explains object views and their benefits.

Object SQL and PL/SQL

Now that you know how to create object types and use them to build columns in relational tables and object tables, the following practice exercises will teach you how to use Oracle8i's object SQL extensions and PL/SQL to construct, update, destroy, and view object data.

EXERCISE 8.7: Constructing a Simple Object

Within a PL/SQL program, you can construct an object using the underlying object type's *constructor* method. Just as with collection types inside a PL/SQL program (see Chapter 5), Oracle8i automatically creates a default constructor method for each object type that has the same name as the type itself. An object type's default constructor method accepts the attributes of the type as parameters. When you call an object type's default constructor method, you must supply a value for each attribute according to positional notation, or specify particular attributes using named notation (just as when you call a stored procedure).

TIP

*If you are unsure of an object type's attributes, you can always use the DESCRIBE command while using SQL*Plus.*

Enter the following anonymous PL/SQL block, which constructs a new sales representative and then outputs each attribute of the new object.

```
DECLARE
  newSalesRep salesRepType;
BEGIN
  newSalesRep := salesRepType(1,'Pratt','Nick',5);
  DBMS_OUTPUT.PUT_LINE('Id: ' || newSalesRep.id);
  DBMS_OUTPUT.PUT_LINE('Last Name: ' || newSalesRep.lastname);
```

```
  DBMS_OUTPUT.PUT_LINE('First Name: ' || newSalesRep.firstname);
  DBMS_OUTPUT.PUT_LINE('Commission: ' || newSalesRep.commission);
END;
/
```

Notice that you can refer to each attribute of an object using dot notation. The output from the preceding program should be as follows:

```
Id: 1
Last Name: Pratt
First Name: Nick
Commission: 5

PL/SQL procedure successfully completed.
```

The newSalesRep object in the previous example is a transient object. A *transient object* exists only while the encompassing PL/SQL program executes. Alternatively, the rows in an object table are *persistent objects* of the table's type because you store them in a database.

Enter the following revision of the previous anonymous PL/SQL block, but this time store the new sales representative as an object in the SALESREPS object table. Notice that the INSERT statement in the PL/SQL block simply references the entire object in its VALUES clause to supply the necessary attribute values for the new object.

```
DECLARE
  newSalesRep salesRepType;
BEGIN
  newSalesRep := salesRepType(1,'Pratt','Nick',5);
  INSERT INTO salesreps
   VALUES(newSalesRep);
END;
/
```

Another way to insert a persistent object into an object table is to use a standard INSERT statement (see Chapter 4). Just supply expressions for each attribute in the object table, or specify a column list and a matching set of expressions. For example, enter the following statements to insert two new sales representatives into the SALESREPS object table, and then commit your work.

```
INSERT INTO salesreps (id, lastname, firstname, commission)
 VALUES (2,'Jonah','Suzanne',5);

INSERT INTO salesreps (id, lastname, firstname, commission)
 VALUES (3,'Greenberg','Bara',5);

COMMIT;
```

To complete this exercise and support subsequent exercises in this chapter, enter the following sequence of statements to insert part objects into the PARTS object table.

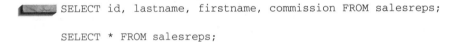

```
INSERT INTO parts
 VALUES (1,'Fax Machine',299,277,50);
INSERT INTO parts
 VALUES (2,'Copy Machine',4895,143,25);
INSERT INTO parts
 VALUES (3,'Laptop PC',2100,7631,1000);
INSERT INTO parts
 VALUES (4,'Desktop PC',1200,5903,1000);
INSERT INTO parts
 VALUES (5,'Scanner',99,490,200);
COMMIT;
```

EXERCISE 8.8: Querying a Simple Object Table

To retrieve object data from a simple object table that has scalar attributes, you can use a standard SELECT command. For example, enter one or both of the following queries of the SALESREPS table to confirm that the new persistent objects inserted in the previous example actually exist.

```
SELECT id, lastname, firstname, commission FROM salesreps;

SELECT * FROM salesreps;
```

The result set should be identical for both queries:

```
       ID LASTNAME             FIRSTNAME            COMMISSION
--------- -------------------- -------------------- ----------
        1 Pratt                Nick                          5
        2 Jonah                Suzanne                       5
        3 Greenberg            Bara                          5
```

EXERCISE 8.9: Constructing More Complex Objects

The examples in the previous exercise demonstrate that it is fairly easy to construct some simple objects. However, things are a bit more involved when you want to build objects that have attributes based on other object types or on REF type modifiers. For example, let's try building some customer objects in this practice exercise.

Recall that the customerType has a complex attribute ADDRESS based on the user-defined addressType, as well as the attribute SALESREP, which is a pointer to a salesRepType object in some other object table. Considering this, you can build a customer object in a PL/SQL block by completing the following steps:

■ To build the new customer object, call the customerType constructor.

■ To build a customer object's ADDRESS attribute, you need to call the addressType constructor within the call to the customerType constructor.

■ You must specify an OID for the new customer's SALESREP attribute. To obtain the OID of the customer's sales representative, use a SELECT ... INTO statement with the special *REF( ) function*, which returns the OID of an object into a salesRepType *REF variable* (a variable that holds a reference to an object, or an OID).

Enter the following anonymous PL/SQL block to build a new customer object and insert it into the CUSTOMERS object table.

```
DECLARE
 newCustomer customerType;
 salesRepRef REF salesRepType; -- ref variable
BEGIN
-- Retrieve OID of sales rep #3 into ref variable
 SELECT REF(s) INTO salesRepRef
 FROM salesReps s
 WHERE id = 3;
-- Construct new customer
 newCustomer := customerType(
  id => 1,
  lastname => 'Joy',
  firstname => 'Harold',
  companyname => 'McDonald Co.',
  address =>addressType('4458 Stafford St.','Baltimore','MD','21209'),
  phone => '410-983-5789',
  fax => NULL,
  email => 'harold_joy@mcdonald.com',
  salesrep => salesRepRef
 );
 INSERT INTO customers
  VALUES(newCustomer);
END;
/
```

Now let's insert another new customer into the CUSTOMERS table, but this time let's accomplish the task with just an INSERT statement (that is, not within a PL/SQL block). Notice in the following example that you can call an object type's constructor in the VALUES clause of an INSERT statement to supply expressions for a complex attribute, and that you can use a subquery to build the VALUES list for the new object. The subquery is necessary to capture the OID of the sales representative for the new customer.

```
INSERT INTO customers
   (id,lastname,firstname,companyname,address,phone,fax,email,salesrep)
   SELECT 2,'Musial','Bill','Car Audio Center',
      addressType('12 Donna Lane','Reno','NV','89501'),
      '775-859-2121','775-859-2121','musial@car-audio.net',
      REF(s)
   FROM salesReps s
   WHERE id = 1;

COMMIT;
```

EXERCISE 8.10: Selecting Data from Complex Table Attributes

To work with a column in a table that is declared using an object type, queries and other DML statements must reference individual column attributes with an extended form of standard dot notation. For example, enter the following query of the CUSTOMERS table to reveal the individual attributes of each customer's address field.

```
SELECT c.id,
   c.lastname,
   c.address.street AS street,
   c.address.city AS city,
   c.address.state AS state,
   c.address.zipcode AS zipcode
 FROM customers c;
```

Notice that you must alias the table that contains the complex attribute, and then use the table alias when referring to individual attributes of an object type. The results of the query should be as follows:

```
ID LASTNAME          STREET               CITY          STATE ZIPCODE
--- ---------------   --------------------  -----------  ----- ----------
  1 Joy               4458 Stafford St.    Baltimore     MD    21209
  2 Musial            12 Donna Lane        Reno          NV    89501
```

EXERCISE 8.11: Navigating Object References in Queries

The benefits of object tables, OIDs, and object references quickly become evident when you want to combine information from related object tables. Rather than build complicated join queries as is necessary with relational models, you can use extended dot notation for attributes of object tables that are object references. Oracle8*i* automatically navigates object references to make coding queries more straightforward. For example, enter the following query to return related information from the CUSTOMERS and SALESREPS object tables.

```
SELECT c.firstname || ' ' || c.lastname AS customer,
    c.salesrep.firstname || ' ' || c.salesrep.lastname AS salesrep
  FROM customers c;
```

The result set is as follows:

```
CUSTOMER                               SALESREP
------------------------------         ------------------------------
Harold Joy                             Bara Greenberg
Bill Musial                            Nick Pratt
```

NOTE
*When Oracle8i navigates an object reference for a
query, the result set is similar to that of an outer join
condition in a relational database system.*

In contrast to a relational system, a developer would need to understand the
relationship between the CUSTOMERS and SALESREPS tables, and then code that
relationship into every query that joins information from the two related tables, such
as (do not enter this query—it is present only for discussion):

```
SELECT c.firstname || ' ' || c.lastname AS customer,
    s.firstname || ' ' || s.lastname AS salesrep
  FROM customers c, salesreps s
  WHERE s.id = c.s_id;
```

EXERCISE 8.12: Retrieving Entire Objects in PL/SQL Programs

PL/SQL programs can retrieve an entire object from an object table into an object
variable of the same type using the *VALUE* function. For example, enter the following
anonymous PL/SQL block that demonstrates the use of the VALUE function.

```
DECLARE
  thisSalesRep salesRepType;
BEGIN
  SELECT VALUE(s) INTO thisSalesRep
  FROM salesReps s
  WHERE s.id = 1;
  DBMS_OUTPUT.PUT_LINE('Id: ' || thisSalesRep.id);
  DBMS_OUTPUT.PUT_LINE('Last Name: ' || thisSalesRep.lastname);
  DBMS_OUTPUT.PUT_LINE('First Name: ' || thisSalesRep.firstname);
  DBMS_OUTPUT.PUT_LINE('Commission: ' || thisSalesRep.commission);
END;
/
```

The program output is as follows:

```
Id: 1
Last Name: Pratt
First Name: Nick
Commission: 5

PL/SQL procedure successfully completed.
```

EXERCISE 8.13: Updating and Deleting Objects in a Table

You can also update and delete objects in an object table using syntax that previous exercises discuss for queries and INSERT statements. For example, enter the following UPDATE statement to modify the address of a customer, and then commit your work.

```
UPDATE customers c
  SET address=addressType('4855 Stafford St.','Baltimore','MD','21209')
  WHERE c.id = 1;

COMMIT;
```

NOTE

If you reissue the query in Exercise 8.9, you can confirm the success of your update.

Now enter the following DELETE statement to delete a sales representative from the SALESREPS table (do not commit your work):

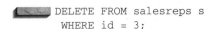

```
DELETE FROM salesreps s
  WHERE id = 3;
```

EXERCISE 8.14: Revealing Dangling REFs

In Exercise 8.4, you learned how to create object type attributes with the REF type modifier, and you also learned that Oracle8*i* does not enforce the integrity of REFs as it does with foreign keys in a typical relational database design. Consequently, an object table based on a type that uses a REF type modifier can be left with dangling REFs. For example, the DELETE statement in the previous exercise creates a dangling REF because a customer in the CUSTOMERS table refers to the OID of the sales representative that you deleted. You can see this fact by submitting the query from Exercise 8.11.

```
SELECT c.firstname || ' ' || c.lastname AS customer,
    c.salesrep.firstname || ' ' || c.salesrep.lastname AS salesrep
  FROM customers c;
```

The result set is as follows:

```
CUSTOMER                         SALESREP
------------------------------   -------------
Harold Joy
Bill Musial                      Nick Pratt
```

Notice how the customer Harold Joy has a null sales representative. You can also reveal dangling REFs by building a query with a WHERE clause that uses the special *IS DANGLING* operator (much like the IS NULL operator). For example, enter the following query to reveal the dangling salesRep REF in the CUSTOMERS table.

```
SELECT id, lastname, firstname
  FROM customers
 WHERE salesrep IS DANGLING;
```

The result set is as follows:

```
       ID LASTNAME             FIRSTNAME
--------- --------------------  --------------------
        1 Joy                  Harold
```

In this case, you can repair the dangling REF by simply rolling back the current transaction that deleted the sales representative (see the previous exercise).

```
ROLLBACK;
```

Now, if you check for dangling salesRep REFs again in the CUSTOMERS table, you will not see any.

```
SELECT id, lastname, firstname
  FROM customers
 WHERE salesrep IS DANGLING;
```

To preserve the integrity of data in a database schema that uses object types and object tables, dangling REFs are a potential problem that you must address. A simple way to prevent dangling REFs for a child table is to define a foreign key in addition to a REF attribute. This way, the referential integrity constraint enforces the relationship between the two tables. At the same time, applications will benefit from the convenience of object navigation provided by REF attributes.

EXERCISE 8.15: Building Collections in a Database

Chapter 5 teaches you how to declare and manipulate transient collections inside PL/SQL programs. You can apply the same set of skills when you need to work with persistent collections in an Oracle database. For example, enter the following anonymous PL/SQL block, which builds a new sales order object for the ORDERS table. Notice that the following example shows how to build a collection of line items for the nested table that is part of the new sales order.

```
DECLARE
  newOrder orderType;
  thisCustomer REF customerType;
  newItem itemType;
  newItems itemListType := itemListType();
  FUNCTION getPartRef (pId IN INTEGER)
    RETURN REF partType IS
      thisPart REF partType;
    BEGIN
      SELECT REF(p) INTO thisPart FROM parts p
        WHERE id = pId;
      RETURN thisPart;
    END getPartRef;
BEGIN
-- Retrieve OID of customer #1 into REF variable
  SELECT REF(c) INTO thisCustomer FROM customers c
    WHERE id = 1;
-- Construct new order
  newOrder := orderType (
    id => 1,
    customer => thisCustomer,
    orderdate => '18-JUN-99',
    shipdate => '18-JUN-99',
    paiddate => '30-JUN-99',
    status => 'F',
    items => NULL);
-- Construct line item #1 and insert it into the newItems collection
    newItems.EXTEND(1);
    newItem := itemType(
      id => 1,
      quantity => 1,
      part =>> getPartRef(3));
    newItems(1) := newItem;
-- Construct line item #2 and insert it into the newItems collection
    newItems.EXTEND(1);
    newItem := itemType(
      id => 2,
      quantity => 1,
```

```
   part => getPartRef(2));
  newItems(2) := newItem;
-- Add collection of items to newOrder
  newOrder.items := newItems;
-- insert the new order into the ORDERS table
INSERT INTO orders
 VALUES (newOrder);
END;
/
```

Although this example might seem complex, take a moment to realize the benefit of being able to insert a sales order, including all of its line items, with a single call to the database server—in a distributed processing environment where applications communicate with Oracle across a network, any way that you can reduce network traffic will reduce network bandwidth requirements and improve overall application performance.

EXERCISE 8.16: Selecting Rows from a Collection in a Database

To work with individual rows in a nested table, SQL statements must always access the outer table using a *flattened subquery,* which is a subquery denoted by the special SQL keyword *THE.* If you are a relational expert, the THE keyword might seem a little strange at first. However, if you read SQL statements that contain flattened subqueries, the use of the THE expression becomes much more intuitive. For example, enter the following query to retrieve the line items from the nested table in the new sales order object.

```
SELECT i.id, i.quantity, i.part.description AS part
  FROM THE(SELECT o.items FROM orders o WHERE o.id = 1) i
  ORDER BY i.id;
```

The result set is as follows:

```
      ID  QUANTITY PART
--------- --------- ---------------
       1         1 Laptop PC
       2         1 Copy Machine
```

EXERCISE 8.17: Manipulating Rows in a Collection with SQL

Although it's a bit tricky, you can also manipulate the rows of a collection using just SQL (without encompassing PL/SQL). Remember that to work with rows in a collection stored in a database, you must use a flattened subquery to build the target for the statement. For example, enter the following statement to insert another line item into the nested table of a sales order. The pseudo-code in the comment makes the use of the THE keyword obvious.

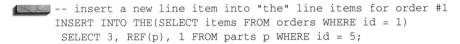

```
-- insert a new line item into "the" line items for order #1
INSERT INTO THE(SELECT items FROM orders WHERE id = 1)
 SELECT 3, REF(p), 1 FROM parts p WHERE id = 5;
```

Similarly, to update a row in a collection, you must use a flattened subquery. For example, enter the following UPDATE statement to change the quantity ordered for the newest line item in our sales order object.

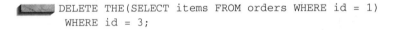

```
-- update "the" line items of order #1
UPDATE THE(SELECT items FROM orders WHERE id = 1)
 SET quantity = 2
 WHERE id = 3;
```

NOTE
To see the changes made by the most recent INSERT and UPDATE statements, resubmit the most recent query, which displays all of the line items in the sales order.

To wrap things up, enter the following DELETE statement, which demonstrates how to delete a specific row in a nested table. Notice again that you must use a flattened subquery to build a target for the DELETE statement.

```
DELETE THE(SELECT items FROM orders WHERE id = 1)
 WHERE id = 3;

COMMIT;
```

Methods

When you specify methods in an object type specification, you implement the methods by creating a corresponding body for the object type. A *method* is nothing more than a procedure or function that is bound to an object type and is meant to encapsulate an object type.

NOTE
With Oracle8i, methods do not truly "encapsulate" object types. That's because applications can use SQL to access objects of a type, rather than accessing objects using corresponding object type methods.

An object type can have different types of methods, including a constructor method, member and static methods, and a map method or an order method. The following sections explain more about each type of method.

An Object Type's Constructor Method

Previous sections in this chapter have already introduced an object type's constructor method. Oracle automatically creates a constructor method for an object type so that you can *instantiate* (construct) new objects of the type. By default, a type's constructor takes the same name as the type itself and has parameters that match the attributes of the object type. See Exercises 8.7, 8.9, and 8.15 for examples of using an object type's constructor method.

Order and Map Methods

Oracle can easily order and compare the data in columns that use standard datatypes, such as NUMBER, DATE, and CHAR. For example, the number 100 comes before 101 when sorting a NUMBER column in ascending order, because 100 is less than 101. The same kind of ordering requires some work on your part before Oracle can order user-defined objects. For example, Oracle cannot order customer records by address unless you explain to Oracle how it can compare two addresses.

```
SELECT c.companyname, c.address.zipcode AS zipcode
 FROM customers c
 ORDER BY c.address;

ORA-22950: cannot ORDER objects without MAP or ORDER method
```

As the previous error message indicates, you must create an object type with either a *map* or an *order* method (but not both) to be able to order and compare objects of the type. Oracle uses an object type's map or order method to determine various outcomes:

- Equality, less-than, and greater-than relations

- BETWEEN and IN predicates

- ORDER BY, GROUP BY, and DISTINCT clauses

- Unique and primary key constraints

NOTE
If you decide to declare an object type without a map or order method, Oracle can perform only equality and inequality comparisons for two objects of the same type. Two objects are equal only when all attributes in each object are identical.

EXERCISE 8.18: Creating and Testing a Map Method

In this exercise, you'll learn how to build a map method, rather than an order method, as the vehicle for comparing objects of an object type. That's because an order method takes a bit more work to code and performs much less efficiently than a map method when comparing many objects of the same type.

Let's try building a map method for the previously declared addressType. First, recall the specification of the addressType that you created in Exercise 8.1 (do not enter the following statement—this type is already in your schema).

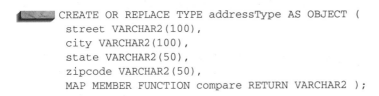

```
CREATE OR REPLACE TYPE addressType AS OBJECT (
   street VARCHAR2(100),
   city VARCHAR2(100),
   state VARCHAR2(50),
   zipcode VARCHAR2(50),
   MAP MEMBER FUNCTION compare RETURN VARCHAR2 );
```

TIP
You can display the specification for an object type, including the attributes of the type and the specification for all of the type's methods, using the SQL*Plus command DESCRIBE.

You must declare the specification for all object type methods in the specification of the object type itself, including the object type's map method. You declare a map method by using the keywords MAP MEMBER FUNCTION, followed by a name for the method. A type's map method does not take any input parameters, and it returns a scalar datatype, such as NUMBER, VARCHAR2, or DATE. In this example, we already declared the addressType with a map method named COMPARE that returns a VARCHAR2 string.

You implement the logic of all object type methods in the object type's body. You create the body of an object type using the SQL command CREATE TYPE

BODY. You can implement the logic of an object type method using PL/SQL, Java, or C. In this example, enter the following statement to implement the logic of the COMPARE map method using PL/SQL.

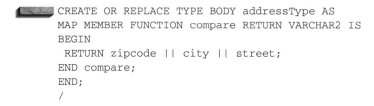

```
CREATE OR REPLACE TYPE BODY addressType AS
MAP MEMBER FUNCTION compare RETURN VARCHAR2 IS
BEGIN
 RETURN zipcode || city || street;
END compare;
END;
/
```

Now, when a query asks to order records by the addresses in a table, Oracle implicitly uses the map method of addressType to order the return set by addresses. For example, enter the following query to display customer information in address order.

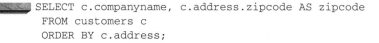

```
SELECT c.companyname, c.address.zipcode AS zipcode
  FROM customers c
  ORDER BY c.address;
```

The result set is as follows:

```
COMPANYNAME          ZIPCODE
-------------------- ----------
McDonald Co.         21209
Car Audio Center     89501
```

NOTE
If you decide at a later time to change the implementation of the map method for the addressType, simply replace the type's body and your new ordering mechanism is in place, without having to recompile applications that depend on it.

Member and Static Methods

Every object type can have one or more member or static methods. In either case, an object type method is nothing more than a stored procedure or function that is tied to the object type itself. An object type's methods typically manipulate the attributes of associated objects in some way.

NOTE
Although you can design object type methods to insert, update, or delete information in a specific object table, doing so makes the object type exclusive to the table. A better design strategy is to build object type methods that manipulate transient objects, and then use SQL or design packages that call object type methods to manipulate persistent objects in specific database tables. You'll see an example of these techniques in subsequent practice exercises of this chapter.

The first step necessary to create methods with an object type is to specify them as part of the object type specification. The specification of an object type's methods is similar to the specification of a PL/SQL package's procedures and functions:

- Each method can be a procedure or a function.

- Each method can have one or more parameters.

- A method that is a function must declare the type of a single return value.

Additionally, each method can be a member method or a static method. If you are familiar with another object-oriented programming language, such as Java, you'll probably recognize this distinction:

- A *member method* acts upon a specific instance of an object type, and has an implicit first parameter called *SELF* that has the same type as the object type itself—the next exercise shows you how to use the SELF parameter in a member method.

- A *static method* acts upon the object type itself, not on instances of the object type. Consequently, you do not have access to the implicit SELF parameter as in a member method.

You implement the logic of an object type's methods in the body of the object type, which you create with the SQL command CREATE TYPE BODY. You can implement the logic of an object type method using PL/SQL, Java, or C.

EXERCISE 8.19: Implementing a Member Method

In this practice exercise, you will implement the logic for the two member methods declared as part of the orderType in Exercise 8.5 (shown again here) using PL/SQL. Do not enter the following statement.

```
CREATE OR REPLACE TYPE orderType AS OBJECT (
  id INTEGER,
  customer REF customerType,
  orderdate DATE,
  shipdate DATE,
  paiddate DATE,
  status CHAR(1),
  items itemListType,
  MEMBER FUNCTION orderTotal RETURN NUMBER,
  MEMBER FUNCTION lineItem (
    quantity IN INTEGER,
    partId IN INTEGER)
  RETURN itemListType
);
/
```

The purpose of the orderTotal method is to calculate and return a total value for all line items in a sales order object. In the next exercise, you will see how the orderTotal method makes it very easy to build a query that displays the total for one or more sales orders.

The lineItem method constructs a collection of line items, containing just the first line item, for a new sales order. In the next exercise, you'll see how the lineItem method makes it easier to create a new sales order using an INSERT statement.

To implement the logic of the orderType's methods, enter the following CREATE TYPE BODY statement.

```
CREATE OR REPLACE TYPE BODY orderType AS
-- Return the total value of an order's line items.
MEMBER FUNCTION orderTotal
 RETURN NUMBER
IS
 returnValue NUMBER;
BEGIN
 SELECT SUM(i.quantity * i.part.unitprice) INTO returnValue
   FROM THE(SELECT o.items FROM orders o WHERE o.id = SELF.id) i;
 RETURN returnValue;
END orderTotal;
-- Return a collection that contains the first line item
-- for an order.
MEMBER FUNCTION lineItem (
    quantity IN INTEGER,
    partId IN INTEGER)
  RETURN itemListType
IS
 thisItemList itemListType;
 thisPart REF partType;
BEGIN
```

```
SELECT REF(p) INTO thisPart
FROM parts p
WHERE p.id = partId;
thisItemList := itemListType(itemType(1, thisPart, quantity));
RETURN thisItemList;
END lineItem;
END;
/
```

EXERCISE 8.20: Using a Method

To use a method that is a function, a SQL statement can simply reference the method anywhere that an expression corresponding to the return type of the function is necessary. For example, enter the following INSERT statement to build a new sales order with its first line item.

```
INSERT INTO orders o
 (id, orderdate, shipdate, paiddate, status, items)
 VALUES (2, '18-JUN-99', NULL, NULL, 'B', o.lineItem(2, 1));
```

Notice how the lineItem method simplifies the creation of a new sales order when using SQL. The lineItem method call in the VALUES clause of the INSERT statement builds a new collection with a single line item and returns this collection for the ITEMS attribute of the new sales order.

To make things clear, the previous INSERT statement did not include an object reference for the new order's customer. Enter the following statement to rectify this situation.

```
UPDATE orders o
 SET customer = (
  SELECT REF(c) FROM customers c WHERE c.id = 2)
 WHERE o.id = 2;
```

Next, enter the following query to test the orderTotal method and display the total value of the two sales orders in the ORDERS table.

```
SELECT o.id, o.orderTotal() AS ordertotal FROM orders o;
```

The result set is as follows:

```
        ID ORDERTOTAL
--------- ----------
         1       6995
         2        598
```

Notice how the orderTotal method greatly simplifies the process of determining an order's total line-item value. A comparable relational query might look similar to the following (do not enter the following query—it is present only to illustrate a point):

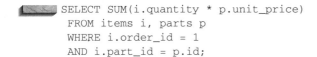

```
SELECT SUM(i.quantity * p.unit_price)
  FROM items i, parts p
  WHERE i.order_id = 1
  AND i.part_id = p.id;
```

NOTE
A PL/SQL program can also call an object type's method just as it would call a stored procedure or function.

Objects and Views

As explained in Chapter 7, a view is a schema object that you might create for several reasons. For example, you could use a view to derive new data, simplify access to a table or set of tables, present table data in a different way, or increase the security of specific columns and rows in a table. Starting with Oracle8, views fully support object extensions: you can create views of object tables, as well as views of relational tables that use object types to declare complex columns. The following sections explain more about using views in an object-relational Oracle8i database.

Object Views of Object Tables

If you decide to implement object tables in your Oracle8i database, you can create an *object view* of any object table that you like. When you create an object view of an object table, each row in the view itself is an object. Furthermore, the OIDs in an object view can be referenced when you add objects to other tables or views in the database. The following practice exercise explains more about building object views based on object tables.

EXERCISE 8.21: Object Views of Object Tables

To build an object view of one or more object tables, you must have an object type to describe the shape of the view. First, let's look at an extremely simple example of an object view. Enter the following statement to create an object view of the PARTS object table using the existing partType to describe the shape of the view.

```
CREATE OR REPLACE VIEW inventory OF partType AS
  SELECT * FROM parts;
```

The declaration of the INVENTORY view is straightforward because there already is an object type available that describes the shape of the new view. When you base an object view on a single object table, it's clear to Oracle that the OID of an object in the view is the OID of the corresponding row in the view's base table.

Now let's look at a slightly more complicated example of an object view. Suppose that you want to create a view that summarizes the number of orders placed by each company. To create an object view that accomplishes your goal, you must first create a new type that describes the shape of the proposed view. Enter the following statement to create a new object type called customerOrderType.

```
CREATE OR REPLACE TYPE customerOrderType AS OBJECT (
  orderCount INTEGER,
  company VARCHAR2(100)
);
/
```

With the new type in place, enter the following statement to create the CUSTOMER_ORDERS view.

```
CREATE OR REPLACE VIEW customer_orders OF customerOrderType
  WITH OBJECT OID (company) AS
  SELECT COUNT(o.id), o.customer.companyname
    FROM orders o
    GROUP BY o.customer.companyname;
```

Notice that the defining query of the view groups the rows in the ORDERS table by customer company names. Consequently, it is unclear how to uniquely identify the objects that the view represents. In this case, it is necessary to specify the *WITH OBJECT OID* clause of the SQL command CREATE VIEW to clearly indicate what attributes of the view type Oracle can use to uniquely identify the OIDs of the object view. In the CUSTOMER_ORDERS view, the clear choice is the COMPANY attribute of the customerOrderType.

Now enter the following query to see how easy it is to display the number of orders placed by each company.

```
SELECT * FROM customer_orders;
```

The result set is as follows:

```
ORDERCOUNT COMPANY
---------- --------------------
         1 Car Audio Center
         1 McDonald Co.
```

Views of Relational Tables

No doubt, many of you reading this book are familiar with using the Oracle7 relational database management system. So let's assume that, after reading the previous sections in this chapter, you decide that Oracle8i's object-oriented database features are the best things since sliced bread. But how do you migrate from Oracle7 and the relational world that you operate in right now? Do you have to scrap all of your previous databases and applications just to reap the benefits of object-oriented database designs? Fortunately, the answer is a resounding No! Oracle8i lets you define views on top of both relational and object tables so that you can smoothly move from a pure relational environment to an object-oriented system. Using views, you can keep all of your data in relational schemas, migrate to new object schemas, or have a mix of both. In any case, applications that use the database will never know the difference.

EXERCISE 8.22: Using Views to Establish Object Abstractions for Relational Data

In most cases, migrating from an existing relational system to an object-relational system is not a one-step process. As you build new information systems, you might want to design new applications to take advantage of Oracle8i's object-oriented database features, but leave existing relational database applications in place. In other words, both the new object-oriented applications and the existing relational applications must coexist and work with the same set of data that is in relational tables. Using views, you can achieve this goal.

To demonstrate, let's first create the traditional CUSTOMERS table in a relational format. Note that the name of the new table includes a trailing underscore (_) so its name does not conflict with the existing CUSTOMERS table in your practice schema.

```
CREATE TABLE customers_ (
  id INTEGER PRIMARY KEY,
  lastname VARCHAR2(100),
  firstname VARCHAR2(50),
  companyname VARCHAR2(100),
  street VARCHAR2(100),
  city VARCHAR2(100),
  state VARCHAR2(50),
  zipcode VARCHAR2(50),
  phone VARCHAR2(30),
  fax VARCHAR2(30),
  email VARCHAR2(100),
  s_id INTEGER
);
```

Enter the following statements to recall how a traditional relational database application works with the CUSTOMERS_ table. Commit your changes so that some data remains in the new table.

```
INSERT INTO customers_
  VALUES (1,'Joy','Harold','McDonald Co.',NULL,'Baltimore','MD',
  '21209','410-983-5789',NULL,'harold_joy@mcdonald.com', 3);

UPDATE customers_
  SET street = '4458 Stafford St.'
  WHERE id = 1;

SELECT id, zipcode FROM customers_;

COMMIT;
```

On the other hand, an object-oriented database application expects to work with a CUSTOMERS table that uses the addressType. The following statements illustrate how an object-oriented database application works with an object-oriented CUSTOMERS table. Afterward, rollback your transaction so that the data in the CUSTOMERS object table remains unaffected.

```
SELECT c.id, c.address.street AS street, c.address.city AS city
  FROM customers c;

UPDATE customers c
  SET c.address.street = '4458 Stafford St.'
  WHERE c.id = 1;

ROLLBACK;
```

To enable the object-oriented database application to work with the relational CUSTOMERS table, you can create a view that establishes the necessary object abstractions. For example, consider the following definition of the CUST view:

```
CREATE OR REPLACE VIEW cust AS
  SELECT c.id, c.lastname, c.firstname, c.companyname,
    addressType(c.street, c.city, c.state, c.zipcode) AS address,
    c.phone, c.fax, c.email, REF(s) AS salesrep
  FROM customers_ c, salesreps s
  WHERE c.s_id = s.id;
```

Now, an application can issue object-oriented queries against the CUST view to retrieve information from the underlying relational table:

```
SELECT c.id, c.address.zipcode AS zipcode
  FROM cust c;
```

The result set is as follows:

```
        ID ZIPCODE
--------- ----------
         1 21209
```

> **NOTE**
> *It's important to realize that the CUST view is not an object view of a relational table—it merely provides an object abstraction for the CUSTOMERS_ relational database table. The next section explains how to create and use object views of relational tables.*

EXERCISE 8.23: Creating Object Views of Relational Tables with OIDs

Oracle8i also allows you to create object views of relational tables. Just as with object views of object tables, you must have an object type that defines the shape of the view that you want to create. As always, the objects of an object view have associated OIDs that other objects in the schema can reference.

Enter the following statements to recreate the CUST view of the relational database table CUSTOMERS_ as an object view.

```
CREATE OR REPLACE TYPE custType AS OBJECT (
  id INTEGER,
  lastname VARCHAR2(100),
  firstname VARCHAR2(50),
  companyname VARCHAR2(100),
  address addressType,
  phone VARCHAR2(30),
  fax VARCHAR2(30),
  email VARCHAR2(100)
);
/

CREATE OR REPLACE VIEW cust OF customerType
  WITH OBJECT OID (id) AS
  SELECT c.id, c.lastname, c.firstname, c.companyname,
    addressType(c.street, c.city, c.state, c.zipcode) AS address,
    c.phone, c.fax, c.email, REF(s)
  FROM customers_ c, salesreps s
  WHERE c.s_id = s.id;
```

With the new view in place, an object-oriented application can use object SQL to reference data that is actually stored in relational tables. For example, enter the following statement to query the new CUST view and navigate an object reference to a customer's sales representative in the SALESREPS object table.

```
SELECT c.firstname || ' ' || c.lastname AS customer,
    c.salesrep.firstname || ' ' || c.salesrep.lastname AS salesrep
 FROM cust c;
```

The result set is as follows:

```
CUSTOMER                        SALESREP
------------------------------- ----------------
Harold Joy                      Bara Greenberg
```

Chapter Summary

This chapter has taught you how to use the most important of Oracle8i's object-oriented database features, including object types, attributes and methods, and object views. By using objects to build application schemas, you can raise the level of abstraction in your database and make it easier for developers to work with application data.

- An object type is a user-defined datatype that serves as a template for objects of the type.

- An object type's attributes describe the data elements in corresponding objects.

- An object type's methods describe a common interface that applications use to work with objects of the type.

- After you declare an object type, you can build columns, tables, views, and other schema objects based on the object type.

PART III

Basic Database Administration

CHAPTER
9

Securing Database
Access

ith any multiuser computer system, security is a particularly important issue to address. Oracle database systems are certainly no exception. Without adequate security controls, malicious users might invade an Oracle database, view confidential information, and make unauthorized changes to database information. This chapter explains the various security features of Oracle8*i* that you can use to control user access to database resources.

- User management and authentication
- Privilege management and roles
- Database resource limits
- User password management

Chapter Prerequisites

To practice the hands-on exercises in this chapter, establish a Linux session as the oracle user, and then start SQL*Plus and run the following command script

location/8istarterkit/SQL/chap09.sql

where *location* is the file directory where you expanded the support archive that accompanies this book. For example, after starting SQL*Plus and connecting as SCOTT, you can run this chapter's SQL command script using the SQL*Plus command @, as in the following example (assuming that your chap09.sql file is in /tmp/8istarterkit/SQL).

```
SQL> @/tmp/8istarterkit/SQL/chap09.sql;
```

Once the script completes successfully, leave the current SQL*Plus session open and use it to perform this chapter's exercises in the order that they appear.

User Management

The first line of defense against unwanted database access is controlling who can access the system in the first place. As you already know from previous chapters in this book, to connect to an Oracle database, a user must have a *username* in the database. The following sections explain more about managing database user accounts.

User Authentication

For each database user, you must indicate how you want Oracle to *authenticate* use of the new account. When someone attempts to connect to a database with a username, Oracle authenticates that the person utilizing the username is authorized to use the account. Oracle can authenticate users via three different techniques: password authentication, operating system authentication, and global user authentication.

Password Authentication

Oracle can authenticate a username with a *password*. When a user starts an application, the application prompts for a username and associated password. Oracle then authenticates the connection request using the user account information managed by the database. Password authentication is common in distributed processing environments when users work with client PCs and connect to an Oracle database server across a network.

When you decide to use password authentication, it's important to have a policy in place that ensures passwords have a certain degree of complexity and that users routinely change them. For more information about managing user passwords, see the "User Account Management" section later in this chapter.

Operating System Authentication

Oracle can authenticate a username using the *operating system* of the computer that's running the database server. When a user starts an application, the application does not request connection information from the user. Instead, the application forwards to Oracle the operating system account information of the user. Oracle then authenticates the connection request by making sure that the operating system user is registered as a user in the database. Operating system authentication is common in Oracle host-based environments when users connect to Oracle using terminals that are directly connected to the database server.

Global User Authentication

Oracle can authenticate a *global username* using an external network service. When a user starts an application and makes a connection request, Oracle authenticates the request with user information managed by an external security service. Oracle8i includes its own security service, *Oracle Security Server*, which you can use to manage global database users. Global user authentication is common in network environments where users require access to several Oracle databases, and the network is not necessarily secure.

EXERCISE 9.1: Creating a User with Password Authentication

You create a database user using the SQL command *CREATE USER*. The following is an abbreviated syntax listing of the CREATE USER command.

```
CREATE USER user
  IDENTIFIED BY password
  [DEFAULT TABLESPACE tablespace]
  [TEMPORARY TABLESPACE tablespace]
  [PASSWORD EXPIRE]
  [ACCOUNT {LOCK|UNLOCK}]
```

Notice that the CREATE USER command lets you create a user with a password, as well as specify various other settings for the new user account that subsequent sections of this chapter will explain. For now, just enter the following CREATE USER statement to create a database user account for a new application developer named Larry Ellison with an initial password of *changethisnow*.

```
CREATE USER lellison
  IDENTIFIED BY changethisnow;
```

EXERCISE 9.2: Changing the Password for a User

Any user can change their own password using the following form of the SQL command *ALTER USER*.

```
ALTER USER user
  IDENTIFIED BY newpassword
```

If you have the necessary privileges as a database administrator, you can also change another user's password with the same command. For example, enter the following ALTER USER statement to change the password for the new LELLISON account.

```
ALTER USER lellison
  IDENTIFIED BY newpassword;
```

A User's Default Tablespace

A tablespace is a logical storage division of a database that organizes the physical storage of database information. (See Chapter 10 for more information about tablespaces.) For each database user, you can set a *default tablespace*. When the user creates a new database object, such as a table or index, and does not explicitly indicate a tablespace for the object, Oracle stores the new database object in the user's default tablespace. Unless you specify otherwise, a user's default tablespace is the SYSTEM tablespace.

A User's Temporary Tablespace

Often, SQL statements require temporary work space to complete. For example, a query that joins and sorts a large amount of data might require temporary work space to build the result set. When necessary, Oracle allocates temporary work space for a user's SQL statements in the user's *temporary tablespace*. Unless you specify otherwise, a user's temporary tablespace is the SYSTEM tablespace.

EXERCISE 9.3: Altering a User's Tablespace Settings

When you create a user with the CREATE USER command, you can explicitly set the user's default and temporary tablespace settings. Subsequently, you can alter a user's default and temporary tablespace settings using the following form of the SQL command ALTER USER.

```
ALTER USER user
  DEFAULT TABLESPACE tablespace
  TEMPORARY TABLESPACE tablespace
```

Exercise 9.1 created the user LELLISON without specifying settings for the user's default and temporary tablespaces; therefore, LELLISON's default and temporary tablespaces are set to the SYSTEM tablespace. As you'll learn subsequently in Chapter 12 of this book, typical database users should not have their default and temporary tablespaces set to the SYSTEM tablespace for performance reasons. Therefore, enter the following ALTER USER statement to change LELLISON's tablespace settings.

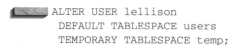
```
ALTER USER lellison
  DEFAULT TABLESPACE users
  TEMPORARY TABLESPACE temp;
```

Locked and Unlocked User Accounts

Oracle lets you *lock* and *unlock* a user account at any time so that you can control database access through the account without having to drop and recreate it. A user cannot connect to Oracle after you lock the user's account. To subsequently allow a user access through an account, you must unlock the account. Why would you want to lock and unlock user accounts?

- You might want to lock a user's account when the user takes a temporary leave of absence from work, but plans on returning in the future.

- When a person leaves your company, you might want to lock the user's account rather than drop the account, especially if the user's schema contains tables and other objects that you want to preserve.

- You typically lock a user account that functions only as a schema for logically organizing all of an application's database objects.

When you create a new database user, the new account is unlocked by default.

NOTE
Later in this chapter, you'll see how to configure Oracle so that it locks a user account automatically after a user's password expires or following a consecutive number of failed connection attempts.

EXERCISE 9.4: Locking and Unlocking a User Account

In Exercise 9.1, the example CREATE USER statement created the new user without specifying whether to lock or unlock the account. Therefore, Oracle creates the user with the default UNLOCK option for the ACCOUNT parameter. For practice, enter the following two ALTER USER statements to lock and then unlock the LELLISON account.

```
ALTER USER lellison
  ACCOUNT lock;

ALTER USER lellison
  ACCOUNT unlock;
```

Default Database Users

This book would be remiss if it did not mention that every Oracle database has two default database user accounts: SYS and SYSTEM.

- The *SYS account* owns the database's data dictionary objects. You should never connect to Oracle using the SYS account unless it is absolutely necessary to install supplemental data dictionary objects owned by SYS. The default password for the SYS account is CHANGE_ON_INSTALL.

- The *SYSTEM account* is the default database administrator account that you can use to get started with a new database. For accountability, it's best to create distinct user accounts capable of database administration rather than use the default SYSTEM account. The default password for the SYSTEM account is MANAGER.

Both the SYS and SYSTEM accounts are all-powerful database administrator accounts that can perform any database operation. Therefore, it is very important to change the default passwords for the SYS and SYSTEM accounts soon after database creation to prevent malicious users from using these accounts.

NOTE
For backward compatibility, Oracle8i also supports the special alias INTERNAL for the SYS account.

Privilege Management

After you create the users for an Oracle database system, they cannot connect to the database server nor do anything of consequence unless they have the *privileges* to perform specific database operations. For example, consider the following limitations:

- A user cannot connect to an Oracle database unless the user has the CREATE SESSION system privilege.

- A user cannot create a table in his or her corresponding schema unless the user has the CREATE TABLE system privilege.

- A user cannot delete rows from a table in a different schema unless the user has the DELETE object privilege for the table.

This short list reveals just some of the different privileges that you can use to control access to operations and data within an Oracle database. The following sections explain more about the different types of database privileges, as well as how to grant them to and revoke them from users.

Types of Database Privileges

If you read the list in the previous section closely, you'll notice that there are two different kinds of privileges that control access to an Oracle database: system privileges and object privileges.

System Privileges

A *system privilege* is a powerful privilege that gives a user the ability to perform some type of system-wide operation. For example, the following examples are just a few of almost 100 system privileges in Oracle8i:

- A user with the CREATE SESSION system privilege can connect to the database server and establish a database session.

- A user with the CREATE TABLE system privilege can create a table in his or her own schema.

- A user with the CREATE ANY TABLE system privilege can create a table in any schema of the database.

- A user with the CREATE ANY TYPE system privilege can create types and associated type bodies in any schema of the database.

- A user with the SELECT ANY TABLE system privilege can query any table in the database.

- A user with the EXECUTE ANY PROCEDURE system privilege can execute any stored procedure, stored function, or packaged component in the database.

- A user with the EXECUTE ANY TYPE system privilege can reference and execute methods of any type in the database.

Because system privileges are very powerful privileges that can affect the security of the entire database system, carefully consider what types of users require system privileges. For example:

- A database administrator is the only type of user that should have the powerful ALTER DATABASE system privilege, a privilege that allows someone to alter the physical structure and availability of the database system.

- Developers typically require several system privileges, including the CREATE TABLE, CREATE VIEW, and CREATE TYPE system privileges to build database schemas that support front-end applications.

- Every user in the system typically has the CREATE SESSION system privilege, the privilege that allows a user to connect to the database server.

At first, the overwhelming number of system privileges might appear intimidating. However, because each system privilege is a focused access right for a specific database operation, it's easy to provide each type of database user with just the right amount of privileges—no more or less power than what is necessary to accomplish their work.

Object Privileges

An *object privilege* is a privilege that gives a user the ability to perform a specific type of operation on a specific database object, such as a table, view, or stored procedure:

- A user with the SELECT object privilege for the CUST view can query the view to retrieve information.

■ A user with the INSERT object privilege for the CUSTOMERS table can insert new rows into the table.

■ A user with the EXECUTE privilege for the partType object type can use the type when building other database objects and execute the type's methods.

These examples are just a few of the object privileges that are available for tables, views, sequences, procedures, functions, packages, object types, and server file directories. Depending on how an application is designed, users might require object privileges for the underlying database objects that the application uses. For example, in a typical order-entry application, a user might need the SELECT, INSERT, UPDATE, and DELETE privileges for the CUSTOMERS, ORDERS, and ITEMS tables, as well as the SELECT and UPDATE privileges for the PARTS table. Because each object privilege is focused on the operation that it permits, you can manage database access with absolute control.

Granting and Revoking Users' Privileges

You can give a user a system or object privilege by *granting* the privilege to the user with the SQL command *GRANT*. To withdraw a privilege from a user, you *revoke* the privilege from the user with the SQL command *REVOKE*. Oracle does not let just anyone grant and revoke privileges to and from users. Consider the following requirements when managing individual system and object privileges for database users:

■ You can grant a user a system privilege only if you have the system privilege with the administrative rights to grant the privilege to other users.

■ You can grant a user a database object privilege only if you own the associated database object or if you have the object privilege with the administrative rights to grant the privilege to other users.

The following practice exercises provide you with more information about using the GRANT and REVOKE commands.

EXERCISE 9.5: Granting a System Privilege to a User

You can grant a system privilege to a user, with or without administrative rights for the privilege, using the following form of the SQL command GRANT.

```
GRANT privilege [, privilege] ...
  TO user [, user] ...
  [WITH ADMIN OPTION]
```

For example, a typical application developer requires the ability to connect to the database and then create tables, views, sequences, and other types of schema objects necessary to support an application. Considering this, enter the following GRANT statement to grant several system privileges to LELLISON.

```
GRANT CREATE SESSION, CREATE TABLE, CREATE VIEW, CREATE ANY INDEX,
   CREATE SEQUENCE, CREATE TYPE
   TO lellison
   WITH ADMIN OPTION;
```

NOTE
To grant a system or object privilege to every user in the database, grant the privilege to the keyword PUBLIC rather than to a specific user. PUBLIC is a special group in an Oracle database that you can use to make a privilege available quickly to every user in the system. However, use this feature carefully so that you do not open up security holes in your database.

EXERCISE 9.6: Revoking a System Privilege from a User

If you make a mistake while granting a user some privileges, or later decide that a user should no longer have a system privilege as part of their *privilege domain* (set of available privileges), you can revoke the system privilege using the following form of the SQL command REVOKE.

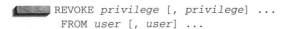

```
REVOKE privilege [, privilege] ...
   FROM user [, user] ...
```

For example, the GRANT statement in the previous practice exercise grants the user LELLISON several system privileges with the ADMIN option. Consequently, LELLISON can use the system privileges to perform database work and can grant the same system privileges to other users at his discretion. Typical application developers should not have the ability to grant system privileges to other database users. Therefore, enter the following REVOKE statement to revoke LELLISON's access to the system privileges granted in the previous exercise.

```
REVOKE CREATE SESSION, CREATE TABLE, CREATE VIEW, CREATE ANY INDEX,
   CREATE SEQUENCE, CREATE TYPE
   FROM lellison;
```

Next, regrant the system privileges to LELLISON, but this time without the ADMIN option.

```
GRANT CREATE SESSION, CREATE TABLE, CREATE VIEW, CREATE ANY INDEX,
    CREATE SEQUENCE, CREATE TYPE
  TO lellison;
```

EXERCISE 9.7: Granting an Object Privilege to a User

You can grant an object privilege for a specific schema object to a user, with or without the right to grant the privilege to other users, using the following form of the SQL command GRANT.

```
GRANT
  { privilege [, privilege] ...
  | ALL [PRIVILEGES] }
  ON {[schema.]object | DIRECTORY directory }
  TO user [, user] ...
  [WITH GRANT OPTION]
```

NOTE

To grant an object privilege, you must own the object or have been granted the object privilege with the GRANT option.

Table 9-1 contains a list of the privileges available for the most common types of schema objects.

Type of Object	Object Privileges	Special Notes
Table	SELECT, INSERT, UPDATE, DELETE, ALTER, INDEX, REFERENCES	The INDEX privilege lets the grantee create an index for the table. The REFERENCES privilege lets the grantee reference the table when declaring a referential integrity constraint. You can grant column-selective privileges for the INSERT, UPDATE, and REFERENCES privileges.

TABLE 9-1. *The Object Privileges for the Most Common Types of Schema Objects in an Oracle8i Database*

Type of Object	Object Privileges	Special Notes
View	SELECT, INSERT, UPDATE, DELETE	You can grant column-selective privileges for the INSERT, and UPDATE privileges.
Sequence	SELECT, ALTER	The SELECT privilege lets the grantee use the sequence to generate and reuse sequence numbers with the sequence's NEXTVAL and CURRVAL pseudo-columns.
Procedure, Function, Package, Object Type	EXECUTE	The EXECUTE privilege for an object type lets the grantee use the object type when building other schema objects and types, and lets the grantee execute the type's methods.

TABLE 9-2.   *The Object Privileges for the Most Common Types of Schema Objects in an Oracle8i Database* (continued)

For example, your current practice schema (PRACTICE09) contains the familiar CUSTOMERS, ORDERS, ITEMS, PARTS, and SALESREPS tables (in other words, your current schema owns these tables). Enter the following statements to grant the user LELLISON various privileges for the tables in your schema.

```
GRANT INSERT, UPDATE, DELETE, SELECT
 ON customers
 TO lellison;

GRANT ALL PRIVILEGES
 ON orders
 TO lellison
 WITH GRANT OPTION;

GRANT SELECT,
 INSERT (id, lastname, firstname),
 UPDATE (lastname, firstname),
 REFERENCES (id)
 ON salesreps
 TO lellison;
```

The first statement grants the INSERT, UPDATE, DELETE, and SELECT privileges for the CUSTOMERS table to LELLISON. The second statement uses the ALL PRIVILEGES shortcut to grant all object privileges for the ORDERS table to LELLISON with the option to grant the table privileges for the ORDERS table to other users. The final statement grants the SELECT, INSERT, UPDATE, and REFERENCES privileges for the SALESREPS table to LELLISON—notice that the INSERT, UPDATE, and REFERENCES privileges are granted for specific columns only.

EXERCISE 9.8: Revoking an Object Privilege from a User

You can revoke an object privilege from a user with the following form of the SQL command REVOKE.

```
REVOKE
  { privilege [, privilege] ...
  | ALL [PRIVILEGES] }
ON {[schema.]object | DIRECTORY directory }
FROM user [, user] ...
[CASCADE CONSTRAINTS]
[FORCE]
```

The CASCADE CONSTRAINTS option indicates that you want to drop all referential integrity constraints created using a REFERENCES object privilege that is being revoked. The FORCE option is necessary when revoking the EXECUTE object privilege for an object type that has table dependencies.

For example, enter the following statement to revoke some of the privileges you granted to LELLISON in the previous practice exercise.

```
REVOKE UPDATE, DELETE ON customers
  FROM lellison;

REVOKE ALL PRIVILEGES ON orders
  FROM lellison;

REVOKE REFERENCES ON salesreps
  FROM lellison
  CASCADE CONSTRAINTS;
```

Privilege Management with Roles

The system and object privileges necessary to use a typical database application can be numerous. When a database application supports a large user population, privilege management can become a big job quickly if you manage each user's privileges with individual grants. To make security administration an easier task, you can use roles. A *role* is a collection of related system and object privileges that you can grant to users and other roles. For example, when you build a new database application, you can create a new role that has the database privileges necessary to run the program. After you grant the role to an application user, the user can start the application to connect to the database and accomplish work. If the privileges necessary to run the application change, all that's necessary is a quick modification of the role's set of privileges. All grantees of the role see the change in the role automatically and continue to have the privileges necessary to use the application.

Predefined Database Roles

Oracle has many predefined roles that you can use to quickly grant privileges to common types of database users. The following is a short list of the five most commonly used predefined database roles that you might use.

CONNECT	A basic user role that lets the grantee connect to the database and then create tables, views, synonyms, sequences, and a few other types of objects in the associated schema.
RESOURCE	Intended for a typical application developer, this role lets the grantee create tables, sequences, data clusters, procedures, functions, packages, triggers, object types, function-based indexes, and user-defined operators in the associated schema.
DBA	Intended for administrators, this role lets the grantee perform any database function, as it includes every system privilege. Furthermore, a grantee of the DBA role can grant any system privilege to any other database user or role.
SELECT_CATALOG_ROLE	Lets the grantee query administrator (DBA_) data dictionary views.
EXECUTE_CATALOG_ROLE	Lets the grantee execute the prebuilt DBMS utility packages.

CAUTION
Although Oracle provides predefined roles to help manage privileges for typical database users, an application that relies on these roles might not necessarily function correctly. That's because you can change a predefined role's privilege set or even drop the role altogether.

User-Defined Roles

You can create as many roles as you need for an Oracle database. After creating a role, you grant privileges and other roles to the role to build the role's set of privileges. Then you grant the role to users so that they have the privileges necessary to complete their jobs.

Enabled and Disabled Roles

A grantee of a role does not necessarily have access to the privileges of the role at all times. Oracle allows applications to selectively enable and disable a role for each individual. After an application *enables* a role for a user, the privileges of the role are available to the user. As you might expect, after an application *disables* a role for a user, the user no longer has access to the privileges of the role. Oracle's ability to dynamically control the set of privileges available to a user allows an application to ensure that users always have the correct set of privileges when using the application.

For example, when a user starts an order-entry application, the application can enable the user's ORDER_ENTRY role so that the user can accomplish work. When the user finishes working, the application can disable the user's ORDER_ENTRY role so that the user cannot use the order-entry application privileges when working with a different application.

Default Roles

Each user has a list of default roles. A *default role* is a role that Oracle enables automatically when the user establishes a new database session. Default roles make it convenient to enable roles that users always require when working with Oracle, no matter which application they use.

Role Authentication

To prevent unauthorized use of a role, you can protect a role with authentication. Oracle can authenticate the use of a role using the same three authentication techniques as with database users: password authentication, operating system authentication, and global role authentication. Oracle authenticates role usage when a user or application attempts to enable the role.

Creating, Managing, and Using Roles

In the previous exercises of this chapter, you granted several system and object privileges directly to a user account. Consider the overhead if you had to repeat this process for 100-plus developers in a large workgroup. To make privilege management easier for the application developers in your system, the next few practice exercises show you how to define a new role called APPDEV that you can grant to application developers' accounts.

EXERCISE 9.9: Creating a Role

To create a new role, you use the SQL command *CREATE ROLE*. The following is an abbreviated version of this command's syntax.

```
CREATE ROLE role
  [NOT IDENTIFIED | IDENTIFIED BY password]
```

Enter the following SQL command to create a new role for application developers in our system.

```
CREATE ROLE appdev
  IDENTIFIED BY yeRtw;
```

> **NOTE**
> *When you create a role, Oracle automatically grants you the role with the administrative rights to alter, drop, and grant the role to other roles and users. Additionally, a role is owned by the system, not the creator of the role.*

EXERCISE 9.10: Granting System Privileges and Roles to a Role

The syntax of the SQL command GRANT for granting system privileges and other roles to a role is basically the same as in Exercise 9.5.

```
GRANT privilege|role [, privilege|role] ...
   TO role [, role] ...
   [WITH ADMIN OPTION]
```

For example, enter the following statement to grant several system privileges to the new APPDEV role.

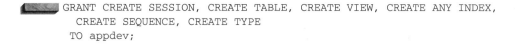

```
GRANT CREATE SESSION, CREATE TABLE, CREATE VIEW, CREATE ANY INDEX,
   CREATE SEQUENCE, CREATE TYPE
   TO appdev;
```

NOTE

If you grant the ADMIN option for a role, the grantee can grant, alter, or drop the role, and can grant the role to other users and roles. To prevent security holes in your system, it is not wise to grant system privileges and roles with administrative rights to other roles.

EXERCISE 9.11: Granting Object Privileges to a Role

The syntax of the SQL command GRANT for granting object privileges to a role is basically the same as in Exercise 9.7—just specify the name of one or more roles rather than one or more users. For example, enter the following statements to grant several object privileges to the new APPDEV role.

```
GRANT INSERT, UPDATE, DELETE, SELECT
   ON customers
   TO appdev;

GRANT ALL PRIVILEGES
   ON orders
   TO appdev;

GRANT SELECT,
   INSERT (id, lastname, firstname),
   UPDATE (lastname, firstname)
   ON salesreps
   TO appdev;
```

NOTE
*Oracle does not permit you to grant the
REFERENCES object privilege for a table
to a role—when a user needs this privilege,
you must grant it to the user directly.*

EXERCISE 9.12: Granting a Role to a User

To grant a role to a user, you use the following syntax of the SQL command GRANT:

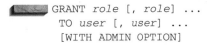

```
GRANT role [, role] ...
  TO user [, user] ...
  [WITH ADMIN OPTION]
```

If you grant the ADMIN option for a role to a user, the user can grant, alter, or drop
the role, and can grant the role to other users and roles. Use this option judiciously.

For example, enter the following SQL statements to create a new database user
account for another application developer, and then grant the APPDEV role to the
new user.

```
CREATE USER rlane
  IDENTIFIED BY changethisnow
  DEFAULT TABLESPACE users
  TEMPORARY TABLESPACE temp
  ACCOUNT UNLOCK;

GRANT appdev TO rlane;
```

With just one grant statement, the new user RLANE has the necessary privileges
to work as an application developer in your database. Furthermore, if you need to
change the privileges for application developers, all that you need to do is grant
privileges to and revoke privileges from the APPDEV role—all grantees of the APPDEV
role will automatically be subject to the new privilege domain of the role.

EXERCISE 9.13: Setting a User's Default Role

When you grant a role to a user, Oracle automatically adds the role to the user's list
of default roles. You can explicitly set a user's list of default roles using the following
syntax of the SQL command ALTER USER.

```
ALTER USER user
  [DEFAULT ROLE
    { role [,role] ...
    | ALL [EXCEPT role [,role] ...]
    | NONE } ]
```

You can specify a role as a user's default role after the user has been granted the role directly—you cannot specify roles received indirectly through other roles. Furthermore, you cannot specify a role as a user's default role if the role is authenticated by the operating system or by a security service—roles authenticated by passwords require no passwords at connect time. Notice that you can specify individual roles, use the ALL clause to specify all or all but a list of roles, or specify no default roles for the user.

NOTE
If a user does not have any default roles with the CREATE SESSION system privilege, you must grant the CREATE SESSION system privilege directly to the user, or else the user will not be able to establish a database session.

Enter the following ALTER USER statement to modify the list of default roles for the new RLANE user account.

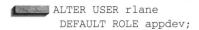

```
ALTER USER rlane
  DEFAULT ROLE appdev;
```

Subsequently, when RLANE connects to your database, Oracle will automatically make available the privileges granted to the APPDEV role.

EXERCISE 9.14: Enabling and Disabling a Role

You can explicitly enable and disable access to the privileges of a role using the SQL command *SET ROLE*. As discussed earlier in this section of the chapter, applications commonly use this command to make sure that application sessions have the appropriate set of privileges for using the application. The syntax of the SET ROLE command is as follows:

```
SET ROLE
  { role [IDENTIFIED BY password] [,role [IDENTIFIED BY password] ... ]
  | ALL [EXCEPT role [,role] ... ]
  | NONE }
```

There are several important points to understand before you use the SET ROLE command:

- Your session can use the SET ROLE command with the ALL option to enable all roles granted to your account. However, when you want to enable a role that requires a password, you must specify the role and its password using the IDENTIFIED BY parameter.

■ You can disable all roles for your session using the NONE option of the SET ROLE command.

■ Oracle automatically disables any role granted to you that you do not enable with the SET ROLE command.

To illustrate the way that the SET ROLE command functions, consider that your current user account (PRACTICE09) has been granted the following roles: CONNECT, RESOURCE, SELECT_CATALOG_ROLE (which has been granted the HS_ADMIN_ROLE), and APPDEV. To display the list of the roles currently enabled by your session, enter the following query of the SESSION_ROLES data dictionary view.

```
SELECT * FROM session_roles;
```

The result set is as follows:

```
ROLE
----------------
CONNECT
RESOURCE
SELECT_CATALOG_ROLE
HS_ADMIN_ROLE
```

Now enter the following SET ROLE statement to enable the APPDEV role and disable the CONNECT and RESOURCE roles for your current SQL*Plus session.

```
SET ROLE appdev IDENTIFIED BY yeRtw;
```

Next, requery the SESSION_ROLES view, and you should see the following result set:

```
ROLE
----------------
APPDEV
```

To enable all of your roles for your current session (CONNECT, RESOURCE, and APPDEV), you must enter the following SET ROLE statement.

```
SET ROLE
   CONNECT,
   RESOURCE,
   SELECT_CATALOG_ROLE,
   appdev IDENTIFIED BY yeRtw;
```

Notice that this SET ROLE statement does not list the HS_ADMIN_ROLE, which is part of the SELECT_CATALOG_ROLE's privilege domain. That's because Oracle automatically enables the roles granted to a role that you explicitly enable.

Resource Limitation

In a multiuser database system, it's prudent to limit each user's access to system resources. Otherwise, one user might consume an inordinate amount of database resources at the expense of other users. For example, when Oracle automatically terminates all database sessions that remain idle for an extended period of time, the server can eliminate unnecessary overhead and provide more memory, CPU cycles, and other system resources to sessions that are performing real work. The following sections explain the features of Oracle that you can use to limit access to several different system resources.

Tablespace Quotas

A user cannot create objects such as tables and indexes in a tablespace unless the user has a *quota* for the tablespace. A tablespace quota limits how much space a user's database objects can consume in the tablespace. A user can have a quota for zero, one, or all tablespaces in the database—it's entirely up to you. When you create or alter a user and give the user a tablespace quota, you set the quota as a specific number of bytes in the tablespace or as an unlimited amount of space in the tablespace.

EXERCISE 9.15: Providing Specific Tablespace Quotas for a User

To give a current user a quota for one or more tablespaces in the system, you can use the following form of the SQL command ALTER USER.

```
ALTER USER user
   [QUOTA {integer [K|M]|UNLIMITED} ON tablespace] ...
```

For example, enter the following statement to provide the user LELLISON with the right to use 5MB of space in the USERS tablespace.

```
ALTER USER lellison
   QUOTA 5M ON users;
```

Now enter the following statement to provide the user RLANE with the right to an unlimited amount of space in the USERS tablespace.

```
ALTER USER rlane
   QUOTA UNLIMITED ON users;
```

EXERCISE 9.16: Granting Unlimited Quota for all Tablespaces

When a user must have an unlimited quota for every tablespace in the database, you can grant the user the UNLIMITED TABLESPACE system privilege, rather than giving the user an unlimited quota for each tablespace in the system. For example, enter the following statement to grant the user RLANE the UNLIMITED TABLESPACE system privilege.

```
GRANT UNLIMITED TABLESPACE TO rlane;
```

NOTE
Oracle does not let you grant the UNLIMITED TABLESPACE system privilege to a role.

Resource Limit Profiles

To control the consumption of several other types of system resources, you can use resource limit profiles. A *resource limit profile* is a set of specific resource limit settings that you assign to one or more database users. Using a resource limit profile, you can limit consumption of the following system resources:

- CPU time (in hundredths of a second), per session or per statement

- Logical disk I/Os, per session or per statement

- Concurrent database sessions per user

- The maximum amount of connect time and idle time (in minutes) per session

- The maximum amount of server memory available to a multithreaded server session

User Account Management

You can use resource limit profiles to enforce several other security policies for database users. Using a resource limit profile, you can control the following settings for each user account that is assigned the profile:

- The number of consecutive failed connection attempts to allow before Oracle locks the account

- The lifetime of the account's password, in days, after which the password expires

- The number of days (grace period) that a user can use an expired password before locking the account

- The number of days that must pass, or the number of times that an account's password must be changed, before the account can reuse an old password

- Whether or not to check an account's password for sufficient complexity to prevent an account from using an obvious password

The Default Profile

Every Oracle database has a *default resource limit profile*. When you create a new database user and do not indicate a specific profile for the user, Oracle automatically assigns the user the database's default profile. By default, all resource limit settings of the database's default profile are set to unlimited; account management settings vary.

When you create a resource limit profile, you can set specific resource limit settings or defer to the corresponding setting of the database's default profile. At any time, you can alter the settings of a database's default profile just like user-defined profiles.

Managing Resource Limit Profiles

Several steps are necessary to configure and enforce resource limitation using profiles in an Oracle database.

1. Enable resource limitation for the database instance.

2. Create one or more profiles.

3. Assign each user's profile.

The following practice exercises teach you how to complete these steps for managing resource limitation, and more.

EXERCISE 9.17: Enabling Resource Limitation

By default, resource limitation is not enforced for your starter database. Therefore, the first step necessary to limit user access to server resources is to enable the enforcement of resource limitation at the instance level. You can enable and disable the enforcement of resource limitation without having to shut down and restart the Oracle service by using the following form of the SQL command ALTER SYSTEM.

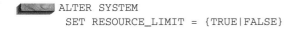

```
ALTER SYSTEM
  SET RESOURCE_LIMIT = {TRUE|FALSE}
```

To enable the enforcement of resource limitation for the current database instance, enter the following ALTER SYSTEM statement.

```
ALTER SYSTEM
  SET RESOURCE_LIMIT = TRUE;
```

NOTE
The example ALTER SYSTEM statement in this exercise enables the enforcement of resource limitation only for the life of the current database instance—if you shut down and restart Oracle, the enforcement of resource limitation is subject to the setting of the RESOURCE_LIMIT parameter in your server's initialization parameter file. If you plan to use resource limitation permanently, edit your server's parameter file and include the following parameter: RESOURCE_LIMIT = TRUE.

EXERCISE 9.18: Creating a Profile

In this exercise, you will create a resource limit profile that you can use with the new application developers in your practice database. To create a new profile, you use the SQL command *CREATE PROFILE*, which has the following syntax:

```
CREATE PROFILE profile LIMIT
  [SESSIONS_PER_USER {integer|UNLIMITED|DEFAULT}]
  [CPU_PER_SESSION {integer|UNLIMITED|DEFAULT}]
  [CPU_PER_CALL {integer|UNLIMITED|DEFAULT}]
  [CONNECT_TIME {integer|UNLIMITED|DEFAULT}]
  [IDLE_TIME {integer|UNLIMITED|DEFAULT}]
  [LOGICAL_READS_PER_SESSION {integer|UNLIMITED|DEFAULT}]
  [LOGICAL_READS_PER_CALL {integer|UNLIMITED|DEFAULT}]
  [COMPOSITE_LIMIT {integer|UNLIMITED|DEFAULT}]
  [PRIVATE_SGA {integer [K|M]|UNLIMITED|DEFAULT}]
  [FAILED_LOGIN_ATTEMPTS {integer|UNLIMITED|DEFAULT}]
  [PASSWORD_LIFE_TIME {integer|UNLIMITED|DEFAULT}]
  [PASSWORD_REUSE_TIME {integer|UNLIMITED|DEFAULT}]
  [PASSWORD_REUSE_MAX {integer|UNLIMITED|DEFAULT}]
  [PASSWORD_LOCK_TIME {integer|UNLIMITED|DEFAULT}]
  [PASSWORD_GRACE_TIME {integer|UNLIMITED|DEFAULT}]
  [PASSWORD_VERIFY_FUNCTION {NULL|function|DEFAULT}]
```

Enter the following statement to create a new resource limit profile:

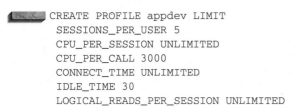

```
CREATE PROFILE appdev LIMIT
  SESSIONS_PER_USER 5
  CPU_PER_SESSION UNLIMITED
  CPU_PER_CALL 3000
  CONNECT_TIME UNLIMITED
  IDLE_TIME 30
  LOGICAL_READS_PER_SESSION UNLIMITED
```

```
LOGICAL_READS_PER_CALL 1000
PRIVATE_SGA 200K;
```

Note the following settings in our new APPDEV profile:

- A profile user can have at most five concurrent database sessions open.

- A profile user session can use an unlimited amount of CPU time, but only 30 seconds (set as 3,000 hundredths of a second) of CPU time per database request. If a call reaches this CPU limit, Oracle stops the operation to prevent further consumption of CPU time by the session.

- A profile user session can remain connected to the instance for an unlimited amount of time without being disconnected, but can remain idle for only 30 minutes before being automatically disconnected.

- A profile user session can perform an unlimited number of logical reads (data block reads from either disk or server memory), but only 1,000 logical block reads per database request. If a call reaches this limit, Oracle stops the operation to prevent further consumption of logical reads by the session.

- A profile user session that connects to the instance using a multithreaded server can allocate and use up to 200K of private memory for the MTS session.

EXERCISE 9.19: Altering Profile Settings

You alter the settings of a profile using the SQL command *ALTER PROFILE*.

```
ALTER PROFILE profile LIMIT
  [SESSIONS_PER_USER {integer|UNLIMITED|DEFAULT}]
  [CPU_PER_SESSION {integer|UNLIMITED|DEFAULT}]
  [CPU_PER_CALL {integer|UNLIMITED|DEFAULT}]
  [CONNECT_TIME {integer|UNLIMITED|DEFAULT}]
  [IDLE_TIME {integer|UNLIMITED|DEFAULT}]
  [LOGICAL_READS_PER_SESSION {integer|UNLIMITED|DEFAULT}]
  [LOGICAL_READS_PER_CALL {integer|UNLIMITED|DEFAULT}]
  [COMPOSITE_LIMIT {integer|UNLIMITED|DEFAULT}]
  [PRIVATE_SGA {integer [K|M]|UNLIMITED|DEFAULT}]
  [FAILED_LOGIN_ATTEMPTS {integer|UNLIMITED|DEFAULT}]
  [PASSWORD_LIFE_TIME {integer|UNLIMITED|DEFAULT}]
  [PASSWORD_REUSE_TIME {integer|UNLIMITED|DEFAULT}]
  [PASSWORD_REUSE_MAX {integer|UNLIMITED|DEFAULT}]
  [PASSWORD_LOCK_TIME {integer|UNLIMITED|DEFAULT}]
  [PASSWORD_GRACE_TIME {integer|UNLIMITED|DEFAULT}]
  [PASSWORD_VERIFY_FUNCTION {NULL|function|DEFAULT}]
```

For example, when you created the new APPDEV profile in the previous exercise, you did not specify any of the password management settings. Enter the following ALTER PROFILE statement to specify the basic password management settings for the new profile.

```
ALTER PROFILE appdev LIMIT
  FAILED_LOGIN_ATTEMPTS 3
  PASSWORD_LOCK_TIME 1
  PASSWORD_LIFE_TIME 30
  PASSWORD_GRACE_TIME 5
  PASSWORD_REUSE_TIME UNLIMITED
  PASSWORD_REUSE_MAX UNLIMITED;
```

The previous statement sets the following password management features:

- A profile user can attempt three consecutive logins without success, after which Oracle automatically locks the account.

- If Oracle locks a profile user's account because of three consecutive failed login attempts, Oracle keeps the account locked for one full day and then automatically unlocks the account.

- The lifetime of a profile user's password is 30 days, plus a grace period of 5 days, after which the user must change the password or else Oracle locks the account.

- A profile user cannot reuse an old password.

NOTE
Oracle8i enforces all password management features that you set with a user's profile, whether or not you enable resource limitation with the ALTER SYSTEM command or the RESOURCE_LIMIT server parameter.

EXERCISE 9.20: Manually Forcing a User's Password to Expire

You can manually force a user's password to expire and require that the user change the password during his or her next session. To accomplish this task, use the following form of the SQL command ALTER USER.

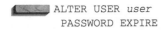
```
ALTER USER user
  PASSWORD EXPIRE
```

For example, enter the following statement to manually expire RLANE's password.

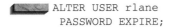
```
ALTER USER rlane
    PASSWORD EXPIRE;
```

EXERCISE 9.21: Using Password Complexity Checking

In the previous exercise, you specified the basic password management settings for a profile. You can also check the complexity of a profile user's password using the PASSWORD_VERIFY_FUNCTION parameter of the SQL commands CREATE PROFILE and ALTER PROFILE. To disable password complexity checking for all profile users, set the profile's PASSWORD_VERIFY_FUNCTION parameter to NULL. To enable password complexity checking for all profile users, set the profile's PASSWORD_VERIFY_FUNCTION parameter to the name of a function that is designed to check password complexity. Oracle supplies a default function that you must create using the utlpwdmg.sql command script located in the $ORACLE_HOME/ rdbms/admin directory. To run this script, start a *different* instance of SQL*Plus (leave your other SQL*Plus session intact) and connect as the user SYS. Once you are connected as SYS, run the utlpwdmg.sql command script. For example, the following command runs the utlpwdmg.sql script:

```
@$ORACLE_HOME/rdbms/admin/utlpwdmg.sql;
```

The utlpwdmg.sql command script creates a PL/SQL stored function named VERIFY_FUNCTION and enables the password management features for the default database profile, including complexity checking with the VERIFY_FUNCTION function. VERIFY_FUNCTION includes some standard checks for password complexity, including the following:

- An account's username and password cannot match.

- A password must be at least four characters in length.

- A password cannot be one of the following common strings: "welcome", "database", "account", "user", "password", "oracle", "computer", or "abcd".

- A password must contain at least one character, one digit, and one punctuation mark.

- A new password must differ from the current password by at least three characters.

After you run the utlpwdmg.sql script, exit this SQL*Plus session and return to your original SQL*Plus session.

Using your original SQL*Plus session (connected as PRACTICE09), alter the new APPDEV profile to enable password complexity checking for all of the profile's users. The following statement alters the APPDEV profile to use the setting of the

PASSWORD_VERIFY_FUNCTION parameter of the database's default profile (which is SYS.VERIFY_FUNCTION).

```
ALTER PROFILE appdev LIMIT
  PASSWORD_VERIFY_FUNCTION DEFAULT;
```

NOTE
When you configure Oracle to check the complexity of user passwords, users should not use the ALTER USER command to change their passwords. See your Oracle documentation for more information about changing user passwords in this setting.

EXERCISE 9.22: Setting a User's Profile

By default, all users are assigned to use the database's default profile. To set a user's profile to another profile, you can use the following form of the SQL command ALTER USER.

```
ALTER USER user
  PROFILE profile
```

For example, using your original SQL*Plus session, enter the following ALTER USER statements to assign the users LELLISON and RLANE to the APPDEV resource limit profiles.

```
ALTER USER lellison
  PROFILE appdev;

ALTER USER rlane
  PROFILE appdev;
```

EXERCISE 9.23: Experimenting with Password Management Settings

At this point, all users in your practice database are subject to various password management checks because the default database profile and the new APPDEV profile have set password management options. In this exercise, let's see what happens when you try to change the password for LELLISON to a very simple password. Enter the following statement.

```
ALTER USER lellison IDENTIFIED BY password;
```

When Oracle tries to execute this statement, it should return the following errors:

```
ORA-28003: password verification for the specified password failed
ORA-20002: Password too simple
```

Now enter the following statement to set an acceptably complex password for LELLISON.

```
ALTER USER lellison IDENTIFIED BY new_password01;
```

EXERCISE 9.24: Altering the Default Database Profile

If you plan to use the default database profile to limit resources or enforce password management, you should pay close attention to the default limits and password management options set for this profile (see Exercise 9.28). You can adjust the default database profile's settings using an ALTER PROFILE statement.

For example, you must disable the password management features of the default database profile so that you can run the SQL command scripts for subsequent chapters without being prompted to change the SYSTEM account's password. To disable password management for the default database profile, enter the following ALTER PROFILE statement.

```
ALTER PROFILE default LIMIT
   PASSWORD_LIFE_TIME UNLIMITED
   PASSWORD_REUSE_TIME UNLIMITED
   PASSWORD_REUSE_MAX UNLIMITED
   PASSWORD_LOCK_TIME UNLIMITED
   PASSWORD_GRACE_TIME UNLIMITED
   PASSWORD_VERIFY_FUNCTION NULL;
```

NOTE

Once you enable the password management features for a profile, Oracle keeps track of when each profile users' password expires, etc., even after you disable password management features for the profile. Consequently, in 30 days, Oracle8i might request that you change the password for existing database accounts such as SYS, SYSTEM, and SCOTT.

Displaying Security Information

The following exercises demonstrate some useful queries that you can use to display information about users, roles, and profiles from your database's data dictionary.

EXERCISE 9.25: Displaying Information About Users

To display information about the users in your database, you can query the DBA_USERS data dictionary view. For example, enter the following statement to reveal the account settings for the LELLISON and RLANE user accounts in the practice database.

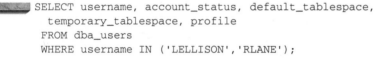
```
SELECT username, account_status, default_tablespace,
  temporary_tablespace, profile
 FROM dba_users
 WHERE username IN ('LELLISON','RLANE');
```

The result set is as follows:

```
USERNAME  ACCOUNT_STATUS  DEFAULT_TABLESPACE  TEMPORARY_TABLESPACE  PROFILE
--------  --------------  ------------------  --------------------  -------
RLANE     EXPIRED         USERS               TEMP                  DEFAULT
LELLISON  OPEN            USERS               TEMP                  DEFAULT
```

EXERCISE 9.26: Displaying Information About Roles

To display information about the roles in your database, you can query the DBA_ROLES data dictionary view. For example, enter the following statement to list information about the CONNECT, RESOURCE, DBA, and APPDEV roles in your database.

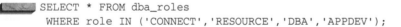
```
SELECT * FROM dba_roles
 WHERE role IN ('CONNECT','RESOURCE','DBA','APPDEV');
```

The result set is as follows:

```
ROLE                          PASSWORD
----------------------------- --------
APPDEV                        YES
DBA                           NO
RESOURCE                      NO
CONNECT                       NO
```

EXERCISE 9.27: Displaying Information About Tablespace Quotas

To display information about the quotas granted for each tablespace in your database, you can query the DBA_TS_QUOTAS data dictionary view. For example, enter the following statement.

```
SELECT tablespace_name, username, bytes, max_bytes
  FROM dba_ts_quotas;
```

The result set for this query should be similar to the following:

```
TABLESPACE_NAME                      USERNAME        BYTES MAX_BYTES
---------------------------------    ----------  --------- ---------
USERS                                PRACTICE09     143360    204800
USERS                                LELLISON            0   5242880
USERS                                RLANE               0        -1
USERS                                PRACTICE08     163840    204800
USERS                                PRACTICE04     143360    204800
USERS                                M1C1           122880    204800
USERS                                PRACTICE05     184320    204800
USERS                                PRACTICE07     122880    204800
```

Notice that the MAX_BYTES column of the DBA_TS_QUOTAS view displays the code "-1" when a user has an unlimited tablespace quota.

EXERCISE 9.28: Displaying Information About Profiles

To display information about profiles and associated resource limit settings, you can query the DBA_PROFILES data dictionary view. For example, enter the following query.

```
SELECT profile, resource_name, limit
  FROM dba_profiles
  WHERE profile = 'APPDEV';
```

The result set is as follows:

```
PROFILE    RESOURCE_NAME             LIMIT
---------- ------------------------- ----------
APPDEV     COMPOSITE_LIMIT           DEFAULT
APPDEV     SESSIONS_PER_USER         5
APPDEV     CPU_PER_SESSION           UNLIMITED
APPDEV     CPU_PER_CALL              3000
APPDEV     LOGICAL_READS_PER_SESSION UNLIMITED
```

```
APPDEV      LOGICAL_READS_PER_CALL      1000
APPDEV      IDLE_TIME                   30
APPDEV      CONNECT_TIME                UNLIMITED
APPDEV      PRIVATE_SGA                 204800
APPDEV      FAILED_LOGIN_ATTEMPTS       3
APPDEV      PASSWORD_LIFE_TIME          30
APPDEV      PASSWORD_REUSE_TIME         UNLIMITED
APPDEV      PASSWORD_REUSE_MAX          UNLIMITED
APPDEV      PASSWORD_VERIFY_FUNCTION    DEFAULT
APPDEV      PASSWORD_LOCK_TIME          1
APPDEV      PASSWORD_GRACE_TIME         5
```

Chapter Summary

This chapter explained the security features of Oracle8i that you can use to limit and monitor access to a database.

- Only a registered database user can access a database once Oracle authenticates a connection request. You create and manage users with the SQL commands CREATE USER and ALTER USER, respectively.

- Once connected to a database, a user can perform only those operations that the user is privileged to execute. You can grant users individual system and object privileges or use roles to group related sets of privileges and more easily manage user privileges. You create roles using the SQL command CREATE ROLE and then grant and revoke privileges to users or roles using the SQL commands GRANT and REVOKE, respectively.

- Resource limit profiles let you limit a user's access to system resources, such as CPU time, disk I/Os, and sessions. You create profiles using the SQL command CREATE PROFILE, and then assign each user to a profile with the SQL commands CREATE USER or ALTER USER.

CHAPTER
10

Managing Database
Space

atabases store information in an organized manner. To store data, an Oracle database uses *storage structures.* An Oracle database has both logical and physical data storage structures that relate to one another.

■ A *logical storage structure* is a conceptual organization of data, such as a database or a table.

■ A *physical storage structure* is a tangible unit of data storage, such as a file or a data block.

In this chapter, you'll learn about the logical and physical storage structures in an Oracle database, including:

■ Tablespaces

■ Data files

■ Control files

■ Data, index, temporary, and rollback segments

■ Extents

■ Data blocks

■ Data partitioning for tables and indexes

Chapter Prerequisites

To practice the hands-on exercises in this chapter, login to your Linux computer using the oracle account. Next, start SQL*Plus and run the following command script

location/8istarterkit/SQL/chap10.sql

where *location* is the file directory where you expanded the support archive that accompanies this book. For example, after starting SQL*Plus and connecting as SCOTT, you can run this chapter's SQL command script using the SQL*Plus command @, as in the following example (assuming that your chap10.sql file is in /tmp/8istarterkit/SQL).

SQL> @/tmp/8istarterkit/SQL/chap10.sql;

Once the script completes successfully, leave the current SQL*Plus session open and use it to perform this chapter's exercises in the order in which they appear.

CAUTION
Carefully read the Warnings screen when running the command script for this chapter. The script drops the PHOTOS tablespace created by a practice exercise later in this chapter. If you are using this script with a database that contains real data in a tablespace named PHOTOS, open and edit the script so that the DROP TABLESPACE command in the script does not conflict with a real tablespace in your database.

Tablespaces and Data Files

A *tablespace* is a logical organization of data within an Oracle database that corresponds to one or more physical *data files* on disk. Figure 10-1 illustrates the relationship between a tablespace and its data files.

When you create a new database object, such as a table or an index, Oracle stores the database object within the tablespace of your choice; when you do not

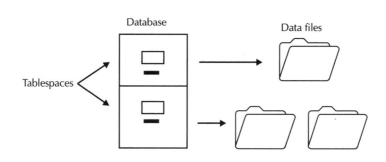

FIGURE 10-1. *Each tablespace in an Oracle database physically stores its data in one or more associated data files*

indicate a specific tablespace for a new database object, Oracle stores the object in your account's default tablespace. See Chapter 9 for more information about setting the default tablespace for a user account.

The physical storage of database objects within a tablespace maps directly to the underlying data files of the tablespace. Figure 10-2 demonstrates how Oracle might store various tables in different tablespaces.

Figure 10-2 shows how Oracle can store data for database objects within tablespaces that have only one data file compared to tablespaces that have multiple data files.

- When a tablespace has only one data file, the tablespace stores the data of all associated objects within the one file.

- When a tablespace has multiple data files, Oracle can store the data for an object within any file of the tablespace. In fact, Oracle might distribute the data of a single object across multiple data files of a tablespace.

The SYSTEM Tablespace

Every Oracle database has at least one tablespace, the *SYSTEM tablespace*. When you create a new Oracle database, you must indicate the names, sizes, and other characteristics of the data files that make up the physical storage for the SYSTEM tablespace.

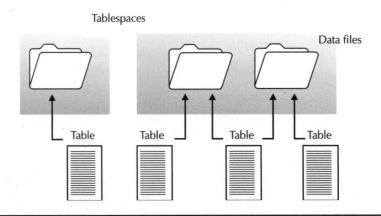

FIGURE 10-2. *Oracle stores objects in a tablespace in one or more data files that comprise the tablespace*

Oracle uses the SYSTEM tablespace for several purposes:

■ Oracle stores a database's data dictionary in the SYSTEM tablespace. As Chapter 7 states, a database's data dictionary is a set of internal system tables that stores information about the database itself. A database's data dictionary also includes other objects that Oracle uses for internal system processing.

■ The SYSTEM tablespace of a database stores the source and compiled code for all PL/SQL programs, such as stored procedures and functions, packages, database triggers, and object type methods. Databases that use PL/SQL extensively should have a sufficiently large SYSTEM tablespace.

■ Database objects such as views, object type specifications, synonyms, and sequences are simple definitions that do not store any data. Oracle stores such object definitions in the data dictionary, which is in the SYSTEM tablespace.

Other Tablespaces

Although they are not required, an Oracle database typically has multiple tablespaces that logically and physically organize the storage of data within the database. Most Oracle databases have different tablespaces to separate storage in the following ways:

■ To separate application data from the internal data dictionary information in the SYSTEM tablespace

■ To separate an application's table data from index data

■ To separate the system's transaction rollback data from other types of data

■ To separate temporary data used during internal system processing from permanently stored data

For example, suppose you are planning to build an Oracle database to support an accounting and a manufacturing application, and each application uses a different set of database tables. One way to organize the database is to create multiple tablespaces that separate the storage of each application's tables and indexes. Figure 10-3 demonstrates this configuration, while also providing distinct tablespaces for the system's temporary and rollback data.

By using multiple tablespaces for different sets of application data, you can manage the data for each application independently. For example, you can back up an active application's data frequently and a less active application's data less frequently.

Database

SYSTEM Tablespace
TEMP Tablespace
ROLLBACK Tablespace
ACCOUNTING Tablespace
ACCOUNTING_INDEX Tablespace
MANUFACTURING Tablespace
MANUFACTURING_INDEX Tablespace

FIGURE 10-3. *Using multiple tablespaces to logically and physically separate the storage of different sets of database information*

NOTE
Your starter database should have the following tablespaces: SYSTEM, TOOLS, USERS, RBS, TEMP, INDX, and DRSYS. Exercise 10.5, later in this chapter, teaches you how to display the names and other information about the tablespaces in your database.

Online and Offline Tablespaces

Oracle lets you control the availability of data in a database on a tablespace-by-tablespace basis. That is, a tablespace can either be online or offline.

- The data in an *online tablespace* is available to applications and databases. Typically, a tablespace remains online so that users can access the information within it.

- The data in an *offline tablespace* is not available to database users, even when the database is available. An administrator might take a tablespace offline to prevent access to an application's data because the tablespace is experiencing a problem, or because the tablespace contains historical data that is typically not required by anyone.

NOTE
A database's SYSTEM tablespace must always remain online because information in the data dictionary must be available during normal operation. If you try to take the SYSTEM tablespace offline, Oracle returns an error.

Permanent and Temporary Tablespaces

Most tablespaces in an Oracle database are permanent tablespaces. A *permanent tablespace* stores information that must persist across individual SQL requests and transactions. For example, a permanent tablespace is necessary to store table, index, or transaction rollback information.

Oracle also lets you create temporary tablespaces in a database. A *temporary tablespace* is a large temporary work space that transactions can use to process complicated SQL operations, such as sorted queries, join queries, and index builds. Rather than inefficiently creating and dropping many small temporary space allocations in a permanent tablespace, Oracle can quickly provide temporary work areas for SQL statements by managing entries in a temporary tablespace's sort segment table.

NOTE
To learn more about temporary tablespaces, see the section "Temporary Segments and Temporary Tablespaces" later in this chapter.

When you create a new tablespace, you can create it as either permanent or temporary. You can always change a current tablespace's type to permanent or temporary, if necessary. If you decide to use a temporary tablespace, Oracle will not use the tablespace until you target the tablespace for temporary operations in one or more users' account settings. See Chapter 9 for more information about specifying a user account's temporary tablespace setting.

Dictionary-Managed and Locally Managed Tablespaces

By default, Oracle uses a database's data dictionary to manage the allocation and reclamation of space within a tablespace. To boost the performance of an active tablespace that frequently allocates and deallocates space for database objects, you can switch a *dictionary-managed tablespace* to a locally managed tablespace. With a *locally managed tablespace*, Oracle uses a bitmap that is part of the tablespace to manage the allocation and reclamation of tablespace space with less overhead than is required by a dictionary-managed tablespace.

Read-Only and Read-Write Tablespaces

When you create a new tablespace, it is always a *read-write tablespace*. That is, you can create, alter, and drop database objects within the tablespace, and applications can query, add, modify, and delete information from the database objects within the tablespace. When applications must actively change data in a tablespace, the tablespace must operate as a read-write tablespace.

In some cases, a tablespace stores historical data that never changes. When a tablespace's data never changes, you can make the tablespace a *read-only tablespace*. Making a static tablespace read-only can protect it from inappropriate data modifications. Making a tablespace read-only can also save time when performing database backups. That's because it's not necessary to back up a read-only tablespace when you back up the other tablespaces of the database.

After you create a new tablespace and add data to it, you can alter the tablespace and make it a read-only tablespace. If necessary, you can always switch a tablespace back to read-write mode so that applications can update the objects within the tablespace.

A Tablespace's Data Files

A data file is a physical storage file on disk for a tablespace in an Oracle database. A tablespace can store all of its data in just a single data file, or a tablespace can have multiple data files to collectively store its data.

When you create a tablespace, you can create one or more data files for the new tablespace. In general, you create a tablespace with multiple data files on different disks to distribute the disk I/O associated with accessing a tablespace's data. This technique is particularly useful when you explicitly partition database data. For more information about data partitioning, see the "Partitioning Large Tables and Indexes" section, later in this chapter.

NOTE
An Oracle database has an upper limit to the number of data files that it can have, and this limit is set during database creation. When planning a database and its tablespaces, make sure that you do not use too many data files to meet the storage requirements for the system, or else you might reach the upper limit for the number of data files.

After you create a tablespace, you can always add more data files to the tablespace to increase its storage capacity. For example, when a tablespace uses data files that do not grow in size, you can allocate additional storage space for the tablespace by creating one or more data files for the tablespace. The following sections provide more information about data file space usage and sizing options.

Use of Data File Space

When you create a new data file for a tablespace, Oracle preallocates the amount of disk space that you specify for the data file. After you create a new data file, it is like an empty data bucket—the file contains no data, but it is a receptacle that is ready to store database information.

Any time you create a new data storage object, such as a table or index in a tablespace, Oracle designates a certain amount of space from the tablespace's data files to the new object. Allocating data file space to a new database object reduces the remaining amount of available free space in the data file. As applications insert and update data in a data storage object, the preallocated space for the object can eventually become full.

If data consumes all of a data storage object's available storage space, Oracle can automatically allocate additional space from the tablespace's data files for the object. Allocating more space to a data storage object to extend the storage capacity of the object further reduces the amount of available free space in the tablespace's data files.

Data File Sizes

In general, the size of a data file remains constant. As objects in a tablespace allocate space from the corresponding data files, the tablespace can become full if all of the data files in the tablespace become full. When applications attempt to insert or update data within a tablespace that's full, Oracle returns errors until more storage space becomes available for the tablespace. To increase the storage capacity of a full tablespace, you have a few different options:

- You can add one or more new data files to the tablespace.

- You can manually resize one or more of the existing data files in the tablespace.

- You can configure one or more of the data files in the tablespace to automatically extend when the tablespace becomes full and requires more space.

Each option has certain advantages and disadvantages. For example, the first two options are fine if you are a watchful administrator who frequently monitors the storage capacity of your database's data files. When you notice that a tablespace is running low on free space, you can add more files to the tablespace or increase the size of one of the tablespace's data files. In contrast, the third option allows a tablespace's storage capacity to grow automatically, without manual assistance. If you choose to manually or automatically extend the storage allocation for a data file, do so conservatively—fragmented allocations of disk space across a disk drive can decrease database performance.

Data File Corruption

Unfortunately, operating system files are always vulnerable to disk and I/O problems. Such problems can corrupt the integrity of a file. At the expense of system performance, you can configure Oracle to detect and log block-level data file corruption.

Online and Offline Data Files

Oracle controls the availability of individual data files of a tablespace. A data file can either be *online* (available) or *offline* (not available). Under normal circumstances, a data file is online. When Oracle attempts to read or write a data file and cannot do so because some type of problem prevents this from happening, Oracle automatically takes the data file offline. The encompassing tablespace remains online, because other data files of the tablespace might still be available. You can take a data file offline manually when a known problem exists. Once the problem is fixed (for example, after a data file recovery), you can bring an offline data file back online manually.

NOTE
The data files of a database's SYSTEM tablespace must always remain online because the data dictionary must always be available during system operation. If Oracle experiences a problem reading or writing a data file in the database's SYSTEM tablespace, the system will not operate correctly until you fix the problem.

Creating and Managing Tablespaces and Data Files

Now that you have a good understanding of tablespaces and data files, the following practice exercises will teach you how to create and manage tablespaces and their data files.

EXERCISE 10.1: Creating a Tablespace

You create a tablespace in an Oracle database using the SQL command *CREATE TABLESPACE*. For the purposes of this exercise, the abbreviated syntax of the CREATE TABLESPACE command is as follows:

```
CREATE TABLESPACE tablespace
  DATAFILE
    'filename' [SIZE integer [K|M]] [REUSE]
      [ AUTOEXTEND
        { OFF
        | ON
          [NEXT integer [K|M]]
          [MAXSIZE {UNLIMITED|integer [K|M]}] } ]
    [, ... other data file specifications ... ]
  [ONLINE|OFFLINE]
  [PERMANENT|TEMPORARY]
```

NOTE
You must have the CREATE TABLESPACE system privilege to create a tablespace.

Notice that when you create a tablespace, you can specify one or more data file specifications for the tablespace, create the tablespace as a permanent or temporary tablespace, and leave the new tablespace in an online or offline state. Assuming that you installed Oracle as instructed in Chapter 2, enter the following statement to create a new tablespace called PHOTOS.

```
CREATE TABLESPACE photos
  DATAFILE
   '/usr/oracle/oradata/oralin/photos1.dbf' SIZE 100K REUSE
     AUTOEXTEND ON NEXT 100K MAXSIZE 1M,
   '/usr/oracle/oradata/oralin/photos2.dbf' SIZE 100K REUSE
  ONLINE
  PERMANENT;
```

NOTE

If you installed Oracle so that the starter database's data files reside in a different directory, modify the file specifications in the previous exercise appropriately.

The previous CREATE TABLESPACE statement creates a new tablespace called PHOTOS with two data files.

- The photos1.dbf file is initially 100K in size, and can automatically extend itself in 100K increments up to 1MB if the tablespace becomes full and an object requests more space in the tablespace.

- The photos2.dbf file is 100K in size and cannot increase in size unless you manually resize the file or enable automatic extension for the file.

- The REUSE option of a data file specification instructs Oracle to reuse the file, if it exists. The example includes this option in each data file specification so that you can repeat this exercise each time you review the chapter.

EXERCISE 10.2: Modifying the Storage Properties of a Data File

You can alter the properties of a data file at any time using the *DATAFILE* clause of the SQL command *ALTER DATABASE*. For the purposes of this exercise, the syntax of this clause in the ALTER DATABASE command is as follows:

```
ALTER DATABASE
  DATAFILE 'filename'
  { RESIZE integer [K|M]
  | AUTOEXTEND
```

```
{ OFF
| ON [NEXT integer [K|M]] [MAXSIZE {UNLIMITED|integer[K|M] } ] } }
```

NOTE
*You must have the ALTER DATABASE system
privilege to use the ALTER DATABASE command.*

For example, enter the following ALTER DATABASE statement to adjust the
automatic extension properties of the photos1.dbf data file.

```
ALTER DATABASE
    DATAFILE '/usr/oracle/oradata/oralin/photos1.dbf'
        AUTOEXTEND ON NEXT 250K MAXSIZE UNLIMITED;
```

Now enter the following ALTER DATABASE statement to manually resize the
photos2.dbf data file.

```
ALTER DATABASE
    DATAFILE '/usr/oracle/oradata/oralin/photos2.dbf' RESIZE 250K;
```

EXERCISE 10.3: Making a Temporary Tablespace

You can switch a permanent tablespace to a temporary tablespace, or vice versa,
using the *PERMANENT* and *TEMPORARY* options of the SQL command *ALTER
TABLESPACE.*

```
ALTER TABLESPACE tablespace
    [PERMANENT|TEMPORARY]
```

NOTE
*You can switch a tablespace from permanent to
temporary only if the tablespace does not contain
any permanent database objects (such as tables
and indexes).*

In your starter database, there is a tablespace named TEMP. By default, this
tablespace is set as a permanent tablespace rather than a temporary tablespace. In
this exercise, enter the following statement to switch the TEMP tablespace to a
temporary tablespace.

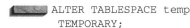
```
ALTER TABLESPACE temp
    TEMPORARY;
```

TIP
To improve performance, it would also be a good idea to set the temporary tablespace setting for all user accounts to the TEMP tablespace. See Chapter 9 for more information about altering the temporary tablespace setting for a user account using the SQL command ALTER USER.

EXERCISE 10.4: Coalescing Free Space in a Tablespace's Data Files

As you create data storage objects in a tablespace and these objects extend their storage capacity, the free space areas in the tablespace's data files can become fragmented and small. Oracle might not be able to complete subsequent free space allocations for new or existing objects if the free space areas on disk are not large enough. To fix this problem, Oracle can coalesce many small adjacent free space areas into fewer, large free space areas. Figure 10-4 illustrates the concept of coalescing free space.

Oracle periodically coalesces a tablespace's free space automatically as an internal system operation. However, you can coalesce a tablespace manually when you know that this operation is necessary, using the *COALESCE* option of the SQL

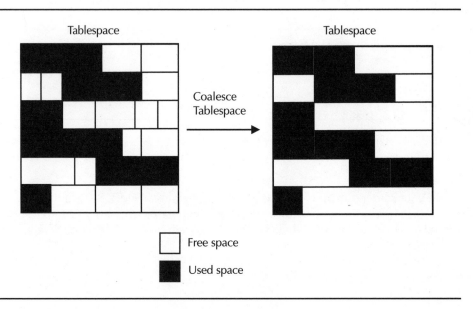

FIGURE 10-4. *Coalescing free space in a tablespace*

command *ALTER TABLESPACE*. For example, enter the following statement to coalesce the RBS tablespace's free space.

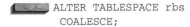

```
ALTER TABLESPACE rbs
  COALESCE;
```

EXERCISE 10.5: Displaying Properties for All Tablespaces

You can display information about your database's tablespaces by querying the DBA_TABLESPACES data dictionary view. For example, enter the following query to display the name, availability status, and type for each tablespace in your database.

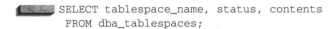

```
SELECT tablespace_name, status, contents
  FROM dba_tablespaces;
```

The result set should be similar to the following:

```
TABLESPACE_NAME      STATUS    CONTENTS
-------------------- --------- ---------
SYSTEM               ONLINE    PERMANENT
TOOLS                ONLINE    PERMANENT
RBS                  ONLINE    PERMANENT
TEMP                 ONLINE    TEMPORARY
USERS                ONLINE    PERMANENT
INDX                 ONLINE    PERMANENT
DRSYS                ONLINE    PERMANENT
PHOTOS               ONLINE    PERMANENT

8 rows selected.
```

NOTE
The STATUS field in the DBA_TABLESPACES view displays either ONLINE or OFFLINE for all read-write tablespaces, and READ ONLY for read-only tablespaces.

EXERCISE 10.6: Displaying Information about Data Files

You can display information about a database's data files by querying the DBA_DATA_FILES data dictionary view. For example, enter the following query to display the name, associated tablespace, size (in bytes), and automatic extension capability of each data file in the database.

```
SELECT file_name, tablespace_name, bytes, autoextensible AS auto
  FROM dba_data_files
  ORDER BY tablespace_name, bytes;
```

Assuming that you installed Oracle as instructed in Chapter 2, the following should be similar to your result set:

```
FILE_NAME                                TABLESPACE_NAME       BYTES AUTO
---------------------------------------- --------------- --------- ----
/usr/oracle/oradata/oralin/drsys01.dbf   DRSYS            20971520 YES
/usr/oracle/oradata/oralin/indx01.dbf    INDX             20971520 YES
/usr/oracle/oradata/oralin/photos1.dbf   PHOTOS             106496 YES
/usr/oracle/oradata/oralin/photos2.dbf   PHOTOS             262144 NO
/usr/oracle/oradata/oralin/rbs01.dbf     RBS              73400320 YES
/usr/oracle/oradata/oralin/system01.dbf  SYSTEM          246022144 YES
/usr/oracle/oradata/oralin/temp01.dbf    TEMP             20971520 YES
/usr/oracle/oradata/oralin/tools01.dbf   TOOLS            10485760 YES
/usr/oracle/oradata/oralin/users01.dbf   USERS            20971520 YES

9 rows selected.
```

EXERCISE 10.7: Controlling Tablespace Availability

You can control the access to a tablespace using the *ONLINE* and *OFFLINE* options of the SQL command *ALTER TABLESPACE*.

```
ALTER TABLESPACE tablespace
  {ONLINE|OFFLINE [NORMAL|TEMPORARY|IMMEDIATE|FOR RECOVER]}
```

When taking an online tablespace offline, you can indicate several options:

■ The default NORMAL option indicates that you want to take the target tablespace offline under normal conditions. You can use the NORMAL option only if all data files of the tablespace are currently online and available without any I/O problems.

■ The TEMPORARY option should be your first choice if you want to take a tablespace offline under abnormal conditions. For example, you might use the TEMPORARY option when one or more data files of the tablespace are offline due to I/O problems. In this case, a recovery operation will be necessary before you can bring the tablespace online again.

■ The IMMEDIATE option should be your last resort when taking a tablespace offline under abnormal conditions.

■ The FOR RECOVER option explicitly indicates that not all data files in the tablespace are available and that you understand that a recovery operation will be necessary to bring the tablespace online. Do not use this option under normal circumstances.

For example, enter the following query, which targets a table stored in the USERS tablespace.

```
SELECT id, description FROM parts;
```

Because the PARTS table is stored in the USERS tablespace, which is online at the moment, the result set for the query should be as follows:

```
       ID DESCRIPTION
--------- ---------------
        1 Fax Machine
        2 Copy Machine
        3 Laptop PC
        4 Desktop PC
        5 Scanner
```

Next, enter the following ALTER TABLESPACE statement to take the USERS tablespace offline.

```
ALTER TABLESPACE users
  OFFLINE NORMAL;
```

Now, reenter the previous query, shown here:

```
SELECT id, description FROM parts;
```

You should see results similar to the following:

```
ERROR at line 1:
ORA-00376: file 5 cannot be read at this time
ORA-01110: data file 5: '/usr/oracle/oradata/oralin/users01.dbf'
```

This error is an indication that the tablespace (or the tablespace's data files) that stores the PARTS table is offline. To bring the USERS tablespace back online, enter the following statement:

```
ALTER TABLESPACE users
  ONLINE;
```

Now, reenter the previous query:

```
SELECT id, description FROM parts;
```

You should again see the following results:

```
       ID DESCRIPTION
--------- ---------------
        1 Fax Machine
        2 Copy Machine
        3 Laptop PC
        4 Desktop PC
        5 Scanner
```

Control Files

Every Oracle database has a *control file*. A database's control file contains information about the physical structure of the database. For example, a database's control file includes the name of the database, as well as the names and locations of all files associated with the database. Oracle also uses a database's control file to keep track of internal system information to log the current physical state of the system, including information about tablespaces, data files, and system backups. A database's control file also logs information about database backups that you make with the Recovery Manager utility (see Chapter 11).

When you create a new database, Oracle creates the database's control file. Subsequently, Oracle updates the database's control file automatically with internal information that it needs to record. Additionally, every time you change a physical attribute of a database, Oracle updates the information in the database's control file. For example, when you create a new tablespace with one or more data files, or add a data file to an existing tablespace, Oracle updates the database's control file to log information about the new data files.

Mirrored Control Files

An Oracle database cannot function properly without its control file. To ensure database availability in the event of an isolated disk failure, Oracle lets you *mirror* a database's control file to multiple locations. When you mirror a database's control file to multiple locations, Oracle updates every copy of the control file at the same time. If one copy of the control file should become inaccessible due to a disk failure, other copies of the control file remain available and permit database processing to continue without interruption.

EXERCISE 10.8: Displaying Your Database's Control File Copies

You can display the names of all control file copies for your database by entering the following query, which targets the V$PARAMETER data dictionary view.

```
SELECT name, value FROM v$parameter
 WHERE name = 'control_files';
```

Assuming that you installed Oracle as instructed in Chapter 2, the following should be your result set:

```
NAME            VALUE
------------    -----------------------------------------
control_files /usr/oracle/oradata/oralin/control01.ctl,
```

```
/usr/oracle/oradata/oralin/control02.ctl,
/usr/oracle/oradata/oralin/control03.ctl
```

Notice that the default configuration for the starter database on Oracle8i for Linux is to create three copies of the control file in the same location. Exercise 11.8 in the next chapter teaches you how to mirror the database's control file to different locations.

Segments, Extents, and Data Blocks

Just as Oracle preallocates data files to serve as the physical storage for tablespaces in a database, Oracle preallocates segments of data blocks as the physical storage for database objects such as tables, indexes, data clusters, and other data storage objects. Oracle allocates groups of contiguous *data blocks* for a database object as *extents*. A *segment* is the collection of all the extents dedicated to a database object. Figure 10-5 demonstrates the relationship between a table and its data segment, extents, and data blocks.

When you create a new data storage object, such as a table or an index, you can indicate the tablespace in which the corresponding segment should be created. Oracle then allocates data blocks from one or more of the data files in use by the target tablespace.

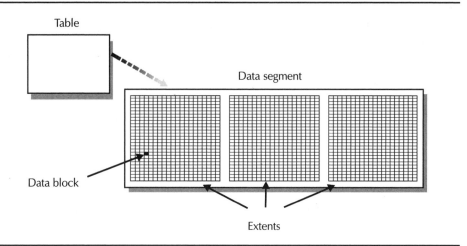

FIGURE 10-5.   *Dedicating physical data storage for a table as extents (groups of contiguous data blocks) in a table's data segment*

Types of Segments in an Oracle Database

An Oracle database can contain many different types of segments, including data segments, index segments, LOB segments, overflow segments, rollback segments, and temporary segments.

- A table stores its data in a *data segment*. If the table has multiple partitions, the table stores its data in a corresponding number of data segments. Additionally, a data cluster stores the data of all tables in the cluster within the cluster's data segment.

- An index stores its data in an *index segment*. If the index has multiple partitions, the index stores its data in a corresponding number of index segments.

- If a table has a column that uses a large object (LOB) datatype, such as CLOB, BLOB, or NCLOB, the table can store corresponding LOB values in a *LOB segment* that is separate from the data segment that holds other field values in the table.

- An index-organized table is a special type of table that stores the rows of a table within an index segment. An index-organized table can also have an *overflow segment* to store rows that do not fit into the original index segment. See Chapter 12 for more information about index-organized tables.

- A *rollback segment* is a special type of segment that Oracle uses to store transaction rollback information. When a user rolls back a transaction, Oracle applies information in a rollback segment to "undo" the transaction's operations.

- Oracle creates and uses a *temporary segment* when processing certain types of SQL statements. A temporary segment is a temporary work space on disk that Oracle can use to store intermediate data during SQL statement processing.

Data Blocks

A *data block* is the unit of disk access for an Oracle database. When you work with a database, Oracle stores and retrieves data on disk using data blocks. For example, when you query a table, Oracle reads into the server's memory all of the data blocks that contain rows in the query's result set.

When you create a database, you can specify the block size that the database will use. A database's block size must be equal to or a multiple of the server's operating system block size. For example, if the server's operating system block size is 512 bytes, the database block size on such a server could be 512 bytes, 1024 bytes, 2048 bytes, and so on.

Data Block Allocation

When you create a new data storage object, such as a table, index, or rollback segment, Oracle allocates one or more extents for the object's segment. An extent is a set of contiguous data blocks in a data file of the tablespace that stores the object's segment. If all data blocks in a segment's existing extents are full, Oracle allocates a new extent (set of blocks) for the segment the next time a transaction requests the storage of some new data.

Data Block Availability, Free Lists, and Free List Groups

Every data and index segment in an Oracle database has one or more data block free lists. A *free list* is a catalog of data blocks that are available to hold new data for the corresponding table, cluster, or index. Figure 10-6 shows how data blocks can go on and off a table's free lists as transactions insert, update, and delete information from a table.

In Figure 10-6, you can see how a data block might go on and off a table's free list. When a transaction wants to insert a new row into the table, all data blocks on the free list are candidates for receiving the data for the new row. As transactions

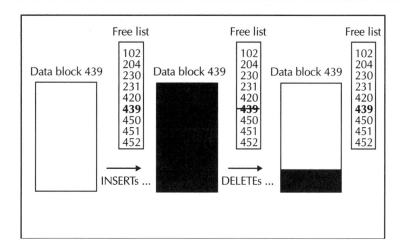

FIGURE 10-6. *A data block going on and off an object's free list, depending on the space available in the block*

insert more and more rows into the table, data blocks eventually become full (or nearly full), such that Oracle removes them from the table's free list. A block can return to the table's free list after a transaction deletes rows from the table, freeing up space in the block.

NOTE
See Exercise 10.13, later in this chapter, which explains how to control when Oracle puts data blocks on a segment's free lists.

When you create a table, cluster, or index, you can indicate the number of free list groups to create for the corresponding segment. A *free list group* is a group of one or more data block free lists for a data storage object's segment. By default, Oracle creates one free list group with one free list per data or index segment. If you are using Oracle with the Parallel Server option, it's possible to reduce contention among servers for free list lookups and improve system performance by creating multiple free list groups with multiple free lists.

Row Chaining and Data Block Size

When you insert a new row into a table, Oracle puts the new row into a data block that's on the table's free list. Optimally, Oracle puts all of a row's data into one data block, assuming that the row can fit within the space of one data block. This way, when you request a row in a table, Oracle has to read only one data block from disk into memory to retrieve all of a row's data.

If a row's length is greater than the data block size, Oracle *chains* the row among two or more data blocks. Figure 10-7 illustrates row chaining.

Row chaining, while unavoidable in this situation, is not desirable. That's because Oracle must read multiple data blocks from disk into memory to access a row's data. More disk I/Os always slows system performance. Therefore, row chaining should be avoided if at all possible.

Typically, the default block size for an installation of Oracle is the optimal setting for most databases. However, databases with certain characteristics can benefit from block sizes that are larger than the default. For example, when many tables in a database will have rows that exceed the default block size, you can reduce the amount of row chaining in the database by creating the database with a larger block size.

Oracle can also create a row chain when you update a row in a table or an index. This type of row chaining happens when both of the following occur:

■ You update the row so that it is longer than the original row, and

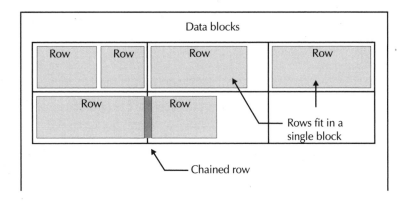

FIGURE 10-7. *Storing pieces of a row in a chain that spans multiple data blocks*

■ The data block that holds the row does not have enough empty space to accommodate the update

When you expect that updates to the rows in a data or index segment will increase row sizes, you can prevent row chaining by reserving extra data block space for updates. See Exercise 10.13, later in this chapter, which explains how to control space usage within data blocks.

Transaction Entries
When a transaction updates a data block of an object, Oracle allocates a transaction entry in the data block. A *transaction entry* is a small amount of space in the header of a data block that Oracle uses to hold internal processing information until the transaction commits or rolls back. Later in this chapter, you'll learn how to fine-tune the way Oracle allocates transaction entries within the data blocks of a table, data cluster, or index.

Managing Storage Settings for Tables and Indexes
With great detail, Oracle lets you control the storage characteristics for all types of segments in a database. Now that you have a general understanding of segments, extents, and data blocks, the practice exercises in this section explain some of the most common tasks that you should consider when creating the tables (data segments) and indexes (index segments) in your database.

NOTE
*Subsequent sections of this chapter discuss
specialized types of segments in an Oracle database,
including rollback segments, LOB segments, and
temporary segments.*

EXERCISE 10.9: Displaying the Segments in Your Schema

You can display information about all of the segments in a database by querying
the DBA_SEGMENTS data dictionary view. For example, enter the following
query to display selected information about the segments in your current schema,
PRACTICE10.

```
SELECT segment_name, segment_type, tablespace_name, extents, blocks
 FROM dba_segments
 WHERE owner = 'PRACTICE10';
```

The result set is as follows:

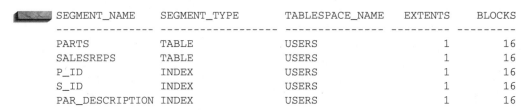

```
SEGMENT_NAME     SEGMENT_TYPE        TABLESPACE_NAME   EXTENTS    BLOCKS
---------------  ------------------  ----------------  ---------  ---------
PARTS            TABLE               USERS                     1         16
SALESREPS        TABLE               USERS                     1         16
P_ID             INDEX               USERS                     1         16
S_ID             INDEX               USERS                     1         16
PAR_DESCRIPTION  INDEX               USERS                     1         16
```

Notice in the result set that there are several segments that correspond to the
tables and indexes in your schema, and that each individual segment consists of
a single extent.

NOTE
*To display information about the segments in
your current schema, you could also query the
USER_SEGMENTS data dictionary view.*

EXERCISE 10.10: Creating a Table in a Specific Tablespace

When you create a new data storage object, such as a table, data cluster, or index,
you can use the *TABLESPACE* parameter of the corresponding CREATE command to
explicitly indicate which tablespace the object's segment should be created within.
Provided that you have the necessary quota in the tablespace and the necessary
privileges to create the object, Oracle completes the request. If you omit a tablespace
specification when creating a new table, data cluster, or index, Oracle creates the
object's segment in your user account's default tablespace.

For example, enter the following CREATE TABLE statement. Use the TABLESPACE parameter to create the ITEMS table in the USERS tablespace.

```
CREATE TABLE items (
  o_id INTEGER,
  id INTEGER,
  p_id INTEGER NOT NULL,
  quantity INTEGER DEFAULT 1 NOT NULL
)
TABLESPACE users;
```

EXERCISE 10.11: Controlling the Number and Size of Extents for a Table

When you create a new table, cluster, or index, you can use the STORAGE clause of the corresponding CREATE command to control several different storage settings related to the allocation of extents for the object's segment. For the purposes of this introductory exercise, an abbreviated form of the *STORAGE* clause for most CREATE commands in SQL is as follows:

```
STORAGE (
  [INITIAL integer [K|M]]
  [NEXT integer [K|M]]
  [MINEXTENTS integer]
  [MAXEXTENTS {integer|UNLIMITED}]
  [PCTINCREASE integer]
```

- Use the *MINEXTENTS* parameter of the STORAGE clause to specify the number of extents to allocate when creating the segment. Oracle must allocate at least one extent when creating a new segment for a table, cluster, or index.

- Use the *MAXEXTENTS* parameter of the STORAGE clause to limit the maximum number of extents that Oracle can ever allocate for the segment.

- You can control the size of the segment's extents. Use the *INITIAL* parameter of the STORAGE clause to set the size of the segment's initial extent. Use the *NEXT* parameter to control the size of subsequent extents. And use the *PCTINCREASE* parameter to specify a growth factor to apply before allocating subsequent extents for the segment.

For example, suppose you know that your order-entry application will need to process a lot of orders every day. In this case, it would be wise to create the ITEMS table with enough storage space to accommodate the expected business. In view of this, let's drop the ITEMS table created in Exercise 10.10 and then recreate it, this time specifying specific storage parameters for the extents of the new table.

```
DROP TABLE items;

CREATE TABLE items (
 o_id INTEGER,
 id INTEGER,
 p_id INTEGER NOT NULL,
 quantity INTEGER DEFAULT 1 NOT NULL
)
 TABLESPACE users
 STORAGE (
  INITIAL 100K
  NEXT 100K
  MINEXTENTS 1
  MAXEXTENTS 10
  PCTINCREASE 50
 );
```

When Oracle creates the data segment for the ITEMS table, the server allocates one initial extent, 100K in size, for the segment. When this initial extent fills, Oracle allocates the next extent, 100K in size, and updates the segment's next extent size to 150K—that is, the current setting of NEXT (100K) increased by PCTINCREASE (50 percent). When a third extent is necessary, Oracle allocates the next extent, 150K in size, and updates the segment's NEXT storage parameter to 225K (that is, 150K increased by 50 percent). Extent allocation for the data segment continues in this manner until Oracle allocates the tenth extent, which is the limit for the number of extents for the segment. Of course, you can alter an object's storage settings, for example, to increase the maximum number of extents for the object.

NOTE
You can also set a segment's MAXEXTENTS storage parameter to UNLIMITED so that the segment can allocate an unlimited number of extents within the encompassing tablespace.

EXERCISE 10.12: Altering Extent Settings for a Table
You can alter many extent settings for a table, cluster, or index using the *STORAGE* clause of the corresponding ALTER command, as follows:

```
STORAGE (
 [NEXT integer [K|M]]
 [MAXEXTENTS {integer|UNLIMITED}]
 [PCTINCREASE integer]
```

Notice that when you alter extent settings for a segment, it does not make sense to alter the segment's INITIAL or MINEXTENTS storage parameters, because the segment already exists. Furthermore, you cannot specify the TABLESPACE parameter in an ALTER command to "move" the segment from its current tablespace to another—if you want to move a data or index segment to another tablespace, you must drop and recreate the associated table, cluster, or index.

In this practice exercise, assume that you have incorrectly set the NEXT and PCTINCREASE storage parameters for the new ITEMS table. Enter the following ALTER TABLE statement to adjust these parameters.

```
ALTER TABLE items
  STORAGE (
  NEXT 200K
  MAXEXTENTS UNLIMITED
  PCTINCREASE 0
  );
```

EXERCISE 10.13: Setting a Table's Data Block Settings

This practice exercise teaches you how to control the use of space within the data blocks of the table, index, or cluster using the PCTUSED, PCTFREE, INITRANS, MAXTRANS, FREELIST GROUPS, and FREELISTS parameters of corresponding CREATE commands.

```
[PCTUSED integer] [PCTFREE integer]
[INITRANS integer] [MAXTRANS integer]
[STORAGE (
   ... other storage parameters ...
   [FREELIST GROUPS integer] [FREELISTS integer]  )]
```

Use the PCTFREE and PCTUSED parameters to control when data blocks go on and off a table's, index's, or cluster's free lists. You can set a maximum threshold using the *PCTFREE* parameter to control how much data block space to reserve for future updates to rows. When a data block becomes PCTFREE full, Oracle removes the block from the corresponding segment's free lists. When you expect that only occasional updates will increase the size of rows, set PCTFREE to a low value (perhaps 5 or 10) so that Oracle fills more space of each data block. However, if you expect frequent updates that will increase the size of rows, set PCTFREE to a high value (perhaps 20 or 30) so that Oracle reserves more block space for the updates to existing rows; otherwise, row chains are likely to occur.

You can set a minimum block threshold using the *PCTUSED* parameter to control when a data block is put back on the corresponding segment's free list. For example, the default PCTUSED for all segments is set to 40 percent. Therefore, when transactions delete rows from a data block so that it becomes only 39 percent full, Oracle puts the block back on the corresponding segment's free lists. When you expect only occasional deletes, set PCTUSED to a high value (perhaps 60) so that data blocks can pop on the free list when the occasional delete happens. However, if you expect frequent deletes, set PCTUSED to a low value (perhaps 40) so that Oracle does not constantly incur the overhead of moving blocks on and off the table's free lists.

NOTE

The sum of the settings for PCTFREE and PCTUSED cannot be greater than 100.

Use the INITRANS and MAXTRANS parameters to tune how Oracle allocates transaction entries within the data blocks of a table, data cluster, or index. The *INITRANS* parameter determines how much data block header space to preallocate for transaction entries. When you expect many concurrent transactions to touch a data block, you can preallocate more space for associated transaction entries and avoid the overhead of dynamically allocating this space when necessary. The *MAXTRANS* parameter limits the number of transactions that can concurrently use a data block. When you expect many transactions to concurrently access a small table (or index), set the table's INITRANS and MAXTRANS parameters to high values (perhaps 5 and 10, respectively) when creating the table. A higher INITRANS setting preallocates more block space for transaction entries, and a higher MAXTRANS parameter allows many transactions to concurrently access the table's data blocks. With large tables, it's less likely that several transactions will access the same data blocks simultaneously. Consequently, the setting for a large table's INITRANS and MAXTRANS parameters can be correspondingly low (perhaps 2 and 5, respectively). With such settings, less space will be reserved for transaction entries and more space in the table's data blocks will be available for data.

Use the FREELIST GROUPS parameter of the STORAGE clause to control the number of free list groups for the segment. Use the FREELISTS parameter to set the number of free lists per group.

To illustrate the use of the PCTUSED, PCTFREE, INITRANS, MAXTRANS, FREELIST GROUPS, and FREELISTS parameters, let's drop and recreate the ITEMS table once more. This time, let's recreate the ITEMS table, setting all possible storage-related parameters, including the storage parameters related to data blocks.

```
DROP TABLE items;

CREATE TABLE items (
```

```
o_id INTEGER,
id INTEGER,
p_id INTEGER NOT NULL,
quantity INTEGER DEFAULT 1 NOT NULL
)
TABLESPACE users
PCTUSED 40 PCTFREE 10
INITRANS 2 MAXTRANS 5
STORAGE (
  INITIAL 100K
  NEXT 200K
  MINEXTENTS 1
  MAXEXTENTS UNLIMITED
  PCTINCREASE 0
  FREELIST GROUPS 1
  FREELISTS 3
 )
;
```

The latest version of the ITEMS table has a single free list group with three data block free lists. The data blocks of the new table save 10 percent of the block for row updates and do not put blocks back on the segment's free lists until the block drops to less than 40 percent used. The data blocks of the new table also preallocate enough space for two transaction entries and allow up to five concurrent transaction entries per block.

EXERCISE 10.14: Setting Defaults for Object Storage

In most cases, storage settings for objects are optional specifications that you can use to control how Oracle stores data for each object. Oracle always has defaults for storage settings. For example, Chapter 9 explains how to set a user's default and temporary tablespaces. When the user creates a new database object and does not explicitly indicate a tablespace for the object, Oracle stores the new object in the user's default tablespace. A user's temporary tablespace is where Oracle allocates temporary work space for the user's SQL statements, whenever necessary.

When you create a new table, data cluster, or index in a tablespace, and choose not to specify extent settings for the new object, the object's segment assumes the default extent storage settings of the tablespace. Using the *DEFAULT STORAGE* clause of the SQL commands CREATE TABLESPACE and ALTER TABLESPACE, you can specify default extent storage settings for a tablespace:

```
DEFAULT STORAGE (
  [INITIAL integer [K|M]]
  [NEXT integer [K|M]]
  [MINEXTENTS integer]
```

```
[MAXEXTENTS {integer|UNLIMITED}]
[PCTINCREASE integer] )
```

For example, enter the following statement to alter the default extent storage settings for the PHOTOS tablespace.

```
ALTER TABLESPACE photos
  DEFAULT STORAGE (
    INITIAL 100K
    NEXT 100K
    MINEXTENTS 3
    MAXEXTENTS 100
    PCTINCREASE 0 );
```

At this point, if you (or another user) create a table, index, data cluster, rollback segment, or temporary segment in the PHOTOS tablespace and do not specify a particular extent storage parameter for the new object, Oracle uses the default extent settings of the encompassing PHOTOS tablespace.

Rollback Segments

Transactions can complete either with a commit or a rollback. Typically, a transaction ends with a *commit*, which permanently records the transaction's changes to the database. A *rollback* undoes all effects of the transaction, as though the transaction never occurred. To provide for transaction rollback, Oracle must keep track of the data that a transaction changes until the transaction commits or rolls back.

Oracle uses a special type of segment called a *rollback segment* (sometimes called an *undo segment*) to record rollback data for a transaction. Should you choose to roll back a transaction, Oracle reads the necessary data from a rollback segment to rebuild the data as it existed before the transaction changed it. Figure 10-8 illustrates how Oracle uses rollback segments to undo the effects of a transaction that is rolled back.

How Oracle Writes to a Rollback Segment

Oracle writes information to rollback segments differently than it does with other types of segments. Figure 10-9 shows how Oracle writes information to the multiple extents in a rollback segment.

As Figure 10-9 shows, a rollback segment is a circle of extents. As transactions write to the *current extent* of a rollback segment and eventually fill it with rollback information, the transactions then *wrap* to the next extent of the segment to continue recording rollback information. If a transaction is so long that it wraps across all extents of a rollback segment and the current extent becomes full, Oracle must allocate an additional extent so that the system does not overwrite earlier rollback information that would be necessary to roll back the long transaction.

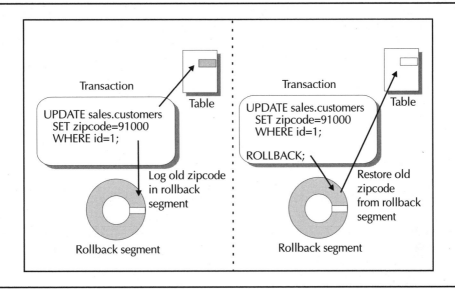

FIGURE 10-8. *Rollback segments keep track of the data that transactions change and facilitate transaction rollback*

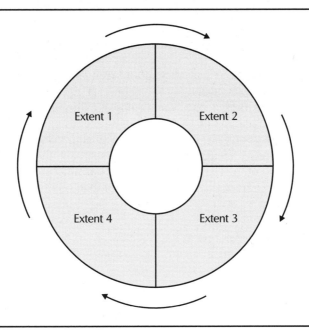

FIGURE 10-9. *Oracle writes rollback information circularly to the extents of a rollback segment*

Oracle can shrink back rollback segments to an optimal number of extents after they grow larger than their original size and once the extra extents are no longer needed. Later in this chapter you'll learn more about specific storage parameters that you can set to control extent allocation and deallocation for rollback segments.

The SYSTEM Rollback Segment

Every Oracle database has at least one rollback segment—the SYSTEM rollback segment. When Oracle creates a new database, it automatically creates the SYSTEM rollback segment in the database's SYSTEM tablespace.

A database's SYSTEM rollback segment alone cannot adequately support a production database system. After you create a new database, you should create additional rollback segments to support the planned transaction loads of the database.

NOTE
The default starter database for Oracle8i Enterprise Edition for Linux contains eight rollback segments (named RBS0 through RBS06) in addition to the SYSTEM rollback segment.

Rollback Segments and Transactions

Typically, an Oracle database has multiple rollback segments that reside in a tablespace specifically set aside for rollback segment data. You can create any number of rollback segments for a database. Each rollback segment can be a different size and can have different storage attributes. You'll learn more about segment storage, including rollback segment storage, later in this chapter.

When you start a new transaction, Oracle automatically assigns it to an available rollback segment in the database. Oracle assigns transactions to rollback segments on a round-robin basis to distribute the load across all available rollback segments.

Once Oracle assigns a transaction to a rollback segment, the segment records the changed data for all of the transaction. Multiple transactions can share a single rollback segment, but a transaction never uses more than one rollback segment.

NOTE
See Exercise 10.18, later in this chapter, which explains how a transaction can choose a specific rollback segment when necessary.

Online and Offline Rollback Segments

Just like tablespaces and data files, a rollback segment is available if it is *online* and unavailable if it is *offline*. Typically, a rollback segment is online so that transactions can use it to record rollback information. However, some administrative operations require that you first take rollback segments offline. For example, to take offline a tablespace that contains rollback segments, you must first take all rollback segments in the tablespace offline. After you bring the tablespace back online, you can then bring the rollback segments back online, as well.

Public and Private Rollback Segments

A rollback segment in a database can be either public or private. A *public rollback segment* is a rollback segment that Oracle automatically acquires access to and brings online for normal database operations. On the other hand, an Oracle instance acquires a *private rollback segment* only if its server parameter file explicitly lists the name of the private rollback segment. Private rollback segments are useful when you are using Oracle's Parallel Server option and want the various servers for the same database to acquire a mutually exclusive set of the database's rollback segments. Unless you use Oracle with the Parallel Server option, it's much easier to create and use public rollback segments.

Deferred Rollback Segments

When a disk problem forces Oracle to take one or more data files offline, it's typical to take associated tablespaces offline so that users do not notice file access errors when using applications. However, when you take a tablespace offline and Oracle cannot access all of the tablespace's data files, Oracle might create a deferred rollback segment in the SYSTEM tablespace. A *deferred rollback segment* contains transaction rollback information that Oracle could not apply to the damaged offline tablespace. Oracle keeps track of this information so that when you recover the damaged tablespace and bring it back online, Oracle can roll back the transactions that affected the tablespace and make its data consistent with the other data in the database.

The Other Functions of Rollback Segments

Oracle also uses rollback segments to provide read-consistent sets of data for concurrent transactions in a multiuser database system and to help during database recovery. To learn more about the function of rollback segments in database recovery, see Chapter 11.

Creating and Managing Rollback Segments

Now that you understand the fundamental concepts related to rollback segments, the next few practice exercises will teach you the basics of creating, managing, and using rollback segments in an Oracle database.

EXERCISE 10.15: Creating a Rollback Segment

To create a rollback segment, you use the SQL command *CREATE ROLLBACK SEGMENT*, which has the following syntax.

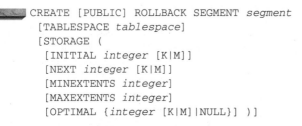

```
CREATE [PUBLIC] ROLLBACK SEGMENT segment
  [TABLESPACE tablespace]
  [STORAGE (
  [INITIAL integer [K|M]]
  [NEXT integer [K|M]]
  [MINEXTENTS integer]
  [MAXEXTENTS integer]
  [OPTIMAL {integer [K|M]|NULL}] )]
```

Notice that when you create a rollback segment, you can specify tablespace and extent storage settings as you can for tables and indexes, using the same TABLESPACE parameter and most of the same parameters in the STORAGE clause. However, because Oracle writes information to the extents of a rollback segment in a circular fashion, and because Oracle can increase and reduce the number of extents in a rollback segment as necessary, there are some special rules for specifying the storage parameters of a rollback segment:

- At all times, a rollback segment can have no fewer than two extents (that is, MINEXTENTS must be equal to or greater than 2).

- Considering that rollback segments can grow, shrink, grow, shrink, and so on, the PCTINCREASE parameter is not available for rollback segments—by default, the growth factor for a rollback segment's extents is set to 0.

- You can set an *optimal size* for a rollback segment using the *OPTIMAL* parameter of the STORAGE clause. If a rollback segment grows larger than its optimal size, Oracle eventually deallocates one or more extents from the segment to shrink it back to its optimal size.

- If you omit a tablespace specification when creating a rollback segment, Oracle creates the segment in the SYSTEM tablespace.

For example, enter the following CREATE ROLLBACK SEGMENT statement to create a public rollback segment and specify its storage settings.

```
CREATE PUBLIC ROLLBACK SEGMENT rb100
  TABLESPACE rbs
```

```
STORAGE (
  INITIAL 100K
  NEXT 200K
  MINEXTENTS 2
  MAXEXTENTS UNLIMITED
  OPTIMAL 1024K );
```

NOTE
When you create a public rollback segment, Oracle records the owner of the segment in the data dictionary as PUBLIC. When you create a private rollback segment, the owner of the segment is your account.

Oracle creates the new RB100 rollback segment in the RBS tablespace with two extents: the first extent is 100K, the second extent is 200K. Furthermore, the segment can grow to an unlimited number of extents (although this limit is bound by the operating system limit of the host server), and Oracle will try to keep the size of the segment at 1024K.

EXERCISE 10.16: Controlling a Rollback Segment's Availability

To control the availability of a rollback segment, you must use the *ONLINE* and *OFFLINE* options of the SQL command *ALTER ROLLBACK SEGMENT*, which has the following syntax:

```
ALTER ROLLBACK SEGMENT segment
  {ONLINE|OFFLINE}
```

For example, after you create a new rollback segment, as in the previous exercise, the rollback segment is left offline. To make the new RB100 rollback segment available to transactions, enter the following statement to bring the segment online.

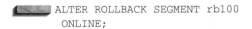

```
ALTER ROLLBACK SEGMENT rb100
  ONLINE;
```

At this point, the rollback segment is available for recording transaction rollback data.

EXERCISE 10.17: Altering a Rollback Segment's Storage Settings

You can alter the extent storage settings for a rollback segment using the *STORAGE* clause of the SQL command *ALTER ROLLBACK SEGMENT*.

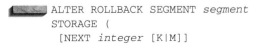

```
ALTER ROLLBACK SEGMENT segment
STORAGE (
  [NEXT integer [K|M]]
```

```
[MINEXTENTS integer]
[MAXEXTENTS integer]
[OPTIMAL {integer [K|M]|NULL}] )
```

For example, enter the following statement to alter the OPTIMAL size of the RB100 rollback segment.

```
ALTER ROLLBACK SEGMENT rb100
STORAGE (OPTIMAL 512K);
```

EXERCISE 10.18: Targeting a Specific Rollback Segment

An application can explicitly target a rollback segment at the very beginning of a new transaction with the *USING ROLLBACK SEGMENT* parameter of the SQL command *SET TRANSACTION*. For example, before starting a large batch operation, you can target a sufficiently large rollback segment in the database. By doing so, you can avoid assigning the large transaction to a small rollback segment and forcing Oracle to allocate additional space for the segment; the end result is that you reduce the overhead necessary to record rollback data for the transaction and improve the performance of the operation.

For example, enter the following statement to start a new transaction that targets the RB100 rollback segment.

```
-- End current transaction with ROLLBACK
ROLLBACK;
SET TRANSACTION USE ROLLBACK SEGMENT rb100;
```

EXERCISE 10.19: Displaying Rollback Segment Information

To display information about rollback segments, you can query the DBA_ROLLBACK_SEGS data dictionary view. For example, enter the following query to display the names and storage settings for all rollback segments in your starter database.

```
SELECT segment_name AS segment,
  tablespace_name AS "TABLESPACE",
  initial_extent AS "INITIAL",
  next_extent AS "NEXT",
  min_extents AS "MIN",
  max_extents AS "MAX",
  status
FROM dba_rollback_segs;
```

The result set is as follows:

```
SEGMENT TABLESPACE   INITIAL      NEXT       MIN       MAX STATUS
------- ---------- ---------- ---------- ---------- ---------- -------
SYSTEM  SYSTEM          57344      57344         2       505 ONLINE
RBS0    RBS            524288     524288         8      4096 ONLINE
RBS1    RBS            524288     524288         8      4096 ONLINE
RBS2    RBS            524288     524288         8      4096 ONLINE
RBS3    RBS            524288     524288         8      4096 ONLINE
RBS4    RBS            524288     524288         8      4096 ONLINE
RBS5    RBS            524288     524288         8      4096 ONLINE
RBS6    RBS            524288     524288         8      4096 ONLINE
RB100   RBS            106496     204800         2     32765 ONLINE

9 rows selected.
```

Unfortunately, the DBA_ROLLBACK_SEGS view does not contain information about a rollback segment's optimal size or corresponding statistics about the number of extent allocations and deallocations—for this information, you must join data from two other data dictionary views, V$ROLLNAME and V$ROLLSTAT. For example, enter the following query:

```
SELECT name, extents, optsize, shrinks, extends, aveshrink
  FROM v$rollname, v$rollstat
  WHERE v$rollname.usn = v$rollstat.usn;
```

Your result set should be similar to the following:

```
NAME            EXTENTS   OPTSIZE   SHRINKS   EXTENDS AVESHRINK
------------ --------- --------- --------- --------- ---------
SYSTEM               7                   0         0         0
RBS0                 8   4194304         0         0         0
RBS1                 8   4194304         0         0         0
RBS2                 8   4194304         0         0         0
RBS3                 8   4194304         0         0         0
RBS4                 8   4194304         0         0         0
RBS5                 8   4194304         0         0         0
RBS6                 8   4194304         0         0         0
RB100                2    524288         0         0         0

9 rows selected.
```

The result set of the most recent query provides you with the information that you need to tune a rollback segment's optimal size. When you notice that rollback segments are extending and shrinking frequently, try increasing the optimal size of the rollback segment to reduce dynamic extent allocations and deallocations that can slow overall server performance.

Temporary Segments and Temporary Tablespaces

SQL statements often require temporary work areas. For example, when you create an index for a large table, Oracle typically must allocate some temporary system space so that it can sort all of the index entries before building the index's segment. When processing a SQL statement that requires temporary work space, Oracle allocates small *temporary segments* from a tablespace in the database. When the statement completes, Oracle releases the segments back to the tablespace so that other objects can use the space. Thus the term "temporary segment."

To optimize temporary segment allocation, you should create one or more temporary tablespaces in your database. (See the section "Permanent and Temporary Tablespaces" earlier in this chapter.) You can think of a temporary tablespace as one large temporary segment that all transactions can use for temporary workspace. A temporary tablespace can more efficiently provide temporary workspace to transactions because Oracle inserts and deletes simple table entries in the temporary tablespace's segment table, rather than physically allocating and deallocating segments on demand.

Unique Data Storage for Multimedia Data

When a table in a database includes a column that uses a LOB datatype (for example, CLOB, BLOB, or NCLOB) or a BFILE datatype, Oracle stores only a small locator inline with each row in the table. A *locator* is a pointer to the location of the actual LOB or BFILE data for the row. For CLOB, BLOB, and NCLOB columns, a LOB locator points to a storage location inside the database; for a BFILE column, a BFILE locator points to an external file managed by the server's operating system. Figure 10-10 illustrates the concept of locators for LOB and BFILE columns.

Notice in Figure 10-10 that a LOB column can have storage characteristics independent of those of the encompassing table. This makes it easy to address the large disk requirements typically associated with LOBs. In this example, the table stores all non-LOB and non-BFILE data for each row together in one tablespace, a LOB column's data in another tablespace, and a BFILE column's data in the server's file system. By doing so, you can distribute the storage of primary table data and related multimedia data to different physical locations (for example, different disk drives) to reduce disk contention and improve overall system performance.

More About LOB Locators

To provide for efficient access to LOB data, Oracle stores a CLOB or BLOB column's pointers within a corresponding B-tree index. By doing so, Oracle can quickly access specifically requested *chunks* (pieces) of individual LOBs in a column.

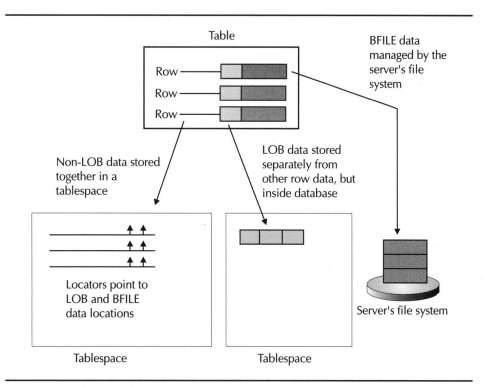

FIGURE 10-10. *Distributing the storage of primary table data and related multimedia data to different physical locations to reduce disk contention*

EXERCISE 10.20: Creating a Table with a LOB Column

When you create a table that has a column that uses the BLOB, CLOB, or NCLOB datatype, you can store the LOB column's data in a LOB segment separate from the table's data segment by specifying the *LOB* clause of the SQL command *CREATE TABLE*. An abbreviated form of the LOB clause is as follows:

```
LOB (column [, column] ... )
{ [segment]
| STORE AS [segment] (
  [TABLESPACE tablespace]
  [{ENABLE|DISABLE} STORAGE IN ROW]
  [STORAGE ( ... ) ]
  [CHUNK integer]
  [PCTVERSION integer]
  [INDEX
  { index
  | [index] (
  [INITRANS integer] [MAXTRANS integer]
```

```
[TABLESPACE tablespace]
[STORAGE ( ... )] ) } ] }
```

The following list briefly describes the parameters of the LOB clause:

- Indicate a list of one or more CLOB, BLOB, or NCLOB columns to which the LOB clause should apply. If you indicate only one column, you can name the LOB segment that Oracle creates for storing the column; however, if you list more than one column, you cannot name the LOB segment.

- Use the *TABLESPACE* parameter of the LOB clause to specify the tablespace that will hold the LOB segment.

- Use the *ENABLE STORAGE IN ROW* option to have Oracle store a LOB value less than 4,000 bytes with the other data in the same row; when a LOB value is greater than 4,000 bytes, Oracle stores the LOB value in the LOB segment. Use the *DISABLE STORAGE IN ROW* option to always store LOB values in the LOB segment, regardless of each LOB value's length.

- Use a *STORAGE* clause to specify several storage parameters that determine the size and number of extents that comprise the segment for a nonclustered table's LOB segment. See Exercise 10.11, earlier in this chapter, for more information about the STORAGE clause and its parameters.

- Use the *CHUNK* parameter to specify the storage allocation unit for a LOB segment. Specify an integer for the CHUNK parameter. The storage allocation unit for a LOB segment is the result of the CHUNK parameter setting multiplied by the database's data block size. For example, when a LOB segment's CHUNK parameter is 10 and the database's data block size is 2K, the storage allocation unit for the LOB segment is 20K. The maximum value of a LOB segment's storage allocation unit is 32K. Additionally, ensure that the extent sizes for a LOB segment (INITIAL and NEXT) are greater than or equal to the storage allocation unit for the segment.

- When a transaction modifies a LOB or part of a LOB, Oracle creates a new version of the LOB's data blocks and leaves the older version of the LOB intact, to support consistent reads of prior versions of the LOB. Use the *PCTVERSION* parameter to control the overall percentage of used LOB data blocks in a LOB segment that are available for versioning of old LOB data. PCTVERSION is a threshold of LOB segment storage space that must be reached before Oracle overwrites older versions of LOB data with newer versions. The default value is 10. When updates to LOBs are infrequent, set PCTVERSION to 5 or lower to minimize the amount of disk space required to store LOBs.

■ Use the INDEX clause to specify the extent storage parameters for the index that Oracle automatically creates for a LOB segment. If you indicate only one column for the LOB clause, you can name the index that Oracle creates for the LOB segment; however, if you list more than one column, you cannot name the index.

To demonstrate the use of the LOB clause in a CREATE TABLE statement, enter the following statement to create a CUSTOMERS table that can store a photograph for each customer record.

```
CREATE TABLE customers (
  id   INTEGER,
  lastname VARCHAR2(100) CONSTRAINT lastname NOT NULL,
  firstname VARCHAR2(50) CONSTRAINT firstname NOT NULL,
  companyname VARCHAR2(100),
  street VARCHAR2(100),
  city VARCHAR2(100),
  state VARCHAR2(50),
  zipcode VARCHAR2(50),
  phone VARCHAR2(30),
  fax VARCHAR2(30),
  email VARCHAR2(100),
  s_id INTEGER CONSTRAINT salesrep NOT NULL,
  photo BLOB
  )
-- storage parameters for data segment
PCTFREE 10 PCTUSED 70
INITRANS 2 MAXTRANS 5
TABLESPACE users
STORAGE (
  INITIAL 100K NEXT 100K
  MINEXTENTS 1  MAXEXTENTS 10
  PCTINCREASE 0
  FREELISTS 3
  )
-- storage parameters for LOB segment
LOB (photo) STORE AS cust_photo (
TABLESPACE photos
  ENABLE STORAGE IN ROW
  STORAGE (
  INITIAL 100K NEXT 100K
  MINEXTENTS 1  MAXEXTENTS 10
  PCTINCREASE 0
  FREELISTS 3
  )
  CHUNK 5
```

```
  PCTVERSION 5
-- storage parameters for index of LOB column
  INDEX photos (
   TABLESPACE indx
   STORAGE (INITIAL 50K NEXT 50K)
  )
)
;
```

Notice the following points about the CREATE TABLE statement in this exercise:

■ The statement specifies storage parameters for the table's data segment using the familiar PCTFREE, PCTUSED, TABLESPACE, INITRANS, MAXTRANS, and STORAGE clause parameters.

■ The statement specifies storage settings for the table's LOB segment using the LOB clause.

■ The statement specifies storage settings for the index of the LOB segment.

Partitioning Large Tables and Indexes

Large tables (and indexes) can create or magnify several problems in production database systems because of their size and storage characteristics. For example, consider the following scenarios:

■ A table becomes so large that associated management operations take longer to complete than the time window that is available.

■ A query requires Oracle to complete a full table scan of a very large table. Application and system performance suffers while Oracle reads the numerous data blocks for the corresponding table.

■ A mission-critical application depends primarily on a single large table. The table becomes unavailable when just a single data block in the table is inaccessible due to a disk failure. An administrator must recover the entire tablespace that contains the table before the table and corresponding mission-critical application can be brought back online.

To help reduce the types of problems that large tables and indexes can create, along with other problems, Oracle8*i* supports *partitioned tables* and *partitioned indexes*.

Partitioned Tables

Oracle8i lets you divide the storage of a table into smaller units of disk storage called *partitions,* as Figure 10-11 shows.

Oracle8i's built-in partitioning features support the *horizontal partitioning* of a table—that is, each partition of a table contains the same logical attributes, including the same set of columns with the same datatypes and the same integrity constraints. However, each table partition is an individual data segment that can have different physical attributes. For example, Oracle can store each partition of a table in separate tablespaces, and the data segment of each partition can have different extent and data block storage settings.

A Table's Partition Key

Every partitioned table has a partition key. A table's *partition key* is a column or ordered set of columns that characterize the horizontal partitioning of table rows. When you create a new table, you specify the table's partition key and configure the table to place rows into available partitions using range partitioning, hash partitioning, or a composite form of range and hash partitioning. The next few sections explain each type of option for table partitioning.

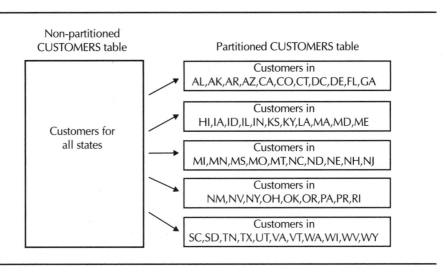

FIGURE 10-11. *Oracle8i lets you horizontally partition a table by storing the table's rows in two or more segments*

Range Partitioning

One way to horizontally partition the data of a table is *range partitioning*. Each partition in the table stores rows according to the partition key values of a row. For example, Figure 10-12 demonstrates how you might partition the rows in the ORDERS table according to the ORDERDATE of each row.

NOTE
To prevent the overhead associated with migrating rows among table partitions, applications should never update data in a table's partition key.

ORDERS table   Logical representation of the ORDERS table

ID	C_ID	ORDERDATE	SHIPDATE	PAIDDATE	STATUS
1	1	JUN-99	JUN-99	JUN-99	F
2	2	JUN-99	JUN-99		B
3	3	JUN-99	JUL-99	JUL-99	F
4	4	JUL-99	JUL-99	JUL-99	F
5	5	JUL-99	JUL-99	JUL-99	F
6	6	JUL-99	JUL-99		F
7	7	AUG-99			B
8	8	AUG-99	AUG-99	AUG-99	F
9	9	AUG-99			B
10	2	AUG-99	AUG-99	AUG-99	F

Partitions contain orders placed in a specific month

ID	C_ID	ORDERDATE	SHIPDATE	PAIDDATE	STATUS
1	1	JUN-99	JUN-99	JUN-99	F
2	2	JUN-99	JUN-99		B
3	3	JUN-99	JUL-99	JUL-99	F

ID	C_ID	ORDERDATE	SHIPDATE	PAIDDATE	STATUS
4	4	JUL-99	JUL-99	JUL-99	F
5	5	JUL-99	JUL-99	JUL-99	F
6	6	JUL-99	JUL-99		F

ID	C_ID	ORDERDATE	SHIPDATE	PAIDDATE	STATUS
7	7	AUG-99			B
8	8	AUG-99	AUG-99	AUG-99	F
9	9	AUG-99			B
10	2		AUG-99	AUG-99	F

Physical storage of the ORDERS table

FIGURE 10-12. *Within range partitioning, Oracle places a row in a partition according to the partition key of the row*

When you create a range-partitioned table, you configure a noninclusive upper bound, or *partition bound*, for each partition in the table. Each partition, except for the first, has an implicit lower value, which is the upper bound of the previous partition. Therefore, it's important to declare table partitions with ranges that ascend in value. For example, in Figure 10-12, each partition of the range-partitioned ORDERS table stores a month's worth of sales order records.

Range partitioning is very useful for managing a large historical table in a data warehouse or decision support system (DSS) database that must keep a revolving set of records that correspond to a particular time interval. For example, you might want to keep the most recent year's sales order records in the ORDERS table of a schema in a DSS. In this case, you could add a new partition every month to the ORDERS table in the DSS to hold the most recent month's records from the production OLTP system. At the same time, you could drop the oldest partition in the ORDERS table to delete the oldest records in the table. Exercise 10.23, later in this chapter, uses this example to teach you how to use range partitioning to maintain a historical table.

Hash Partitioning

Another way to partition the data of a table is *hash partitioning*. To place a row in a hash-partitioned table, Oracle8i first applies a hash function to the partition key of the row and then uses the resulting hash value to determine which partition will hold the row. For example, Figure 10-13 shows a version of the ITEMS table that uses hash partitioning.

All things considered, hash partitioning is a good choice when your primary goal is to improve the response time of SQL statements that target the table. That's because hash partitioning typically distributes the rows of the table uniformly among all available partitions, which you can create on different physical disk drives to reduce contention for disk access during full table scans. Hash partitioning is also useful when the data of a large table is not suitable for range partitioning—for example, when the data is not evenly spread among ranges of partition key values, or when historical management of table data is not called for.

Composite Partitioning

When you require the management benefits of range partitioning but would also like to receive the performance benefits of hash partitioning, you can combine the two forms of partitioning in the same table. When you use *composite partitioning* with a table, Oracle first partitions the rows of the table into ranges, and then stripes the rows within a partition into subpartitions using hash partitioning.

Creating and Managing Partitioned Tables

Now that you have a basic understanding of range, hash, and composite partitioning for tables, the next few practice exercises teach you how to get started by creating range- and hash-partitioned tables.

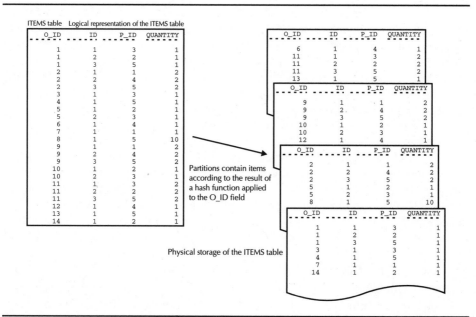

ITEMS table   Logical representation of the ITEMS table

Partitions contain items
according to the result of
a hash function applied
to the O_ID field

Physical storage of the ITEMS table

FIGURE 10-13. *With hash partitioning, Oracle places a row in a partition according to the result of applying a hash function to the row's partition key*

EXERCISE 10.21: Creating a Range-Partitioned Table

This exercise and the following two teach you how to manage a fictitious ORDERS historical table in a DSS database with range partitioning. To create a range-partitioned table, you must use the *PARTITION BY RANGE* clause of the SQL command *CREATE TABLE*. An abbreviated form of the syntax of the PARTITION BY RANGE clause is as follows:

```
CREATE TABLE table
  ( ... columns and constraints ... )
  PARTITION BY RANGE (column [, column] ... )
    ( PARTITION [partition]
       VALUES LESS THAN ({values list|MAXVALUE})
       [PCTFREE integer] [PCTUSED integer]
       [INITRANS integer] [MAXTRANS integer]
       [TABLESPACE tablespace]
       [STORAGE ( ... )]
    [, ... ] )
```

The PARTITION BY RANGE clause lets you specify one or more PARTITION clauses to specify the characteristics of each table partition. For each successive partition, you indicate the partition bound using the VALUES LESS THAN parameter—each value in the partition bound must be a literal or a TO_DATE() or RPAD() function with a constant argument. You can also indicate storage settings for each partition using familiar storage settings such as the PCTFREE and TABLESPACE parameters and a STORAGE clause.

NOTE
You can also indicate the partition bound of the last partition in a range-partitioned table using the MAXVALUE keyword rather than a values list. In this case, the last partition in the table stores all rows with a partition key value greater than the upper bound of the next-to-last partition. Additionally, when a table's partition key accepts nulls, Oracle sorts rows with null partition keys greater than all other values except MAXVALUE.

Enter the following CREATE TABLE statement to create a range-partitioned version of the ORDERS table.

```
CREATE TABLE orders (
  id INTEGER,
  c_id INTEGER NOT NULL,
  orderdate DATE DEFAULT SYSDATE NOT NULL,
  shipdate DATE,
  paiddate DATE,
  status CHAR(1) DEFAULT 'F' )
PARTITION BY RANGE (orderdate)
( PARTITION jun1999
    VALUES LESS THAN (TO_DATE('07-01-1999','MM-DD-YYYY'))
    TABLESPACE users,
  PARTITION jul1999
    VALUES LESS THAN (TO_DATE('08-01-1999','MM-DD-YYYY'))
    TABLESPACE users,
  PARTITION aug1999
    VALUES LESS THAN (TO_DATE('09-01-1999','MM-DD-YYYY'))
    TABLESPACE users);
```

This example statement creates the ORDERS table with three partitions to hold sales order records for the months of June, July, and August of 1999.

EXERCISE 10.22: Understanding How Oracle Places Rows into a Range-Partitioned Table

To see how Oracle places the rows of a table into the various partitions of the range-partitioned ORDERS table, let's insert some rows with ORDERDATE values that correspond to the different partition ranges in the table. Enter the following statements:

```
INSERT INTO orders
  VALUES (1,1,'18-JUN-1999','18-JUN-1999','30-JUN-1999','F');
INSERT INTO orders
  VALUES (2,2,'23-JUL-1999',NULL,NULL,'B');
INSERT INTO orders
  VALUES (3,3,'08-AUG-1999','08-AUG-1999','08-AUG-1999','F');
```

> **NOTE**
> *When a table's partition key is a date column, you must specify the partition key of a row using a date format that includes the month, day, and four-digit year.*

The PARTITION parameter of the SQL command SELECT lets you target rows in a specific partition. For example, enter the following query to see only the rows in the JUL1999 partition of the ORDERS table.

```
SELECT *
  FROM orders
  PARTITION (jul1999);
```

The result set is as follows:

```
       ID      C_ID ORDERDATE SHIPDATE  PAIDDATE  STATUS
--------- --------- --------- --------- --------- ------
        2         2 23-JUL-99                     B
```

Notice that Oracle correctly placed the record with an ORDERDATE of 23-JUL-1999 into the JUL1999 partition. If you wish, you can modify the preceding query to display the records in the other partitions of the ORDERS table.

Now try to insert another sales order into the ORDERS table with the following INSERT statement.

```
INSERT INTO orders
  VALUES (4,4,'04-SEP-1999','04-SEP-1999','04-SEP-1999','F');
```

In this example, Oracle returns an error, because the ORDERDATE of the new record is higher in value than the partition bound of the last partition in the table.

```
ORA-14400: inserted partition key is beyond highest legal partition key
```

You cannot store the new record until you create a new partition for the table with a higher partition bound.

EXERCISE 10.23: Managing a Range-Partitioned Historical Table

This final exercise concerning range partitioning teaches you how to roll in and roll out historical data in the range-partitioned ORDERS table of a fictitious DSS database. In this example, you will see how to add a new partition to the ORDERS table to accept records for the month of September, 1999, and then drop the partition that contains the oldest sales records.

First, let's add a new partition to the ORDERS table to accept records for the month of September, 1999. To add a new partition to a range-partitioned table, you use the *ADD PARTITION* clause of the SQL command *ALTER TABLE*.

```
ADD PARTITION [partition]
  VALUES LESS THAN ({values list|MAXVALUE})
  [PCTFREE integer] [PCTUSED integer]
  [INITRANS integer] [MAXTRANS integer]
  [TABLESPACE tablespace]
  [STORAGE ( ... )]
```

For example, enter the following statement to add the new SEP1999 partition to the ORDERS table.

```
ALTER TABLE orders
  ADD PARTITION sep1999
    VALUES LESS THAN (TO_DATE('10-01-1999','MM-DD-YYYY'))
    TABLESPACE users;
```

Now, retry the last INSERT statement of the previous exercise, and the ORDERS table will accept the new row.

```
INSERT INTO orders
  VALUES (4,4,'04-SEP-1999','04-SEP-1999','04-SEP-1999','F');
```

Next, let's see how to drop the partition that contains the oldest sales records of the ORDERS table. To drop a partition from a table, you use the *DROP PARTITION* parameter of the SQL command *ALTER TABLE*. For example, enter the following statement to drop the JUN1999 partition and all records in the partition from the ORDERS table.

```
ALTER TABLE orders
  DROP PARTITION jun1999;
```

The examples in the previous three exercises explain just a few of the many different management operations available for range-partitioned tables. See your Oracle documentation for more information about other management operations related to range-partitioned tables, including how to convert a nonpartitioned table to a partitioned table (and vice-versa), how to split or merge partitions in the middle of a range-partitioned table, and how to delete all rows in an individual partition of a table.

EXERCISE 10.24: Creating a Hash-Partitioned Table

In this exercise, let's create yet another version of the ITEMS table—this time, a hash-partitioned version. To create a hash-partitioned table, you use the *PARTITION BY HASH* clause of the SQL command *CREATE TABLE*.

```
PARTITION BY HASH (column [, column] ... )
  { PARTITIONS integer STORE IN (tablespace [, tablespace] ... )
  | ( PARTITION [partition]
      [PCTFREE integer] [PCTUSED integer]
      [INITRANS integer] [MAXTRANS integer]
      [TABLESPACE tablespace]
      [STORAGE ( ... )]
    [, ... ] ) }
```

Notice that the PARTITION BY HASH clause lets you specify the partitions of a hash-partitioned table using two different techniques:

- Use the PARTITIONS clause to specify a number of partitions and a list of a corresponding number of tablespaces for the partitions. In this case, all partitions have the same extent storage parameters.

- Specify a list of partitions using PARTITION clauses when you want to specify names and individual extent storage settings for each partition in the table.

TIP
To obtain the best distribution of rows among table partitions, create a hash-partitioned table with an even number of partitions (for example, 2, 4, 6, ...).

Enter the following series of statements to drop the existing ITEMS table, and then create a new hash-partitioned version of the table.

```
DROP TABLE items;

CREATE TABLE items (
 o_id INTEGER,
 id INTEGER,
 p_id INTEGER NOT NULL,
 quantity INTEGER DEFAULT 1 NOT NULL )
 PARTITION BY HASH (o_id)
 ( PARTITION item1 TABLESPACE users,
   PARTITION item2 TABLESPACE users,
   PARTITION item3 TABLESPACE users,
   PARTITION item4 TABLESPACE users );
```

EXERCISE 10.25: Confirming the Distribution of Rows in a Hash-Partitioned Table

In this exercise, let's insert some rows into the hash-partitioned ITEMS table and then confirm the distribution of rows. Enter the following INSERT statements to insert line items into the ITEMS table that correspond to the four sales orders in the ORDERS table.

```
INSERT INTO items VALUES (1,1,3,1);
INSERT INTO items VALUES (1,2,2,1);
INSERT INTO items VALUES (1,3,5,1);
INSERT INTO items VALUES (2,1,1,2);
INSERT INTO items VALUES (2,2,4,2);
INSERT INTO items VALUES (2,3,5,2);
INSERT INTO items VALUES (3,1,3,1);
INSERT INTO items VALUES (4,1,5,1);
```

Now enter the following queries to reveal how Oracle8i's hash function distributes the rows among the available partitions.

```
SELECT * FROM items PARTITION (item1);
SELECT * FROM items PARTITION (item2);
SELECT * FROM items PARTITION (item3);
SELECT * FROM items PARTITION (item4);
```

When you examine the result sets for these queries, you should notice that some partitions do not have any rows (yet), while others have rows for various line items according to their O_ID value. If you insert more and more rows into the ITEMS table, the number of rows in each partition will eventually even out.

Partitioned Indexes

Chapter 7 of this book introduced the advantage of creating one or more indexes for the columns in a table—using indexes, you can reduce the amount of disk I/O necessary to locate a specific row or set of rows in the corresponding table, which translates to faster response times for SQL statements that target the table. If you create an index for a large table, you should also know that Oracle8i supports the horizontal partitioning of an index using range, hash, or composite partitioning. Just as with tables, each partition of an index has the same logical attributes (index columns), but can have different physical characteristics (tablespace placement and storage settings). An index's partition key and the type of partitioning option that you choose for the index determines which partition Oracle stores index entries within. An index's partition key must include one or more of the columns that define the index.

Partitioned Index Options

Should you always create partitioned indexes for partitioned tables? What columns should a partitioned index incorporate? How should you structure the partitions in an index? These are good questions to answer before deciding how to index the partitioned tables in your database.

First things first. It doesn't always make sense to partition an index of a partitioned table. In general, you should consider a partitioned index when the index itself is large enough to justify partitioning, or when you frequently manage partitions of a table and you want the index to be available for SQL statements that happen during administrative tasks.

Choosing the key columns for a partitioned index is no different from choosing the key columns for a nonpartitioned index—index the columns in a table that SQL statements use within a WHERE clause's search criteria. You'll learn more about indexes and general guidelines for indexing in Chapter 12 of this book.

Once you decide to create a partitioned index for a table, you must then decide how to structure the index's partitions. Considering the plethora of options that Oracle8i offers for indexes and partitioning, determining the best option for an index can get confusing. The following sections introduce you to the fundamental options available and provide you with some basic considerations for each option.

Global Indexes   A nonpartitioned index of a partitioned table is called a global index. As the name implies, a partition in a *global index* contains index entries that correspond to rows that originate from two or more partitions of a partitioned table. Figure 10-14 illustrates a nonpartitioned global index of a partitioned table.

You can also create a global partitioned index. A *global partitioned index* has partitions that do not match the partitions in the associated table. For example, to consolidate the number of partitions in an index of a range-partitioned table, the index entries in each partition of the global index might correspond to the rows in three successive partitions in the associated table.

In general, global indexes are useful for improving the response times of SQL statements that target rows in many partitions of a partitioned table. However, the administration and availability of a global index can be affected when you modify the associated table. For example, if you load new data into a single partition of a table that has a global index, you might need to rebuild the entire global index to synchronize it with the new table data.

Equi-Partitioned Objects and Local Indexes   Two or more database objects are *equi-partitioned* if they have identical logical partitioning attributes. For example,

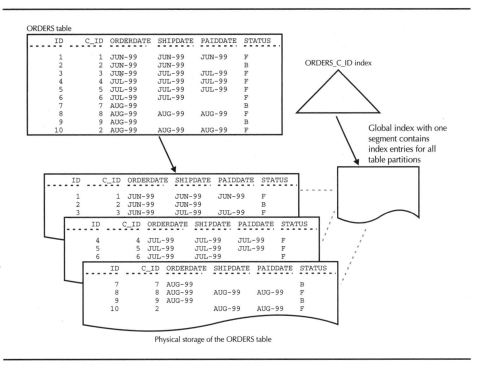

FIGURE 10-14.   *A nonpartitioned index of a partitioned table*

a range-partitioned table and an associated range-partitioned index would be equi-partitioned if they have the same number of partitions, the same data ranges for each partition, and the same columns defining their respective partition keys.

When you equi-partition an index with its table, all keys in a particular index partition refer only to the rows in the corresponding table partition—thus, a partitioned index that is equi-partitioned with its table is a *local partitioned index*. Oracle can use the local index partitions to generate excellent query plans. Additionally, an administrator affects the availability of only one index partition when performing a maintenance operation on a table partition. Figure 10-15 illustrates an equi-partitioned table and a local index.

Equi-partitioned tables and local indexes can provide benefits for administration and data availability because an administrative operation that affects a specific table partition will affect the corresponding index partition only. For example, if you perform a bulk data load into the range-partitioned historical table in a DSS database, and the load updates data in just one table partition, you only have to rebuild the corresponding index partition. All other partitions of the index remain available and valid, because the data load does not affect the rows that correspond to the index entries in other partitions of the index.

Creating and Managing Partitioned Indexes

The following two practice exercises teach you how to create normal (B-tree) indexes for the partitioned ORDERS and ITEMS tables created in Exercises 10.21 and 10.24.

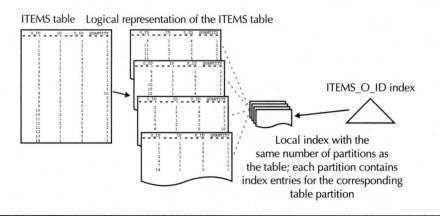

FIGURE 10-15. *Each partition of a local index contains index entries that correspond to rows in the same partition of its table*

EXERCISE 10.26: Creating Global Indexes

To create a global index for a table, you use various forms of the SQL command *CREATE INDEX*. For example, to create a nonpartitioned global index for a table, you create the index without any special syntax. Enter the following statement to create a nonpartitioned global index for the C_ID column of the range-partitioned ORDERS table.

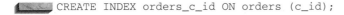

```
CREATE INDEX orders_c_id ON orders (c_id);
```

To create a range-partitioned global index for a table, you use the *GLOBAL* keyword followed by the *PARTITION BY RANGE* clause of the SQL command *CREATE INDEX*. The syntax of the PARTITION BY RANGE clause in the CREATE INDEX command is identical to the same clause in the CREATE TABLE command, listed in Exercise 10.21. For example, enter the following statement to create a partitioned global index of the ORDERDATE column in the ORDERS table.

```
CREATE INDEX orders_orderdate ON orders (orderdate)
  GLOBAL
  PARTITION BY RANGE (orderdate)
  ( PARTITION q11999
      VALUES LESS THAN (TO_DATE('04-01-1999','MM-DD-YYYY'))
      TABLESPACE users,
    PARTITION q21999
      VALUES LESS THAN (TO_DATE('07-01-1999','MM-DD-YYYY'))
      TABLESPACE users,
    PARTITION q31999
      VALUES LESS THAN (TO_DATE('10-01-1999','MM-DD-YYYY'))
      TABLESPACE users,
    PARTITION q41999
      VALUES LESS THAN (MAXVALUE)
      TABLESPACE users );
```

NOTE
The last partition in a range-partitioned global index must use the MAXVALUE keyword.

In the preceding example, notice that each partition in the range-partitioned global index of the ORDERS table contains index entries that correspond to sales records for each fiscal quarter, rather than to each month, as with the associated range-partitioned ORDERS table. This query would be appropriate if queries frequently analyze rows in the ORDERS table by quarter.

EXERCISE 10.27: Creating Local, Equi-Partitioned Indexes

Creating a local, equi-partitioned index of a partitioned table is very simple—all you need to do is include the *LOCAL* keyword when creating the index with the SQL command *CREATE INDEX*. For example, enter the following statement to create a local, equi-partitioned index for the hash-partitioned ITEMS table.

```
CREATE INDEX items_o_id ON items (o_id) LOCAL;
```

In this example, Oracle creates the ITEMS_O_ID index with four partitions (ITEM1, ITEM2, ITEM3, ITEM4) in the USERS tablespace—refer to the CREATE TABLE statement in Exercise 10.24 if you do not remember the specific partitions in the hash-partitioned ITEMS table.

Chapter Summary

This chapter has explained the logical and physical database storage structures, including databases, tablespaces, data files, control files, segments, extents, and data blocks.

■ Tablespaces are logical storage divisions within an Oracle database. You create and manage tablespaces using the SQL commands CREATE TABLESPACE and ALTER TABLESPACE.

■ Each tablespace has one or more data files to physically store its data. You can specify the names and properties of a tablespace's data files when you create the tablespace with the CREATE TABLESPACE command. You can subsequently add data files to a tablespace or change the storage characteristics of a data file using the ALTER DATABASE and ALTER TABLESPACE commands.

■ A segment is the collection of data blocks for a data storage object, such as a table, data cluster, index, or rollback segment. An extent is a set of contiguous data blocks allocated to an object's segment. A data block is the unit of physical disk access for an Oracle database.

■ When you create a database object, such as a table, you can explicitly specify storage parameters that determine how Oracle allocates extents for the object's segment and storage parameters that determine how Oracle uses the space within the data blocks of the object's segment.

■ Oracle uses a rollback segment to record rollback data for a transaction. If you choose to roll back a transaction, Oracle reads the necessary data from a rollback segment to "undo" the effects of the transaction. You create and manage rollback segments with the SQL commands CREATE ROLLBACK SEGMENT and ALTER ROLLBACK SEGMENT.

■ A database's control file keeps track of internal system information about the physical structure of the database.

Additionally, you learned how to partition the data of large tables and indexes to improve the performance and manageability associated with these objects.

CHAPTER
11

Database Protection

hen you bet your business on some software, it had better have the capability to protect your valuable data from any type of problem—from simple system crashes that are the result of unexpected power outages to more serious problems, such as hard-disk failures. This chapter explains the sophisticated database backup and recovery mechanisms of Oracle that you can use to protect and repair your databases. Topics in this chapter include the following:

- Possible failures to prepare for
- The transaction log
- The database's control file
- Database backups
- Database recovery

Chapter Prerequisites

To practice the hands-on exercises in this chapter, login to your Linux computer using the oracle account. You do not have to run a script to prepare for this chapter's exercises. However, there are a couple of points to consider before completing any of the practice exercises in this chapter:

- It is very important that you perform all of the exercises in this chapter, in the order given.
- You may not be able to repeat several of the exercises in this chapter that focus on database configuration. After all, once you configure the database in a certain way, it doesn't make any sense to reconfigure it the same way again!

In addition, please pay close attention to the special Caution notes that appear throughout this chapter before several practice exercises.

Different Types of Problems

Before you begin learning about Oracle's database protection mechanisms, you should have a general idea of the types of problems that can adversely affect your database system. Knowing what types of problems are possible will help you to better protect your Oracle databases from an unfortunate catastrophe.

System and Server Crashes

Perhaps the most common type of problem that affects the availability of computer systems are crashes. A *crash* is the sudden failure of the system in question. Unexpected power failures, software bugs, and operating system process failures are inevitable problems that commonly cause crashes. For example, a bug in your computer's operating system might cause an Oracle background process to suddenly fail, which, in turn, causes the entire Oracle instance to crash—this type of crash is commonly called a *database instance crash*.

In general, Oracle instance crashes do not damage physical database structures permanently. The primary problem with an instance crash is that all of the work and data in the instance's memory at the time of the crash is lost, unless the data was written to disk. For example, when an Oracle database instance crashes, all of the data in the instance's buffer cache that was not yet written back to the data files is lost forever. However, this isn't a cause for alarm—later in this chapter you'll see that the database's transaction log contains data on disk that can recover all committed work lost during a simple instance crash.

NOTE
You'll learn more about an instance's buffer cache in Chapter 12.

File Loss from User Error, Corruption, or Disk Failure

The loss of an important database file due to operator error, file corruption, or a disk failure is a serious problem that you must be prepared for, even though it might never occur. For example, let's say you're working overtime, you're tired, and you accidentally delete a data file. You won't be able to recover from this user error unless you are ready:

- To restore the lost data file, you must have a database backup that contains the deleted data file.

- To recover all work committed since the backup was taken, you must have the necessary transaction log groups.

Oracle's database backup and recovery mechanisms include all that you need in order to completely protect and recover your database from any type of file loss.

Site Disaster

A company that uses Oracle to run its entire business might have particularly strict requirements for the protection of its data. Such requirements often include contingency plans to prepare for total site disasters that result from earthquakes, fires, and other natural or unnatural catastrophes. Later in this chapter, you'll learn how Oracle's standby database feature can provide the necessary protection.

Overview of Oracle's Database Protection Mechanisms

Before explaining the specifics of the many database protection features of Oracle that you'll learn about in this chapter, let's take a brief look at them and understand how they function together to protect an Oracle database. Figure 11-1 introduces the primary database protection features: database backups and the transaction log.

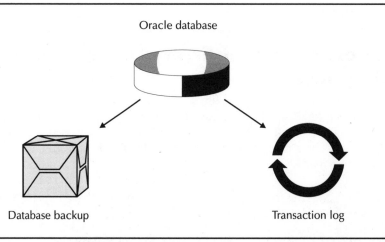

FIGURE 11-1. *Database backups and the transaction log (or redo log) are the primary features of Oracle that enable you to recover a database from problems*

■   Regular and frequent database backups make it possible to restore files that are lost due to user error, file corruption, or disk failures.

■   The database's transaction log, often called the redo log, is a group of operating system files that record the database changes made by committed transactions. During the commit of a transaction, Oracle writes enough information in the transaction log to "redo" the transaction's work, should the database require recovery.

An Example Backup and Recovery Scenario

With a database backup and the transaction log, Oracle can recover the database from all types of problems, even serious problems such as a disk crash. To better understand the function of database backups and the transaction log, let's study a brief example of how you can protect and recover an Oracle database from a disk failure:

■   Every night, you back up your Oracle database. Among other files, each database backup includes a backup of all the database's data files.

■   One day, a disk crashes that contains one of the database's data files. Consequently, a part of the database is unavailable and needs recovery. Although it is not necessary, you shut down the database so that you can perform the recovery.

■   First, you address the disk with the problem. Unfortunately, you have a serious disk failure and must replace the broken drive with a new drive.

■   Next, you use the most recent database backup to *restore* the lost data file to the replacement disk drive. However, the restored version of the data file is missing the work of transactions that committed *after* the backup was taken.

■   Finally, you perform database recovery. Guided by information in the database's control file, Oracle reads the transaction log to "redo" (apply) the work of past committed transactions to the restored data file, which *recovers* the data file and makes it current.

■   After completing database recovery, you open the database and make it available to applications.

This concise example gives you a general understanding of how an Oracle database's transaction log, control file, and database backups all play an important role during database recovery. Subsequent sections of this chapter explain how to configure the database's transaction log and control file, as well as perform database backup and recovery.

The Transaction Log or Redo Log

An Oracle database's *transaction log*, also called the *redo log*, is an important component of the database that protects the work of all committed transactions. The job of the transaction log is to immediately record the changes made by committed transactions. Should the database need recovery from an instance crash, disk failure, or some other type of problem, Oracle reads the transaction log during an appropriate recovery operation to "redo" the work of all committed transactions that are missing from the database.

Transaction Log Structure

The transaction log of a database is a group of operating system files on the host computer. As Figure 11-2 illustrates, a database's transaction log is made up of two or more log groups. Together, this set of log groups is often called the *online transaction log* or *online redo log*.

Each *log group* in the online log is a set of one or more identical operating system files that records the log entries of committed transactions. During server startup, LGWR chooses one of the groups in the online log and then uses the group to begin recording log entries. The log group being written to by LGWR at any given time

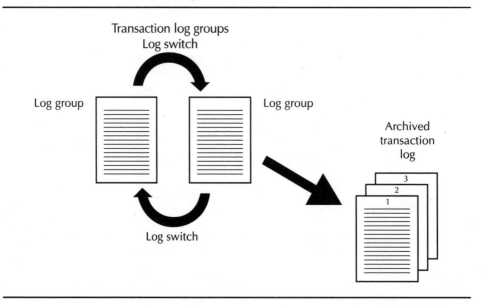

FIGURE 11-2. *An Oracle database's online log contains two or more log groups*

is the *current log group*. A log group has a static size and eventually fills with information. Once LGWR fills the current log group, Oracle performs a *log switch*. During a log switch, Oracle closes the current log group, opens the next log group, and begins writing log entries to the new current log group.

NOTE
To optimize the logging of transaction redo entries, Oracle sometimes allows LGWR to write an open transaction's redo entries in anticipation of a commit. Therefore, at any given time, the transaction log might contain a small number of changes to the database made by uncommitted transactions. However, Oracle notes these redo entries appropriately so that if database recovery is necessary, the server automatically clears the uncommitted changes from the database.

To enable Oracle to recover from damage to a database's data files, you must configure the server to permanently archive online log groups after they fill. Operating in this mode after a log switch, the archiver (ARCH) background server process archives the previous current group as a file on a disk or backup media (tape, for example). Oracle names each archived log group with a unique *log sequence number*, which serves as a permanent record of the log entries written to the group. The sequence of log groups that Oracle continuously generates by archiving log groups as they fill is called the *archived transaction log, archived redo log,* or *offline redo log.* Most Oracle databases archive log groups to offer full protection from media failures—you can refer to this mode of operation as either *ARCHIVELOG mode* or operating with *media recovery enabled.* To further protect the archived transaction log, you should move or copy your database's archived log files to offline storage, such as tape. Later in this chapter, you'll learn more about how you can back up a database's archived transaction log.

CAUTION
When you choose to operate your database with media recovery disabled, or in NOARCHIVELOG mode (not archiving log groups), you can boost server performance a small degree. However, the consequences can be significant, because this means Oracle can protect your database from simple system crashes only and not from more serious problems, such as disk failures.

After Oracle fills the final log group in the online log, LGWR performs a log switch back to the first log group, and then recycles through the log groups in the same order as before. When Oracle reuses a log group to record log entries, LGWR overwrites the previous entries in the group. If you have configured your server to archive log groups after they fill, the log entries are preserved as part of the database's archived log. By cyclically using and reusing the log groups in the database's transaction log, an Oracle database server can continuously record transaction log entries in a relatively small, predefined amount of disk space.

Log Members and Fault Tolerance

The transaction log is a critical component in Oracle's database protection scheme. To prevent an isolated disk failure from damaging the log groups in the transaction log, you can *mirror* the transaction log by creating log groups with multiple *members* (files) that reside on different disks. Figure 11-3 shows a mirrored transaction log with log groups that contain multiple members.

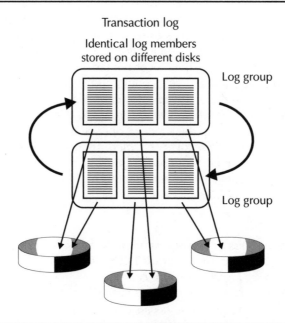

FIGURE 11-3. *To protect a transaction log from an isolated disk failure, you can create log groups with multiple members on different disks*

As Figure 11-3 shows, all members of a log group are replicas—as LGWR writes to a log group that has multiple members, LGWR writes to all members concurrently. Should one of the members in the current log group become damaged due to a disk failure or user error, LGWR can continue to write to the log group as long as one or more of the members are available.

When you operate your database server to archive filled log groups, ARCH reads one or more of the members in a mirrored log group to create an archived copy of the group. To protect the archived log from single points of failure, you can also mirror the archived log. That is, you can configure ARCH to write two or more replicas of each filled log group to distinct offline archive areas.

Checkpoints

Periodically, Oracle performs a *checkpoint*. During a checkpoint, DBWR writes all modified data blocks in the instance's buffer cache back to the data files that contain those blocks. The purpose of a checkpoint is to establish mileposts of transaction consistency on disk. After performing a checkpoint, Oracle knows that the changes made by all committed transactions have been written to the database's data files. Therefore, a checkpoint indicates how much of the transaction log's redo entries Oracle must apply if a simple server crash occurs and database recovery is necessary.

Oracle performs checkpoints at different times and at different levels. For example, Oracle automatically performs a *database checkpoint* during each log switch. During a database checkpoint, DBWR writes all modified data blocks in the buffer cache back to all of the database's data files. In contrast, when you take a tablespace offline, Oracle performs a *tablespace checkpoint*. During a tablespace checkpoint, DBWR writes the modified data blocks in the buffer cache that correspond to data files of that tablespace only.

NOTE
The next chapter teaches you more about checkpoints and how to control when database checkpoints happen.

Managing the Transaction Log

Now that you have a solid understanding of the concepts related to an Oracle database's transaction log, the following exercises will teach you how to get started managing your database's online log groups and log archiving.

EXERCISE 11.1: Displaying Current Log Configuration Information

To display useful information about your database's current transaction log configuration, you can use the *LIST* option of the special SQL*Plus command

ARCHIVE LOG. Start SQL*Plus and establish a SYSDBA-privileged administrator session using the steps in Exercise 3.5. Next, enter the following statement:

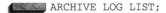 ARCHIVE LOG LIST;

If you have not altered your starter database's default log configuration, the results of the previous statement should be similar to the following:

```
Database log mode            No Archive Mode
Automatic archival           Enabled
Archive destination          /usr/oracle/dbs/arch
Oldest online log sequence   23
Current log sequence         25
```

Notice that, by default, the starter Oracle8i database on Linux operates in NOARCHIVELOG mode—in other words, with media recovery disabled. If you want to protect your database from the possibility of disk failure, you'll have to switch the database to operate permanently with media recovery enabled, and then you can configure how the log groups will be archived as they fill. The next few exercises teach you how to perform these tasks.

EXERCISE 11.2: Switching a Database's Log Mode and Configuring Log Archiving

To switch a database's log mode, you need to complete several steps in the following order:

1. Shut down the current instance of your starter database.

2. Modify several log-configuration parameters in your server's initialization parameter file to prepare the database for archiving filled log groups.

3. Start a new instance and mount the starter database to the instance, but do not open the database.

4. Use the ARCHIVELOG option (or NOARCHIVELOG option) of the SQL command ALTER DATABASE to switch the database's log mode.

5. Open the database.

This exercise teaches you how to perform each of the steps in the preceding list so that you can enable media recovery for your starter database.

First, shut down the current instance of your starter database using the SQL*Plus command SHUTDOWN, as in Exercise 3.7. Using a SYSDBA-privileged SQL*Plus session, enter the following statement to shut down your current database instance:

```
SHUTDOWN IMMEDIATE;
```

After a few seconds, you should see the following results, which indicate that Oracle has shut down:

```
Database closed.
Database dismounted.
ORACLE instance shut down.
```

At this point, exit your current SQL*Plus session:

```
EXIT;
```

Next, you need to open and edit your starter database's initialization parameter file, $ORACLE_HOME/dbs/initoralin.ora. (Review Exercise 3.10 if you are not sure how to open and edit your database's parameter file.) Once you open initoralin.ora in a text editor such as vi, search for the following block of text:

```
# log_archive_start = true
# log_archive_dest_1 = "location=/usr/oraInventory/admin/oralin/arch"
# log_archive_format = arch_%t_%s.arc
```

Once you switch your database's log mode to operate with media recovery enabled (in ARCHIVELOG mode), you need to configure Oracle to archive log groups as they fill, so that Oracle can reuse online log groups as transaction logging continues. The critical server parameters to set for transaction log archiving include LOG_ARCHIVE_START, LOG_ARCHIVE_DEST_#, and LOG_ARCHIVE_FORMAT.

- The *LOG_ARCHIVE_START* parameter determines whether ARCH automatically archives filled log groups after log switches. Once you enable media recovery for a database, you should set LOG_ARCHIVE_START to TRUE. If you set this parameter to FALSE, it's up to you to constantly monitor the instance and manually archive log groups as they fill. Be forewarned that if you fail to archive filled log groups in a timely fashion, Oracle will not be able to reuse a filled log group, which in turn suspends all database operations.

- Each *LOG_ARCHIVE_DEST_#* parameter determines a location to which ARCH archives log groups as they fill. Although the parameter allows you to specify locations using several different parameters, formats, and options, the most typical specification is one that uses the LOCATION parameter to target an operating system location, such as a directory on a disk. When you plan to operate the database with media recovery enabled, you should have at least one of these parameters—for example, LOG_ARCHIVE_DEST_1. For redundant protection of archived logs, you can configure up to five of these parameters—for example, LOG_ARCHIVE_DEST_2, LOG_ARCHIVE_DEST_3, and so on. See your Oracle documentation for more information about this parameter and its options.

■ The *LOG_ARCHIVE_FORMAT* parameter determines the filename format that Oracle uses to generate unique filenames for archived log files. If you wish, you can customize archived log filenames by changing the parameter's setting; however, in most cases the default setting is fine, thus relieving you of the need to explicitly set the parameter. If you want to override the default filename format, see your Oracle documentation for more information about the parameters that you specify as part of LOG_ARCHIVE_FORMAT to uniquely name archived log files.

To use the default archiving parameters in your starter database's initialization parameter file, simply uncomment the lines shown above by removing the #s at the beginning of each line so that they appear as follows.

```
log_archive_start = true
log_archive_dest_1 = "location=/usr/oraInventory/admin/oralin/arch"
log_archive_format = arch_%t_%s.arc
```

If for some reason you want to further edit the settings for these parameters, make appropriate modifications. Finally, save your edits, and exit your text editor.

At this point, you must start a new instance and mount the database to the instance, but do not open the database. First, start a new SQL*Plus session and establish a SYSDBA-privileged administrator session as in Exercise 3.5. Alternatively, if your Linux user account is a member of the OSDBA operating system group, you can establish a SYSDBA-privileged connection to a local Oracle instance by specifying the username INTERNAL. In this case, Oracle communicates with Linux to authenticate your administrator connection and the password as oracle. Either way, SQL*Plus will display a message that you are connected to an idle instance. Next, you can start up a new instance and mount the database using the *MOUNT* option of the SQL*Plus command STARTUP, as described in Exercise 3.6. Remember to specify the *PFILE* parameter to identify the location of your parameter file.

```
STARTUP MOUNT PFILE=$ORACLE_HOME/dbs/initoralin.ora;
```

Once this operation is complete, you should see results similar to the following:

ORACLE instance started.

```
Total System Global Area    56012784 bytes
Fixed Size                     69616 bytes
Variable Size               38993920 bytes
Database Buffers            16777216 bytes
Redo Buffers                  172032 bytes
Database mounted.
```

Finally, you can switch your database's log mode using the *ARCHIVELOG* option or *NOARCHIVELOG* option of the SQL command *ALTER DATABASE*. For example, enter the following statement to switch your starter database to ARCHIVELOG mode (media recovery enabled):

ALTER DATABASE ARCHIVELOG;

NOTE
Once you switch a database's log mode, always operate the database in this mode. There is no good reason to switch between log modes frequently.

Next, open the database to make it available, using the *OPEN* option of the SQL command *ALTER DATABASE*:

ALTER DATABASE OPEN;

To confirm your changes, repeat the steps listed in Exercise 11.1. An ARCHIVE LOG LIST statement should display results similar to the following:

```
Database log mode              Archive Mode
Automatic archival             Enabled
Archive destination            /usr/oraInventory/admin/oralin/arch
Oldest online log sequence     23
Next log sequence to archive   25
Current log sequence           25
```

Notice in the results above that the database now operates with media recovery enabled (ARCHIVELOG mode) and automatically archives log files, as they fill, to the location /usr/oraInventory/admin/oralin/arch. Also, notice that the display shows the log sequence number for the oldest online log group, the sequence number of the current online log group, and the sequence number of the next log group that will be archived (in this case, the current log group).

TIP

Any time that you make a structural or operational change to your database (such as changing the database's log archiving mode), it is a good idea to back up the database both before and after the change so that you can recover the database if a problem occurs. See the sections later in this chapter that discuss database backup and recovery.

EXERCISE 11.3: Forcing a Log Switch

Immediately upon opening your starter database for the first time after enabling media recovery with automatic archiving, you will probably not notice any archived log files in your archive destination. Oracle does not need to archive an online log group until transactions generate enough log entries to fill the current online log group and cause a log switch.

To test the new log mode and automatic archiving, let's force a log switch to happen using the *SWITCH LOGFILE* option of the SQL command *ALTER SYSTEM*. Using your current SYSDBA-privileged SQL*Plus session, enter the following statement:

```
ALTER SYSTEM SWITCH LOGFILE;
```

Subsequently, take a look in your log archive destination (for example, /usr/oraInventory/admin/oralin/arch) and you should see a new archived log file. For example, enter the following HOST command from your SQL*Plus session:

```
HOST ls /usr/oraInventory/admin/oralin/arch
```

NOTE

*The SQL*Plus command HOST lets you execute an operating system command from your computer's operating system from within SQL*Plus.*

The archived log file's name should be similar to the following:

```
arch_1_25.arc
```

NOTE
You will have the appropriate privileges to access the archive log destination if your Linux session is through the oracle account. Otherwise, your Linux user account must have the appropriate group permissions to list the files in the $ORACLE_HOME directory and subdirectories.

The trailing portion of the generated filename (in this case, 25) is the sequence number that corresponds to the online log group that was archived.

NOTE
If you use an ARCHIVE LOG LIST statement after forcing a log switch, you'll notice that the current online log sequence has been incremented by one.

EXERCISE 11.4: Permanently Saving Archived Log Files

The example configuration for log archiving in previous practice exercises shows how to archive filled online log groups to a single archive destination on disk. To permanently protect the availability of the database's archived log files and to free up valuable disk space on your server, you should periodically move archived log files to offline storage, such as a tape or CD-ROM. See Exercise 11.11, later in this chapter, which teaches you how to back up archived log files.

CAUTION
If you do not periodically move archived log files to offline storage, and your system generates enough archived log files to consume all available disk space at the archive log destination, your database instance will suspend operations until enough space is available to archive filled online log groups.

EXERCISE 11.5: Examining a Database's Online Log Group Structure

A database's data dictionary contains several views that you can query to display information about the current configuration and status of your database's online log groups, including the V$LOG and V$LOGFILE views. Using your current

SYSDBA-privileged SQL*Plus session, enter the following query to display the names of all log members in each group of your starter database:

```
COLUMN member FORMAT a50;

SELECT group#, member FROM v$logfile
  ORDER BY group#;
```

NOTE
*The FORMAT parameter of the SQL*Plus command COLUMN, used in the previous example, lets you set the display width of a column in a query's result set.*

Unless you have altered the configuration of your starter database's online log groups, your results should be similar to the following:

```
GROUP# MEMBER
--------- --------------------------------------------------
      1 /usr/oracle/oradata/oralin/redo03.log
      2 /usr/oracle/oradata/oralin/redo02.log
      3 /usr/oracle/oradata/oralin/redo01.log
```

Notice from these results that there are three online log groups for your starter database, and that each online log group has only one member. If you want to protect your online redo log from a single point of failure, you'll need to create two or more members for each online log group, as the next exercise demonstrates.

EXERCISE 11.6: Creating Log Groups with Multiple Members

As the previous exercise shows, the default online log groups for the starter database have only one member each. If the disk containing the log members were to crash, you might lose the data necessary to subsequently recover the database. In this exercise, you'll learn how to add members to log groups and establish a more fault-tolerant online log configuration.

For ideal fault tolerance, each log group should have two or more members and should store the members of a log group on a mutually exclusive set of disk storage systems. For example, if a log group has two members, place each member of the log group on different disks managed by different controllers—do not place them on the same disk, or on different disks controlled by the same disk controller.

NOTE
If your starter database operates on a computer with only one disk, then you cannot fulfill the recommended log group configuration. However, you can still learn how to configure log groups with multiple members by completing this exercise—just store the log members somewhere on the same disk, but realize that this is not the optimal configuration.

To add log members to a log group, you use the *ADD LOGFILE MEMBER* clause of the SQL command *ALTER DATABASE*. A simplified syntax listing of the ADD LOGFILE MEMBER clause follows.

```
ALTER DATABASE
 ADD LOGFILE MEMBER
 ('filename' [REUSE] [,'filename' [REUSE]] ... )
 TO { GROUP integer
    | 'filename' }
```

Notice that you can specify filenames for one or more new members of a log group, and you can indicate the log group to target by the group's unique ID or by specifying the filename of one of the existing members in the group. Also notice that you do not have to indicate a file size for the new members—Oracle automatically makes the new members match the existing member(s) in the group. For example, assuming that your Linux computer has a file system location /u/oradata/oralin, enter the following statements to add new log members to each of the log groups of the starter database.

```
ALTER DATABASE
 ADD LOGFILE MEMBER '/u/oradata/oralin/redo01.log'
  TO '/usr/oracle/oradata/oralin/redo01.log';

ALTER DATABASE
 ADD LOGFILE MEMBER '/u/oradata/oralin/redo02.log'
  TO '/usr/oracle/oradata/oralin/redo02.log';

ALTER DATABASE
 ADD LOGFILE MEMBER '/u/oradata/oralin/redo03.log'
  TO '/usr/oracle/oradata/oralin/redo03.log';
```

NOTE
When you add log members to log groups, Oracle automatically creates the new files with the ownership and default group setting of the Linux user account that owns the Oracle installation—for example, the user oracle and the group oinstall. Furthermore, all file system locations that store Oracle database files, such as data files, log members, and control files, should be owned by the user and group that owns the Oracle installation.

At this point, each log group in the database's online log has two members—one in the /usr partition and one in the /u partition. If one of the drives were to crash and no other part of the database was affected, Oracle could continue to log transactions using the intact members of the online log groups. You can confirm your new configuration by using the query in Exercise 11.5—the results of this query should be similar to the following:

```
GROUP# MEMBER
--------- -------------------------------------------------
    1 /usr/oracle/oradata/oralin/redo03.log
    1 /u/oradata/oralin/redo03.log
    2 /usr/oracle/oradata/oralin/redo02.log
    2 /u/oradata/oralin/redo02.log
    3 /usr/oracle/oradata/oralin/redo01.log
    3 /u/oradata/oralin/redo01.log
```

TIP
Again, any time that you make a structural or operational change to your database (such as adding a member to a log group), it is a good idea to back up the database both before and after the change so that you can recover the database if a problem occurs. See the sections later in this chapter that discuss database backup and recovery.

This exercise concludes your introduction to configuring an Oracle database's online transaction log and log archiving. Now let's turn our attention to protecting the database's control file.

The Database Control File

The information in a database's control file describes the physical structure of the database. Oracle also uses information in the database's control file to guide various types of database recovery operations. When using Oracle's Recovery Manager utility, Oracle also uses a database's control file to record information about administrative operations such as database backups. Because the control file has such important functions, it's no wonder that a database cannot function properly without its control file.

To protect a database's control file and database availability from disk failures, you should always mirror the database's control file to multiple locations, just as you do with the log groups in a database's online transaction log. When you mirror a database's control file to multiple locations, Oracle updates every copy of the control file at the same time. If one copy of the control file becomes inaccessible due to a disk I/O problem or failure, other copies of the control file remain available and permit database processing to continue without interruption.

EXERCISE 11.7: Mirroring the Database Control File

By following the steps in Exercise 10.8, you can see that the default configuration of your Oracle8i database for Linux has three copies of the database control file:

```
COLUMN name FORMAT a13;
COLUMN value FORMAT a42;

SELECT name, value FROM v$parameter
 WHERE name = 'control_files';
```

NOTE
The COLUMN statements format the display width of the NAME and VALUE columns.

Your results should be similar to the following:

```
NAME          VALUE
------------- --------------------------------------------------
control_files /usr/oracle/oradata/oralin/control01.ctl,
              /usr/oracle/oradata/oralin/control02.ctl,
              /usr/oracle/oradata/oralin/control03.ctl
```

However, it is important to note that all copies of the database's control file reside in the same directory on the same disk. If this disk were to crash, the database's control file would be lost and complete database recovery would be difficult or impossible. In view of this vulnerability, you need to perform the following steps to move one of the control file copies to a different drive to better protect the availability of the database's control file in the event of an isolated disk crash.

1. Shut down the database instance.

2. Move one of the control file copies to a different drive.

3. Edit the CONTROL_FILES parameter in the database's parameter file (/usr/oracle/dbs/initoralin.ora).

4. Restart the instance and open the database.

This exercise teaches you how to perform each of the steps in the preceding list.

First, use your existing SYSDBA-privileged SQL*Plus session to issue a SHUTDOWN statement and shut down the database, as in Exercise 3.7:

```
SHUTDOWN IMMEDIATE;
```

Once the database shuts down, you can exit SQL*Plus:

```
EXIT;
```

The next step is to move one of the control file copies to a different drive. For example, using a shell session (as the oracle user) and the cp command, copy the file /usr/oracle/oradata/oralin/control02.ctl to /u/oradata/control02.ctl.

```
cp /usr/oracle/oradata/oralin/control02.ctl /u/oradata/control02.ctl
```

If the filenames and directory names in the example do not match those on your computer, make appropriate substitutions and note the new file locations.

NOTE
To repeat, all file system locations that store Oracle database files, such as data files, log members, and control files, should be owned by the user and group that owns the $ORACLE_HOME location—for example, the user oracle and the group oinstall.

After moving one of the control file copies to a different location, you need to open and edit your database's initialization parameter file, /usr/oracle/admin/oralin/

pfile/initoralin.ora. (Review Exercise 3.10 if you are not sure how to open and edit your database's parameter file.) Once you open initoralin.ora in a text editor, search for the CONTROL_FILES parameter. In my starter database, the CONTROL_FILES parameter setting appears similar to the following:

```
control_files = ("/usr/oracle/oradata/oralin/control01.ctl",
"/usr/oracle/oradata/oralin/control02.ctl",
"/usr/oracle/oradata/oralin/control03.ctl")
```

NOTE
The control filenames in your starter database may differ, depending on the location where you installed Oracle8i.

Update the CONTROL_FILES parameter setting so that the file specification of the file that you moved earlier is correct. For example, the updated CONTROL_FILES parameter for my starter database is as follows:

```
control_files = ("/usr/oracle/oradata/oralin/control01.ctl",
"/u/oradata/oralin/control02.ctl",
"/usr/oracle/oradata/oralin/control03.ctl")
```

Once you make the necessary changes, save the file and exit your text editor. At this point, you can restart the instance and open the database. First, start a new SQL*Plus session and establish a SYSDBA-privileged administrator session (for example, connect using the INTERNAL account). Next, start up a new instance, and mount and open the database using the OPEN option of the SQL*Plus command STARTUP as in Exercise 3.6. Don't forget to specify the PFILE parameter to identify the location of your parameter file.

```
STARTUP OPEN PFILE=$ORACLE_HOME/dbs/initoralin.ora;
```

If the database opens successfully, you did everything correctly. You can confirm the mirrored configuration of your control file copies by resubmitting the query used earlier in the exercise:

```
COLUMN name FORMAT a13;
COLUMN value FORMAT a42;

SELECT name, value FROM v$parameter
 WHERE name = 'control_files';
```

Your results should be similar to what's shown in the following code.

```
       NAME            VALUE
       ------------    -------------------------------------------------
       control_files   /usr/oracle/oradata/oralin/control01.ctl,
                       /u/oradata/oralin/control02.ctl,
                       /usr/oracle/oradata/oralin/control03.ctl
```

Introduction to Backup and Recovery Options

Once you mirror the log groups in your database's online log, configure log archiving, and mirror the database's control file for fault tolerance, you can turn your attention to database backup and recovery. Table 11-1 lists the tools and techniques that you can use to back up and recover databases with Oracle8i Enterprise Edition for Linux.

Because Recovery Manager does not function properly with the version of Oracle8i distributed with this book, subsequent sections of this book teach you how to perform database backup and recovery using a combination of SQL and operating system commands rather than with Recovery Manager.

Tool	Description
Recovery Manager (RMAN)[*]	Tool for backing up, restoring, and recovering both local and remote Oracle databases. You can use the RMAN command line interface to enter commands interactively to back up databases or run jobs that automate regular database backups. RMAN also supports unique features, such as parallel processing for faster backup operations, and incremental backups. RMAN is automatically installed with Oracle8i Enterprise Edition, and it is the recommended tool for both Oracle8 and Oracle8i.
Operating system backups and restores	Using a combination of SQL and operating system commands, you can back up Oracle databases. Prior to Oracle8, OS backups were the only method for performing Oracle database backups.

[*] Does not function properly with Oracle8.1.6 Enterprise Edition on Linux

TABLE 11-1. *Database Backup and Recovery Options for Oracle8i Enterprise Edition on Linux*

Database Backups

Database backups are an important part of a comprehensive database protection strategy. In general, a *database backup* is a copy of the files that comprise the database. If you damage or lose a file that is part of a database, you can extract a copy of the lost file from a database backup to restore the file in the database.

Types of Database Backups

Considering the tools and techniques available for database backup and recovery (RMAN, OS backup and restore), understanding the many terms, equivalent terms, and concepts related to various types of database backups can be very confusing for a novice. To make things relatively simple, this chapter will focus on performing the most typical types of database backups using a combination of SQL and operating system commands. Table 11-2 and the next few sections introduce the generic database backup terminology that you should understand before continuing.

Whole Database Backups

A *database backup,* or *whole database backup,* includes a copy of all database data files and the database's control file. A whole database backup is the most common type of backup that you perform to protect an Oracle database. With Oracle, you can make two different types of database backups: an open database backup and a closed database backup.

Open Database Backups   An *open database backup,* also called a *hot database backup,* is a database backup that you perform while the database is open and operational. Open database backups are useful for environments in which high availability is required by one or more applications. You cannot perform an open database backup unless you *always* operate your database with media recovery enabled (that is, in ARCHIVELOG mode).

Because the data in the data files of an open database backup are being modified by transactions throughout the course of the backup, the backup is said to be *inconsistent* or *fuzzy.* That is, there is not a single transaction-consistent time point to which all data blocks correspond. Don't worry, though. After restoring a data file from an inconsistent database backup, Oracle's recovery mechanism regenerates missing transactions so that all data blocks in the file are in a transaction-consistent state that corresponds with all other data blocks in the database.

Closed Database Backups   A *closed database backup* is a database backup that you perform after a planned database shutdown. A closed database backup is an option for systems where high availability is not critical.

Type of Backup (Synonyms)	Description
Database backup (Whole database backup)	Includes all data files of all tablespaces, as well as the database's control file. *This is the most common type of backup that you perform to protect a database.*
Open database backup (Hot database backup) (Inconsistent database backup)	Database backup taken while the database is open and operational. Because the data in the backup does not correspond to any single transaction-consistent time point, the backup is said to be *inconsistent*.
Closed database backup (Cold database backup) (Consistent database backup)	Database backup taken after you shut down the database cleanly (that is, after a planned shutdown that completes normally). Because the data in the backup corresponds to a transaction-consistent time point, the backup is said to be *consistent*.
Tablespace backup	Includes all data files of a tablespace.
Online tablespace backup (Hot tablespace backup) (Inconsistent tablespace backup)	Tablespace backup taken while the database is open and the tablespace is online. Online tablespace backups are also called *hot tablespace backups* or *inconsistent tablespace backups*.
Offline tablespace backup (Consistent tablespace backup)	Tablespace backup taken while the database is open but the tablespace is offline. If you take a tablespace offline cleanly, a subsequent offline backup of the tablespace is considered *consistent*.
Data file backup (Data file copy)	Backup of a single data file.

TABLE 11-2. *General Oracle Database Backup Terms and Concepts to Understand*

NOTE
A closed database backup is also the only option for databases that operate without media recovery enabled (that is, in NOARCHIVELOG mode). In this case, a closed database backup includes all of the database's data files, online log members, and the database's control file.

To perform a closed database backup, the preceding shutdown of the database must complete normally—you cannot perform a closed database backup after a system crash or an abnormal shutdown. During a normal database shutdown, Oracle rolls back any open transactions, performs a database checkpoint, and then closes the database's data files and control file. All files that comprise the database are in a transaction-consistent state with one another. Therefore, a closed database backup is often called a *consistent database backup*.

Tablespace Backups
Oracle also lets you back up individual tablespaces in a database. A *tablespace backup* is a backup of all the data files that comprise the tablespace. Tablespace backups are useful when you want to back up particular divisions of a database that applications modify more frequently than others.

When your database always operates with media recovery enabled, you can perform two different types of tablespace backups: online tablespace backups and offline tablespace backups.

Online Tablespace Backups   An *online tablespace backup*, also called a *hot tablespace backup*, is a tablespace backup that you perform while the database is open and the tablespace is online. Because the data in the tablespace can be modified as the backup progresses, the backup is said to be *inconsistent*.

Just as with open database backups, an online tablespace backup is useful when high availability is a must. Rather than shutting down the database or taking a tablespace offline for a backup, you simply back up the tablespace while applications are using it.

Offline Tablespace Backups   An *offline tablespace backup* is a tablespace backup that you perform while the database is open but the tablespace is offline.

If you take a tablespace offline normally (that is, if Oracle can successfully perform a tablespace checkpoint and close all associated data files), the backup data generated from an offline tablespace backup is consistent.

Backing Up Databases

The following series of exercises teach you how to use a combination of SQL and operating system commands to back up your starter database. The exercises in this section of the chapter teach you how to

- back up an online tablespace
- back up the database's control file
- back up archived log files
- back up related database files
- automate a complete online database backup

EXERCISE 11.8: Preparing a Storage Space for Database Backups

In this chapter's exercises, you will learn how to create backup files of your database in some disk location. To prepare for the exercises in this section of the chapter, you should create a directory to organize your database backup files. *Using a shell session as the oracle user*, create a backup directory on a disk partition that has at least 1GB of available free space. For example, the following mkdir command creates a backup directory in the directory structure of the $ORACLE_BASE location.

```
mkdir $ORACLE_BASE/admin/oralin/backup
```

NOTE

For safe keeping, system backup files are normally stored on some type of offline media, such as tape, rather than a disk location. If possible, consider moving backup files to offline storage both for safe keeping and to free up disk space on your server.

EXERCISE 11.9: Backing Up an Online Tablespace

The data files of a tablespace are the operating system files that store all data within the tablespace. Consequently, it is very important to make regular backups of the data files of the tablespaces in your database. To back up an individual tablespace's data files while the tablespace is online, you must complete the following steps:

1. Obtain a list of the tablespace's data files.

2. Put the tablespace in online backup mode.

3. Use operating system commands to back up the tablespace's data files.

4. Remove the tablespace from online backup mode.

To list the data files for each tablespace in your database, use your current SYSDBA-privileged SQL*Plus session to issue the following commands:

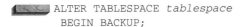

```
COLUMN file_name FORMAT a45;
COLUMN tablespace_name FORMAT a20;

SELECT file_name, tablespace_name
  FROM dba_data_files
 ORDER BY tablespace_name;
```

The results of the previous query should be similar to the following:

```
FILE_NAME                                     TABLESPACE_NAME
--------------------------------------------- -----------------
/usr/oracle/oradata/oralin/drsys01.dbf        DRSYS
/usr/oracle/oradata/oralin/indx01.dbf         INDX
/usr/oracle/oradata/oralin/photos1.dbf        PHOTOS
/usr/oracle/oradata/oralin/photos2.dbf        PHOTOS
/usr/oracle/oradata/oralin/rbs01.dbf          RBS
/usr/oracle/oradata/oralin/system01.dbf       SYSTEM
/usr/oracle/oradata/oralin/temp01.dbf         TEMP
/usr/oracle/oradata/oralin/tools01.dbf        TOOLS
/usr/oracle/oradata/oralin/users01.dbf        USERS

9 rows selected.
```

To prepare an online tablespace for backup, you can use the following syntax of the SQL command ALTER TABLESPACE.

```
ALTER TABLESPACE tablespace
  BEGIN BACKUP;
```

For example, using your current SYSDBA-privileged SQL*Plus session, enter the following command to prepare the SYSTEM tablespace for an online tablespace backup.

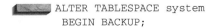
```
ALTER TABLESPACE system
   BEGIN BACKUP;
```

After an online tablespace is in online backup mode, you can back up the tablespace's data files using operating system commands or a backup utility of your choice. For example, the previous query shows that the SYSTEM tablespace has just one data file, /usr/oracle/oradata/oralin/system01.dbf. Considering this, enter the following HOST command (all on one line) from within your current SQL*Plus session to create an archive that backs up the data file of the SYSTEM tablespace.

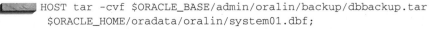
```
HOST tar -cvf $ORACLE_BASE/admin/oralin/backup/dbbackup.tar
   $ORACLE_HOME/oradata/oralin/system01.dbf;
```

NOTE
Substitute an appropriate path in the preceding example if you created a different backup directory in Exercise 11.8. Also, if disk space is at a premium on your system, add the -z option to your tar command to filter the archive creation through the gzip compression utility or archive directly to tape if a tape drive is available on your system.

Once you complete the backup of your online tablespace, it is very important to use the following syntax of the SQL command ALTER TABLESPACE to remove the tablespace from online backup mode.

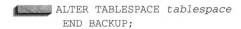
```
ALTER TABLESPACE tablespace
   END BACKUP;
```

For example, using your current SYSDBA-privileged SQL*Plus session, enter the following command to remove the SYSTEM tablespace from online backup mode.

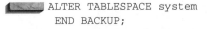
```
ALTER TABLESPACE system
   END BACKUP;
```

CAUTION
The first and final steps in this exercise are very important. If an online tablespace is not placed in backup mode before you make data file backups, the backup files are worthless. On the other hand, if you forget to remove an online tablespace from backup mode after making data file backups, you can inadvertently damage the database.

To back up an entire Oracle database while it is online, you must complete the steps in this exercise for every online tablespace—see Exercise 11.13 for additional information on performing a complete online database backup with multiple online tablespaces.

NOTE
To back up a tablespace that was taken offline normally with ALTER TABLESPACE ... OFFLINE NORMAL, simply back up the tablespace's corresponding data files. In other words, you do not need to place an offline tablespace in backup mode before backing up the tablespace's data files.

EXERCISE 11.10: Backing Up the Database's Control File

A database's control file is critical to the ongoing operation of the database. Even if you mirror your database's control file on physically independent storage devices, it is very important to make backups of the database's control file, especially after you make database structural modifications, such as the addition of a tablespace or data file, or the modification of your database's online log structure. To back up an Oracle database's control file, you can use the following syntax of the SQL command ALTER DATABASE:

```
ALTER DATABASE
  BACKUP CONTROLFILE TO 'filename' [REUSE];
```

The REUSE option is useful if you want to overwrite an existing file. For example, using your current SYSDBA-privileged SQL*Plus session, enter the following command to make a backup of your database's control file:

```
ALTER DATABASE
  BACKUP CONTROLFILE TO '$ORACLE_BASE/admin/oralin/backup/controlbkup.ctl' REUSE;
```

NOTE
Substitute an appropriate path in the preceding example if you created a different backup directory in Exercise 11.8.

EXERCISE 11.11: Backing Up Archived Log Files

Earlier exercises in this chapter explain how to enable media recovery for your database and automatically archive online log groups as they fill. To fully protect your database's archived log files and free up disk space in the archiving destination, you should periodically back up the archived log files to offline storage, such as tape or CD-ROM, as quickly as possible, to protect their availability. Use appropriate operating system commands to complete this operation.

For example, the following operating system command archives all archive log files in the archive log destination to tape:

```
tar -cv $ORACLE_BASE/admin/oralin/arch/*
```

Afterwards, you can delete the archive log files from the archive log destination to free disk space on your computer.

TIP

When you make database backups of any type, you should carefully document what each backup contains, when the backup was completed, and other pertinent information. Subsequently, if database recovery is necessary, you can review your notes to quickly ascertain what backups you will need to use during database recovery.

EXERCISE 11.12: Backing Up Related Database Files

The previous three exercises teach you how to back up the most important database files, including data files, archived log files, and the database's control file. However, a good backup strategy will also protect other files related to database operation, including the following:

- Database parameter files, including $ORACLE_HOME/dbs/initoralin.ora or equivalent

- The database's password file, $ORACLE_HOME/dbs/orapworalin.ora or equivalent

Why Not Backup Online Log Files?

You might be wondering why the exercises in this chapter do not mention anything about backing up the files that comprise the database's online log. That's because the exercises in this chapter assume that you operate your database with media recovery (that is, log archiving) enabled and with a mirrored online log to protect the online log groups from isolated disk failures. In this type of configuration, the online log is adequately protected from everything but a complete site disaster.

- Net8 configuration files, including
  $ORACLE_HOME/network/admin/tnsnames.ora,
  $ORACLE_HOME/network/admin/sqlnet.ora,
  $ORACLE_HOME/network/admin/listener.ora)

- Custom SQL command scripts (for example, backup scripts)

- Other files related to system configuration (for example, /etc/oratab,
  /etc/rc.d/init.d/dbora)

Use operating system commands or your favorite backup utility to create
backups of the files in the preceding list. The next exercise also has an example
backup script that protects the files in this list.

EXERCISE 11.13: Automating a Complete Online Database Backup

The previous exercises in this section of the chapter introduce how to back up the
individual components of an Oracle database. In this exercise, you will learn how
to automate the backup of all database components at once, using a SQL command
script. Automating database backups with scripts make routine database backups
easy to perform and make errors less likely.

The exact commands inside a backup script for an Oracle database will always
be unique because of installation options and other variables. However, a sound
database backup script will complete the following steps:

1. Back up each tablespace's data files.

2. Back up the database's control file.

3. Back up related database files.

The following is an example backup script that you can use to back up the
starter database on your Linux computer. A copy of this script is distributed as part
of this book's archive, and it is available in the *8iStarterKit_Home*/scripts directory.

```
/********************************************************/
/* DESCRIPTION: Backup script for default database.     */
/* USAGE: Execute in SYSDBA-privileged SQL*Plus session. */
/********************************************************/
PROMPT Backing up database to tar
PROMPT $ORACLE_BASE/admin/oralin/backup/backup001.tar

PROMPT Backing up SYSTEM tablespace ...
PROMPT
ALTER TABLESPACE system BEGIN BACKUP;
HOST cp $ORACLE_HOME/oradata/oralin/system01.dbf $ORACLE_BASE/admin/oralin/backup/.
ALTER TABLESPACE system END BACKUP;

PROMPT SYSTEM tablespace backed up.
PROMPT
```

```
PROMPT Backing up TOOLS tablespace ...
PROMPT

ALTER TABLESPACE tools BEGIN BACKUP;
HOST cp $ORACLE_HOME/oradata/oralin/tools01.dbf $ORACLE_BASE/admin/oralin/backup/.
ALTER TABLESPACE tools END BACKUP;

PROMPT TOOLS tablespace backed up.
PROMPT

PROMPT Backing up TEMP tablespace ...
PROMPT

ALTER TABLESPACE temp BEGIN BACKUP;
HOST cp $ORACLE_HOME/oradata/oralin/temp01.dbf $ORACLE_BASE/admin/oralin/backup/.
ALTER TABLESPACE temp END BACKUP;

PROMPT TEMP tablespace backed up.
PROMPT

PROMPT Backing up USERS tablespace ...
PROMPT

ALTER TABLESPACE users BEGIN BACKUP;
HOST cp $ORACLE_HOME/oradata/oralin/users01.dbf $ORACLE_BASE/admin/oralin/backup/.
ALTER TABLESPACE users END BACKUP;

PROMPT USERS tablespace backed up.
PROMPT

PROMPT Backing up RBS tablespace ...
PROMPT

ALTER TABLESPACE rbs BEGIN BACKUP;
HOST cp $ORACLE_HOME/oradata/oralin/rbs01.dbf $ORACLE_BASE/admin/oralin/backup/.
ALTER TABLESPACE rbs END BACKUP;

PROMPT RBS tablespace backed up.
PROMPT

PROMPT Backing up DRSYS tablespace ...
PROMPT

ALTER TABLESPACE drsys BEGIN BACKUP;
HOST cp $ORACLE_HOME/oradata/oralin/drsys01.dbf $ORACLE_BASE/admin/oralin/backup/.
ALTER TABLESPACE drsys END BACKUP;

PROMPT DRSYS tablespace backed up.
PROMPT

PROMPT Backing up INDX tablespace ...
PROMPT

ALTER TABLESPACE indx BEGIN BACKUP;
HOST cp $ORACLE_HOME/oradata/oralin/indx01.dbf $ORACLE_BASE/admin/oralin/backup/.
ALTER TABLESPACE indx END BACKUP;

PROMPT INDX tablespace backed up.
PROMPT
```

```
PROMPT Backing up PHOTOS tablespace ...
PROMPT

ALTER TABLESPACE photos BEGIN BACKUP;
HOST cp $ORACLE_HOME/oradata/oralin/photos01.dbf $ORACLE_BASE/admin/oralin/backup/.
HOST cp $ORACLE_HOME/oradata/oralin/photos02.dbf $ORACLE_BASE/admin/oralin/backup/.
ALTER TABLESPACE photos END BACKUP;

PROMPT PHOTOS tablespace backed up.
PROMPT

PROMPT Backing up database control file ...
PROMPT

ALTER DATABASE BACKUP CONTROLFILE TO
'$ORACLE_BASE/admin/oralin/backup/controlbkup.ctl' REUSE;

PROMPT Database control file backed up.
PROMPT

PROMPT Backing up miscellaneous files ...
PROMPT

HOST cp $ORACLE_HOME/dbs/initoralin.ora $ORACLE_BASE/admin/oralin/backup/.
HOST cp $ORACLE_HOME/dbs/orapworalin $ORACLE_BASE/admin/oralin/backup/.
HOST cp $ORACLE_HOME/network/admin/*.ora $ORACLE_BASE/admin/oralin/backup/.
HOST cp /etc/oratab $ORACLE_BASE/admin/oralin/backup/.
HOST cp /etc/rc.d/init.d/dbora $ORACLE_BASE/admin/oralin/backup/.

PROMPT Miscellaneous files backed up.
PROMPT

PROMPT Creating compressed archive backup001.tar ...
PROMPT

HOST tar -czvf $ORACLE_BASE/admin/oralin/backup/backup001.tar
$ORACLE_BASE/admin/oralin/backup/*
```

NOTE
If you did not install Oracle using the same directory structure or name as in Chapter 2, or you chose a different backup location in Exercise 11.8, you will need to make appropriate modifications to the commands in the preceding script.

Notice that the example script, when backing up several online tablespaces, completes the steps in Exercise 11.9 for each online tablespace, one at a time. In other words, it does not attempt to place several or all of the online tablespaces in backup mode, back up the data files, and then remove the tablespaces from backup mode—doing things this way can generate an extraordinary amount of server overhead when your system is busy, and it can consequently limit the performance of applications during an online database backup.

TIP
To free space in your backup location, remember to delete temporary backup files after you archive the files to permanent offline storage.

The backup script in this exercise is an extremely simple example of how you can automate database backups. As you become more familiar with Oracle and database backup, you will most likely want to build more sophisticated scripts as shell scripts to allow for variables and command line arguments.

Logical Database Backups

To supplement the physical, block-by-block backups of a database's data files, archived log groups, and the control file, you can make logical backups of an Oracle database's data. A *logical backup* is a backup of database information that corresponds to the specific schemas and schema objects in the database (for example, tables). To make and use logical database backups, you use the Oracle utilities Export and Import.

The Export Utility

Using Oracle's *Export* utility, you can logically back up all or a subset of data in an Oracle database. For example, Export lets you selectively export

- all objects in the database
- the objects in a specific schema
- a single table

You can export database information while the database is open and in use. Export ensures that the export data for an individual table is consistent with itself. However, when you export a schema or the entire database while the database is open and being modified, the export data that you generate is not necessarily consistent—if all export data must be consistent, you must take additional measures to ensure that an Export file is a transaction-consistent snapshot of the data that you are exporting. This means that applications and their transactions cannot make any changes to the database data that you are exporting until after the export operation completes. This requirement alone can severely affect database concurrency.

The Import Utility

To recover lost data from an Export file, you use the companion Oracle utility, *Import*. With Import, you can read an Export file to restore specific database tables, schemas, or an entire database.

The Proper Use of Export and Import

Oracle's Export and Import utilities should never be your first or complete choice to protect an Oracle database. That's because an export of a database, schema, or table can never guarantee complete recovery from a database failure. It is very important to understand that after you import data from an Export file, there is no recovery process to complete—the work of all committed transactions that completed after you performed the export is lost forever. For these reasons, use database exports only as a supplement to true database backups and transaction logging.

Other Uses for Export and Import

Besides using Export and Import for supplemental database protection, you can use the utilities to move data from one database to another. For example, when you configure different databases in an Oracle distributed database system to replicate large amounts of data using Oracle's data replication features, you can use the Export and Import utilities to initially transfer data between sites during configuration. In many cases, the use of Export and Import is also necessary when migrating an existing Oracle database to a newer release of Oracle.

Database Recovery

Hopefully, your database will never have a problem, and you will never have to use the transaction log and database backups to recover lost work. However, if you do, rest assured that Oracle has the necessary mechanisms to complete the job. The following sections explain Oracle's database recovery mechanisms and options that you can use to repair a damaged database. Subsequent exercises teach you how to simulate the loss of a data file and recover it.

Roll-Forward and Roll-Back Recovery Stages

All types of database recovery include two stages: roll-forward and roll-back. Figure 11-4 illustrates what happens during the roll-forward and roll-back recovery stages.

During the *roll-forward recovery*, Oracle applies the necessary archived and online log groups to "redo" all committed transactions not present in the current data files of the database. When you are recovering from a simple system crash, all necessary log entries are present in the current set of online log groups. After more serious damage, such as a disk failure, you might need to use backup data files and archived log groups to complete the roll-forward recovery.

After roll-forward recovery, Oracle must perform *roll-back recovery*. During roll-back recovery, Oracle uses information in the database's rollback segments to "undo" the database changes made by any transactions that were open (uncommitted) when the system crashed. After roll-back recovery completes, the database contains all work as of the last committed transaction before the problem that necessitated the recovery.

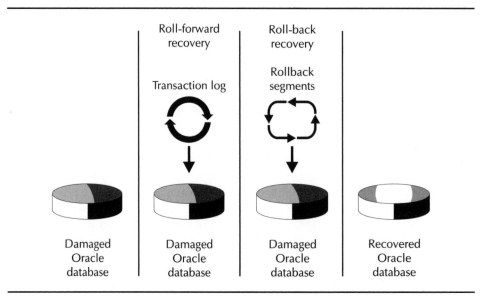

FIGURE 11-4. *A database recovery includes two stages: roll-forward and roll-back*

Now that you have a general understanding of how Oracle performs all database recovery operations, Table 11-3 and the following sections explain more specifically the different types of database recovery situations.

Type of Recovery	Description
Crash recovery	The automatic recovery operation that Oracle performs to recover from a simple system crash.
Media recovery (Disk failure recovery)	A recovery operation that is necessary after one or more of a database's data files are lost. Before performing a media recovery, you typically have to restore one or more lost data files from a backup set or switch to available image copies.
Complete recovery (Database, tablespace, or data file recovery)	A recovery operation that recovers the work of all committed transactions.

TABLE 11-3. *Summary of Oracle's Recovery Mechanisms*

Type of Recovery	Description
Incomplete recovery (Point-in-time, cancel-based, or change-based recovery)	A recovery operation that recovers only some of the work of committed transactions.
Database recovery (Closed database recovery)	A database recovery is a type of complete recovery that recovers lost work in all data files of the database. You perform a database recovery while the database is mounted but closed.
Tablespace recovery (Open database recovery)	A tablespace recovery is a type of complete recovery that recovers lost work in all data files of a specific tablespace. You can perform a tablespace recovery while the database is open and the damaged tablespace is offline, or while the database is mounted but closed.
Data file recovery (Open database recovery)	A data file recovery is a type of complete recovery that recovers lost work in a specific data file. You can perform a data file recovery while the database is open and the damaged tablespace is offline, or while the database is mounted but closed.
Time-based recovery (Point-in-time recovery)	A time-based recovery is a type of incomplete recovery that recovers the work of committed transactions in a database up to a specific point in time (for example, up to Monday at 8:05 A.M., just before a user dropped an important table).
Change-based recovery	A change-based recovery is a type of incomplete recovery that recovers the work of committed transactions in a database up to a specific system change number (SCN).
Cancel-based recovery	A cancel-based recovery is a type of incomplete recovery that recovers the work of committed transactions in a database up to the application of a specific log group.

TABLE 11-3. *Summary of Oracle's Recovery Mechanisms* (continued)

Crash Recovery

Unfortunately, power failures and software problems are common events that can cause an Oracle database server to crash unexpectedly. When a system crash happens, your Oracle instance does not shut down cleanly. More specifically, at the time of the crash, the server might be managing many open transactions that have modified database information. Additionally, during a system crash, Oracle does not have time to perform a database checkpoint to make sure that all modified data blocks in the server's buffer cache are written back to the database's data files safely. Considering these side effects of a system crash, it's likely that the data in the data files of the database will be inconsistent and missing some changes made by committed transactions—the database's transaction log will contain the only permanent records of some committed transactions. Database recovery is thus necessary.

After a system crash, Oracle automatically performs crash recovery as part of the subsequent server startup. To perform *crash recovery*, Oracle uses the redo entries in the online transaction log to perform roll-forward recovery on the existing, intact data files of the database (by definition, a system crash does not permanently damage any of the database's data files). After performing the roll-back recovery stage, crash recovery is complete and Oracle automatically opens the database for general use. Although it might take longer to start up Oracle after a system crash, crash recovery is completely transparent and happens without any work on your part.

Media Recovery: Recovery from File Damage

After a disk failure or a user error causes the loss of one or more of a database's data files, you must perform a *media recovery* operation. During a typical media recovery, you must perform the following steps:

1. Fix all hardware problems.

2. Restore lost data files.

3. Make available the transaction log groups necessary to perform recovery.

4. Perform an appropriate media recovery operation.

The following sections explain each step in more detail.

NOTE
Recovery from the loss of a data file is not possible unless you always operate the database with media recovery enabled (that is, in ARCHIVELOG mode). When you choose to operate the database with media recovery disabled (that is, you choose not to archive filled transaction log groups), database recovery is not possible from media failures. Your only option is to perform a restore operation using the most recent closed database backup. Understand that if this is the case, the work of all committed transactions performed since the backup is lost forever.

Fix Hardware Problems

After you lose one or more data files because of a hardware failure, you should fix the hardware problem if it might prevent the server from operating properly in the future. For example, if a disk drive crashes and you want to continue to use the drive for the database, you should either fix or replace the drive before performing recovery.

Restore Lost Data Files

Before you can recover a lost file, there must be an intact version of the file in place to recover. When a database's data files are lost because of a hardware failure or a user error, you must restore copies of all damaged data files from the most recent backup.

Mount Necessary Archived Log Groups

After you restore a data file from a backup, Oracle must recover the file by performing roll-forward and roll-back recovery. Depending on how long ago the backup of the data file was made and how much work has been done since the backup, roll-forward recovery of the restored data file might involve applying a significant number of redo entries from the database's archived and online logs. Therefore, you must ensure that all of the archived log groups necessary to complete recovery of the damaged data file are available. To meet this requirement, you should restore (mount) archived log files from backups to the archive log destination *before* starting recovery.

Perform Database Recovery

After you prepare for recovery from media failure by fixing hardware and restoring necessary data files and archived log groups, you can start a database recovery operation using SQL*Plus and the DBA command RECOVER. Once you start a database recovery, Oracle will carry out the stages of database recovery and fix your damaged database. The following sections explain several different types of media recovery operations.

Complete Recovery

A *complete recovery* operation is one that recovers the work of all committed transactions. Complete recovery operations, including database recovery, tablespace recovery, and data file recovery, are the most typical types of recovery used when a problem damages a database.

Database Recovery

The simplest way to recover all lost work in a database using only one operation is to perform a database recovery. A *database recovery* is a type of complete recovery that recovers lost work in all data files of the database. Oracle identifies data files that require media recovery and automatically recovers them by applying information in the database's offline and online redo logs.

A database recovery is appropriate when many data files of the database require recovery and the database can be unavailable during the recovery operation. To perform a database recovery, the database is mounted but closed.

Tablespace Recovery

When selected portions of a database have been damaged and high availability is a requirement, consider using tablespace recovery. A *tablespace recovery* is a type of complete recovery that recovers lost work in all data files of a specific tablespace. You can use SQL*Plus and the DBA command RECOVER to perform a tablespace recovery while the database is open and the damaged tablespace is offline, or while the database is mounted but closed.

NOTE

If a problem damages any data file of the SYSTEM tablespace, the database cannot operate properly. Therefore, you must shut down the database after such a failure; you cannot perform tablespace recovery of the SYSTEM tablespace while the database is open.

Data File Recovery

When a single data file has been damaged, consider using a data file recovery. A data file recovery is a type of complete recovery that recovers lost work in a specific data file. You can use SQL*Plus and the DBA command RECOVER to perform a data file recovery while the database is open and the damaged tablespace is offline, or while the database is mounted but closed.

NOTE
You cannot recover a damaged data file of the SYSTEM tablespace while the database is open.

Incomplete Recovery

In most situations, Oracle applies all available transaction log groups to perform a complete database recovery (for example, with database, tablespace, or data file recovery). In rare circumstances, you might consider performing an incomplete recovery operation. When you perform an incomplete recovery, Oracle recovers the work of only some of the committed transactions by applying a limited amount of the redo entries in the database's transaction log.

For example, assume that on Monday at 8:06 A.M., you accidentally drop an important database table—no other damage has been done to the database. If you have a recent Export file that contains the table, you can import the table to recover nicely from this problem. However, if you do not use Export to perform supplemental database backups (see the section "Logical Database Backups" earlier in this chapter for more information about the Export utility), you can still recover the lost table by performing an incomplete recovery operation. For example, you might restore the entire database from the most recent backup to a different computer, and then perform a point-in-time recovery up to the time 8:05 A.M. Then, you could export the table and import it back into the production database to recover from your mishap.

Oracle supports three different types of incomplete recovery: time-based recovery, change-based recovery, and cancel-based recovery.

Time-Based Recovery

A *time-based recovery*, sometimes called a *point-in-time recovery*, is a type of incomplete recovery that recovers the work of committed transactions in a database up to a specific point in time (for example, up to Monday at 8:05 A.M., just before a user dropped an important table).

Change-Based Recovery

A *change-based recovery* is a type of incomplete recovery that recovers the work of committed transactions in a database up to a specific *system change number* (SCN). Oracle assigns a unique SCN to every transaction that commits. If you know the SCN of the last transaction that you want to include in a database recovery, you can perform change-based recovery.

Cancel-Based Recovery

A *cancel-based recovery* is a type of incomplete recovery that recovers the work of committed transactions in a database, up to the application of a specific log group. To perform cancel-based recovery, you must be able to indicate the last log sequence to apply as part of the recovery.

What About Damage to Log Groups and the Control File?

If you read the previous section closely, you'll notice that there is no mention of the fact that serious failures might damage the database's transaction log groups and its control file. You might be asking yourself what type of database recovery is necessary after these types of files are damaged or lost.

If you mirror the database's online and archived transaction log, as well as the database's control file, on different disks to protect them from isolated disk failures and user errors, you'll never have to worry about recovering from the loss of these critical database files. As long as one copy of a log group or control file is always accessible, the database can continue to function properly without interruption.

In contrast, when you lose a data file, database recovery is usually necessary because Oracle does not provide any facility to mirror data files. Oracle can always perform database recovery as long as you have a backup of the lost data file and at least one copy of all log groups and the database's control file.

After a disk failure, the database's transaction log or control file might become unprotected (that is, unmirrored). For example, if you mirror the database's control file to two different disks, and one disk fails, the control file would now be unprotected because there is no mirror copy. When such situations arise, the most urgent step that you can take is to reconfigure the database's log groups and control file and protect them with at least one mirror copy. Otherwise, the database is vulnerable to an isolated disk failure.

NOTE
Even when you mirror the database's transaction log groups and control file, the database theoretically still remains vulnerable to total site disasters (for example, fires, floods, and other catastrophes). If these types of situations worry you, consider using Oracle's standby database feature or data replication for ultimate database protection—the following section discusses these advanced database protection features of Oracle8i.

Database Protection for Mission-Critical Databases

Oracle's backup and recovery mechanisms can protect a database from almost any type of failure that occurs. However, if you plan to use Oracle to manage your entire business and support mission-critical applications, you might want to design a database protection strategy with some additional contingency plans. For example, will you be able to recover your business's lost data if an earthquake totally destroys your building? If so, how long will it take for you to actually recover any damaged databases, and is this time window satisfactory to your business's customers and workers? Fortunately, Oracle has a couple of features that can satisfy even the most extreme high-availability requirements. The next couple of sections discuss these features: standby databases and subset failover sites.

Standby Databases

A *standby database* is a database that mirrors a *primary database*. In a standby database configuration, the primary database is open and in use with applications, while the standby database is closed and perpetually in a special standby database recovery mode. If a failure of some type happens to make the primary database unavailable, you can activate the standby database immediately, and applications can continue to work after switching connections. Figure 11-5 illustrates a standby database configuration.

In a standby database configuration, both the primary database and the standby database operate with media recovery enabled. As the primary database archives a

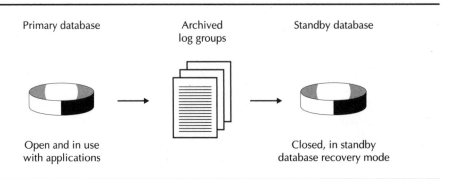

Primary database   Archived   Standby database
                          log groups

Open and in use   Closed, in standby
with applications   database recovery mode

FIGURE 11-5. *A standby database configuration*

transaction log group, you transfer the log to a standby database site as soon as possible. Once you have an archive log group at the standby database site, you can apply it to the standby database to make the standby database a more recent version of the primary database.

NOTE
Starting with Oracle8i, you can automate the process of transferring logs from the primary database site to the standby database site and then applying them to the standby database.

To protect a database's availability from complete site disasters, such as floods, fires, and earthquakes, you must operate the primary and standby databases on different computers at physically different locations. Additionally, you should prepare your system's network configuration so that clients can connect to the standby database should a site switchover be necessary.

Failover Sites and Data Replication

Oracle's standby database feature is a good solution when you need to protect the availability of an entire database from extreme situations, such as site disasters. However, some environments might not need the full database protection that a standby database configuration supports, or require the standby database to always be available for database access by applications. In such circumstances, consider using Oracle's advanced data replication features to create a failover site, instead. Oracle's advanced data replication features are beyond the scope of this book—see your Oracle documentation for more information.

Recovering Databases

Now that you have a general idea of Oracle's recovery mechanisms, the following series of exercises teach you how to recover your starter database from a simulated system crash, and then from the simulated loss of a data file.

The exercises in this section build upon the previous exercises in this chapter. In other words, you will not be able to complete the following exercises unless you configure your starter database to operate with media recovery enabled (ARCHIVELOG mode) and to archive online log groups as they fill, and you have a backup that includes all data files in the database.

Important Warning: Before You Start ...

The following exercises are about to show you how to purposely damage an Oracle database so that you can practice performing database recovery. Considering that you might make a mistake during the subsequent database recovery process, please do not attempt to perform the following exercises using a database that contains important data. Instead, you should use these exercises to practice your database recovery skills within the confines of an isolated test database environment, or using a database that you can afford to lose should you make a mistake.

EXERCISE 11.14: Simulating a System Crash and Performing Crash Recovery

As mentioned previously, a system crash is an unexpected or otherwise abrupt shutdown of Oracle, such that the instance does not have time to roll back current transactions, disconnect users, and leave the database's data in a clean state. To simulate a system crash, you can use the *ABORT* option of the SQL*Plus command *SHUTDOWN*.

Assuming that you are working with your starter database, and it is an isolated database not in use with other users and applications, simulate a system crash by entering the following command using your current SYSDBA-privileged SQL*Plus session:

```
SHUTDOWN ABORT;
```

Once Oracle aborts the instance, you should see the following message:

```
ORACLE instance shut down.
```

At this point, pretend that a temporary power failure has just happened, causing your Linux computer to restart. Crash recovery for your starter database automatically happens when you restart an instance and open the database. For example, using your existing SYSDBA-privileged SQL*Plus session, enter the following command to restart the instance and open the database:

STARTUP OPEN PFILE=$ORACLE_HOME/dbs/initoralin.ora;

The output from the command should be similar to the following:

```
Oracle instance started.

Total System Global Area      56012784 bytes
Fixed Size                       69616 bytes
Variable Size                 38993920 bytes
Database Buffers              16777216 bytes
Redo Buffers                    172032 bytes
Database mounted.
Database opened.
```

Your database is now available and completely operational for server users and applications.

NOTE
If you configure your Oracle database service to automatically start up when Linux restarts (see Exercise 3.17), after an authentic crash of your Linux computer Oracle will automatically restart and perform crash recovery without any administrative intervention.

EXERCISE 11.15: Simulating a Lost Data File and Performing Tablespace Recovery

This last exercise of the chapter is the most challenging exercise yet in this book. This exercise teaches you how to simulate the loss of a data file so that you can practice performing media recovery with an open database.

NOTE
You will not be able to complete this exercise unless you configure your starter database to operate with media recovery enabled (ARCHIVELOG mode) and to archive online log groups as they fill, and you have a backup of all data files in the database.

This exercise will take you through the following steps:

1. Check to make sure that the intended backup contains all data files in your database.

2. Restore all archived log files necessary to complete the recovery.

3. Take the INDX tablespace offline in your starter database.

4. Delete the data file that corresponds to the INDX tablespace.

5. Restore the data file of the INDX tablespace.

6. Try to bring the "damaged" INDX tablespace back online.

7. Recover the damaged INDX tablespace while the remainder of the database is open and available.

8. Bring the recovered INDX tablespace back online.

The first step in this exercise is to ensure that you have a backup that you can use to recover your database. If you made your backup using the steps exactly as in Exercise 11.13, you can use the following command from a shell prompt to list the contents of your archive.

```
tar -tzvf $ORACLE_BASE/admin/oralin/backup/backup001.tar
```

Before you continue, make sure that you have a backup that contains all data files in your starter database. If you do not have one, complete Exercise 11.13 successfully before continuing with this exercise.

Once you have a backup that contains all data (referred to hereafter as "the backup"), the next step is make sure that all archived log files that Oracle generated just before and since the backup was taken are available in the archive log destination. This may require that you extract some logs from any backups that you took as part of Exercise 11.11.

At this point, let's pretend that for some reason, the data file that corresponds to the INDX tablespace has been lost. If this were true, the database's alert file and applications would most likely display Oracle-related error messages that indicate the name of the damaged tablespace or data file(s). When you notice this type of problem, you should immediately take the corresponding tablespace offline to avoid frightening application users with all sorts of errors that they know nothing about. To take the INDX tablespace offline, enter the following command using your current SYSDBA-privileged SQL*Plus session:

```
ALTER TABLESPACE indx OFFLINE NORMAL;
```

NOTE

In a genuine situation where a data file has been lost, you might need to use the OFFLINE TEMPORARY, OFFLINE IMMEDIATE, or OFFLINE FOR RECOVER options to successfully take the damaged tablespace offline, as described in Exercise 10.7.

Next, you can simulate the loss of the INDX tablespace's data file by simply deleting the file. For example, using a shell session as the oracle user, use the rm command to delete the indx01.dbf file:

```
rm $ORACLE_HOME/oradata/oralin/indx01.dbf
```

NOTE

Substitute an appropriate path in the preceding command if you installed your starter database in a different directory on your computer.

The next step is to restore the "lost" data file of the damaged INDX tablespace using an operating system command or your backup utility. For example, if you created your backup exactly as in Exercise 11.13, you can extract a copy of the missing indx01.dbf data file to $ORACLE_HOME/oradata/oralin using the following commands:

```
cd /
tar -xzvf $ORACLE_BASE/admin/oralin/backup/backup001.tar
cp $ORACLE_BASE/admin/oralin/backup/indx01.dbf $ORACLE_HOME/oradata/oralin
```

NOTE

The previous commands assume that your backup is named backup001.tar, is available in the $ORACLE_BASE/admin/oralin/backup directory on your computer, and that your database's data files are in $ORACLE_HOME/oradata/oralin—make appropriate modifications to the previous commands if your backup is named differently, is stored on tape, or your system's directory structure differs. Also, you can extract just the usr/oraInventory/admin/oralin/backup/indx01.dbf file, rather than all files in the archive, to save time.

Once you restore the damaged indx01.dbf data file from your backup, enter the following SQL command using your current SYSDBA-privileged SQL*Plus session just to see what error messages appear when you try to bring the INDX tablespace back online with the restored version of the indx01.dbf data file.

```
ALTER TABLESPACE indx ONLINE;
```

After submitting this SQL command, you should see error messages similar to the following:

```
ERROR at line 1:
ORA-01113: file 6 needs media recovery
ORA-01110: data file 6: '/usr/oracle/oradata/oralin/indx01.dbf'
```

Before commencing recovery, you can make things a bit more automatic by issuing the following command using your current SYSDBA-privileged SQL*Plus session:

```
SET AUTORECOVERY ON;
```

This command tells SQL*Plus that all necessary archived logs are available in the archive log destination, and that it should automatically apply them during recovery rather than prompting you for filenames.

Finally, it's time to recover the "damaged" INDX tablespace. To recover a specific tablespace, use the *TABLESPACE* parameter of the DBA command *RECOVER*. For example, enter the following command to recover the INDX tablespace:

```
RECOVER TABLESPACE indx;
```

Once you start a database recovery with the SQL*Plus AUTORECOVERY system variable set to ON, you should see messages similar to the following, indicating the progress of your recovery.

```
ORA-00279: change 197150 generated at 07/03/2000 16:07:52 needed for thread 1
ORA-00289: suggestion : /usr/oraInventory/admin/oralin/arch/arch_1_10.arc
ORA-00280: change 197150 for thread 1 is in sequence #10


ORA-00279: change 197179 generated at 07/05/2000 08:47:14 needed for thread 1
ORA-00289: suggestion : /usr/oraInventory/admin/oralin/arch/arch_1_11.arc
ORA-00280: change 197179 for thread 1 is in sequence #11
ORA-00278: log file '/usr/oraInventory/admin/oralin/arch/arch_1_10.arc' no
longer needed for this recovery


ORA-00279: change 217181 generated at 07/05/2000 15:22:57 needed for thread 1
```

```
ORA-00289: suggestion : /usr/oraInventory/admin/oralin/arch/arch_1_12.arc
ORA-00280: change 217181 for thread 1 is in sequence #12
ORA-00278: log file '/usr/oraInventory/admin/oralin/arch/arch_1_11.arc' no
longer needed for this recovery


ORA-00279: change 217278 generated at 07/06/2000 10:18:53 needed for thread 1
ORA-00289: suggestion : /usr/oraInventory/admin/oralin/arch/arch_1_13.arc
ORA-00280: change 217278 for thread 1 is in sequence #13
ORA-00278: log file '/usr/oraInventory/admin/oralin/arch/arch_1_12.arc' no
longer needed for this recovery


Log applied.
Media recovery complete.
```

The messages that you see during your recovery will vary, depending on the number of archived logs that Oracle needs to apply during roll-forward recovery for the indx01.dbf data file. The final message is the important one—it indicates that your recovery operation was successful! Upon the successful completion of media recovery, you can bring the formerly damaged INDX tablespace back online using the following SQL command:

```
ALTER TABLESPACE indx ONLINE;
```

Congratulations! You just recovered your database from the loss of a specific data file.

Chapter Summary

Protecting an Oracle database from unforeseen problems is one of the most important jobs that you can perform as a database administrator. This chapter has explained the many features of Oracle that you can use to back up, restore, and recover databases when inevitable problems affect your system.

- A database's transaction log records the changes made by committed transactions.

- A database backup is a collection of all of the files that comprise the database. If you damage or lose a file that is part of a database, you can extract a copy of the lost file from a database backup to restore the file in the database.

- A database recovery operation recovers the work lost due to some type of problem. Configured correctly, Oracle can recover a database from all types of problems, including simple system crashes, more serious disk failures, and even complete site disasters.

CHAPTER
12

Basic Tuning

lthough you probably do not have a need to tune your test starter database to achieve any type of performance enhancement as you learn about Oracle8i, it is a good idea to become familiar with the concepts and steps necessary to do some basic tuning for future reference. This chapter explains how to tune the following components of an Oracle8i database application system:

- Access to database tables with indexes and other optional database objects

- Application SQL

- The database instance, including disk I/O and memory structures

Chapter Prerequisites

To practice the hands-on exercises in this chapter, you need to complete the following steps:

1. Start SQL*Plus and connect as SYS. See Chapter 9 for more information about the SYS account.

2. Once you establish a connection as SYS, run the $ORACLE_HOME/sqlplus/admin/plustrce.sql command script using the SQL*Plus command @. For example, after starting a SQL*Plus session and connecting as SYS, enter the following command:

```
SQL> $ORACLE_HOME/sqlplus/admin/plustrce.sql;
```

Running this script creates the PLUSTRACE role, which is necessary to complete one of the exercises in this chapter.

3. To practice the hands-on exercises in this chapter, you need to start a Linux session as the oracle user, and then start SQL*Plus and run the following command script

location/8iStarterKit/SQL/chap12.sql

where *location* is the file directory where you expanded the support archive that accompanies this book. For example, after starting SQL*Plus and connecting as SCOTT, you can run this chapter's SQL command script using the SQL*Plus command @, as in the following example (assuming that your chap12.sql file is in /tmp/8istarterkit/SQL).

```
SQL> @/tmp/8istarterkit/SQL/chap12.sql;
```

Once the script completes successfully, leave the current SQL*Plus session open and use it to perform this chapter's exercises in the order that they appear.

What Is Tuning?

As you start building real systems with Oracle8i, there comes a time when you'll need to focus on tuning the system to achieve acceptable performance for the system's users. The fundamental goal of computer application system tuning should be to minimize the *appreciable* amount of time that an application user must wait while the application processes a request; when you accomplish this goal, the application does not unnecessarily limit the productivity of the user.

Before starting to tune a database application system based on Oracle8i, you must understand that there are several distinct components of the system to tune: data access, application logic, and the database server itself. Incredibly large and complex books have been written that encompass hundreds or thousands of pages to teach you how to squeeze every last bit of performance out of an Oracle-based application system. However, before you overwhelm yourself with too many details, realize that you can achieve the most noticeable performance gains by performing some very simple tuning. The sections of this chapter teach you the fundamental concepts and steps necessary to tune each application component.

NOTE
The performance of the network in a distributed application can also affect an application's performance. See Chapter 3 for more information about configuring Oracle's Net8 networking software, as well as setting up Oracle8i to accept network connections.

Tuning Table Access

One focus of application performance tuning concentrates on making sure that Oracle can access the information in database tables as quickly as possible. Typically, disk I/O is the primary bottleneck that determines the speed of table access—the less disk I/O required to access table data, the better the dependent applications will perform. Because of this, one goal of application tuning is to minimize the amount of disk access that applications must perform when working with database tables. This section of the chapter explains several types of database structures that you can use to reduce disk I/O when applications access tables.

Indexes

As Chapter 7 explains (in the "Indexes" section), using table indexes is the most common technique for reducing the amount of disk I/O necessary to find specific rows in a table, and thus for improving the performance of table access. Please reread that section of the book if you need a review of the basic concepts of indexing.

Oracle8i supports several different types of indexes to satisfy many types of application requirements, including B-tree (normal) indexes, reverse key indexes, bitmap indexes, index-organized tables, and function-based indexes. The following sections explain more about the various types of indexes that you can create for a table's columns.

Normal (B-Tree) Indexes

The default and most common type of index for a table column is a B-tree (or normal) index. See the "B-Tree Indexes" section in Chapter 7 for more information about normal indexes and for a simple practice exercise that shows you how to create a normal index.

Reverse Key Indexes

When keys are sequential in a B-tree index, the distribution of keys in the index's tree structure can become one-sided and make the index inefficient (see Figure 7-4 for an illustration of a B-tree index structure). In this case, you can create a reverse key B-tree index to better balance the distribution of sequential keys. In a *reverse key index*, the storage of bytes for each key value is the reverse of what they would normally be in a standard B-tree index.

Bitmap Indexes

Another indexing option for the columns in a table is a bitmap index. A *bitmap index* is a B-tree index that stores bitmaps rather than key values. Each bitmap is a series of bits that are either on (1) or off (0). A bitmap index includes bitmaps for each distinct value in the column or set of columns that is in the index.

To illustrate the storage structure of a bitmap index, consider the following query of the ITEMS table. To make the example easier to understand, the query uses the SQL function *ROWNUM* to display the row number of each row in the ITEMS table as a pseudo-ROWID (authentic ROWIDs are more difficult to interpret). The query also displays the ID of the part ordered in each line item.

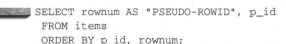

```
SELECT rownum AS "PSEUDO-ROWID", p_id
  FROM items
  ORDER BY p_id, rownum;
```

The results of this query would be as follows:

```
PSEUDO-ROWID        P_ID
------------    ----------
           4             1
          12             1
          14             1
           2             2
           9             2
          17             2
          20             2
          24             2
           1             3
           7             3
          10             3
          18             3
          19             3
           5             4
          11             4
          15             4
          22             4
           3             5
           6             5
           8             5
          13             5
          16             5
          21             5
          23             5

24 rows selected.
```

Now consider a bitmap index of the P_ID column in the ITEMS table. If each bitmap in the index stores bits for 12 rows in the table, Figure 12-1 illustrates the series of bitmaps in the index for the distinct P_ID (part ID) key values 1, 2, 3, 4, and 5.

Examine each bitmap in the index and carefully compare them with the results of the previous query. You should notice that when the associated key value is present for the row, the bit is turned on (1) in the bitmap (match the pseudo-ROWIDs with the P_IDs of each row)—otherwise, the bit is turned off (0).

While bitmap indexes are useful, bitmap indexes are an option to consider only in specific situations. In general, bitmap indexes work best with columns that have just a few distinct values relative to the total number of rows in the table. The more distinct values that an indexed column contains, the more bitmaps in the index, and the more space needed to store the index. Additionally, because of the way that Oracle must lay out a bitmap index, bitmap indexes are useful typically only for decision support and data warehouse applications that query data. Bitmap indexes should not be created to support applications that frequently insert and update data.

Key	Start ROWID	End ROWID	Bitmap
1	1	12	000100000001
1	13	24	010000000000
2	1	12	010000001000
2	13	24	000010010001
3	1	12	100000100100
3	13	24	000001100000
4	1	12	000010000010
4	13	24	001000000100
5	1	12	001001010000
5	13	24	100100001010

FIGURE 12-1.   *A simple bitmap index*

Function-Based Indexes

In addition to creating straightforward B-tree and bitmap indexes for columns in a table, Oracle8*i* also lets you create B-tree and bitmap indexes based on expressions that you build using one or more columns in the table. For each row in a table, a *function-based index* of the table materializes and stores the value of an expression along with the row's ROWID. A function-based index is a handy performance structure that you can use to increase the performance of queries and DELETE statements that frequently use the same expression in their search criteria (WHERE clauses).

The expression that you specify for a function-based index can have the following properties:

■ The expression can be an arithmetic expression, using standard arithmetic operators.

■ The expression can employ one or more built-in SQL functions, excluding group functions such as AVG, COUNT, MAX, MIN, STDDEV, SUM, and VARIANCE.

■ The expression can employ one or more user-defined PL/SQL functions, declared either as stand-alone functions or as public functions that are part of a PL/SQL package. Additionally, each user-defined function in the expression must be a *deterministic* function—see your Oracle documentation for more information about declaring deterministic functions.

Index-Organized Tables

When you create a B-tree or bitmap index for a table, Oracle creates a separate index segment to store the index's data, separate from the associated table's data. Another indexing option is to create a table *within* a B-tree index—in other words, as an index-organized table. In an *index-organized table*, each index entry contains a key value and its corresponding row data (rather than the row's ROWID, as in a normal index). Index-organized tables must have a primary key, which serves as the index for the structure. Figure 12-2 illustrates the structure of an index-organized table.

In general, index-organized tables are appropriate only for applications that manage complex or unstructured data, and thus require some form of cooperative indexing. With *cooperative indexing*, the application must be able to interpret the non-key values that are part of each index entry. Spatial data and online analytical processing (OLAP) applications are examples of applications that manage complex data and can benefit from the use of index-organized tables.

Creating and Managing Indexes

The following practice exercises teach you how to create a normal index and a function-based index.

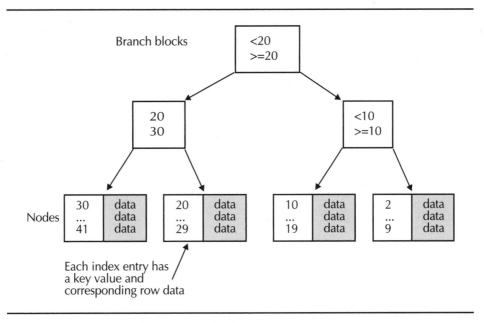

FIGURE 12-2. *An index-organized table*

EXERCISE 12.1: Creating Normal Indexes

To create a normal index for a table, you use the SQL command *CREATE INDEX*. An abbreviated form of the CREATE INDEX command for creating a normal index, including storage parameters (see Chapter 10), is as follows:

```
CREATE INDEX [schema.]index
 ON { [schema.]table
 ( column [ASC|DESC] [, column [ASC|DESC]] ... )
 [PCTFREE integer]
 [INITRANS integer] [MAXTRANS integer]
 [TABLESPACE tablespace]
 [STORAGE (
 [INITIAL integer [K|M]]
 [NEXT [K|M]]
 [MINEXTENTS integer]
 [MAXEXTENTS {integer|UNLIMITED}]
 [PCTINCREASE integer]
 [FREELIST GROUPS integer] [FREELISTS integer]  )
```

NOTE

Also see Exercise 7.18, which teaches you the basics of creating a normal (B-tree) index for a column in a table.

Suppose that queries frequently request specific records from the ORDERS table according to the ORDERDATE field of a sales order, as shown here:

```
-- Show orders placed on June 21, 1999 (equality search)
SELECT id
 FROM orders
 WHERE orderdate = '21-JUN-99';

-- Show orders placed in June of 1999 (range search)
SELECT id, orderdate, status
 FROM orders
 WHERE orderdate BETWEEN '01-JUN-99' AND '30-JUN-99';
```

Assuming that the ORDERS table contains many rows, you could improve the response time of such equality and range-comparison queries by creating a normal index for the ORDERDATE column of the ORDERS table. Enter the following statement to create the index:

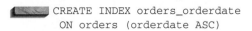

```
CREATE INDEX orders_orderdate
 ON orders (orderdate ASC)
```

```
PCTFREE 5
INITRANS 3 MAXTRANS 10
TABLESPACE users
STORAGE (
  INITIAL 50K NEXT 50K
  MINEXTENTS 1 MAXEXTENTS 10
  PCTINCREASE 0
  FREELIST GROUPS 1 FREELISTS 2  );
```

In certain situations, you might need to create a composite index. A *composite index* is an index that contains concatenated key values of two or more columns in the same table. You can create a composite index for up to 32 columns.

NOTE
Even though a composite index can contain up to 32 columns, the total size of the largest concatenated key value must be less than 1/3 the total data block size.

When you create a composite index, carefully consider the order of the columns in the index. Most important, make sure that the leading column in the index is the column that queries most often specify in the condition of a WHERE clause to search for rows in the table. Oracle does not automatically use a composite index when SQL statements request rows by a non-leading column in a composite index.

For this practice exercise, let's assume that there are many sales representatives in the SALESREPS table, and queries frequently request specific rows in the table using each sales representative's last-name/first-name combination. In this case, create a composite index that consists of the LASTNAME and FIRSTNAME columns in the SALESREPS table by entering the following CREATE INDEX statement:

```
CREATE INDEX salesrep_names
  ON salesreps (lastname, firstname);
```

EXERCISE 12.2: Creating a Function-Based Index

Consider the following query of the CUSTOMERS table that identifies information about a specific customer record, based on the uppercase version of a customer's LASTNAME field.

```
SELECT id, lastname, firstname, phone
  FROM customers
  WHERE UPPER(lastname) = 'CLAY';
```

In this case, a normal index of the LASTNAME field would not be optimal because the index contains each customer record's LASTNAME field as it exists in the record itself (in other words, in all uppercase letters, in all lowercase letters, or in a mixed case of letters). Consequently, to do a comparison with an index of the LASTNAME column, Oracle needs to convert each key in the index to uppercase letters and then compare the resulting string to the search criteria.

Assuming that case-insensitive searches like the query in this exercise are common with the LASTNAME column of the CUSTOMERS table, a more efficient solution would be to create a function-based index that indexes the uppercase version of each customer's LASTNAME. A function-based index is an index of an expression rather than of the simple scalar values in a column. For example, enter the following statement to index the uppercase LASTNAME values in the CUSTOMERS table:

```
CREATE INDEX customer_upper_lastname
  ON customers (UPPER(lastname));
```

Now, when you run the example query, Oracle simply compares the precomputed, uppercased, index key values to the search criteria to find the target rows.

There are several important prerequisites that you must meet to create and then use function-based indexes with Oracle8*i*. First, to create function-based indexes based on tables in your schema, you must have the QUERY REWRITE system privilege—the prerequisite command script for this chapter grants your practice account the privilege so that you can complete this exercise. Additionally, for Oracle to make use of function-based indexes, the instance's or session's QUERY_REWRITE_ENABLED parameter must be set to TRUE, and the QUERY_REWRITE_INTEGRITY parameter must be set to TRUSTED. The prerequisite command script for this chapter uses two ALTER SESSION statements to set the practice session's parameters as necessary—see your Oracle documentation for more information about these server parameters. And finally, you must use cost-based optimization to take advantage of function-based indexes—see the section "Tuning SQL" later in this chapter, which discusses Oracle's optimizer.

Data Clusters

Oracle8*i* offers data clusters as an alternative to indexing, which can minimize disk I/O for table access. A *data cluster* is a unique way of storing table data. In a data cluster, Oracle clusters the related rows of one or more tables together in the same data block. Figure 12-3 shows an example of a data cluster.

The motivation for using a typical data cluster is to store together on disk the rows that an application commonly uses together. When the application requests the set of rows, Oracle can retrieve all the requested rows with perhaps one or just a few disk I/Os. For example, you might use a data cluster to "prejoin" the ORDERS and ITEMS tables in a data warehouse. When a sales analysis application requests historical information about specific sales orders, Oracle could read the data for a specific order with only one disk I/O. In contrast, when related rows are stored unclustered in random data blocks across a disk, several disk I/Os are necessary to complete the application's request.

As Figure 12-3 shows, every data cluster has a *cluster key*. A data cluster's key is a column or set of columns that determines how to cluster data. The cluster key in this example is the related order ID column of both tables.

Oracle offers two different types of data cluster organizations: indexed data clusters and hash data clusters. The following sections explain more about each type of data cluster.

Indexed Data Clusters

In an *indexed data cluster*, Oracle physically stores a row in the cluster according to the row's cluster key value. For example, when you cluster the ORDERS and

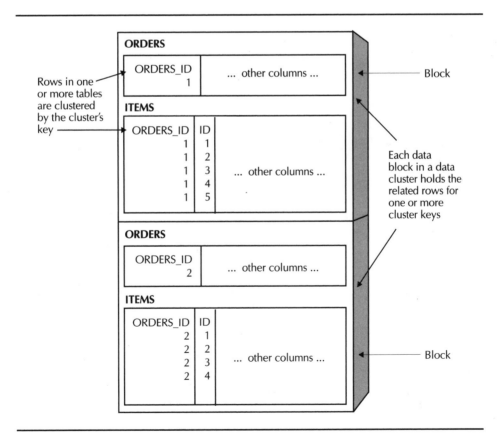

FIGURE 12-3. *A data cluster*

ITEMS tables by order IDs, Oracle clusters each order along with its associated line items in a separate data block. Figure 12-3 illustrates an indexed data cluster of the ORDERS and ITEMS tables.

Hash Clusters

The motivation for hash clustering is a little bit different than with indexed data clusters. In a *hash data cluster*, Oracle physically stores a row in the cluster according to the result of applying a *hash function* to the row's cluster key value. Oracle stores all rows that produce the same hash function result in the same data block(s) or *hash bucket*. When an application looks for a specific row in a hash-clustered table, Oracle applies the hash function to the selection criteria and immediately knows which bucket contains the row. The server can then access the target row with only one disk I/O. Unlike with indexed data clusters, hash data clusters typically store the rows of just one table.

NOTE
Chapter 10 explains hash partitioning. Within a hash partitioned table, Oracle stores the rows of the table in different partitions (physical data segments) according to a hash function. In some ways, a table stored in a hash data cluster is similar. Within a hash data cluster, Oracle stores the rows of the table in different data blocks according to a hash function; however, all of the data blocks in a hash cluster are part of the same data segment.

Using Data Clusters Appropriately

As with the different types of indexes that Oracle offers, index and hash clusters have particular settings in which they work better than others:

■ Indexed data clusters have been available for many releases of Oracle. In most cases, indexed data clusters produce only minimal gains in application performance. Consequently, developers typically opt to use indexes or hash clusters rather than indexed data clusters to improve application performance.

■ Similar to bitmap indexes, a hash cluster has a rigid physical structure that does not work well when applications make extensive inserts and updates to table data.

■ The previous example of a hash cluster shows how hash clusters can dramatically improve the performance of application queries that use exact match searches, or equality searches. In contrast, hash clusters perform poorly for queries that look for ranges of rows. Oracle can resolve range searches much better using B-tree indexes.

Tuning SQL

Once you supplement the tables in a schema with indexes and data clusters to minimize the disk I/O necessary to find specific rows in a table, you can turn your attention to tuning the SQL that particular applications use. This section explains how Oracle optimizes SQL statement execution and what you can do to make your SQL execute more efficiently.

The Optimizer: Executing SQL Statements

To execute SQL statements optimally, Oracle has an internal system feature called the *optimizer*. When you issue a SQL statement, the Oracle optimizer determines one or more *execution plans* that it can use to execute the statement. After comparing the *costs* of execution for each plan, Oracle then executes the statement using the plan with the lowest relative cost, which typically executes the fastest. Consequently, you and all application users receive excellent response time for SQL statement execution.

Optimizer Statistics

To determine the best execution plans for statements, Oracle examines statistics in the data dictionary concerning the data with which the statement works. To generate and keep the optimizer statistics current, you must *analyze* the tables, indexes, and other data storage objects in application schemas. When you analyze an object, Oracle generates statistics for the object and stores them in the data dictionary so that the statistics are available to the optimizer. For example, when you analyze a table, Oracle generates statistics for the number of rows in the table, the amount of physical storage space used to store the table, and more. Statistics can get out of date as applications insert, update, and delete information from tables and indexes. Therefore, it's important to regularly analyze application objects to make their statistics representative of the corresponding objects.

Optimizer Choices

Depending on the SQL statement, Oracle's optimizer might be able to find several different ways to execute a SQL statement. Simple statements are likely to have one or just a few execution plan options. More complicated SQL statements typically present more execution plan options.

For example, consider a CUSTOMERS table that has an index for the STATE column. When you issue a query to find all of the customers who live in the state of California, the optimizer can pick from two execution plans:

- Oracle can execute the statement by performing a *full table scan*—that is, Oracle can read every row in the table and return only the records for customers who live in California.

- Oracle can execute the statement using the index on the STATE column— that is, Oracle can quickly search the index for customers who live in California and then read and return only the requested customer records.

At a glance, you might naively assume that using an available index is always optimal, and that Oracle's optimizer would always choose the second option to execute the example query. However, this might not always be the case. For example, consider what execution plan would be optimal if all or the large majority of your customers live in California. In this case, looking up customers in a state index to find just the California customers, only to find that all of the customers already live in California, would be a relative waste of time. Therefore, to make intelligent choices, Oracle's optimizer uses the statistics in the data dictionary.

Hints and Optimizer Control

In certain circumstances, Oracle's optimizer might not be able to choose the optimal execution plan for a statement. In such cases, you can influence and control the optimizer's choices using hints. A *hint* is a specially formatted comment within an SQL statement that instructs Oracle's optimizer how to execute the statement. For example, you might include a hint in a query that tells Oracle to execute the query using an available index. You'll see an example of using such a hint in a subsequent practice exercise of this section.

Basic SQL Tuning

Now that you understand the fundamental concepts of Oracle's optimizer, the following practice exercises teach you to do the following:

- Generate optimizer statistics for the objects in your practice schema

- Display the execution plans that the optimizer picks for some SQL statements

- Influence the execution of some SQL statements with hints

Rules-Based Optimization

For backward compatibility with older applications, Oracle8i's optimizer can also determine statement execution plans using a rules-based approach rather than a cost-based approach. When using *rules-based optimization*, Oracle's optimizer chooses an execution plan for a statement after ranking all available access paths to the requested data. To build applications that perform well when using the rules-based approach, you must know intimately the relative ranking of all possible statement constructs, and then write SQL that takes advantage of the lower-ranked constructs. To avoid this additional complexity, you should rely on cost-based optimization and avoid rules-based optimization.

EXERCISE 12.3: Generating Basic Optimizer Statistics with the ANALYZE Command

The first thing that you can do to help Oracle execute an application's SQL as fast as possible is to generate basic statistics for the application's tables, indexes, and clusters—without these statistics, Oracle's optimizer cannot make the best possible decisions. To avoid unnecessary or untimely performance hits, Oracle does not automatically generate and refresh optimizer statistics. Instead, you must generate optimizer statistics for your database objects.

One way to generate optimizer statistics for a table, index, or cluster is to use the SQL command *ANALYZE*. For the purposes of this exercise, an abbreviated syntax listing of the ANALYZE command is as follows:

```
ANALYZE
  { INDEX [schema.]index [[SUB]PARTITION partition]
  | TABLE [schema.]table [[SUB]PARTITION partition]
  | CLUSTER [schema.]cluster }

  { COMPUTE STATISTICS
  | ESTIMATE STATISTICS [SAMPLE integer {ROWS|PERCENT}] }

  [FOR TABLE]
  [FOR ALL [LOCAL] INDEXES]
```

The key parts to understand of the ANALYZE command include the following:

■ The *INDEX, TABLE,* and *CLUSTER* parameters identify the index, table, or cluster to analyze, respectively. You can also analyze selected partitions and subpartitions of partitioned tables and indexes.

■ Use the *COMPUTE STATISTICS* option to compute statistics for the target table, index, or cluster using all data in the target. Alternatively, use the *ESTIMATE STATISTICS* option to estimate statistics for the target using a default or specific number of rows in the target—the ESTIMATE STATISTICS option is primarily useful when analyzing very large tables and indexes to reduce the amount of time necessary to gather statistics.

■ When analyzing a table, the FOR TABLE option indicates that you want to generate statistics for the table.

■ When analyzing a table, the FOR ALL INDEXES option indicates that you want to generate statistics for all indexes of the table.

NOTE

Be careful! If you do not specify either the FOR TABLE or FOR ALL INDEXES option with an ANALYZE statement, Oracle generates statistics for the table, for all indexes of the table, as well as for all columns (histograms) in the table. See the next exercise for more information about histograms and column statistics.

Enter the following ANALYZE statement to compute statistics for the CUSTOMERS table in your current practice schema, as well as for all indexes of the CUSTOMERS table.

```
ANALYZE TABLE customers
  COMPUTE STATISTICS
  FOR TABLE
  FOR ALL INDEXES;
```

Next, enter the following ANALYZE statement to estimate statistics for the ORDERS table based on 15 percent of the rows in the table. The statement will also estimate statistics for all indexes of the ORDERS table.

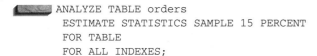
```
ANALYZE TABLE orders
    ESTIMATE STATISTICS SAMPLE 15 PERCENT
    FOR TABLE
    FOR ALL INDEXES;
```

EXERCISE 12.4: Using Histograms to Improve Column Selectivity

In most cases, simple ANALYZE statements, such as those in the previous exercise, generate the basic statistics that Oracle's optimizer needs to make good decisions when determining how to execute a given query or SQL statement. However, the basic statistics generated by a simple ANALYZE command cannot convey the selectivity of columns and indexes that contain an irregular distribution of values. To reveal the selectivity of columns with uneven distributions of data, you can use some special syntax in the ANALYZE command's optional FOR clause to generate height-balanced *histograms* for the columns of a table.

```
[FOR ALL [INDEXED] COLUMNS [SIZE integer]]
[FOR COLUMNS [SIZE integer]
   column [SIZE integer] [, column [SIZE integer]] ... ]
```

The key parts to understand of the FOR clause include the following:

- The *FOR ALL COLUMNS* clause indicates that you want to generate statistics (histograms) for all columns in the table. Specify the INDEXED option to generate histograms for all indexed columns only.

- The *FOR COLUMNS* clause indicates a list of one or more columns that require statistics (histograms).

- Specify the *SIZE* parameter of either clause to indicate the number of buckets (bands) in each histogram. The default setting of 75 is typically adequate.

Even though our practice schema is relatively simple, and histograms are not actually necessary for any column, let's generate a histogram anyway so that you know how to accomplish the task when the need arises in the future. Enter the following ANALYZE statement to generate a histogram for the ZIPCODE column in the CUSTOMERS table.

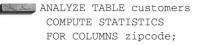
```
ANALYZE TABLE customers
    COMPUTE STATISTICS
    FOR COLUMNS zipcode;
```

CAUTION
When working with tables that contain many rows, histograms can take quite a long time to generate and subsequently update. Build histograms only when you know that queries reference a column in a large table as the search criteria, and the column contains an irregular distribution of values.

EXERCISE 12.5: Using the DBMS_STATS Package

Periodic analysis of an application's tables, indexes, and clusters is an ongoing maintenance task that keeps associated statistics current and ensures maximum application performance throughout the life cycle of the application. When an application schema contains a great number of tables, indexes, and clusters, it can get tedious to submit individual ANALYZE statements that target every schema object. Additionally, the ANALYZE command itself does not offer any syntax that you can use to "play" with statistics in order to examine how the optimizer will behave in different conditions. To provide additional flexibility and functionality when analyzing tables and indexes, Oracle8i offers the *DBMS_STATS* package. The many procedures in the DBMS_STATS package let you do several things:

- Gather statistics quickly for large tables and indexes using parallel processing

- Gather statistics for all tables and indexes in a schema or in the database using one procedure call

- Store gathered statistics in the data dictionary or in a user statistics table external to the data dictionary

- Display or manually modify the statistics in the data dictionary or in a user statistics table

- Import and export statistics from one database to another

This practice exercise introduces just a few of the basic features of the DBMS_STATS package to get you started. First, enter the following PL/SQL block that calls the *GATHER_SCHEMA_STATS* procedure of the DBMS_STATS package to compute statistics for all tables and indexes in the current practice schema:

```
BEGIN
  DBMS_STATS.GATHER_SCHEMA_STATS (
    ownname => 'PRACTICE12',
    estimate_percent => NULL,
```

```
  method_opt => NULL,
  cascade => TRUE
 );
END;
/
```

Notice the following important points in this example:

- To compute statistics, you must set the ESTIMATE_PERCENT parameter to NULL.

- To gather basic table and index statistics only (that is, use no histograms), you must set the METHOD_OPT parameter to NULL.

- To gather statistics for indexes as well as tables in the schema, set the CASCADE parameter to TRUE.

Next, assume that some time has gone by and you want to update the statistics for just the ORDERS table. You can do this using an ANALYZE statement or by entering the following PL/SQL block that calls the *GATHER_TABLE_STATS* procedure of the DBMS_STATS package:

```
BEGIN
 DBMS_STATS.GATHER_TABLE_STATS (
  ownname => 'PRACTICE12',
  tabname => 'ORDERS',
  estimate_percent => NULL,
  method_opt => NULL,
  cascade => TRUE );
END;
/
```

Now let's use the *GET_TABLE_STATS* procedure of the DBMS_STATS package to display some of the statistics that we gathered with the previous two procedure calls. Enter the following PL/SQL block to print out the basic statistics in the data dictionary for the CUSTOMERS table:

```
DECLARE
 rows NUMBER;
 blocks NUMBER;
 length NUMBER;
BEGIN
 DBMS_STATS.GET_TABLE_STATS (
  ownname => 'PRACTICE12',
  tabname => 'CUSTOMERS',
  numrows => rows,
```

```
  numblks => blocks,
  avgrlen => length
 );

 DBMS_OUTPUT.PUT_LINE('Analysis Summary for Table');
 DBMS_OUTPUT.PUT_LINE('Table Rows: ' || rows);
 DBMS_OUTPUT.PUT_LINE('Table Blocks: ' || blocks);
 DBMS_OUTPUT.PUT_LINE('Avg Row Length (bytes): ' || length);
END;
/
```

The results will be as follows:

```
Analysis Summary for Table
Table Rows: 10
Table Blocks: 1
Avg Row Length (bytes): 115

PL/SQL procedure successfully completed.
```

Similarly, enter the following PL/SQL block that calls the *GET_INDEX_STATS* procedure of the DBMS_STATS package to display the statistics for one of the indexes of the CUSTOMERS table.

```
DECLARE
 rows NUMBER;
 leafblocks NUMBER;
 distinctkeys NUMBER;
 avgleafblocks NUMBER;
 avgdatablocks NUMBER;
 clustering NUMBER;
 height NUMBER;
BEGIN
 DBMS_STATS.GET_INDEX_STATS (
  ownname => 'PRACTICE12',
  indname => 'CUSTOMER_UPPER_LASTNAME',
  numrows => rows,
  numlblks => leafblocks,
  numdist => distinctkeys,
  avglblk  => avgleafblocks,
  avgdblk  => avgdatablocks,
  clstfct => clustering,
  indlevel => height );

 DBMS_OUTPUT.PUT_LINE('Analysis Summary for Index');
 DBMS_OUTPUT.PUT_LINE('Rows: ' || rows);
 DBMS_OUTPUT.PUT_LINE('Leaf Blocks: ' || leafblocks);
```

```
DBMS_OUTPUT.PUT_LINE('Distinct Keys: ' || distinctkeys);
DBMS_OUTPUT.PUT_LINE('Average # Leaf Blocks/Key: ' || avgleafblocks);
DBMS_OUTPUT.PUT_LINE('Average # Data Blocks/Key: ' || avgdatablocks);
DBMS_OUTPUT.PUT_LINE('Clustering Factor: ' || clustering);
DBMS_OUTPUT.PUT_LINE('Index Height: ' || height);
END;
/
```

The results will be as follows:

```
Analysis Summary for Index
Rows: 10
Leaf Blocks: 1
Distinct Keys: 10
Average # Leaf Blocks/Key: 1
Average # Data Blocks/Key: 1
Clustering Factor: 1
Index Height: 0

PL/SQL procedure successfully completed.
```

As you can see from the most recent two procedure calls, our CUSTOMERS table and supporting indexes are rather small. This will lead to very boring execution plans in the next exercise. To play "what if" and make things a bit more interesting in the next practice exercise, enter the following PL/SQL block to alter the statistics for the CUSTOMERS table using the *SET_TABLE_STATS* procedure of the DBMS_STATS package.

```
DECLARE
  rows NUMBER := 10000;
  blocks NUMBER := 650;
  length NUMBER := 108;
BEGIN
  DBMS_STATS.SET_TABLE_STATS (
   ownname => 'PRACTICE12',
   tabname => 'CUSTOMERS',
   numrows => rows,
   numblks => blocks,
   avgrlen => length
  );
END;
/
```

This call to the SET_TABLE_STATS procedure updates the statistics for the CUSTOMERS table to make it appear as though the table has 10,000 rows (instead of just 10) stored in 650 data blocks (instead of just one).

CAUTION
If you are trying to force Oracle's optimizer to execute a particular statement one way or another, it's typically not a wise idea to change the real statistics for a table. While you might be able to make one statement execute a particular way with a specific set of fictitious table statistics, the same set of statistics could very well cause all other statements that target the table to execute poorly. A better way to control Oracle's optimizer for specific problem statements is to use hints. Exercise 12.7 will demonstrate the use of a hint.

The examples in this exercise quickly introduce you to just some of the functionality available via the DBMS_STATS package. Make sure you read your Oracle documentation for more information about all available procedures in the package, their parameters, and so on.

EXERCISE 12.6: Displaying a Statement's Execution Plan

Now that there are some statistics in place for the optimizer, let's take a look at how Oracle executes a SQL statement so that we can learn more about how the optimizer works. To display the execution plan that Oracle's optimizer chooses for a SQL statement, you can use the SQL command *EXPLAIN PLAN*. The EXPLAIN PLAN command provides an interface that you can use to store information about statement execution plans in a database table. The database table that you create for EXPLAIN PLAN output must have a specific format. You can easily create a table with the format required to store EXPLAIN PLAN output by running the *utlxplan.sql* command script located in your installation's $ORACLE_HOME/rdbms/admin directory. For example, using your current SQL*Plus session, enter the following statement to run the utlxplan.sql command script:

```
@$ORACLE_HOME/rdbms/admin/utlxplan.sql;
```

The utlxplan.sql script creates a table called *PLAN_TABLE* in your current schema. After running the script, you should see the following message:

```
Table created.
```

With your PLAN_TABLE in place, you are now ready to start "explaining" SQL statements. But rather than use the clunky EXPLAIN PLAN command, itself, along with subsequent queries of the PLAN_TABLE table, this practice exercise shows you how to use a handy interface to the EXPLAIN PLAN command provided through SQL*Plus. Whenever you want to display the execution plan for a statement in your SQL*Plus session, simply set SQL*Plus's *AUTOTRACE* system variable to ON EXPLAIN.

```
SET AUTOTRACE ON EXPLAIN;
```

NOTE
To use the SQL*Plus AUTOTRACE feature, your account must have access to the PLUSTRACE role. The prerequisite command scripts for this chapter create this special role and then grant your practice account this role so that you can complete this practice exercise.

Now, when you execute a SQL statement, SQL*Plus automatically uses the SQL command EXPLAIN PLAN to store the execution plan for the current statement in your PLAN_TABLE and then displays the execution plan steps in a hierarchical format that is easy to read. For example, enter the following query of the CUSTOMERS table:

```
SELECT id, lastname, firstname, phone
  FROM customers
 WHERE UPPER(lastname) = 'CLAY';
```

The results will be as follows:

```
    ID LASTNAME         FIRSTNAME         PHONE
--------- --------------- --------------- -----------
     9 Clay             Dorothy           916-672-8700

Execution Plan
----------------------------------------------------------
        0
SELECT STATEMENT Optimizer=CHOOSE (Cost=2 Card=101 Bytes=10908)
        1                0
  TABLE ACCESS (BY INDEX ROWID) OF 'CUSTOMERS' (Cost=2 Card=101 Bytes=10908)
        2                1
    INDEX (RANGE SCAN) OF 'CUSTOMER_UPPER_LASTNAME' (NON-UNIQUE)
(Cost=1 Card=101)
```

To read execution plans, read from the bottom line up. In this example, the execution plan happens as follows:

1. Perform a *range scan* of the function-based index CUSTOMER_UPPER_LASTNAME index to find the ROWIDs of the rows that match the search criteria.

2. Using the ROWIDs found in the previous step, access just the blocks in the table that contain the corresponding rows, and return the requested data.

This execution plan is just what you might expect, given that we created a function-based index specifically for case-insensitive searches of customer last names in Exercise 12.2. However, remember that in the Exercise 12.5, you manually changed the statistics for the CUSTOMERS table to reflect a table with 10,000 rows in 650 data blocks. How do you think the optimizer would execute the same query if the original statistics were restored? Find out by entering the following commands:

```
-- refresh statistics for CUSTOMERS table
ANALYZE TABLE customers
 COMPUTE STATISTICS
 FOR TABLE;

-- repeat the query
SELECT id, lastname, firstname, phone
 FROM customers
 WHERE UPPER(lastname) = 'CLAY';
```

With the refreshed statistics, the results of the second query and its execution plan should appear as follows:

```
      ID LASTNAME          FIRSTNAME        PHONE
--------- --------------- --------------- -----------
       9 Clay              Dorothy          916-672-8700

Execution Plan
----------------------------------------------------------
          0
SELECT STATEMENT Optimizer=CHOOSE (Cost=1 Card=1 Bytes=115)
          1                0
   TABLE ACCESS (FULL) OF 'CUSTOMERS' (Cost=1 Card=1 Bytes=115)
```

Notice in this new execution plan, the optimizer chooses to perform a full table scan of the CUSTOMERS table to find the requested row. This makes sense, because all of the rows for the table are in a single data block. In other words, it would actually cost more to read the blocks of the index and then read the data block of the table anyway.

This very simple exercise has shown you how to reveal optimizer execution plans using the SQL command EXPLAIN PLAN via the SQL*Plus AUTOTRACE feature. The exercise also demonstrates how the current statistics for tables and other objects can significantly affect the choices that Oracle's optimizer makes.

EXERCISE 12.7: Using a Hint

From time to time, you might find that when diagnosing a problem SQL statement, Oracle's optimizer makes a bad choice for one reason or another. In this case, you can force Oracle's optimizer to execute the statement your way by including one or more hints. For example, even though the final query in the previous exercise executes using a full table scan rather than an index range scan of the available CUSTOMER_UPPER_LASTNAME index, you can force the query to execute with the index by including an *INDEX hint*. The syntax for the INDEX hint is as follows:

```
--+INDEX(table index [, index] ... )
```

For example, using your current SQL*Plus session with AUTOTRACE set to ON EXPLAIN, enter the following version of the query from the previous exercise that includes a hint to use the CUSTOMER_UPPER_LASTNAME index.

```
SELECT --+INDEX(customers customer_upper_lastname)
  id, lastname, firstname, phone
FROM customers
WHERE UPPER(lastname) = 'CLAY';
```

The results of executing the query with the hint should be as follows:

```
       ID LASTNAME         FIRSTNAME        PHONE
--------- --------------- --------------- ------------
        9 Clay             Dorothy          916-672-8700


Execution Plan
----------------------------------------------------------
          0
SELECT STATEMENT Optimizer=CHOOSE (Cost=2 Card=1 Bytes=115)
          1                0
  TABLE ACCESS (BY INDEX ROWID) OF 'CUSTOMERS' (Cost=2 Card=1 Bytes=115)
          2                1
    INDEX (RANGE SCAN) OF 'CUSTOMER_UPPER_LASTNAME' (NON-UNIQUE) (Cost=1
Card=1)
```

Notice that the hint forced the optimizer to execute the statement with the index, even though this execution plan is higher in cost than it would be to execute the statement with a simple full scan of the CUSTOMERS table (a full scan of one data block).

The INDEX hint is one of many hints that you can use when tuning SQL statements. Oracle has hints that let you force full table scans, index searches in ascending or descending order, hash cluster scans, and joins of tables using several different techniques. See your Oracle documentation for a complete list of available hints and their syntax.

To complete this exercise, enter the following statement to turn off your current SQL*Plus session's AUTOTRACE feature so that execution plans do not display in the subsequent exercises in this chapter.

 SET AUTOTRACE OFF;

Tuning the Database Instance

Once you tune an application's SQL statements, the final system component to tune is the database server, itself. This section explains the concepts you'll need to understand and the steps necessary to perform some basic database instance tuning.

Primary Bottlenecks

The potential response time of an Oracle database instance is limited primarily by two potential bottlenecks in the system: disk I/O and resource contention.

Disk I/O

Disk access, or disk I/O, is a necessary evil in all computer systems. Why? To permanently store data, the computer must write the data to a disk. To subsequently read the data, the computer must retrieve the information from the disk. But relatively speaking, disk I/O is typically one of the slowest operations that a computer can perform. Therefore, the less disk access that is necessary, the faster a computer and applications using the computer will appear to perform. Oracle uses several different types of memory caches to reduce unnecessary disk I/O and improve overall performance.

Resource Contention

When two or more processes try to use the same resource, contention can result, which makes one of the processes wait for the other to finish. Oracle has many different types of resources over which applications and users can contend. Examples of such database system resources include memory, processor cycles, disk and file access, network communication, and others.

Memory Areas and Data Caching

To minimize disk access and speed up the performance of computer systems, applications typically create *random access memory* (RAM) areas that temporarily *cache* (store) data stored on disk. An application can manipulate data in a memory cache almost instantly and can then consolidate relatively slow disk access operations only when necessary or when it is most efficient. By using memory caches, the applications and the entire system can perform much more quickly.

Caching Concepts and Benefits

Before learning about the specific memory areas that an Oracle instance creates and uses, it's useful to learn a bit more about how data caching works. Figure 12-4 illustrates the key concepts of data caching.

A *cache hit* (or cache *get*) happens when an application requests data that is already in the memory cache. A cache hit is good because disk access is not necessary to work with the requested data. On the other hand, a *cache miss* happens when an application requests data that is not in the cache, so a disk read

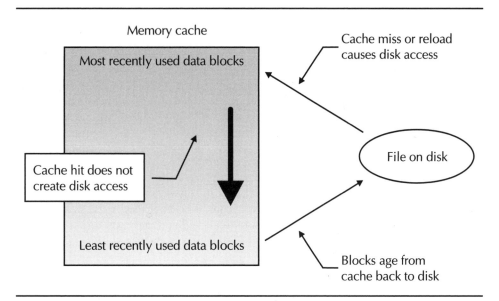

FIGURE 12-4. *To cache data, an application uses a caching algorithm that maximizes cache hits and minimizes cache misses and cache reloads*

is necessary to put the data into the cache. A cache reload is very similar to a cache miss. A *cache reload* happens when an application requests data that was in the cache, but has since been *aged* from the cache (has been written back to disk)—therefore, the application must read the data from disk back into memory. As you might imagine, the fewer the cache misses and reloads, the less disk access and the better the system will perform.

A memory cache is typically a fixed chunk of memory that does not grow or shrink in size. Consequently, there is a limit as to how much data the cache can hold. If the memory cache is full of data and some new data must be read into the cache, the application must decide which blocks to age from the cache to make room for the new data. To keep the most frequently used data blocks in memory and minimize the number of cache misses and reloads, the application implements an intelligent *caching algorithm* that decides when to age blocks from the cache. A common caching algorithm is the *most-recently used/least-recently used* (MRU/LRU) *caching algorithm*. Basically, this algorithm keeps the most recently used data blocks in the cache and writes the least recently used blocks back to disk when more space is necessary.

Oracle8i Memory Areas

Oracle is a database management system that typically manages large amounts of data. To perform optimally, Oracle creates and uses many different memory caches to minimize disk I/O and maximize server performance, including the buffer cache, the library cache, the dictionary cache, program global areas, and sort areas. The following sections explain each of the memory areas of an Oracle instance.

The Buffer Cache

An Oracle instance's *buffer cache* is typically the largest server memory area. The buffer cache stores database information that application transactions have recently requested. Figure 12-5 shows an instance's buffer cache.

When you update a row in a table, a foreground server process reads the data block that contains the row from a data file on disk into the buffer cache. Then, the foreground server can modify the data block in server memory. Should another user's transaction request to update the same row or another row in the same data block, the buffer cache already contains the block and can avoid disk access. Eventually, the DBWR writes *dirty* (modified) data blocks back to the data files. See the section "The Database Writer (DBW*n*)" in Chapter 3 for more information about how DBWR works.

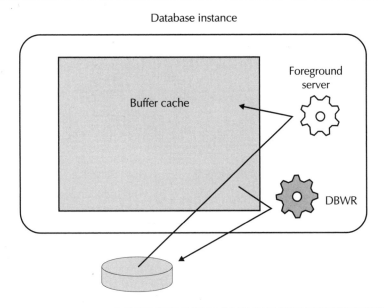

Database instance

Buffer cache

Foreground
server

DBWR

FIGURE 12-5.   *Foreground server processes read data into an Oracle instance's buffer cache to perform database work. Eventually, the DBWR background process writes dirty data blocks from the buffer cache back to the database's data files*

The Shared Pool

An instance's *shared pool* memory area is another primary server memory area. An instance's shared pool has two components: the library cache and the dictionary cache. Figure 12-6 and the following sections describe an instance's shared pool.

The Library Cache   The *library cache* stores and shares parsed representations of the most recently executed SQL statements and PL/SQL programs. For example, when you issue a SQL statement, Oracle parses the statement and determines the most efficient execution plan for the statement. Then, Oracle caches the statement in the shared pool. If another user issues the same statement, Oracle can share the statement already in memory rather than perform identical steps to execute the statement again. By caching statements in memory, Oracle's *shared SQL* reduces the server overhead necessary to execute a set of application statements.

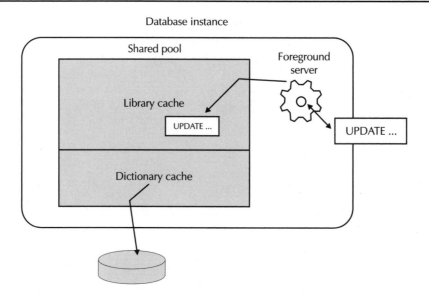

FIGURE 12-6. *An instance's shared pool contains two memory areas: the library cache and the dictionary cache*

The Dictionary Cache   During system processing, Oracle continually requests and updates information in the database's data dictionary. To maximize the performance of the system's internal operations, an Oracle instance's *dictionary cache* stores the most recently used data dictionary information.

System Global Area (SGA)
The *system*, or *shared, global area* (SGA) encompasses the buffer cache and the shared pool. Therefore, the SGA is a general term that you can use to refer to all of the shared memory used by an Oracle instance.

Program Global Area (PGA)
For each connected client, Oracle creates a private memory area called a *program*, or *private, global area* (PGA). A PGA is a relatively small amount of server memory that holds session-specific information. For example, a client's server thread uses its PGA to hold the state of the session's program variables and packages.

Sort Areas
The previous chapter explains how Oracle uses temporary segments (or a temporary tablespace) as work space to sort a large amount of information for ordered queries, index builds, and other demanding server operations. Oracle uses temporary segments

only when it cannot complete the entire operation in a sort area. A *sort area* is a small amount of server memory that a session can use as a temporary workspace.

Basic Database Instance Tuning

Now that you have a general idea of the primary performance bottlenecks to watch out for and the memory caches that Oracle uses to minimize disk I/O, the following exercises teach you how to perform some basic database instance tuning.

EXERCISE 12.8: Checking for Improper User Account Settings

One of the most common sources of contention in an Oracle instance results from the improper configuration of user accounts. Unfortunately, when you create a new user account, the default setting for the user's default and temporary tablespace is the SYSTEM tablespace, the same tablespace that stores the data dictionary. If you do not explicitly set a new user's default and temporary tablespace to a tablespace other than SYSTEM, ongoing user operations, such as temporary segment allocation, will compete for access to the SYSTEM tablespace data files with internal Oracle processes that need to manage the data dictionary. This situation can really slow things down, especially when many users have improper configurations.

To generate a list of users with improper tablespace settings, enter the following query:

```
SELECT username, default_tablespace, temporary_tablespace
  FROM dba_users
 WHERE username != 'SYS'
   AND ( default_tablespace = 'SYSTEM'
       OR temporary_tablespace = 'SYSTEM');
```

The results of your query should be something similar to the following:

```
USERNAME                      DEFAULT_TABLESPACE   TEMPORARY_TABLESPACE
----------------------------  -------------------  --------------------
OUTLN                         SYSTEM               SYSTEM
DBSNMP                        SYSTEM               SYSTEM
MTSSYS                        SYSTEM               SYSTEM
AURORA$ORB$UNAUTHENTICATED    SYSTEM               SYSTEM
DEMO                          SYSTEM               SYSTEM
ORDSYS                        SYSTEM               SYSTEM
ORDPLUGINS                    SYSTEM               SYSTEM
MDSYS                         SYSTEM               SYSTEM
CTXSYS                        SYSTEM               SYSTEM
PRACTICE12                    USERS                SYSTEM

10 rows selected.
```

Once you find a user with improper tablespace settings, you can adjust the settings using the SQL command ALTER USER, as demonstrated in Exercise 9.3. For example, the prerequisite command script for this chapter purposely creates the user PRACTICE12 with the TEMPORARY TABLESPACE setting as SYSTEM so that the previous query returns at least one row. To change the PRACTICE12 account's temporary tablespace setting, enter the following ALTER USER statement.

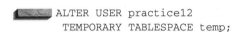

```
ALTER USER practice12
  TEMPORARY TABLESPACE temp;
```

EXERCISE 12.9: Distributing Files for Minimal Contention

When you install Oracle8i Enterprise Edition for Linux as instructed in Chapter 2, the installer creates all of the starter database's database files, log members, and control files on the same disk. Storing all of a database's files on one disk not only sets up your system for a lot of contention for disk access, but also makes your database vulnerable to a single disk failure (see Chapter 11).

For both performance and safety reasons, a computer that supports a production database system should have multiple disk drives, and you should distribute your database's files among the available drives. For example, consider a computer that has three disk drives: data1, data2, and data3. Table 12-1 demonstrates one possible file distribution scheme for your starter database that would reduce contention for disk access and provide extra levels of protection for database availability, should an isolated disk failure occur.

Disk data1	Disk data2	Disk data3
SYSTEM tablespace data files	USERS tablespace data files	INDX tablespace data files
RBS tablespace data files		TEMP tablespace data files
One member of each log group	One member of each log group	One member of each log group
One copy of the control file	One copy of the control file	One copy of the control file

TABLE 12-1. *One Possible File Distribution Scheme for a Typical Starter Database Using Three Distinct Disk Drives*

There are a few key points to notice about the example file-distribution scheme:

■ Each online log group has a member on each one of the three disk drives, providing three access points for each log group.

■ The database has a control file copy on each one of the three disk drives, providing three access points for the control file.

■ The data files for the various tablespaces are spread across the available disk drives to distribute database I/O and reduce contention among competing database operations.

Because this book cannot assume that your system has multiple disk drives, it is impossible for the exercise to provide step-by-step instructions for moving the data files of the starter database. If your system does have multiple drives, then the steps for moving an existing data file's tablespace are as follows:

1. Back up the entire database, including the database's control file.

2. Shut down the current database instance.

3. Restart the instance and mount the database, but do not open the database.

4. For each data file that you want to move, copy the file to the new location using operating system commands.

5. For each data file that you moved in the previous step, use the *RENAME FILE* parameter of the SQL command *ALTER DATABASE* to rename the file's pointer in the database's control file.

6. Reopen the database.

7. Back up the entire database, including the database's control file.

To supplement the directions in this exercise, please read your Oracle documentation, which includes more information about renaming and relocating database files.

EXERCISE 12.10: Altering the Size of the Database Buffer Cache

One of the easiest ways to tune the performance of an Oracle server is to correctly size the instance's buffer cache. The objective is to make the buffer cache large enough so that it can hold the set of database information most frequently used by applications, but not excessively large so that it hoards all of the host computer's memory. Many server parameters are available to help tune an instance's buffer cache settings and configure the buffer cache with specialized memory areas.

Although it is beyond the scope of this book to explain all of these parameters and configurations, this exercise teaches you how to do some very basic database buffer cache tuning by controlling its overall size.

During server startup, Oracle8*i* sizes the instance's buffer cache using the following server parameter settings:

```
Database Buffer Cache Size = DB_BLOCK_BUFFERS * DB_BLOCK_SIZE
```

- The DB_BLOCK_SIZE parameter sets the data block size for the database. The default block size for the starter database on Linux is 8K. Once you create a database, you cannot alter the database's block size without recreating the entire database.

- The DB_BLOCK_BUFFERS server parameter sets the number of buffers to allocate for the instance's buffer cache. Each buffer cache is DB_BLOCK_SIZE in size.

To check the current size of your instance's buffer cache, enter the following query:

```
SELECT bytes AS "BUFFER CACHE (BYTES)"
  FROM v$sgastat
  WHERE LOWER(name) = 'db_block_buffers'
    AND pool IS NULL;
```

The results for the default starter database on Linux should be as follows:

```
BUFFER CACHE (BYTES)
--------------------
            16777216
```

Notice that the buffer cache is more than 16MB, a sizeable cache if all you are doing is using the database to learn Oracle8*i* and nothing more. To decrease the size of the buffer cache, complete the following steps:

1. Open your database's parameter file ($ORACLE_HOME/dbs/initoralin.ora) in a text editor (see Exercise 3.10).

2. Search for the DB_BLOCK_BUFFERS parameter setting, which is most likely set to 2,048 (the default value specified by the installer).

3. Edit the DB_BLOCK_BUFFERS parameter setting to 150, a setting that can cache a little more than 1MB worth of data. Of course, if your system supports the activities of more than one person and performs real work, 150 might be

too low. Exercise 12.14 teaches you how to monitor the performance of important instance statistics, such as the buffer cache miss ratio, so that you can size the buffer cache correctly.

4. Save the parameter file, but leave it open in the text editor for the next exercise.

NOTE
The changes that you make to your database's parameter file do not have any effect on the current instance. A subsequent exercise will instruct you to shut down and restart the instance with the new buffer cache size.

EXERCISE 12.11: Altering the Size of the Shared Pool

Like the buffer cache, Oracle8i sizes your instance's shared pool using the setting of a server parameter—in this case, the SHARED_POOL_SIZE server parameter. Enter the following query to determine the current size of your instance's shared pool and the amount of memory in the shared pool that is not being used.

```
SELECT 'TOTAL SIZE' AS "SHARED POOL",
    ROUND(value/1024/1024,2) AS megabytes
  FROM v$parameter
  WHERE UPPER(name) = 'SHARED_POOL_SIZE'
UNION
SELECT 'UNUSED PORTION' AS description,
    ROUND(bytes/1024/1024, 2) AS megabytes
  FROM v$sgastat
  WHERE pool = 'shared pool'
    AND name = 'free memory';
```

The results from this query should be similar to the following:

```
SHARED POOL     MEGABYTES
--------------  ---------
TOTAL SIZE             15
UNUSED PORTION      9.56
```

Notice in this example that about 9.5MB of the shared pool has never been used. Based on these statistics, which show that the unused portion of the shared pool is a significant portion of the overall shared pool size, you can reclaim some unused memory by decreasing the setting of the SHARED_POOL_SIZE parameter.

TIP
*Configuring the shared pool size is particularly
significant when you plan to use server-side PL/SQL
and Java extensively within your Oracle environment.
In this type of system, more shared-pool memory is
typically necessary for the library cache.*

Continuing from the previous exercise, complete the following steps using your text editor with the open parameter file of your database:

1. Search for the SHARED_POOL_SIZE parameter, which should be set to 15,728,640 (bytes).

2. Edit the SHARED_POOL_SIZE parameter setting to the new setting in bytes. With Oracle8i, you can also set the SHARED_POOL_SIZE using the K and M suffixes to indicate a number of kilobytes or megabytes, respectively (for example, 10M). Exercise 12.14 will teach you how to monitor the performance of important instance statistics, such as the library cache and dictionary cache miss ratios, so that you can determine when the shared pool is the correct size.

3. If you make changes to the parameter file, save it, then leave it open for the next exercise.

NOTE
*The changes that you make to your database's
parameter file do not have any effect on the current
instance. A subsequent exercise will instruct you to
shut down and restart the instance with the new
shared pool size.*

EXERCISE 12.12: Altering the Sort Tuning Parameters

All sessions that connect to an Oracle instance have a small sort area available in server memory. When a query sorts a small number of rows with an ORDER BY or GROUP BY clause, Oracle can sort the result set in the session's sort area in memory. Alternatively, Oracle automatically uses temporary segments to provide larger amounts of temporary work space for sorting during more demanding statement processing, including CREATE INDEX statements and SELECT statements that include an ORDER BY, DISTINCT, GROUP BY, UNION, INTERSECT, or MINUS clause. However, be aware that frequent use of temporary segments can generate a significant amount of disk I/O and detract from overall server performance. Therefore, it is useful to minimize the number of sorts that go to temporary segments, if possible.

The easiest way to reduce the number of sorts on disk is to increase the size of each user's in-memory sort area. You can adjust the size of the in-memory sort areas that Oracle creates for user sessions with the SORT_AREA_SIZE parameter. The default sort-area size setting for your Oracle8i starter database on Linux should be 65K, which is typically adequate. In Exercise 12.14, you'll learn how to monitor the number of sorts that happen in memory and the number of sorts that use temporary segments (on disk). If you see a great number of sorts that use temporary segments, try increasing the setting for SORT_AREA_SIZE in small increments to see if more sorts can happen in memory.

To complete this exercise, save your database's parameter file and then close the file and your text editor.

EXERCISE 12.13: Shut Down and Restart a New Instance

The previous exercises made some changes to your database's parameter file. As the notes in each exercise indicate, these configuration changes will not take place until after you shut down and restart the server. After establishing a SYSDBA-privileged SQL*Plus session, shut down and restart Oracle as outlined in Exercises 3.7 and 3.6, respectively.

EXERCISE 12.14: Monitoring Memory Cache Statistics

The most recent exercises have taught you how to tune several of your starter database's memory caches and configuration settings. To make good decisions as you tune your instance, you need statistics that tell you about the current performance of the system. You can collect the tuning statistics that you need by querying some data dictionary views, including V$SYSSTAT (for database buffer cache and sorting statistics), V$ROWCACHE (for dictionary cache statistics), and V$LIBRARYCACHE (for library cache statistics). The following script, available as *8iStarterKit_Home*/scripts/tune.sql, shows you how to query these views for the necessary statistics.

```
/***************************************************************/
/* SCRIPT TO DISPLAY TUNING STATISTICS FOR THE BUFFER CACHE, */
/* SHARED POOL, AND SORTS                                    */
/***************************************************************/
COLUMN name FORMAT A20;

CLEAR SCREEN;
PROMPT DATABASE BUFFER CACHE STATISTICS:
SELECT
    SUM(DECODE(name, 'physical reads',value,0)) AS misses,
```

```
    SUM(DECODE(name, 'db block gets',value,0)) +
    SUM(DECODE(name, 'consistent gets',value,0)) AS hits,
    ROUND(100*(1-SUM(DECODE(name, 'physical reads',value,0)))/
     (SUM(DECODE(name, 'db block gets',value,0)) +
    SUM(DECODE(name, 'consistent gets',value,0))) ),2) AS "HIT RATIO"
  FROM v$sysstat
 WHERE name IN
 ('db block gets','consistent gets','physical reads');
PROMPT  DICTIONARY CACHE STATISTICS:
SELECT SUM(getmisses) AS misses,
   SUM(gets) AS "HITS (EXECUTIONS)",
   ROUND(100*(1-(SUM(getmisses)/SUM(gets))),2) AS hit_ratio
  FROM v$rowcache;
PROMPT  LIBRARY CACHE STATISTICS:
SELECT SUM(reloads) AS misses,
   SUM(pins) AS "HITS (EXECUTIONS)",
   ROUND(100*(1-(SUM(reloads)/SUM(pins))),2) AS hit_ratio
  FROM v$librarycache;
PROMPT SORTING STATISTICS:
SELECT name, value
  FROM v$sysstat
 WHERE name IN ('sorts (memory)', 'sorts (disk)');
```

The queries in this script provide you with the statistics that you'll need to correctly size the database instance's buffer cache, shared pool, and sort areas. After running the server for a couple of hours after startup under normal system conditions, start SQL*Plus and establish a session using the SYSTEM account, then run the tune.sql script periodically. You should see output that looks similar to the following:

```
DATABASE BUFFER CACHE STATISTICS:

  MISSES      HITS HIT RATIO
--------- --------- ---------
    7844     42883     81.71

DICTIONARY CACHE STATISTICS:

  MISSES HITS (EXECUTIONS) HIT_RATIO
--------- ----------------- ---------
     364             10597     96.57

LIBRARY CACHE STATISTICS:
```

```
    MISSES HITS (EXECUTIONS) HIT_RATIO
--------- ----------------- ---------
       11            60234     99.98
```

SORTING STATISTICS:

```
NAME                    VALUE
------------------- ---------
sorts (memory)           5123
sorts (disk)                0
```

In this output, look for the following red flags:

- If the buffer cache hit ratio is less than 90 percent, increase the size of the buffer cache (the DB_BLOCK_BUFFERS parameter).

- If the dictionary cache hit ratio is less than 95 percent, increase the size of the shared pool (the SHARED_POOL_SIZE parameter).

- If the library cache hit ratio is less than 90 percent, it could be that the shared pool is too small. However, the high number of misses relative to hits could also be the result of applications starting up or applications that are not well written to take advantage of shared SQL. You can try increasing the size of the shared pool (the SHARED_POOL_SIZE parameter); however, if this does not remedy the situation, consult your Oracle documentation or a tuning book for more information about tuning applications so that they use the shared pool better.

- If the number of sorts on disk is significant, try increasing the sort area size for all database sessions (the SORT_AREA_SIZE parameter). However, increase this parameter in small increments, especially if your system supports many concurrent user sessions, to avoid taking away too much memory from other instance caches.

Chapter Summary

This chapter has introduced you to some of the most basic concepts and steps related to Oracle application and database-instance tuning. In this chapter, you learned how to do the following:

- Minimize extra disk I/O from full-table scans using indexes and data clusters

- Help Oracle's optimizer perform well with up-to-date statistics

- Examine execution plans for SQL statements, and influence optimizer behavior with hints

- Alter the size of a database instance's buffer cache, shared pool, and sort areas

- Query the data dictionary to monitor the caching efficiency of a database instance's buffer cache, shared pool, and sort areas

Index

NOTE: Page numbers in *italics* refer to illustrations or charts.

Knowledge is power. To which we say,

crank up the power.

Are you ready for a power surge?

Accelerate your career—become an **Oracle Certified Professional** (OCP). With Oracle's cutting-edge *Instructor-Led Training*, *Technology-Based Training*, and this *guide*, you can prepare for certification faster than ever. Set your own trajectory by logging your personal training plan with us. Go to **http://education.oracle.com/tpb**, where we'll help you pick a training path, select your courses, and track your progress. We'll even send you an email when your courses are offered in your area. If you don't have access to the Web, call us at 1-800-441-3541 (Outside the U.S. call +1-310-335-2403).

Power learning has never been easier.

ORACLE
University

Get Your **FREE** Subscription to *Oracle Magazine*

Oracle Magazine is essential gear for today's information technology professionals. Stay informed and increase your productivity with every issue of *Oracle Magazine*. Inside each **FREE,** bimonthly issue you'll get:

- Up-to-date information on Oracle Database Server, Oracle Applications, Internet Computing, and tools
- Third-party news and announcements
- Technical articles on Oracle products and operating environments
- Development and administration tips
- Real-world customer stories

Three easy ways to subscribe:

1. Web   **Visit our Web site at www.oracle.com/oramag/.** **You'll find a subscription form there, plus much more!**

2. Fax   Complete the questionnaire on the back of this card and fax the questionnaire side only to **+1.847.647.9735.**

3. Mail   Complete the questionnaire on the back of this card and mail it to P.O. Box 1263, Skokie, IL 60076-8263.

If there are other Oracle users at your location who would like to receive their own subscription to *Oracle Magazine*, please photocopy this form and pass it along.

☐ YES! Please send me a FREE subscription to *Oracle Magazine*.   ☐ NO

To receive a free bimonthly subscription to *Oracle Magazine*, you must fill out the entire card, sign it, and date it (incomplete cards cannot be processed or acknowledged). You can also fax your application to **+1.847.647.9735. Or subscribe at our Web site at www.oracle.com/oramag/**

SIGNATURE (REQUIRED)	X	DATE	

NAME		TITLE	
COMPANY		TELEPHONE	
ADDRESS		FAX NUMBER	
CITY		STATE	POSTAL CODE/ZIP CODE
COUNTRY		E-MAIL ADDRESS	

☐ From time to time, Oracle Publishing allows our partners exclusive access to our e-mail addresses for special promotions and announcements. To be included in this program, please check this box.

You must answer all eight questions below.

1 What is the primary business activity of your firm at this location? *(check only one)*
- ☐ 03 Communications
- ☐ 04 Consulting, Training
- ☐ 06 Data Processing
- ☐ 07 Education
- ☐ 08 Engineering
- ☐ 09 Financial Services
- ☐ 10 Government—Federal, Local, State, Other
- ☐ 11 Government—Military
- ☐ 12 Health Care
- ☐ 13 Manufacturing—Aerospace, Defense
- ☐ 14 Manufacturing—Computer Hardware
- ☐ 15 Manufacturing—Noncomputer Products
- ☐ 17 Research & Development
- ☐ 19 Retailing, Wholesaling, Distribution
- ☐ 20 Software Development
- ☐ 21 Systems Integration, VAR, VAD, OEM
- ☐ 22 Transportation
- ☐ 23 Utilities (Electric, Gas, Sanitation)
- ☐ 98 Other Business and Services
  _____

2 Which of the following best describes your job function? *(check only one)*
CORPORATE MANAGEMENT/STAFF
- ☐ 01 Executive Management (President, Chair, CEO, CFO, Owner, Partner, Principal)
- ☐ 02 Finance/Administrative Management (VP/Director/ Manager/Controller, Purchasing, Administration)
- ☐ 03 Sales/Marketing Management (VP/Director/Manager)
- ☐ 04 Computer Systems/Operations Management (CIO/VP/Director/ Manager MIS, Operations)

IS/IT STAFF
- ☐ 07 Systems Development/ Programming Management
- ☐ 08 Systems Development/ Programming Staff
- ☐ 09 Consulting
- ☐ 10 DBA/Systems Administrator
- ☐ 11 Education/Training
- ☐ 14 Technical Support Director/ Manager
- ☐ 16 Other Technical Management/Staff
- ☐ 98 Other _____

3 What is your current primary operating platform? *(check all that apply)*
- ☐ 01 DEC UNIX
- ☐ 02 DEC VAX VMS
- ☐ 03 Java
- ☐ 04 HP UNIX
- ☐ 05 IBM AIX
- ☐ 06 IBM UNIX
- ☐ 07 Macintosh
- ☐ 09 MS-DOS
- ☐ 10 MVS
- ☐ 11 NetWare
- ☐ 12 Network Computing
- ☐ 13 OpenVMS
- ☐ 14 SCO UNIX
- ☐ 24 Sequent DYNIX/ptx
- ☐ 15 Sun Solaris/SunOS
- ☐ 16 SVR4
- ☐ 18 UnixWare
- ☐ 20 Windows
- ☐ 21 Windows NT
- ☐ 23 Other UNIX _____
- 99 ☐ **None of the above**

4 Do you evaluate, specify, recommend, or authorize the purchase of any of the following? *(check all that apply)*
- ☐ 01 Hardware
- ☐ 02 Software
- ☐ 03 Application Development Tools
- ☐ 04 Database Products
- ☐ 05 Internet or Intranet Products
- 99 ☐ **None of the above**

5 In your job, do you use or plan to purchase any of the following products or services? *(check all that apply)*
SOFTWARE
- ☐ 01 Business Graphics
- ☐ 02 CAD/CAE/CAM
- ☐ 03 CASE
- ☐ 05 Communications
- ☐ 06 Database Management
- ☐ 07 File Management
- ☐ 08 Finance
- ☐ 09 Java
- ☐ 10 Materials Resource Planning
- ☐ 11 Multimedia Authoring
- ☐ 12 Networking
- ☐ 13 Office Automation
- ☐ 14 Order Entry/Inventory Control
- ☐ 15 Programming
- ☐ 16 Project Management
- ☐ 17 Scientific and Engineering
- ☐ 18 Spreadsheets
- ☐ 19 Systems Management
- ☐ 20 Workflow

HARDWARE
- ☐ 21 Macintosh
- ☐ 22 Mainframe
- ☐ 23 Massively Parallel Processing
- ☐ 24 Minicomputer
- ☐ 25 PC
- ☐ 26 Network Computer
- ☐ 28 Symmetric Multiprocessing
- ☐ 29 Workstation

PERIPHERALS
- ☐ 30 Bridges/Routers/Hubs/Gateways
- ☐ 31 CD-ROM Drives
- ☐ 32 Disk Drives/Subsystems
- ☐ 33 Modems
- ☐ 34 Tape Drives/Subsystems
- ☐ 35 Video Boards/Multimedia

SERVICES
- ☐ 37 Consulting
- ☐ 38 Education/Training
- ☐ 39 Maintenance
- ☐ 40 Online Database Services
- ☐ 41 Support
- ☐ 36 Technology-Based Training
- ☐ 98 Other _____
- 99 ☐ **None of the above**

6 What Oracle products are in use at your site? *(check all that apply)*
SERVER/SOFTWARE
- ☐ 01 Oracle8
- ☐ 30 Oracle8*i*
- ☐ 31 Oracle8*i* Lite
- ☐ 02 Oracle7
- ☐ 03 Oracle Application Server
- ☐ 04 Oracle Data Mart Suites
- ☐ 05 Oracle Internet Commerce Server
- ☐ 32 Oracle *inter*Media
- ☐ 33 Oracle JServer
- ☐ 07 Oracle Lite
- ☐ 08 Oracle Payment Server
- ☐ 11 Oracle Video Server

TOOLS
- ☐ 13 Oracle Designer
- ☐ 14 Oracle Developer
- ☐ 54 Oracle Discoverer
- ☐ 53 Oracle Express
- ☐ 51 Oracle JDeveloper
- ☐ 52 Oracle Reports
- ☐ 50 Oracle WebDB
- ☐ 55 Oracle Workflow

ORACLE APPLICATIONS
- ☐ 17 Oracle Automotive
- ☐ 35 Oracle Business Intelligence System
- ☐ 19 Oracle Consumer Packaged Goods
- ☐ 39 Oracle E-Commerce
- ☐ 18 Oracle Energy
- ☐ 20 Oracle Financials
- ☐ 28 Oracle Front Office
- ☐ 21 Oracle Human Resources
- ☐ 37 Oracle Internet Procurement
- ☐ 22 Oracle Manufacturing
- ☐ 40 Oracle Process Manufacturing
- ☐ 23 Oracle Projects
- ☐ 34 Oracle Retail
- ☐ 29 Oracle Self-Service Web Applications
- ☐ 38 Oracle Strategic Enterprise Management
- ☐ 25 Oracle Supply Chain Management
- ☐ 36 Oracle Tutor
- ☐ 41 Oracle Travel Management

ORACLE SERVICES
- ☐ 61 Oracle Consulting
- ☐ 62 Oracle Education
- ☐ 60 Oracle Support
- ☐ 98 Other _____
- 99 ☐ **None of the above**

7 What other database products are in use at your site? *(check all that apply)*
- ☐ 01 Access
- ☐ 02 Baan
- ☐ 03 dbase
- ☐ 04 Gupta
- ☐ 05 IBM DB2
- ☐ 06 Informix
- ☐ 07 Ingres
- ☐ 08 Microsoft Access
- ☐ 09 Microsoft SQL Server
- ☐ 10 PeopleSoft
- ☐ 11 Progress
- ☐ 12 SAP
- ☐ 13 Sybase
- ☐ 14 VSAM
- ☐ 98 Other _____
- 99 ☐ **None of the above**

8 During the next 12 months, how much do you anticipate your organization will spend on computer hardware, software, peripherals, and services for your location? *(check only one)*
- ☐ 01 Less than $10,000
- ☐ 02 $10,000 to $49,999
- ☐ 03 $50,000 to $99,999
- ☐ 04 $100,000 to $499,999
- ☐ 05 $500,000 to $999,999
- ☐ 06 $1,000,000 and over

If there are other Oracle users at your location who would like to receive a free subscription to *Oracle Magazine*, please photocopy this form and pass it along, or contact Customer Service at **+1.847.647.9630**

Form 5

OPRESS

ORACLE SOFTWARE LICENSE AGREEMENT

YOU SHOULD CAREFULLY READ THE FOLLOWING TERMS AND CONDITIONS BEFORE BREAKING THE SEAL ON THE DISC ENVELOPE. AMONG OTHER THINGS, THIS AGREEMENT LICENSES THE ENCLOSED SOFTWARE TO YOU AND CONTAINS WARRANTY AND LIABILITY DISCLAIMERS. BY USING THE DISC AND/OR INSTALLING THE SOFTWARE, YOU ARE ACCEPTING AND AGREEING TO THE TERMS AND CONDITIONS OF THIS AGREEMENT. IF YOU DO NOT AGREE TO THE TERMS OF THIS AGREEMENT, DO NOT BREAK THE SEAL OR USE THE DISC. YOU SHOULD PROMPTLY RETURN THE PACKAGE UNOPENED.

LICENSE: ORACLE CORPORATION ("ORACLE") GRANTS END USER ("YOU" OR "YOUR") A NON-EXCLUSIVE, NON-TRANSFERABLE DEVELOPMENT ONLY LIMITED USE LICENSE TO USE THE ENCLOSED SOFTWARE AND DOCUMENTATION ("SOFTWARE") SUBJECT TO THE TERMS AND CONDITIONS, INCLUDING USE RESTRICTIONS, SPECIFIED BELOW.

You shall have the right to use the Software (a) only in object code form, (b) for development purposes only in the indicated operating environment for a single developer (one person) on a single computer, (c) solely with the publication with which the Software is included, and (d) solely for Your personal use and as a single user.

You are prohibited from and shall not (a) transfer, sell, sublicense, assign or otherwise convey the Software, (b) timeshare, rent or market the Software, (c) use the Software for or as part of a service bureau, and/or (d) distribute the Software in whole or in part. Any attempt to transfer, sell, sublicense, assign or otherwise convey any of the rights, duties or obligations hereunder is void. You are prohibited from and shall not use the Software for internal data processing operations, processing data of a third party or for any commercial or production use. If You desire to use the Software for any use other than the development use allowed under this Agreement, You must contact Oracle, or an authorized Oracle reseller, to obtain the appropriate licenses. You are prohibited from and shall not cause or permit the reverse engineering, disassembly, decompilation, modification or creation of derivative works based on the Software. You are prohibited from and shall not copy or duplicate the Software except as follows: You may make one copy of the Software in machine readable form solely for back-up purposes. No other copies shall be made without Oracle's prior written consent. You are prohibited from and shall not: (a) remove any product identification, copyright notices, or other notices or proprietary restrictions from the Software, or (b) run any benchmark tests with or of the Software. This Agreement does not authorize You to use any Oracle name, trademark or logo.

COPYRIGHT/OWNERSHIP OF SOFTWARE: The Software is the confidential and proprietary product of Oracle and is protected by copyright and other intellectual property laws. You acquire only the right to use the Software and do not acquire any rights, express or implied, in the Software or media containing the Software other than those specified in this Agreement. Oracle, or its licensor, shall at all times, including but not limited to after termination of this Agreement, retain all rights, title, interest, including intellectual property rights, in the Software and media.

WARRANTY DISCLAIMER: THE SOFTWARE IS PROVIDED "AS IS" AND ORACLE SPECIFICALLY DISCLAIMS ALL WARRANTIES OF ANY KIND, EITHER EXPRESS OR IMPLIED, INCLUDING, BUT NOT LIMITED TO, THE IMPLIED WARRANTIES OF MERCHANTABILITY, SATISFACTORY QUALITY AND FITNESS FOR A PARTICULAR PURPOSE. ORACLE DOES NOT WARRANT, GUARANTEE OR MAKE ANY REPRESENTATIONS REGARDING THE USE, OR THE RESULTS OF THE USE, OF THE SOFTWARE IN TERMS OF CORRECTNESS, ACCURACY, RELIABILITY, CURRENTNESS OR OTHERWISE, AND DOES NOT WARRANT THAT THE OPERATION OF THE SOFTWARE WILL BE UNINTERRUPTED OR ERROR FREE. ORACLE EXPRESSLY DISCLAIMS ALL WARRANTIES NOT STATED HEREIN, NO ORAL OR WRITTEN INFORMATION OR ADVICE GIVEN BY ORACLE OR OTHERS SHALL CREATE A WARRANTY OR IN ANY WAY INCREASE THE SCOPE OF THIS LICENSE, AND YOU MAY NOT RELY ON ANY SUCH INFORMATION OR ADVICE.

LIMITATION OF LIABILITY: IN NO EVENT SHALL ORACLE OR ITS LICENSORS BE LIABLE FOR ANY DIRECT, INDIRECT, INCIDENTAL, SPECIAL OR CONSEQUENTIAL DAMAGES, OR DAMAGES FOR LOSS OF PROFITS, REVENUE, DATA OR DATA USE, INCURRED BY YOU OR ANY THIRD PARTY, WHETHER IN AN ACTION IN CONTRACT OR TORT, EVEN IF ORACLE AND/OR ITS LICENSORS HAVE BEEN ADVISED OF THE POSSIBILITY OF SUCH DAMAGES. SOME JURISDICTIONS DO NOT ALLOW THE EXCLUSION OF IMPLIED WARRANTIES OR LIMITATION OR EXCLUSION OF LIABILITY FOR INCIDENTAL OR CONSEQUENTIAL DAMAGES SO THE ABOVE EXCLUSIONS AND LIMITATION MAY NOT APPLY TO YOU.

TERMINATION: You may terminate this license at any time by discontinuing use of and destroying the Software together with any copies in any form. This license will also terminate if You fail to comply with any term or condition of this Agreement. Upon termination of the license, You agree to discontinue use of and destroy the Software together with any copies in any form. The Warranty Disclaimer, Limitation of Liability, and Export Administration sections of this Agreement shall survive termination of this Agreement.

NO TECHNICAL SUPPORT: Oracle is not obligated to provide and this Agreement does not entitle You to any updates or upgrades to, or any technical support or phone support for, the Software.

EXPORT ADMINISTRATION: You acknowledge that the Software, including technical data, is subject to United States export control laws, including the United States Export Administration Act and its associated regulations, and may be subject to export or import regulations in other countries. You agree to comply fully with all laws and regulations of the United States and other countries ("Export Laws") to assure that neither the Software, nor any direct products thereof, are (a) exported, directly or indirectly, in violation of Export Laws, either to countries or nationals that are subject to United States export restrictions or to any end user who has been prohibited from participating in the Unites States export transactions by any federal agency of the United States government; or (b) intended to be used for any purposes prohibited by the Export Laws, including, without limitation, nuclear, chemical or biological weapons proliferation. You acknowledge that the Software may include technical data subject to export and re-export restrictions imposed by United States law.

RESTRICTED RIGHTS: The Software is provided with Restricted Rights. Use, duplication or disclosure of the Software by the United State government is subject to the restrictions set forth in the Rights in Technical Data and Computer Software Clauses in DFARS 252.227-7013(c)(1)(ii) and FAR 52.227-19(c)(2) as applicable. Manufacturer is Oracle Corporation, 500 Oracle Parkway, Redwood City, CA 94065.

MISCELLANEOUS: This Agreement and all related actions thereto shall be governed by California law. Oracle may audit Your use of the Software. If any provision of this Agreement is held to be invalid or unenforceable, the remaining provisions of this Agreement will remain in full force.

YOU ACKNOWLEDGE THAT YOU HAVE READ THIS AGREEMENT, UNDERSTAND IT, AND AGREE TO BE BOUND BY ITS TERMS AND CONDITIONS. YOU FURTHER AGREE THAT IT IS THE COMPLETE AND EXCLUSIVE STATEMENT OF THE AGREEMENT BETWEEN ORACLE AND YOU.

Oracle is a registered trademark of Oracle Corporation.

Register for the *Oracle Technology Network* (OTN)

Oracle Technology Network ("OTN") is the primary technical source for developers building Oracle-based applications. As an OTN member, you will be part of an online community with access to technical papers, code samples, product documentation, self-service technical support, free software, OTN-sponsored Internet developer conferences, and discussion groups on up-to-date Oracle technology. Membership is FREE! Register for OTN on the World Wide Web at

```
http://technet.oracle.com/register/oraclepress_linux/
```